CONFUCIAN ROLE ETHICS

SUNY series in Chinese Philosophy and Culture
Roger T. Ames

CONFUCIAN ROLE ETHICS
A VOCABULARY

ROGER T. AMES

Cover: *Xiaodao*, the prime moral imperative in the Confucian tradition that references the intergenerational embodiment of a continuing culture. Calligraphy by Ni Peimin.

© The Chinese University of Hong Kong, 2011
This edition is published by arrangement with The Chinese University Press.
This edition is for sale in North America only.

Published by State University of New York Press, Albany

All rights reserved

Printed in the United States of America

No part of this book may be used or reproduced in any manner whatsoever without written permission. No part of this book may be stored in a retrieval system or transmitted in any form or by any means including electronic, electrostatic, magnetic tape, mechanical, photocopying, recording, or otherwise without the prior permission in writing of the publisher.

For information, contact State University of New York Press, Albany, NY
www.sunypress.edu

Library of Congress Cataloging-in-Publication Data

Names: Ames, Roger T., author
Title: Confucian role ethics : A vocabulary / Roger T. Ames, author.
Description: Albany : State University of New York Press, [2020] | Series: SUNY series in Chinese Philosophy and Culture | Includes bibliographical references and index.
Identifiers: LCCN 2020917049 (print) | ISBN 9781438481760 (pbk : alk. paper)
Further information is available at the Library of Congress.

10 9 8 7 6 5 4 3 2 1

Dedication

For D. C. Lau, and his CUHK family

The ordinary lives of these extraordinary people teach us more of Confucian role ethics than any book could pretend to do.

Contents

Acknowledgments   xi
Preface   xiii

I. **Introduction: "Appreciating" Confucianism**   1
1. A Historically Appreciated Confucianism   1
2. Leibniz's Appreciation of Confucian China   5
3. Whatever Happened to Wisdom?   8
4. Western Enlightenment Rationality: The Internal Critique   13
5. A "Depreciated" Confucianism   18
6. The Necessity of Informed Generalizations in Making Cultural Comparisons   20
7. The Inevitability of Analogy in Making Cultural Comparisons   35
8. Wholesale and Retail Analogies, Associative and Contrastive Analogies   38

II. **An Interpretive Context for Understanding Confucianism**   41
1. Correlative Thinking as Common Sense   41
2. The *Book of Changes* (*Yijing* 易經) and Chinese Natural Cosmology   49
3. Correlative Cosmology and Traditional Chinese Medicine (TCM)   56
4. Correlative Cosmology as an Ecological Cosmology: From "Things" to "Gerunds" and "Vital Relations"   61
5. Correlative Cosmology as a Moral Cosmology: *This* Focus (*de* 德) and *Its* Field (*dao* 道)   66
6. Correlative Cosmology as a Religious Cosmology: The Emergence of Cultural Exemplars   69

7.	The Collateral and Constitutive Nature of Relationality	71
8.	Confucian Creativity: "What Makes *This* Life Significant"	76
9.	Tang Junyi 唐君毅 and Chinese Process Cosmology	77

III. The Confucian Project: Attaining Relational Virtuosity — 87

1.	"Human *Beings*" or "Human *Becomings*"?	87
2.	Setting the Project: The *Great Learning* (*Daxue* 大學)	92
3.	"Family" as the Governing Metaphor	96
4.	The Discursive Nature of Family Relations	98
5.	Achieving Personal Identity through Embodying (*ti* 體) Propriety (*li* 禮) in One's Roles and Relations	102
6.	The Liberating Role of Friendship	114
7.	The Embeddedness and Growth of "Human Becomings"	121
8.	"Human Becomings" as *Creatio in Situ*	126
9.	Tang Junyi 唐君毅 on "Human Nature" (*renxing* 人性) *as* Conduct	128
10.	Our Uncommon Assumptions	134
11.	The *Mencius* (*Mengzi* 孟子) and "Human Becomings"	136
12.	The *Five Modes of Proper Conduct* (*Wuxingpian* 五行篇) as a Window on the *Mencius*	143
13.	The Pragmatic Notion of Relational Person: An Associative and Contrastive Analogy	147
14.	Making Better Sense of the Notions of "Root," "Source," "Potential," and "Cause"	154

IV. Confucian Role Ethics — 159

1.	On the Source of "Principles" and "Virtues": Value as Growth in Relations	159
2.	A Son Covers for His Father: And Being "True" Lies in Doing So	163
3.	A Flourishing Harmony (*he* 和)	168
4.	Propriety in Roles and Relations (*li* 禮) as a Source of Face and of a Sense of Shame	171
5.	Gerundive Persons as Evolving Configurations of Roles (*ren* 仁)	175
6.	*Ren* 仁 as the Expedient in the Way of Acting	179
7.	"Virtues" as "Virtuosity": The Optimizing of Meaning in Roles and Relations	180
8.	The Beginnings of Moral Competence: Family Roles as Ethical Injunctions	183
9.	A Preemptive Vision of the Consummate Life	189
10.	An Explanatory Vocabulary for Confucian Role Ethics	193

11.	*Shu* 恕: "Putting Oneself in the Other's Place"	194
12.	*Zhong* 忠: "Doing One's Utmost"	200
13.	*Yi* 義: "Optimal Appropriateness"	201
14.	*Xin* 信: "Making Good on One's Word"	205
15.	*De* 德: "Excelling Morally"	206

V. Confucian Human-Centered Religiousness — 211

1. Getting Past Transcendence: Distinguishing Process Cosmology from Substance Ontology — 211
2. Privileging Gerundive Language: Knowing *How* — 218
3. Abjuring Clarity on *tian* 天 and *di* 帝 — 221
4. Cosmic Origins: Genealogical Cosmogony and Its "Epistemogony" — 225
5. Meaning and Value: Confucian A-Theistic Religiousness — 231
6. Confucian Religiousness: The Flower of Inspired Living — 236
7. The Nature of Creativity: Confucian Religiousness as Co-Creativity — 241

Epilogue: The Limits of Confucian Role Ethics — 257

Notes — 269
Bibliography of Works Cited — 311
Index — 323

Acknowledgments

It is with real joy that I hasten to acknowledge the extraordinary hospitality that I enjoyed at New Asia College under the stewardship of Henry N. C. Wong and his colleagues, Peter J. L. Man and Nixon W. K. Fok, who did such a marvelous job in organizing the 2008 Ch'ien Mu lectures. In the Philosophy Department at CUHK I have always been treated as one of the family, and number my colleagues there among my closest personal and professional friends: Cheung Chan-fai, Kwan Tze-wan, Kwong-loi Shun, Lau Kwok-ying, Lao Kwok-keung, Liu Xiaogan, Wang Qingjie, and Pollyanna So. Along the way as I struggled to bring the manuscript to closure, I was grateful for the critical comments and the encouragement that I received from my three good friends, Henry Rosemont Jr., George H. Rudebusch, and Danny Coyle who are absolved of any responsibility for a colleague who got their one corner but sometimes could not find the other three. Working with Chinese University Press in the production of this handsome volume has been a delight for me, and I must in particular thank my editor Luke Ramón Krawec for his serious eye and for his pleasant professionalism. As always, I owe a debt to my wonderful family and to my exceptional students for their forbearance as they have listened patiently to many different iterations of the ideas found in these pages.

Preface

I was much honored to be invited to give the 2008 Ch'ien Mu (Qian Mu) 錢穆 Lectures at The Chinese University of Hong Kong. My set of presentations on that happy occasion was called "Appreciating Confucianism." The double entendre introduced into the title by the word "appreciate" is calculated to express my underlying motivation in expanding upon those lectures in the preparation of this present monograph.

I will certainly want to "appreciate" the narrative of one of the world's longest lived cultural traditions. That is, I will in these pages endeavor to appraise and to give a robust account of the uniqueness and the worth of Confucianism as a cultural narrative, and in offering this summary of it, to acknowledge as best I can its magnitude and its complexity. To this end, in the introductory chapter I reflect upon the problem of making responsible cultural comparisons, concluding that we need as best we can to allow the texts under scrutiny to tell their story within their own cultural narrative. In the second chapter that follows I then use the *Great Tradition* (*Dazhuan* 大傳) commentary on the *Book of Changes* (*Yijing* 易經), Traditional Chinese Medicine, and Tang Junyi's account of natural Chinese cosmology as overlapping resources for defining those persistent cosmological assumptions that provide an interpretive context for the evolution of Confucian philosophy, and that allow us imperfectly for sure, but with imagination, to take the Confucian tradition on its own terms. In a third chapter under the heading of "The Confucian Project: Attaining Relational Virtuosity," I rehearse the Confucian vision of the consummate ethical life as it is grounded in a distinctive, relational conception of role-bearing persons—an understanding of person that stands in stark contrast to the foundational individualism that began in classical Greece and, evolving over the centuries, has in one guise or another grounded and underlies much of current ethical, social, and political theory. In the fourth chapter titled "Confucian Role Ethics" I explore the ways in which, in Confucian philosophy, intimate family feelings serve as the entry point for developing moral competence, giving this tradition a distinctly different vocabulary and profile from principle-based and virtue-based ethical theories. And again, the fifth chapter is comprised of a discussion of Confucian religiousness wherein I try to show the symbiotic and coterminous relationship between achieved personal worth within the flourishing family, and the profoundly human-centered (indeed, "a-theistic") religiosity that makes this Confucianism "religiousness" a significant, world-affirming alternative to the more familiar Abrahamic, God-centered "religions." It is the cultivation, attainment, and contribution of this unique personal worth to the cosmos that become one's primary warrant for the intense sense of belonging that is the substance of felt religiousness. Finally, in an epilogue I seek to assess critically Confucian role ethics and ask after the strengths and the limitations of this specifically Confucian version of role ethics as it has been articulated in the early canonical texts. My understanding of the responsibility of the philosophical enterprise is that it should not only help us to understand different points of view, but also make a recommendation as to which ideas we ought to endorse. This evaluation will hopefully serve as a critical point of departure for constructing a more adequate and inclusive account of role ethics in the future.

But attempting herein to provide an adequate assessment of this Confucian tradition is only the initial phase in "appreciating" Confucianism. In parsing the meaning of the word "appreciate," there is a second even more significant connotation of this term that I want to register and to bring into play. "To appreciate" can be the opposite of "to depreciate." That is, an understanding of Confucian role ethics that makes this position available for the contemporary professional discourse on ethics will, I believe, appreciate role ethics in the sense of investing it with additional value and meaning.

In an essay contributed to a Festschrift for Herbert Fingarette titled

"Rights-Bearing Individuals and Role-Bearing Persons," my long-time collaborator and finest of friends, Henry Rosemont Jr., began in earnest to develop the theme of this present volume—the idea of Confucian role ethics. He began as any good Confucian philosopher would by making an observation about how we as human beings actually live our lives as radically contextualized, situated, relationally-constituted persons. In his words:

> We are all born and reared in a specific cultural community, each with its language, values, religious orientation, customs, traditions, and concomitant ideas of what it is to be a human being. There are not, in short, any culturally independent human beings. Each of us has specific hopes, fears, joys, sorrows, values, and views which are inextricably linked to our definitions of who and what we are, and these definitions have been overwhelmingly influenced by the cultural community of which we are a part.[1]

Confucian philosophy requires such an allegiance to the notion of ordinary experience as both its point of initial departure and as its ultimate source of adjudication in its articulation of the ethical life. This being the case, the prescriptive definition of the abstract, rights-bearing individual that grounds rights-talk couched in the concept-cluster of "liberty," "autonomy," "individual," "principles," "rationality," and so on, as those conditions essential to the decision-making of moral agents, is a vocabulary without counterpart within the canons of classical Confucian. Some version of this reductive Cartesian profile has dominated Western theorizing about moral and religious thinking for the past three centuries in spite of the fact that this disembodied, purely logical, abstracted caricature of what it is to be a person has little relevance to the real "hopes, fears, joys, sorrows, values, and views" of flesh and blood human beings in their best efforts to live significant lives. This untenable model of the human experience constitutes a serious concern for Rosemont, and for Fingarette too, in the way in which universal human rights are being articulated, advocated, and justified, and more broadly, in the way in which the discourse on ethical theory continues. Paraphrasing their exchange, both of these scholars acknowledge that the doctrine of human rights is a powerful and valuable set of guidelines while at the same time arguing that a predominant preoccupation with this approach to solving social and political problems has had many unwelcome outcomes, and blinds us to the constructive potential of other orientations.[2]

As an alternative, Confucian starting point for reflecting on the ethical life, and in stark contrast to the abstract and reductive rights-bearing individual, Rosemont introduces what he calls the role-bearing person:

> But for the early Confucians there can be no me in isolation, to be considered abstractly: I am the totality of roles I live in relation to specific others.... Taken collectively, they weave, for each of us, a unique pattern of personal identity, such that if some of my roles change, others will of necessity change also, literally making me a different person.[3]

In articulating this relationally constituted notion of person, Rosemont argues vigorously for the social, transactional, and interdependent nature of achieved human identity:

> Moreover, seen in this socially contextualized way, it should become clearer that in an important sense I do not achieve my own identity, am not solely responsible for becoming who I am. Of course, a great deal of personal effort is required to become a good person. But nevertheless, much of who and what I am is determined by the others with whom I interact, just as my efforts determine in part who and what they are at the same time.[4]

In this seminal essay, Rosemont argues for the contemporary relevance of a Confucian philosophy that addresses directly the question of how to optimize the possibilities inherent in the real conditions of the human experience. He leaves us with two challenging questions. First, what is the cluster of concepts within the early Confucian canons that on their own terms give full expression to this notion of Confucian roles ethics? This present monograph is a modest attempt to respond to this preliminary yet essential task of defining the vocabulary of Confucian role ethics. The second challenge—how to articulate a new and inclusive concept-cluster that draws critically from all of our cultural resources—is undoubtedly the greater assignment. In Rosemont's own words:

> I do not wish to imply that the early Confucian writings are the be-all and end-all for finding answers to the multiplicity of questions I have posed.... Some Western philosophical concepts will, and should remain with us;

some others will have to be stretched, bent, and/or extended significantly in order to represent more accurately non-Western concepts and concept-clusters; and still other Western philosophical concepts may have to be abandoned altogether in favor of others not yet extant, but which will issue from future research as new (and old) concept clusters are advanced and examined. [5]

The next stage in the effort to give full expression to role ethics as a new and compelling vision of the ethical life will require a sustained conversation between Confucian philosophy and existing Western ethical theories that is able to draw creatively upon these very different ways of thinking about the refinement and evaluation of human conduct.

Below I will have occasion to reference the work of the contemporary philosopher, Tang Junyi 唐君毅, who makes much of the existentially informed dimension of our evolving understanding of what it means to become consummately human. Tang's argument—a sound Confucian argument—is that we learn to become persons most fundamentally by becoming persons, and in the process, seek for a vocabulary that can do justice to the achievement. And as Rosemont observes in his characterization of Confucian role ethics, becoming a person is something that we either do together in our roles and relations, or not at all.

In my career as a student of Chinese philosophy, I have over the years had occasion to study and to teach in many institutional environments that have aspired uniquely to embody Confucian values. In this context, I have had the good fortune to enjoy many sustained friendships that have given me insight into what it means as persons to become one together. These wonderful life-transforming collaborations more than any canonical texts have been an object lesson for me in attempting to understand and to find the language to express the notion of the relationally constituted person as the site and the substance of Confucian role ethics. I have also had available to me the model life of my teacher and mentor, Professor D. C. Lau, and the precious friendship of his CUHK family, to whom this book is respectfully dedicated.

I

Introduction: "Appreciating" Confucianism

A Historically Appreciated Confucianism

The philosopher and teacher, Kongfuzi 孔夫子, latinized as "Confucius," lends his name to the English (but not the Chinese) expression of this tradition called "Confucianism." Confucius was certainly a flesh-and-blood historical person who lived, taught, and died some twenty-five centuries ago, consolidating in his own time a formidable legacy of wisdom that has been passed down and applied through the ages to shape the character of an entire culture. In and of itself, the profoundly personal model of Confucius remembered by his protégés through those intimate snapshots of his life collected in the middle chapters of the *Analects* has its own value and meaning. But then, as Confucius reportedly said of himself, most of what he had to offer had ancient roots, and that he was one who was inclined to follow the established path rather than strike out in new directions.[1] Indeed it is perhaps for this reason that in the Chinese language itself the tradition is not identified specifically with Confucius as "Confucianism," but rather with the *ru* 儒 literati class who over the centuries provided the cultural tradition with its evolving "literati learning" (*ruxue* 儒學). And consistent with Confucius's own premises, this legacy called *ruxue*—the always-porous core of an aggregating Chinese culture—is both vital and corporate. That is, Confucianism has been appropriated, commented upon, reinterpreted, and reauthorized by each of some eighty generations of Chinese scholars and intellectuals that across the ages have contributed their own best thoughts to this "literati learning" as a continuous, living tradition.

Hence, for us in the first decades of the twenty-first century, "appreciating" Confucianism means no more or less than participating in this evolutionary process at a juncture when Confucian values will as never before emerge on the world stage as a cultural force to be reckoned with. In our own much-troubled historical moment, in the wake of the unrelenting holocaust of the twentieth century, it behooves us all to find whatever resources we can within human culture to do much better than we have done in making the most of the human experience. This living Confucian legacy is one substantial resource for informing and inspiring new directions in human culture, a legacy that for the past two centuries and largely for economic and political reasons, has been muted and ignored. The contention of this monograph then, is that we are entering upon a transitional period of enormous proportions with the imminent emergence of a new cultural order, and that Confucianism offers us philosophical assets that can be resourced and applied to serve not only the renaissance of a revitalized Chinese culture, but also the interests of world culture more broadly. Thus, in identifying, elaborating upon, and applying those elements within this continuing Confucian tradition that can be brought into productive conversation with cultural narratives that lie beyond it, we will find that it can serve as a significant source for the enrichment of our own ways of thinking and living. At the same time, this integrative process will further "appreciate" Confucianism itself by offering it opportunities for its own creative growth and innovation.

"Appreciation" as "increase in value" is not new in the evolution of Confucianism. Historically, marked growth occurred within the tradition itself when in the fourth century BCE a shrewd early proponent of this tradition named Xunzi 荀子 co-opted the disputational vocabulary of the Mohists to strengthen his Confucian arguments, adapted the military terminology of the Strategists to prioritize his Confucian values, and applied the regulative rigor and strictness of the Legalists to bring discipline to his vision of the Confucian project of personal cultivation. All of Xunzi's philosophical appropriation was done in service to a newly fortified Confucianism that emerged in the Western Han dynasty (206 BCE–9 CE) to become a state ideology that would persist for nearly two millennia. For Xunzi, such broad assimilation directed at exploiting and ingesting the intellectual resources of precisely those philosophical lineages best able to compete with Confucianism was a deliberate and ultimately successful strategy used to enhance and to galvanize an emerging, syncretic tradition.

This kind of appreciation of Confucianism has also occurred from without as two waves of "Western learning" have rolled up upon the Confucian shore to create tide pools and ecotones in which cultural experimentation has flourished. The first wave of Western learning began during the Eastern Han dynasty (25–220) when the challenge of South Asian Buddhist ideas reset the agenda for a Chinese culture broadly, and in the centuries to follow, produced a responsive and hybridic neo-Confucianism (*daoxue* 道學) that was inspired by Buddhist approaches to personal growth and transformation. The neo-Confucians of the Song (960–1279) and Ming (1368–1644) dynasties certainly railed against their own thin caricature of the foreign Buddhist teachings, but at the same time, by absorbing and elaborating upon the spiritual resources of this competing tradition, they redefined their own lofty aspirations of sagehood. And of course in this encounter between Confucianism and Buddhism, thoroughly sinified lineages of Buddhism such as Huayan 華嚴, Sanlun 三論, and Chan 禪宗 also produced a much-appreciated Chinese Buddhism that in one form or another has continued to spread throughout the East Asian world and beyond, down to our present day.

The second wave of Western learning arrived in a set that began in the late sixteenth century with the classical learning and science of the Jesuits who were led in their first encounter by Matteo Ricci. This first surge was followed a century and a half later by the broad arts and sciences curriculum of the Protestant missionaries, and then again in another wave by the timely translations of evolutionary theories undertaken by scholars such as Yan Fu 嚴復 who sought the liberalization of Chinese culture by appeal to Western science and democracy. This second set has continued to wash up on China's shores in the twentieth and twenty-first centuries with the competing ideologies of Marxist socialism and democratic capitalism, and with the influence of decidedly Western taxonomies and theoretical models that continue to hold sway within the Chinese academy. The thoroughly comparative doctrines of many if not most of the twentieth-century Chinese philosophers who since the 1980s have come to be known as the "New Confucians"—the *xinruxuejia* 新儒學家—are self-conscious amalgams of traditional Chinese ideas and substantial borrowings from systematic Western philosophy. There is the attempt of Xiong Shili 熊十力 to revitalize Confucianism through a synthesis of Yogacara Buddhism with Western and Chinese ideas, the complex and critical appropriation of Kant by Mou Zongsan 牟宗三, the imaginative applications of Hegel and Whitehead by Tang Junyi 唐君毅, the eclectic and creative assimilation of much of the history of Western philosophy by Fang Dongmei 方東美, and on it goes. There is no question that Confucianism has in many ways become more formidable because of this continuing appropriation of elements of Western learning, although it is a criticism well made that the systematized, intellectualized, and theorized iteration of Confucian ideas in imitation of abstract Western philosophical theory by some of these New Confucians has to an important degree set Confucianism adrift from its anchor in the daily lives of the people.

In this essay, I will argue that the long-postponed impact of Confucian values on different aspects of the world's philosophical and cultural traditions is now on the horizon, and that a creative fusion of Confucianism with other narratives will follow behind the rise of China as a contemporary economic and political force.[2] As Confucian values spread to become a global cultural factor in our own time, it will not only be the other traditions it encounters that will be altered, challenged, and enriched. Indeed, Confucianism itself will continue to be transformed in the process.

Before we attempt to anticipate more specifically what Confucianism will have on offer in reconfiguring the shape of world civilization in our own time, we might do well to address an immediate objection that this claim about the pending influence of Confucian values might provoke. Some critics of old China might worry that such an assertion is to advocate for an effete and antiquarian tradition that many have come to see as a burden weighing down the new China as it finally takes its place at the table of nations. Others will certainly see notions such as "Confucian role ethics" and "Confucian democracy" as oxymoronic. For them, a less corrupt and more democratic China, if it ever comes to be, will be a decidedly post-Confucian phenomenon. For yet others, they will dismiss this claim about the imminent impact of Confucian values on world culture as the prediction of a perhaps well-intended, but fatally naïve foreign convert with an idealization of Cathay that has failed to register the sometimes shrill but always passionate voices of the courageous reformers of the New Culture movement at the beginning of the last century. Indeed, they will say, such an inflation of Confucianism is undoubtedly the fantasy of a romantic who has failed to take adequate account of the painful humiliation Confucian China suffered in its resistance first to decades of an escalating foreign imperialism and more recently to the ineluctable forces of modernity.

Leibniz's Appreciation of Confucian China

Perhaps the best answer to this concern that I am predicting too much influence from Confucian philosophy on an evolving world culture is to recall an earlier European advocate of the fundamental worth of this tradition. In anticipating this impending rise of Chinese cultural influence today, we might remember that centuries ago, Gottfried Wilhelm Leibniz, a comparative philosopher of a former age and anything but a naïve romantic, attempted to make productive sense of Confucian China for the culture of his own time and place.[3] Leibniz was a universalist of the first order, and thus an unlikely source of appreciation for a usually pragmatic Confucian culture. Politically Leibniz was a federalist, religiously an ecumenicalist, and linguistically he searched for and saw in the ancient polyphonetic Chinese script a language of what he thought to be ideographs that might possibly reveal the "universal characteristic" of both the universe and the structure of the mind through which to unify the communication of the world.[4] He saw parallels between the dyadic *yinyang* 陰陽 lines of the hexagrams in the *Book of Changes* and the binary arithmetic system he had been developing as a basis for his infinitesimal calculus, and he discovered a shared biblical chronology that began in antiquity with the parallel flood myths of Noah recounted in Genesis, and Yu the Great (Da Yu 大禹), reputed to be the founder of the Xia dynasty.

In the last year of his life (1716), perhaps anticipating a better place at the Lord's table, Leibniz wrote his *Discourse on the Natural Theology of the Chinese*.[5] In this treatise, he argues that Chinese civilization early on had been quite properly Christian, but that the Chinese population had "strayed from the truth and even from their own antiquity."[6] In reflecting on the early Confucian doctrines that everywhere celebrate "Heaven" (*tian* 天), Leibniz concludes that the tradition "is pure Christianity, insofar as it renews the natural law inscribed in our hearts."[7] Unfortunately for China, continues Leibniz's argument, intervening cultural distractions and Confucian hubris have led modern China and its Mandarins into a kind of theoretical and religious amnesia in which they knew neither the demonstrable science of the mind nor the Truth of their own God. The universalistic and rationalistic impulses behind Leibniz's contribution to the Western philosophical tradition have led some scholars to dismiss his interest in China as at best a condescending cultural appropriation, and at worst, a kind of cultural imperialism. In short, as this story goes, his motivation for turning to the Far East was simply a matter of corroboration, and thus his celebration of China amounts to nothing more than an appeal to another high culture as a means of demonstrating the truth of his own European universal indices. But those who would tell such a story should know their Leibniz better.

In the Preface to the *Novissima Sinica* written during the period of 1697–99, an astute and penetrating Leibniz offers a synoptic comparison of the contributions of European and Chinese culture that would satisfy even the most optimistic interpreters of this antique Chinese culture. Leibniz allows that in technologies, crafts, and artifacts, we Europeans stand on equal ground with the Chinese, with each people having "knowledge which it could with profit communicate to the other."[8] In theoretical disciplines such as mathematics, logic, metaphysics, and in particular, theology, however, there is a clear European superiority. Indeed, we Europeans "excel by far in the understanding of concepts which are abstracted by the mind from the material."[9] We own the theoretical sciences and surpass the Chinese in those rational tools of the intellect that lead us to demonstrable truth, whilst the Chinese struggle with a kind of empirical geometry owned by most artisans.

As a reluctant aside, Leibniz offers a second area in which Europe overshadows the China of his day. For it is much to Europe's shame, he laments, that we have a decided advantage in the military arts. Leibniz allows that this particular superiority is not out of ignorance or incompetence on the part of the Chinese, but rather is a matter of deliberate choice, and it is to their credit, for as a people they properly "despise everything which creates or nourishes ferocity in men."[10]

In fact, this Chinese antipathy toward conflict and belligerence

I · Introduction: "Appreciating" Confucianism

is not unrelated to what Leibniz perceives to be this culture's greatest achievement. On Leibniz's reading, the Chinese excel in the pursuit of civil philosophy where Chinese "civilization" has set a standard far superior to that of Europe. In his own words:

> But who would have believed that there is on earth a people who, though we are in our view so very advanced in every branch of behavior, still surpass us in comprehending the precepts of civil life? Yet now we find this to be so among the Chinese, as we learn to know them better. And so if we are their equals in the industrial arts, and ahead of them in contemplative sciences, certainly they surpass us (though it is almost shameful to confess this) in practical philosophy, that is, in the precepts of ethics and politics adapted to the present life and use of mortals. Indeed, it is difficult to describe how beautifully all the laws of the Chinese, in contrast to those of other peoples, are directed to the achievement of public tranquility and the establishment of social order, so that men shall be disrupted in their relations as little as possible.... Certainly the Chinese above all others have attained a higher standard. In a vast multitude of men they have virtually accomplished more than the founders of religious orders among us have achieved within their own narrow ranks.[11]

On Leibniz's estimation, China's ongoing achievements in practical philosophy enabled them to excel in the establishment and maintenance of social order at all of its many different levels: familial, communal, political, and religious. Leibniz attributes this inspiring public virtuosity to the way in which observing *li* 禮—that is, being committed to the pursuit of propriety in one's familial and communal roles and relationships—functions to produce a religious *ethos* in the human community.

> So great is obedience toward superiors and reverence toward elders, so religious, almost, is the relation of children toward parents, that for children to contrive anything violent against their parents even by word, is almost unheard of.... Moreover, there is among equals, or those having little obligations to one another, a marvelous respect, and an established order of duties. To us, not enough accustomed to act by reason and rule, these smack of servitude; yet among them, where these duties are made natural by use, they are observed gladly.[12]

Considering the relatively limited information on China available to Leibniz in his own time, this philosopher, resisting his own formalist philosophical proclivities that might have inclined him steeply in the opposite direction, was indeed a surprisingly keen and honest observer of the human experience. In advancing his own generalizations about both European and Chinese cultures, he saw a clear contrast between the value invested in those abstract, theoretical disciplines in the European academy that are in search of axiomatic-deductive demonstration and the more aesthetic and pragmatic applications of the Chinese tradition—a distinction that broadly distinguishes a European confidence in the dividends of the rational sciences from those alternative rewards that can be derived from virtuosity in the art of living itself. In fact, it was more than a fundamental sympathy and respect for Chinese culture that led Leibniz to defend Matteo Ricci's advocacy of an accommodationist Christianity in the long simmering Rites Controversy that came to a boil in Rome towards the end of Leibniz's own life. Leibniz's commitment to accommodationism was based upon his conviction that the precepts of any universal civil philosophy that would seek to construct a framework for optimizing the social, political, and indeed religious life of human beings in community would do well to take into account the substantial accomplishments of Chinese culture in this same effort.

Whatever Happened to Wisdom?

Reflecting on the cultural contrast between Europe and China offered by Leibniz in *Novissima Sinica*, we might say that while he is celebrating European culture for achieving superiority in abstract knowledge and demonstrable truth, he is at the same time extolling the Chinese tradition for surpassing Europe in a kind of practical wisdom—that is, "in the precepts of ethics and politics adapted to the present life and use of mortals."[13] The language that Leibniz appeals to in making these thick cultural generalizations about the differences in the evolution of the European and Chinese narratives has its historical background. It takes us back to the commitment made to *eidos*, *theoria*, and *episteme*, the building blocks of a metaphysical realism, in the metaphysics and epistemology of early Greek philosophy in which the ideal is equated with the most real. This idealism is apparent in Leibniz's own description of the European achievement:

In the profundity of knowledge and in the theoretical disciplines we are their superiors. For besides logic and metaphysics, and the knowledge of things incorporeal, which we justly claim as peculiarly our province, we excel by far in the understanding of concepts which are abstracted by the mind from the material.... The Chinese are thus seen to be ignorant of that great light of the mind, the art of demonstration...[14]

If we look back to the beginnings of the discipline of philosophy in ancient Greece, we might observe that Pythagoras certainly celebrated the contemplation of abstract, theoretical science, but for him such speculations were inseparable from and subordinate to religious practices based upon assumptions about the immortality of the human soul, to periodical ascetic observances, to a complex program of social and political reform, to sustained ethical reflection, to the pleasures of music and the benefits of a strict physical regimen, and even to rigorous dietary prescriptions and prohibitions. For historians telling the story of this period of human flourishing, the eloquent Pythagoras and his holistic, practical way of life could be most aptly described as *philosophia*—"the love of wisdom." But what happened in this Western philosophical narrative to the original meaning of "philosophy" (*philosophia*) as "the love of wisdom"—an understanding that the role of philosophy is to seek the authentication of the theoretical in practical application so as to conduce to the enjoyment of the human experience?

Pythagoras's comprehensive vision of the good life faded with time, and what had been for him a truly "philosophical" journey—that is, a quest for a practical wisdom informed by theoretical knowledge—gave way to quite a different kind of pilgrimage. Precisely how we are to parse this change in the occupation of the philosopher from philosophy as an ethical and spiritual way of life to discursive philosophy has been the preoccupation of several of Pierre Hadot's recent contributions. Hadot argues that pervasively among the ancient thinkers, "Philosophy is not wisdom, but a way of life and discourse determined by the *idea* of wisdom."[15] With the melding of the Greek and the Christian traditions, medieval scholastic philosophy was placed in the service of theology, and reverence for the theoretically and spiritually abstract meant that in the fullness of time, practical wisdom, rhetoric, and the aesthetic were relegated to the down side of a prevailing dualism. In this narrative we witness that a growing preoccupation with ontological and metaphysical questions led to a more rarified and pointed search for an abstract, unconditioned knowledge, and its promise of certainty. *Logos* that had originally encompassed both *ratio* and *oratio*—both rational explanation and rhetoric—became weighted on the side of the former. And in many circles, *philosophia*, "the love of wisdom," had for all intents and purposes become *philoepisteme*, "the love of knowledge." Apodictic knowledge and truth had become the vocabulary of systematic philosophy, and "wisdom" became and remains today a seldom-referenced term in the corridors of philosophy within the Western academy. While professional philosophy among its central interests continues to teach and do research in "metaphysics" and "epistemology," "sophiology" has yet to find a place in the curriculum, and in our age of educational assessment wisdom is not usually stipulated as a desired student outcome.[16]

This early shift in the self-understanding of Western philosophy has not gone unnoticed in the internal critique of its twentieth century revolution.[17] Alfred North Whitehead diagnoses what he calls the "fallacy of misplaced concreteness" as that error in reasoning committed when the formally abstracted is taken to be what is real and concrete—that is, when the ideal is taken to be what is *really* real.[18] Whitehead rehearses the history and the consequences of this "fatal virus" that has come to inhibit our understanding of the intrinsic, constitutive, and productive nature of relatedness. He accuses Plato, Aristotle, and Epicurus of being "unaware of the perils of abstraction" that render knowledge closed and complete, and that in fact precludes the possibility of attaining wisdom in the ordinary affairs of the day. According to Whitehead, "the history of thought" that he associates with these great men

> ... is a tragic mixture of vibrant disclosure and of deadening closure. The sense of penetration is lost in the certainty of completed knowledge. This dogmatism is the antichrist of learning. In the full concrete connection of things, the characters of the things connected enter into the character of the connectivity which joins them.[19]

What Whitehead means here by a "sense of penetration" that is compromised by assumptions about the certainty of knowledge is the creative advance made possible by achieving productive relations among unique particulars. Indeed, for Whitehead it would be this cultivated, creative application of our understanding of how things can best relate to each other that would be the source and the substance of wisdom.

Whitehead uses friendship as an example of a relationship that is constituted by the unique character of the two persons involved, where the continuity of a real meaningful friendship is a matter of vibrant disclosure in which two persons "appreciate" each other in the most concrete sense of this term. That is, in their friendship they substantially enlarge and increase the weight and measure of each other. Importantly, the realization of this vital relationship is not at the expense of their personal uniqueness and integrity, but indeed a consequence of it. Integrity, as it applies here, means both the persistent particularity of each friend, and their "becoming one together" in the friendship. And such integrity is at once the substance of a real relationship and a source of cosmic meaning. In the growth of this achieved friendship, it is ultimately the dynamic configuration of a living friendship that has become what is most concrete, and it is persons taken as discrete individuals that has become the abstraction.

This understanding of relationality as intrinsic, constitutive, and productive is what Whitehead means by an "aesthetic" as opposed to a "rational" sense of order. For Whitehead any aesthetic achievement aspires to the fullest disclosure of the particular details in the totality of the achieved effect—in this case, the "connectivity" of the friendship itself.[20] If the assumption has been that "knowledge" is to be discovered in the rational comprehension of some abstract and universal truth, then it is in the pragmatic and aesthetic project of harmonizing concrete relationships and in the optimizing of the productivity of these relations that the ultimate source of "wisdom" can be found. There is for Whitehead real wisdom to be found in a "true" friendship.

Whitehead criticizes the classical Greek aesthetic sensibility harshly for losing sight of the balance needed between the particular details and the achieved harmony:

> The enjoyment of Greek art is always haunted by a longing for the details to exhibit some rugged independence apart from the oppressive harmony. In the greatest examples of any form of art, a miraculous balance is achieved. The whole displays its component parts, each with its own value

enhanced; and the parts lead up to a whole, which is beyond themselves, yet not destructive of themselves.[21]

When we turn to the art of being most fully human, disclosure in our relationships is what makes this family and this community meaningful, or said more dynamically, is what makes these radically embedded relationships a situated case of "meaning making." Any understanding of harmony that demands conformity at the expense of a disclosing particularity in so doing sets limits on the possibility of attaining wisdom, and is for this reason, quite literally, life-threatening. As Whitehead observes:

> Our lives are passed in the experience of disclosure. As we lose this sense of disclosure, we are shedding that mode of functioning which is the soul. We are descending to mere conformity with the average of the past. Complete conformity means the loss of life. There remains the barren existence of inorganic nature.[22]

The thrust of what Whitehead is saying here is that the productive harmony achieved by optimizing relationships—indeed, a shared and joyful wisdom—can only emerge out of the real, reciprocated experiences of always unique-yet-overlapping persons. As such, wisdom will always be collateral rather than unilateral, correlative rather than univocal, a case of disclosure rather than closure. Wisdom is primarily concrete and local, and only then abstractable as a kind of functional knowledge.

A summary clarification to be made here for comparative philosophy is that registering the difference among the details is a critical factor in achieving a truly aesthetic harmony, and that an exaggerated emphasis upon commonality at the expense of difference threatens the very possibility of real harmony. Indeed, achieving and sustaining a robust harmony is dependent upon the ongoing, effective correlation of difference. This being said, Whitehead is not advocating the concrete details over the abstract arrangement of them. Instead, he is recommending the restoration of an optimum and inclusive balance between the concrete and the abstract to compensate for what in Greek metaphysics had become an undue emphasis on the latter at the expense of the former.[23]

As we continue in our exploration of Confucianism's vision of the consummate life, what we will find is that to the degree that the narrative of Western philosophy has stressed the abstract and the impartial as standards for ethical adjudication, and to the degree that the narrative of Confucian philosophy has emphasized the more concrete partiality of family feeling as the source of our moral sensibilities, they will have much to say to each other. Indeed, it is precisely this difference in emphasis that anticipates an important compensatory role for Confucianism in the imminent recasting of the world cultural order.

Western Enlightenment Rationality: The Internal Critique

Unfortunately, Leibniz's appreciation of the different but complementary value of the disparate worlds produced by a European deductive rationalism on the one hand, and a Confucian bottom-up aestheticism on the other, was lost on most of the heirs to the Industrial Revolution who came to see their own Enlightenment rationality as the only game in town. Indeed, the modern European understanding of the Confucian tradition that evolved in the nineteenth and twentieth centuries was a much distorted caricature produced by framing Confucian culture with an idealism not its own and by overwriting it with Europe's own top-down assumptions. Hegel is a good example of a philosopher who in his dialectically driven teleology is wedded to a theoretical-deductive understanding in ethics and most everything else. For him, the Chinese are not even immoral—they are amoral—because, lacking any sense of personal autonomy, they are unable to affirm for themselves the authority of any moral precept. According to Hegel, for the Chinese:

> Moral distinctions and requirements are expressed as Laws, but so that the subjective will is governed by these Laws as by an external force. Nothing subjective in the shape of disposition, Conscience, formal Freedom, is recognized. Justice is administered only on the basis of external morality, and Government exists only as the prerogative of compulsion.... Morality is in the East likewise a subject of positive legislation, and although moral prescriptions (the *substance* of their Ethics) may be perfect, what should be internal subjective sentiment is made a matter of external arrangement.... While *we* obey, because what we are required to do is confirmed by an *internal* sanction, there the Law is regarded as inherently and absolutely valid without a sense of the want of this subjective confirmation.[24]

This construal of Chinese morality as being purely objective without regard for subjective confirmation echoes Hegel's criticism of the excessive abstractness of Kant's Moral Law in formalizing our natural moral intuitions by assuming the application of pure rational thought without reference to the concrete beliefs, institutions, and traditions that shape our thinking. What Hegel is not considering in the Confucian case, of course, is that ritual norms (*li*) differ fundamentally from the notion of law in that, far from being external in their moral force, they require a process of appropriation, personalization, and internalization—an insight that we have seen was not lost on Leibniz. Indeed, it is precisely because of this personal confirmation that governing through ritual norms is a considered strategy for providing a basis for the self-ordering of the community that precludes the need for any external coercion.[25]

In any case, the influence of this Hegelian picture of an Oriental despotism in which all authority lies with the emperor has had enormous play in the way in which Chinese history, politics, and philosophies have come to be understood within the Western academy, and is still alive and well as an interpretive framework.[26] Further, the Enlightenment assumptions about the nature of order that inspired this interpretation of a Chinese despotism have had consequences for the Western philosophical tradition itself that are more dire than simply an interpretive problem reflected in the misconstrual of the Chinese cultural tradition. Indeed, the issue runs much deeper, precipitating as it has the internal revolution within twentieth-century Western philosophy.

The Leibnizean valorization of the theoretical-deductive sciences as the hallmark of the European self-understanding perpetuated an entrenched and indeed fallacious way of thinking that came increasingly under assault in the twentieth-century self-critical phase of the Western philosophical narrative. William James for example, himself an heir to an Emersonian celebration of process and particularity, expresses concern about the consequences of investing so much in this refined rationalist approach to knowing our world that makes of philosophy "a kind of marble temple shining on a hill":[27]

> The theorizing mind tends always to the over-simplification of its materials. This is the root of all that absolutism and one-sided dogmatism by which both philosophy and religion have been infested.[28]

I · Introduction: "Appreciating" Confucianism

In fact, James was a process philosopher who argued for overcoming a substance understanding of "things" by giving equal status to the conjunctions and transitions that obtain among them, and who suggested that every sentence should end with "and...". For a philosopher who is reputed to have defined philosophy as "the peculiarly stubborn attempt to think clearly," James's notion of clarity was not so simple. Indeed, with deep respect for the complexity of the human experience, he takes his challenge to rationalism to be the nub of his own philosophical contribution:

> It is ... the reinstatement of the vague and inarticulate to its proper place in our mental life which I am so anxious to press on the attention.[29]

And real vestiges of this entrenched rationalist prejudice seem alive and well in our contemporary philosophical discourse. In reflecting upon alternative conceptions of persons in his evaluation of contemporary rights talk, for example, Henry Rosemont gives voice to what he takes to be the limitations of recommending an abstractive, rationalistic model of the discrete human being to alternative cultural traditions. He states:

> In the first place, the view of human beings as autonomous, rational individuals would be seen by a great many of the world's peoples as simply false. Utilizing an impoverished—and largely bureaucratic—technical vocabulary emphasizing law, abstract logic, the formation of policy statements, and employing altogether implausible hypothetical examples, contemporary rights-based moral and political philosophers, it would be argued, are no longer grounded in the real hopes, fears, joys, sorrows, ideas, and attitudes of flesh-and-blood human beings. Since the time of Descartes, Western philosophers have increasingly abstracted a purely cognizing activity away from concrete persons and determined that this use of logical reasoning in a disembodied "mind" is the choosing, autonomous essence of individuals, which is philosophically more foundational than are actual persons; the latter being only contingently who they are, and therefore of no great philosophical importance.[30]

The uncritical commitment to a Leibnizian rationalism in its various forms rehearsed by Rosemont here, is in fact one bit of faulty reasoning so recalcitrant and so persistently exercised by the philosophical elite that John Dewey, one of the earliest thinkers to be consistently critical of this particular *deformation profesionelle*, dubbed it "*the* philosophical fallacy." Simply put, *the* philosophical fallacy is committed whenever the outcome of a process is presumed to be antecedent to that process—whenever some ostensive "principle" is identified, isolated, and abstracted from the flow of experience and is then used anachronistically and reduplicatively to rationalize an always-emergent history. Dewey from early on saw as "the most pervasive fallacy of philosophical thinking" the error of ignoring the historical, developmental, and contextualizing aspects of experience. The methodological problem as he saw it is "the abstracting of some one element from the organism which gives it meaning, and setting it up as absolute" and then proceeding to revere this one element "as the cause and ground of all reality and knowledge."[31]

Notable examples of this fallacy are the Empiricist assumption that bare sense data are the beginning points of knowledge rather than mere abstractions constructed from the wholeness of primitive feelings, or the Rationalist prejudice that the coherence and stability won from the control of the precarious aspects of existence are the ground rather than the outcome of human practices, as when a divinely ordered cosmos is presumed to be the model for human personal and social order rather than the reverse. Suffice to say that *the* philosophical fallacy exists anytime the *terminus ad quem* is placed before the *terminus a quo*. Why, pondered the curious tourist, were so many American Civil War battles fought in national parks?

In fact, we philosophers are urged by the responsibilities of our office to warn against all fallacious forms of reasoning. But like the preacher who, come Monday, commits the very sins he railed against the day before, we are ourselves rarely delivered from the idols of the mind. Sometimes the fallacy is overlooked by polite conspiracy—as when we allow the author of this book to call the last pages written the "Preface," or when we give the name "Pre-Socratic philosophers" to those early Greek thinkers who in some seemingly ineluctable way anticipated the questions that would preoccupy the agora's barefoot philosopher. In such cases, the fallacy seems both innocent and harmless.

Moreover, given the extreme difficulty of avoiding this fallacious bit of reasoning in which we anachronistically take the outcome of experience to be its antecedent, we may be justified in often overlooking it, for as William James quoting Kierkegaard insists: "We live forwards …

but we understand backwards."[32] And in Lewis Caroll's *Through the Looking-Glass*, the White Queen says to Alice: "It's a poor sort of memory that only works backwards." Jorge Luis Borges too worries over how the outcome of experience is always present in our understanding of the past when he concludes that "life is essentially anachronistic."

As on almost every other issue, of course, philosophers are likely to disagree as to precisely when the conditions leading to the commission of *the* philosophical fallacy obtain. A strong ontological disposition, sustained by a distinction between the orders of knowing and of being, will suggest that it is always appropriate to place Being before those beings of the world through which Being itself is made manifest. The teleologist might find in some "far off Divine event" the ground as well as the goal of understanding, or perhaps anticipate the perfectibility of the "ready-made" human being in the actualization of a given potential.

One of the more pernicious of the many instances of *the* philosophical fallacy involves the kind of anachronism that reads history narrowly backwards from a given theoretical construct, finding at the origins of a historical narrative what in fact is merely one of the reflective fruits of that narrative. Such are the prejudices of teleological historiographies: Marxist, Hegelian, Christian, and indeed scientific. And corollary to this reading of history backwards is the myth that history "can be read sideways."[33] That is to say, there is a belief as widespread as it is mistaken that institutions such as the family, for example, have developed the same the world over. Since we assume that the family as an institution in our own experience has gone from being more oppressive to more liberating, we can thus learn about the evolution of the Western family by studying its more "primitive" antecedents elsewhere on the globe. Such is Marcel Mauss's understanding of the hard-won construction of the sacred Enlightenment person (*personne*) in its relation to other traditional conceptions of person:

> From a simple masquerade to the mask, from a "role" (*personage*) to a "person" (*personne*), to a name, to an individual; from the latter to a being possessing metaphysical and moral value; from a moral consciousness to a sacred being; from the latter to a fundamental form of thought and action—the course is accomplished.... It is formulated only for us, among us. Even its moral strength—the sacred character of the human "person" (*personne*)—is questioned, not only throughout the Orient, which has not

yet attained the level of our sciences, but even in the countries where this principle was discovered. We have great possessions to defend. With us the idea could disappear.[34]

Such Enlightenment thinking tends to condescend in seeing other strategies for organizing the human experience as proto- or pre-rational, thus in effect taking "traditional" to mean at best "pre-enlightened," and at worst, "unenlightened."

These are not only the more damaging forms taken by *the* philosophical fallacy, they are also the most difficult to avoid. After all, if one is to achieve any coherence in the construction of a historical narrative, one must appeal to some pattern of meanings, where the presumption of natural necessity can elevate that abstracted pattern to be the putative object of systematic knowledge. In any event, what Dewey saw long ago as *the* philosophical fallacy has become the philosophical issue of our day. An internal critique continues to be waged against *the* philosophical fallacy within professional Western philosophy under the many banners of hermeneutics, existentialism, post-structuralism, phenomenology, post-modernism, neo-pragmatism, neo-Marxism, deconstructionism, feminist philosophy and so on, taking as a shared target what Robert Solomon has called "the transcendental pretense"—*the* philosophical fallacy variously expressed as theo-ontological thinking, idealism, essentialism, formalism, objectivism, foundationalism, structuralism, transcendentalism, absolutism, logocentrism, the master narrative, the Myth of the Given, and all such foundational appeals on the carrousel of systematic philosophies.[35]

A "Depreciated" Confucianism

As we will find in the exploration of Confucian role ethics that follows, the Confucian vision of the consummate life has its own limitations, but *the* philosophical fallacy—the rationalization of the ethical life by appeal to antecedent moral principles—is not one among them. As first observed by Leibniz so long ago, rather than looking to Confucianism for abstract ethical theory, our appreciation of Confucian China might be better focused on its capacity to inspire the daily lives of the people, and in so doing, to realize a religiousness "in a vast multitude of men" that is of a quality greater "than the founders of religious orders among us have achieved."³⁶ For Leibniz, Confucianism's potential contribution to world culture lies in the various symbiotic areas of civil philosophy: ethics, social and political philosophy, and philosophy of religion.

But an uncritical advocacy of Confucianism in and of itself is not what will be offered in these pages. We all know that the stock value of Confucianism has risen and fallen across its long career, and has just as often been depreciated as appreciated by its erstwhile adherents. In the broadest terms, we can argue that Chinese history has never (and probably never will) live up to the lofty vision laid down in the canonical Confucian texts. Confucius himself during his lifetime despaired at having yet to meet "anyone who is truly fond of consummate conduct" (*ren* 仁) or "anyone who is truly steadfast" (*gang* 剛),³⁷ and it is unlikely that many consummate and steadfast persons who have reached Confucius's high expectations have lived in the interim.³⁸

Internally, Confucianism has all too often been appropriated by the powers-that-be to reinforce class and gender inequities. More than a fair share of despotic rulers have ruled imperial China over the centuries and have oppressed generations in the name of Confucian values. And in Chinese homes, patriarchy has often reduced the complex notion of "family reverence" (*xiao* 孝) to blind obedience and unquestioning loyalty to adult males. Indeed, such a depreciation of Confucianism continues today. In our own times, it has been depreciated from within when a patriarchal and patronizing Singapore government manages to transform this living Confucian tradition into a dry-as-bones catechism—a form of political indoctrination to be foisted upon witless school children for their ostensive moral edification.³⁹

Confucianism has also been depreciated from without as, in the process of being introduced into the Western academy, its key philosophical vocabulary and terms of art have been overwritten with the values of an Abrahamic religiousness not its own, thereby reducing Confucianism in the eyes of many to a necessarily anemic, second-rate form of Christianity. Witness the standard formula of translations: *tian* 天 is "Heaven," *li* 禮 is "ritual," *yi* 義 is "righteousness," *dao* 道 is "*the* Way," *ren* 仁 is "benevolence," *de* 德 is "virtue," *xiao* 孝 is "filial piety," and so on. In sum, such a vocabulary conjures forth a pre-established, single-ordered and divinely sanctioned cosmos guided by the hand of a righteous God that ought to inspire human faith and compliance.

There have been subsequent efforts by some scholars to rescue an uprooted and transplanted Confucianism from this Christian soil. But the result has often been to reconstruct its ideas and values through the prism of an Orientalism that would ostensibly save the integrity of Confucianism by dismissing its profoundly religious dimensions, and in so doing, reduce it to a kind of secular humanism. Or perhaps worse, in reading Confucianism's inclusive and provisional approach to philosophical understanding as unstructured and indeterminate, such interpreters are given to reducing its holistic sensibilities to mysticism and the occult.

The consequence, then, of this overtly Christianized and then Orientalized reading of the Confucian vocabulary has located the study of this tradition within Western seats of higher learning in religion and area studies departments rather than as a proper part of the philosophy curriculum, and has relegated translations of the Confucian texts to the "New Age" and suspect "Eastern Religions" corners of our bookstores. In attempting to provide a more nuanced explanation of these same Confucian terms, Qian Mu is adamant that this vocabulary expressing the unique and complex Confucianism vision of a consummate life simply has no counterpart in other languages.[40] Qian Mu's point in making this claim is not to argue for cultural purism and incommensurability; on the contrary, he would allow that with sufficient exposition (the ambitious objective of this present monograph), the Confucian world can be "appreciated" in important degree by those from without. Qian Mu's claim is on behalf of the uniqueness and the value of a tradition that has defined its own terms of art through the lived experience of its people over millennia, and anticipates the real difficulty we must face in attempting to capture its complex and organically related vocabulary in other languages without substantial qualification and explanation.

The Necessity of Informed Generalizations in Making Cultural Comparisons

Confucianism is further being depreciated today from another rather unlikely source—that is, from earnest interpreters of this tradition, some of whom are as committed to the enduring value of Confucian philosophy as Qian Mu was, but who would disagree fundamentally with his claims about the difficulty of cultural translation. I want to contest the resistance among some contemporary scholars to sanction the thick cultural generalizations we have seen made by both Leibniz and Qian Mu that I believe are necessary if we are to respect the rich differences that obtain among traditions and if we are to avoid as best we can an impoverishing cultural reductionism.

Some sinologists think that we do well to abjure generalizations about Chinese history and culture altogether. Indeed, Paul Goldin indicts many of the most distinguished sinologists of the past century as offering "an updated Orientalism" for their attempt to provide an interpretive context for understanding Chinese culture. He charges these scholars with presenting "China as a reified foil to a reified West, an antipodal domain exemplifying antithetic mores and modes of thought."[41] As an alternative, Goldin would argue that

> ... if there is one valid generalization about China, it is that China defies generalization. Chinese civilization is simply too huge, too diverse, and too old for neat maxims.[42]

I think such an approach, while aspiring after an ostensive interpretive objectivity, advocates nothing short of a naïve realism. Hilary Putnam dismisses outright this extreme kind of realism by not only rejecting the idea that we could ever arrive at an understanding of such a mind-independent reality, but also that such an object of understanding would in fact even constitute reality. He argues that

> ... elements of what we call "language" or "mind" *penetrate so deeply into what we call "reality" that the very project of representing ourselves as being "mappers" of something "language-independent" is fatally compromised from the start.* Like Relativism, but in a different way, Realism is an impossible attempt to view the world from Nowhere.[43]

Putnam continues by insisting that this kind of human penetration and transformation of our environments extends to our attention and valorization of the world in which we live, requiring us to accept our own reflexivity as "beings who cannot have a view of the world that does not reflect our interests and values."[44] As we will discover in chapter three, the Confucian position of "embodying our experience" (*ti* 體) and "pursuing a ritual propriety in our roles and relations" (*li* 禮) differs from Putnam only in that it is more radical, going beyond the twentieth-century philosophical preoccupation with "language" and "mind" to claim that our entire psychophysical persons are involved in the process of assimilating and transforming the world as it is experienced. Our further argument would be that cultural differences in thinking and living are fundamental to this transformative process, and affect in a vital way any attempt we might make to interpret other cultures.

We must be self-conscious of what we bring to the enterprise of exploring another cultural tradition. There is a failure of interpreters to be conscious of and to take fair account of their own Gadamerian "prejudices." They offer the excuse that they are relying on some "objective" lexicon when the truth of the matter is that this lexicon is itself heavily colored with cultural biases, thereby betraying their readers not once, but twice. That is, not only do they fail to provide their readers with the actual meaning of the text, but further and with undeterred confidence they offer up a *hasenpfeffer* (German rabbit stew) rather than the promised *char siu* duck.

This self-consciousness in interpretation is not to distort the Chinese philosophical tradition and its process cosmology, but to endorse its fundamental premises. Just as each generation selects and carries over earlier thinkers to reshape them in their own image, each generation reconfigures the classical canons of world philosophy to its own needs. We too are inescapably people of a time and place.

In contrast to a naïve realism that pretends to a view from Nowhere, I would contend that the canopy of an always-emerging cultural vocabulary is itself rooted in and grows out of a deep and relatively stable soil of unannounced assumptions sedimented over generations into the language, the customs, and the life forms of a living tradition. And further, I would argue that to fail to acknowledge the fundamental character of cultural difference as an erstwhile safeguard against the sins of "essentialism" or "relativism" or "Orientalism" is not itself innocent. Indeed, ironically, such an antagonism to cultural generalizations leads to the uncritical essentializing of one's own contingent cultural assumptions and to the insinuating of them into one's interpretations of the ways of thinking and living of other traditions.[45]

This same point can be made another way. I would maintain that the only thing more dangerous than striving to make responsible cultural generalizations is failing to make them. Generalizations do not have to preclude appreciating the richness and complexity of always evolving cultural traditions; in fact, it is generalizations that locate and inform specific cultural details and provide otherwise sketchy historical developments with the thickness of their content. There is no alternative in making cultural comparisons to an open, hermeneutical approach that is ready to modify always provisional generalizations with the new information that additional detail yields as it is read and understood within the grid of interpretation. Philosophical interpreters must sensitize the student of Chinese philosophy to the ambient uncommon assumptions that have made the Chinese philosophical narrative so different from our own. It is these assumptions that inform the philosophical vocabulary and set parameters on their meanings.

If Ludwig Wittgenstein is insightful in suggesting that "the limits of our language are the limits of our world," then perhaps we need more language to capture, inform, and facilitate the understanding and application of these cultural generalizations. To take a familiar example, we know that by developing a nuanced understanding of a classical Greek vocabulary—*logos, nous, physis, kosmos, eidos, alethea*, and so on—we are able to get behind Descartes and at least in degree, give classical Greek texts their own integrity and read them in a more sophisticated way. By generating and constructing a glossary of key philosophical terms around which the Chinese texts are woven, we will be better able to locate these seminal documents in their own intellectual landscape. Indeed, we will need this vocabulary to explore and define Confucian role ethics if we are indeed to take this vision of the consummate life on its own terms.

Are these generic assumptions that inform the vocabulary of Confucian role ethics essential and unchanging? Such a claim would violate the premises of the underlying Chinese process cosmology and the language that gives it expression. Recently, and specifically in reference to the classical Chinese language, the distinguished sinologist Angus Graham concludes that in reporting on the eventful flow of correlative cosmology, "The sentence structure of Classical Chinese places us in a world of process about which we ask ... 'Whence?' and also, since it is moving, 'At what time?'"[46]

It is for this reason that I have consistently advocated a holistic, narrative understanding of Chinese culture as being more revealing of its underlying cultural assumptions than a merely analytical approach that tends to isolate and decontextualize elements which are always situated within a particular time and place. Using the language of the *Book of Changes*, we must be able to appreciate both the flux (*bian* 變) and the persistence (*tong* 通) that define this Chinese philosophical narrative, without abandoning either one for the sake of the other.

In a sustained effort to allow Chinese philosophy to have its own voice, over the past century our best interpreters of Chinese culture have been struggling to construct an interpretive context for reading the canons. This interpretive context begins by clarifying the cultural presuppositions we are likely to bring to the Chinese texts, and then continues by attempting to articulate those uncommon assumptions that make Chinese cosmology distinctive and different from our own philosophical narrative. In recent years, some serious scholarship has been offered that disputes the value of this search for the always-imperfect but often corroborating generalizations being made by these same scholars.

To take one example: In Michael Puett's monograph, *To Become a God: Cosmology, Sacrifice, and Self-Divinization in Early China*, he rehearses and then sets aside the attempts of these earlier sinologists to provide a cultural framework for interpreting classical Chinese texts and the historical events that locate them in time and place.

Puett describes one such group of prominent interpreters of Chinese culture as belonging to the "evolutionary paradigm"—Max Weber, Fung Yu-lan, Karl Jaspers, and most recently, Heiner Roetz. On Puett's reading, these scholars share a commitment to taking a kind of universal rationality as the gold standard, and then attempt to weigh and measure the development of Chinese culture against it. Ultimately these interpreters either assert that China too has evidenced the transition from the proto-rational to the rational, or they dispute such a claim. For Puett, Karl Jaspers, who argues that the emergence of the idea of transcendence created a universal form of consciousness, has been the most influential exemplar of this evolutionary framework. In Jaspers' *The Origin and Goal of History*, he develops the notion of the Axial Age (800–200 BCE) in which human beings for the first time experience "absoluteness in the depths of selfhood and the lucidity of transcendence."[47] Philosophers who would advocate this understanding of culture as a universal history emphasize the emergence of a common consciousness among traditions rather than the growth of assumptions that would make them distinctive.

Indeed, when for Jaspers, both the "origins" and the "goal" of history are already predetermined, one wonders in what sense such a thesis can be described in any meaningful way as "evolutionary." Evolution entails an open, continuing, and contingent process of transformation where, through genetic drift, the spontaneous emergence of novelty produces unexpected hybridic forms. Jaspers instead offers us a doctrine of universal history in which, through an ineluctable process of convergence, a universal form of consciousness arises. This is the familiar idealization of history driven by teleological necessity. Indeed, I would describe the assumptions of this group of rationalists as a kind of "cultural essentialism" that, given their universalistic pretence, cannot escape their own ethnocentrism.

But Puett chooses to describe yet another set of interpreters as positing a "cultural essentialism": Granet, Mote, Needham, Graham, K. C. Chang, and Hall and Ames.[48] What this group of interpreters shares in common is the belief that there is a distinctive yet always-evolving way of thinking that needs to be taken into account in understanding a holistic Chinese cosmology. Further, they assert that this dynamic Chinese cosmology posits a world that is naturalistic, autogenerative, and self-construing without appeal to some external metaphysical principle as its unilateral source of order.

We might take Marcel Granet, the earliest sinologist to give clear voice to this position, as an example. According to Puett, Marcel Granet seeks to defend Chinese philosophy as a viable way of organizing and explaining the human experience "by arguing that it was based on a cosmology radically different from, but nonetheless as important as, the cosmology that dominated the West."[49] In identifying and articulating the conditions of this early Chinese cosmology, Granet insists that there is "no world of transcendent principles outside the human realm."[50] Puett further observes that Granet "read these cosmological notions not as a particular historical development during the Han but as indications of Chinese thinking in general.... Then, in the final quarter of the book

[*La pensée Chinoise*], Granet looks at individual thinkers, beginning with Confucius. Each thinker is presented as building on a particular aspect of this 'Chinese' cosmology. In other words, instead of presenting cosmology as a late development building on or reacting against earlier figures like Confucius, Granet reads correlative thinking as the guiding principle of all Chinese thought."[51]

When Puett here suggests that correlative Chinese cosmology is a development peculiar to the Han dynasty, does he mean that such a cosmology emerged *ex nihilo*—that thinkers prior to the Han are without a worldview that in some way anticipates the application of a continuing common sense in the articulation of an elaborate cosmology during the Han? In chapter two, I will cite David Keightley who *contra* Puett argues at length for a continuity in ways of thinking between the Shang dynasty (1600–1046 BCE) and the formative period of Chinese philosophy during the Zhou (1045–256 BCE) and Han dynasties (206 BCE–220 CE).[52] Again, to describe "correlative thinking" as the application of a "principle" would render such thinking as a species of rationalism. But correlative thinking means very different things in different contexts. To appreciate what is at issue in this debate, we need to maintain a clear distinction between the ahistorical implications of rational or logical thinking that is analytical, and that seeks closure in patterns of fixed regularity, and the historical entailments of correlative thinking that is synthetic, and that seeks open-ended, aesthetic disclosure in *ad hoc* unities constituted by unique details. This distinction is captured in the difference Whitehead asserts in defining a logical and an aesthetic order, where the former as an act of closure is universalistic, while the latter as an act of disclosure is radically historicist.[53] Logic requires a notion of strict identity as the ground for its essentialism; art only allows for analogical relations among unique particulars. And since Granet and the other interpreters who share his approach are self-consciously historicist in tracing the evolution of this common sense through the corpus of canonical texts and again historicist in their understanding of its application to and elaboration in different dimensions of the Chinese experience, including the cosmologies made explicit in the Han dynasty, where is the essentialism?

Puett goes on to rehearse this same distinction between the rational and aesthetic sensibilities that Hall and Ames refer to as the difference between first and second problematic thinking and again the difference between analogical and causal thinking. Puett allows that through such distinctions, like Granet before them, Hall and Ames "attempt to 'illumine the contrasting assumptions shaping classical Chinese and Western culture.'"[54] True enough. And that like Graham, Hall and Ames "see each of these ways of thinking as existing to some degree in both Chinese and Western cultures, and ... are thus able to argue that Chinese thought is something that can be fully assimilated into contemporary Western thinking."[55] Again confirmed. But if essentialism is to be understood as a generalization stating that certain properties possessed by a population are universal and exclusive to them, that these same properties are not dependent on context, and that again such properties entail a relativism and incommensurability among cultures, how can Puett describe any of these scholars as proferring a "cultural-essentialist model" of interpretation? The account of these interpreters instead sounds like an open and inclusive pluralism. And given that this characterization of Chinese culture anticipates a productive dialogue among importantly different cultural narratives, I would in fact describe it as "evolutionary" in the best sense of that term.

Puett criticizes what he takes to be "the central dangers of contrastive approaches such as that of Hall and Ames," claiming that "building such a contrastive framework requires taking particular texts out of context and reading them as assumptions of the entire cultures being compared."[56] For Puett, "All of these interpretive strategies—reading in terms of schools, essentialized definitions of culture, evolutionary frameworks—have the consequence of erasing the unique power that particular claims had at the time."[57]

We would ask: How does the claim that people who have a shared language, culture, and history are likely to have some common philosophical assumptions preclude not only the possibility but also the probability that they also have important differences that, in our reading of their canons, also need to be registered and appreciated? How does insisting that texts must be read within the ambiance of these shared cultural assumptions take them out of context or preclude our understanding of the differences that obtain among them?

But perhaps the more important question is: What does Puett

offer us as an alternative strategy for responsible cultural comparisons? Allowing Puett to speak for himself:

> In short, I am recommending that we dispense with both of the frameworks discussed above—both the contrastive and the evolutionary models. We should instead work toward a more nuanced approach in which we make no *a priori* assumptions regarding single statements made in single texts and the significance of individual claims.[58]

This can only mean that, like Goldin, Puett proposes we forego any cultural generalizations and just read the texts as they present themselves to us. But following Hilary Putnam in rejecting the very possibility of this "view-from-Nowhere" realism, we would insist that our own interests and values guide our interpretations in a palpable way, and that they enable us to see only what we would see. Henry Thoreau reflects on this unavoidably collaborative nature of acquiring new knowledge in the human experience:

> A man receives only what he is ready to receive, whether physically or intellectually or morally.... We hear and apprehend only what we already half know.... Every man thus *tracks himself* through life, in all his hearing and reading and observation and traveling. His observations make a chain. The phenomenon or fact that cannot in any wise be linked with the rest which he has observed, he does not observe.[59]

Puett's determining thesis is that correlative cosmology arises dialectically when what was exclusively *two*—the divine Ancestoral One and the human world—becomes *one*: that is, when human beings aspire "To Become a God."

> What is going on in Chinese correlative thought is precisely an attempt to pull together elements perceived to be distinct—an attempt to claim a form of continuity prevailing against disparate entities.[60]

Puett applies his methodology to the *Taiyishengshui* 太一生水, a fragmentary document recovered in 1993 as an integral element in the Guodian *Daodejing* 郭店道德經. Even though he allows that in this document "the Great One pervades everything and is both the mother and the aligner of the myriad things,"[61] he arrives at a familiar single-source, One-behind-the-many, unilateral cosmogony in which the correlative relationship between the Great Ancestral One and the waters and everything else that is born of this progenitor is not taken to be a significant factor. On Puett's interpretation:

> In this cosmology, neither humans nor spirits affect the environment: the cosmos is simply a set of natural forces that respond to one another. Sages are simply those who understand these processes properly understanding the Great One—whose style name is "the Way." ... There is an inherent alignment in the cosmos, generated and maintained by the Great One, that provides the basis for human action. Power and knowledge are thus to be gained not by appropriating the powers of spirits but by understanding and subordinating oneself to the patterns of the cosmos."[62]

For Puett, the *Daodejing* too "is based on generation from an original ancestor, the Way."[63] The overriding consideration that ostensively distinguishes the *Taiyishengshui* and the *Daodejing* is whether or not the human being accords with or contrives to usurp the powers of the independent divine force, the Way. In Puett's words:

> The debate will turn then to issues such as What is the relationship of human to this One? Do they simply conform to the patterns of the One, or can they achieve power by means of the One as well?[64]

For Puett, what distinguishes the doctrine espoused in the *Daodejing* from *Taiyishengshui* is the putative capacity of the sage to take on the powers of the One and to thereby gain control over both the people and the cosmos by virtue of this Promethean hubris:

> By holding fast to the Way, the adept is able to make all things submit to him, to control the populace with resorting to overt commands, and even to bring Heaven and Earth into harmony. He becomes, in a sense, like the ancestor: he is able to generate order and cause everything to submit to him.[65]

Unlike the sage in *Taiyishengshui* who simply understands and conforms to a pre-existing cosmic order, the sage in the *Daodejing* deceptively accords

> ... with the ancestor in order to gain its powers and create an order of his own choosing.... He thus gains power over both: the natural world, like the human world, submits to him, not the other way around.... He thereafter

fools people into thinking the subsequent phenomena they witness are natural, when in fact they are simply his wishes.[66]

This cynical interpretation of the *Daodejing* is not a new one, and on my reading, is not a good one either. As early as Han Fei and as recent as Herrlee Creel, we have been offered what the latter author describes as a "purposive" Daoism that celebrates deceit, personal ambition, and political control as the intended meaning of this text.[67] On my reading, such a contrived interpretation does not do justice to the cosmological and political profundity of this classic document.[68]

Let me appeal to another prominent voice as one more example of a resolute resistance to generalizations as a relevant factor in any attempt to express the distinctiveness of our cultural traditions. The quantum difference between Confucian and Christian cultural sensibilities and the practical implications of these differences is certainly not lost on Zhang Longxi 張隆溪, a hugely erudite scholar of comparative literature who is as intellectually comfortable in the cultural classics of the Western narrative as he is in the Chinese canons. He allows for this degree of difference when he observes:

> Judging from the tenacious grip of Confucianism on the Chinese mind in late imperial China and the negligible number of Chinese converts whom the missionaries succeeded in proselytizing, no one can overlook the enormous gap between Chinese and Western cultural traditions.[69]

At the same time, Zhang has argued consistently that the asserting of radical difference he quite properly ascribes to the interpretation of the Chinese language and culture by comparative philosophers with whom I would identify, is "purist" and leads to "relativism" and thus, incommensurability. Zhang Longxi states with confidence that while we will never find strict identity among cultures, we can find "equivalencies":

> Linguistic and cultural differences between China and the West are obvious, that is, in the etymological sense of "standing in the way" (*ob viam*) like obstacles, and it is the task of translation to clear the way for understanding and communication by discovering equivalent formulations underneath the changing surface of differences.[70]

What makes the formulation of such equivalents possible for Zhang is an acknowledged sameness in thinking among cultures:

> Against such an overemphasis on difference and cultural uniqueness ... I would like to argue for the basic translatability of languages and cultures.... Only when we acknowledge different peoples and nations as equal in their ability to think, to express, to communicate, and to create values, we may then rid ourselves of ethnocentric biases ...[71]

In making his case for "equivalencies," the target of Zhang's ire is Arthur Wright and "those who present views more or less similar to Wright's," with myself and my collaborators being prominent in his indictment. Citing Wright as his immediate example, Zhang's complaint is against positing different modes of thinking and speaking:

> Here the cultural difference between the Chinese and the Western is formulated as fundamentally distinct ways of thinking and speaking, as the ability, or lack of it, to express abstract ideas.[72]

For Zhang, an even more egregious example of exaggerated difference is Jacques Gernet, who would describe the tension between Christianity and Chinese thinking as not only one "of different intellectual traditions but also of different mental categories and modes of thought."[73] Again, taking one specific terminology as an example, Zhang suggests that those who would assert that the Chinese language does not have an adequate equivalent to translate the protean Abrahamic concept of "God" are in fact claiming "that the very idea of God or divinity is inconceivable in the Chinese mind and inexpressible in the Chinese language."[74]

It is not that Zhang and I have different goals. Indeed, Zhang, in arguing for cultural translatability, is advocating a position that I and many of the other objects of his criticism endorse whole-heartedly in everything we say and do. We are not all "purists" or "relativists," and it would be anything but fair to associate us with the likes of the anti-accommodationist Franciscan Father Antonio de Caballero whom Zhang takes to be representative of cultural incommensurability. Zhang describes the arrogant and dismissive Caballero as "the staunch purist who insistently demands the unadulterated essence of the original" for whom anything less is "merely aping the Truth."[75] What separates we self-confessed cultural pluralists (rather than "purists") from Zhang are what we take to be several troubling implications of his basic assumptions about how the translation between and among cultural traditions is to be carried out.

To begin with, one might argue that the bugbear of "essentialism" that properly worries Zhang is itself, like any strict philosophical notion of "universalism," largely a culturally specific deformation. Indeed, universalism is closely associated with "the transcendental pretense" described above as a fallacy pervasive in the pre-Darwinian Western philosophical narrative that is immediately aligned with what Dewey has called "*the* philosophical fallacy." After all, we can only "essentialize" (rather than analogize) if we are predisposed to believe there are such things as "essences," a way of thinking about things that did not recommend itself to the formative thinkers of classical China. Essentialism itself arises from familiar classical Greek assumptions about ontology as "the science of being," and from the application of strict identity as the principle of individuation. It is this notion of "essences" that grounds Platonic idealism and the Aristotelian doctrine of species (*eidos*) as natural kinds.

Again, Zhang's claim about peoples and cultures being "equal" in their ability to think is intended to be inclusive and liberating and respectful, and while such assurances might be salutary for some scholars, such an assertion is anything but innocuous. To claim that other traditions have culturally specific modalities of thinking is *not* to claim that such traditions do not know how to think unless we ourselves believe that in fact there is only one way of thinking, and that this way of thinking—that is, *our* way of thinking—is the only way. The uncritical assumption that other cultures must think the same way as we do is for me the very definition of essentialism and ethnocentrism. I would contend that it is precisely the recognition and appreciation of the degree of difference obtaining among cultures in living and thinking that properly motivates cultural translation in the first place, and that ultimately rewards the effort. Surely arguing that there are culturally contingent modalities of thinking can be pluralistic rather than relativistic, and can be accommodating rather than condescending. At the very least, if the field of comparative studies is to provide us with the mutual enrichment that it promises, we must strive with imagination to take other cultures on their own terms and appreciate fully the differences that obtain among them.[76]

And acknowledging what Whitehead has described as "the perils of abstraction," I would maintain that the kind of rich aesthetic harmony achieved when we are able to find the proper balance between concreteness

I · Introduction: "Appreciating" Confucianism

and abstraction and between unique detail and a productive coherence requires that we exercise our imagination in identifying and respecting the differences among cultures. Without the possibilities made available to us by these protean differences, we are left with a lifeless and insipid sameness.[77]

Thirdly, much of Zhang's exasperation seems to arise from interpreters such as Arthur Wright and Jacques Gernet (and I dare say me and my collaborators) who, in allowing for "fundamentally distinct ways of thinking and speaking," would claim (using Zhang's language) that the difference between the Chinese and Western cultures is "the ability, or lack of it, to express abstract ideas."[78] For Zhang, those who would allow for alternative modalities of thinking that place a different degree of emphasis on the functional value of abstraction are guilty of a clear debasement of the Chinese language and culture:

> The Chinese language, as seen in this formulation, appears to be a language of concrete things and specific objects, a language bogged down in matter and unable to rise above the ground of materiality and literality toward any spiritual height. The judgment is thus not on Chinese translation of particular foreign words and concepts, but on the very nature and ability of the Chinese language as a whole.[79]

Here, on my reading of Zhang, he is buying into two dualistic assumptions common to a tradition grounded in Greek ontology. First, in disallowing "distinct ways of thinking and speaking" he is locating cultural differences in the "content" and "objects" of thought rather than in its subjective instrument, as though "thinking" and "what is thought about" are somehow distinct. The implication here is that modes of thinking are essentially separable from the content of thinking by virtue of some pre-cultural faculties of the human mind and some *a priori* categories that structure it. And a further familiar assumption entailed by this distinction is that some definition of the human "mind" is not only an inclusive universal, but is also what is most distinctively and most valuably human. Such an exclusive mind/body and theory/praxis dualism has never been a distraction in a Chinese correlative *yinyang* cosmology in which mind/body (*shenxin* 身心) and theory/praxis (*zhixing* 知行) have been taken to be collaborative, coterminous, and mutually entailing aspects of experience. Indeed, the continuity and wholeness of experience is defined in terms of "forming and functioning" (*tiyong* 體用), and "flux and persistence" (*biantong* 變通)—cosmological assumptions that preclude any strictly dualistic categories.

A corollary assumption implicit in Zhang's critique, again itself profoundly dualistic, is that the theoretical and spiritual idealities entertained by this essentialized conception of mind are superior to practical efficacy in our everyday experience, and that entertaining these abstractions elevates us closer to the mind of God. Such abstraction as the work of intellection in its theoretical assent is somehow more real and refined than embodied concrete experience, providing us with a quality of knowledge uncontaminated by the changing world whence these abstractions arise, and from a Confucian perspective, to which they perhaps ought to owe their allegiance. Indeed Zhang is endorsing the superiority and the arrogance of a theo-ontological tradition that has defined itself as being preoccupied by abstractions—a tradition that assumes its interpretation of the human experience is more noble and spiritual than one that pursues practical wisdom and the alternative spiritual and religiousness sensibilities produced therefrom.

At the end of the day, the irony is that Zhang is affirming for Confucian philosophy precisely the long-lived and hobbling fallacy that many twentieth- and now twenty-first-century Western philosophers have been struggling to put to rest within our own narrative. As players in the internal critique raging within Western philosophy today, contemporary philosophers are attempting to reverse the gravity of theoretical ascent, and to reinstate what was left behind.

But I am not done. Fourthly, Zhang Longxi is eliding an important distinction we might borrow from Saussure between *langue* (language) and *parole* (speech), a division between the evolved, theoretical, and conceptual structure of a language system that is shaped by an aggregating intelligence over millennia and that makes speech possible, and the application of any natural language in the individual utterances we make.[80] We pluralists need this distinction to galvanize our claim that the Chinese language has not developed and does not have available to it either an indigenous concept or a term that can be used to capture the Abrahamic notion of "God," while at the same time allowing us to insist that the same Chinese language has all of the semantic and syntactic resources necessary to give a fair account of such an idea. What we are saying about this absence in the *langue* of the Chinese language is precisely what Qian Mu is quite properly saying about the want of a Western vocabulary to adequately speak Confucianism. You cannot say "*li* 禮" in English, or in German either, although you can say lots about it in both languages.

Finally, in disqualifying our claim of disparity in the relative value that different cultures invest in abstract conceptualizations, Zhang inadvertently saves Confucianism from what I would take to be an entirely appropriate critique. It precludes a salutary criticism of the limits of Confucianism made by many scholars late and soon, Western and Chinese alike, with the philosopher Bertrand Russell and the sociologist Ambrose King (Jin Yaoji 金耀基) being prominent among them. In these pages I want to join these scholars in advocating a revitalized Confucian moral philosophy adequate to the complexities of the modern world that complements its traditional emphasis upon family feeling as both the entry point and the substance of moral competence with a more robust framework of regulative ideals directed at preempting the all-too-frequent misuse of intimate relationships that gives rise to nepotism, cronyism, and other forms of social and political corruption. Just as intimacy needs the restraining complement of integrity, concrete family feelings require the guiding complement of some form of more general ideals.

But at the end of the day, that Zhang Longxi and I can think differently about cultural translation is perhaps itself to advocate for a healthy pluralism. That is, the competing positions we have taken on the issue of cultural translatability can certainly be seen as cautionary, if not in some respects compensatory for one another. If we can rise above the exclusivity of our critical dialectic, we might well concede that there is merit to each of our positions, and that we would certainly have less if we had only one of them.

The Inevitability of Analogy in Making Cultural Comparisons

Abandoning the assumption then that we all think pretty much alike (a first step in appreciating Confucianism), is to attempt as best we can to take this tradition on its own terms and to try to give an adequate account of it as it has evolved. But if, as I have claimed above, cultural reductionism has been a longstanding obstacle in the introduction of

Confucianism into the Western academy, how do we avoid this problem and get beyond it? Indeed, if cross-cultural translation is by definition collaborative, symbiotic, and transformative, what would it mean to take Confucianism on its own terms?

Alexander Pope, in *An Essay on Man*, asks: "What can we reason, but from what we know?" Adapting this question with license to our present task, we might allow that we can only know what we do not know by invoking what we do know. This means that cross-cultural understanding must proceed analogically with each tradition having to find within its own resources a vocabulary that enables it to restate in some always-imperfect way the philosophical and cultural assets of the tradition that it would understand better. Appropriate directly from other cultures we cannot; analogize we must.

Encountering the unsummed richness of the original texts themselves, we as interpreters are always people of a specific place and time. As such, any cross-cultural interface will in itself be a formula for an inescapable cultural reductionism. And certainly our too-hastily-constructed interpretive strategies and overarching theories, "philosophical" and otherwise, when applied in the practice of cultural and textual translation, cannot help but put concrete detail at some considerable risk. When Robert Frost remarks that "what is lost in translation is the poetry," I think that as an artist he is quite properly concerned that translation is a literary transaction that at best makes poetry different, and that most often, makes it less.

Further, a rather natural question that arises for me and my likeminded collaborators who would seek to interpret Confucianism for the Western academy is this: In our attempt to get past earlier putatively reductive readings of the Chinese corpus are we not in fact just substituting one Western philosophical reading of these texts for another? Are we not "rescuing" the Chinese tradition from an uncritical Greek or Cartesian reading, or a more calculated Christian understanding of the tradition, only to overwrite it with our own pragmatic, process assumptions?[81]

Indeed, in order to optimize our always-imperfect efforts at translation, we will always need a commitment to a Heideggerian *destruktion* in which we struggle to recover the situated, primordial meanings of the key philosophical terminology by dissolving the concealing calcifications and by "polishing" these terms back to their genuine luster. This process is "conservative" in the archaeological sense of recovering as much contextualizing detail as possible, and is "radical" as we pursue the root meanings within the soil of Chinese culture that are themselves alive and have grown along with the semantic foliage. In spite of our real interpretive limitations, we must, to the extent that we can, accord with the principle of logical charity and struggle with imagination to allow a text that belongs to another cultural narrative to reveal its own poetry—the bottomlessness of its own unmediated detail and particularity. But a resolute commitment to recovering the ostensively "objective" specificity of the text is not enough.

First, the image of Jorge Luis Borges's "Funes the Memorious" comes to mind, raising the question of whether can we actually "think" particularity without mediating its concrete detail with one interpretive prolepsis or another.[82] It is only possible in some degree and to some extent to escape our own facticity and to read these texts with a naiveté and innocence unburdened by our own cultural assumptions. Perhaps instead of pretending to an impossible objectivity, we need a hermeneutical openness in the project of cultural interpretation. Surely the most savvy interpreter is Bacon's bee, who must mediate between the textual specificity of Bacon's ant, hopelessly lost as it is in the inexhaustible details of phrase and meaning, and the always tenuous web of contextualizing generalizations spun by Bacon's spider. That is, beyond the necessary commitment to respecting the particularity of the text, we are in need of Gadamer's hermeneutical sensibilities that begin from an awareness of our own prejudgments, and that allow for both textual detail and interpretive generalizations in the ongoing and inevitable process of fusing cultural horizons.[83]

Indeed, it can be argued that interpretation—literally, a "go-between negotiation"—emerges analogically through establishing and aggregating a pattern of truly productive correlations between what we know and what we would know. Such correlations can be productive or otherwise, to the extent that they are a source of increased or reduced meaning. And if such "wit" is pursued effectively, we actually achieve a modicum of wisdom itself when we are able to accumulate and optimize these meaningful correlations effectively in our own life situations.

Wholesale and Retail Analogies, Associative and Contrastive Analogies

Of course, if analogize we must, at the same time we must also allow that not all analogies are equally apposite. As we have argued above in rehearsing the career of Chinese philosophy within the Western academy, poorly chosen comparisons can be a persisting source of distortion and of cultural condescension. A heavy-handed and impositional "Christian," "Heideggarian," and yes, even "Pragmatic" or "Whiteheadian" reading of Chinese philosophies betrays the reader not once but twice by distorting both the Chinese tradition and the Western analog in the comparison. Even so, we have no choice but to identify productive analogies that, with effort and imagination, can in the fullness of time be qualified and refined in such a way as to introduce culturally novel ideas into our own world in order to enrich our own ways of thinking and living.

In so doing, we need to be analogically retail and piecemeal rather than working in whole cloth. That is, when for example we turn to the *Zhongyong* 中庸, in which the human being is celebrated as co-creator with the heavens and the earth, we might find analogy with Whitehead in his concern to reinstate a viable notion of "creativity" as an important human value.[84] At the same time we might be keenly aware that when the same Whitehead in explanation of this creativity invokes the primordial nature of God and the Eternal Objects sustained in His mind, the long shadow of Aristotelian teleology sets a real limit on the relevance of this dimension of Whitehead's thought for classical Chinese processual cosmology.

Further, as we can see from these two references to Whitehead, analogies can be productive of both associations and contrasts, and we can learn much from both. Indeed, while Aristotle's teleology and his reliance upon formal logic as the method of achieving demonstrable truth might serve as clear points of contrast with Chinese philosophies, his resistance to Platonic abstraction in promoting an aggregating practical wisdom does resonate productively with one of the central issues in classical Confucian moral philosophy: a commitment to the cultivation of excellent habits in thinking and feeling. In this project of cultural translation, we do well to pick and choose our analogies carefully—but pick and choose we must.

And taking one further turn on the hermeneutical circle, such analogical explorations and appropriations are by no means passive. Going back to Frost, while translation is always pursued at real risk to both rhyme and reason, surely what can be *found* in translation is also an additional measure of meaning and elegance. Try as we might, we cannot avoid to some degree "making up" our interpretation and "making over" the text with it. But at the same time, one way or another, there is always the possibility of enlarging the meaning of the text in making it our own. To thus "appreciate" the text means not only to become aware of its scale and sophistication, but also to become creatively responsive to it, and in the process of becoming intimate with it, to add our own unique value that expands the text further. For example, in the first half of the twentieth century, Arthur Waley, as a translator of Tang dynasty poetry and Noh plays, became a prominent literary personality among the Bloomsbury group with such notables as T. S. Eliot, Virginia Woolf, E. M. Forster, Lytton Strachey, and Roger Fry. His inclusion among such company was due to his capacity to provide elegant interpretation of premodern Asian culture for a world audience and to elevate this new art to global status.

Indeed, the *Zhongyong* is made more meaningful because it is read and "translated" creatively as the "Unwobbling Pivot" by Ezra Pound, and it is made more meaningful by us too. And reinforcing the premise that creativity is always collateral, the process is itself recursive. Ezra Pound's idiosyncratic engagement with Tang dynasty poetry—the inspiration and encouragement for Waley's later foray—presaged the new twentieth-century form of free verse that came to be called modernism and imagism and vectorism that marks our own contemporary Western poetic sensibility. And yes, it is this Western modernism that more recently has inspired new generations of Chinese poets to abandon a traditional formalism and write contemporary Chinese poetry in free verse. Just as Chinese poets are inspired by a creative Western appropriation of their own traditional Chinese poetry, so we too can come to see our Whitehead and our Aristotle in a different and brighter light by coming to know the *Zhongyong* better. And so the circle turns.

Since cross cultural comparisons are necessarily analogical, both cultures in the relationship stand to quite literally "appreciate" each other in the sense that they can accrue an increasing dividend of meaning in their continuing conversation. Thick and robust relations—both personal and cultural—are the ultimate source of growth in this world, enriching the family, the community, the cosmos, and certainly Confucianism as well.

II

An Interpretive Context for Understanding Confucianism

Correlative Thinking as Common Sense

In the first chapter, I argued that there is a resilient substratum sedimented over time into our natural languages that makes cultural traditions distinctive, and that acknowledging this phenomenon is a necessary starting point for making productive cultural comparisons. It is this persistent worldview conveyed in the structure and the content of the language that continues a cultural identity as a shared and unifying common sense. And further, to identify and to articulate this cosmology as a prism of underlying, always-protean cultural assumptions, far from establishing an incommensurable gap among traditions, can in fact serve us well as a preventative against the essentialism and reductionism that are the hallmarks of cultural relativism.

Nathan Sivin has observed that "man's prodigious creativity seems to be based on the permutations and recastings of a rather small stock of ideas."[1] In this chapter, I will argue that the correlative thinking first described by Marcel Granet in *La pensée Chinoise* as a modality of Chinese thinking and later elaborated upon at length by Angus Graham in his *Disputers of the Tao* seems to belong to this small but fertile inventory.[2] Indeed, I will contend that the long history and development of correlative thinking within the Chinese cultural tradition parallels the defining force of an early Greek metaphysical realism in shaping the categories and the grammar of the Western philosophical narrative. Again, Sivin finds a similar contrast between China and Greece in his reflections on the emergence of Chinese and Western science:

Scientific thought began, in China as elsewhere, with attempts to comprehend how it is that although individual things are constantly changing, always coming to be and perishing, nature as a coherent order not only endures but remains conformable to itself. In the West the earliest such attempts identified the unchanging reality with some basic stuff out of which all the things around us, despite their apparent diversity, are formed. In China the earliest and in the long run the most influential scientific explanations were in terms of time. They made sense of the momentary event by fitting it into the cyclical rhythms of natural process.[3]

Henry Rosemont and I have argued elsewhere that Sivin's observation here can be extended to include not only scientific, but ethical discourse as well. The atomistic "basic stuff" as the "unchanging reality" of the scientific West has its counterpart ethically in the moral and religious culture with the notion of the self-sufficient and immortal soul that begins in Greece as early as Pythagoras. We have argued that the Chinese made sense of personal identity not by asserting the existence of an essential and individuating soul, but correlatively by locating personal conduct within "the cyclical rhythms of natural process," where the cultural and social are integral dimensions of this natural cosmology.[4]

What then is the vintage and what has been the resilience of correlative thinking in the proto-Chinese culture that is appealed to in explanation of both the natural and the human worlds? What in the early Chinese lived-world, we might ask, propelled "the permutations and recastings" of this correlative mode of thinking as it spread from centers of specific kinds of knowledge to produce an explanatory vocabulary in so many areas of ordinary Chinese activity: medical therapies, calligraphy and painting, architecture and gardens, literary tropes and style, mantic practices, military logistics and the prosecution of warfare, culinary preparations, ritual performances, *fengshui*, and so on?

William James, himself a dedicated process thinker, provides us with his own reflections on both change and cultural persistence. As a liberated, post-Darwinian pragmatist, he is determined to overcome our retrospective rationalist and empiricist ways of organizing the human experience that he believes have saddled us philosophically with a "block universe"—his expression for a closed, pre-determined world devoid of any real novelty or spontaneity. By attempting to reinstate "process"—

that is, the relevance of change, particularity, creativity, and the ongoing emergence of an always-novel order—James is trying to take us beyond default assumptions about some foundational, permanent, and transcendent reality that have over millennia insinuated themselves into our language and our worldview. But even in thus trying to escape the dead hand of permanence, James is keenly aware that acknowledging the reality of change must itself be qualified by a cognizance of a persistence or "equilibrium" in human ways of rationalizing the life experience that he calls "common sense." He offers us this observation:

> My thesis now is this, *that our fundamental ways of thinking about things are discoveries of exceedingly remote ancestors, which have been able to preserve themselves throughout the experience of all subsequent time.* They form one great stage of equilibrium in the human mind's development, the stage of *common sense.*[5]

James then goes on to rehearse what he takes to be the basic categories of this entrenched "common sense," this distilled wisdom passed on by our progenitors: "things, kinds, sameness or difference, minds, bodies, subjects and attributes, causal influence, the fancied, the real," and so on. Although we might be properly critical of James for taking the familiar categories of our own common sense—indeed, the default vocabulary of a metaphysical realism—as definitive of the "human mind" without taking genuine cultural differences into account, his basic point about the thickness of culture is still well made. Sedimented across the centuries into our ways of thinking and living is a persistent deep stratum, an abiding internal impulse that grounds more apparent changes. To be sure, this "common sense" has itself always been vulnerable to the ineluctable process of change, but relatively speaking, it is also resilient and enduring.

John Dewey in rehearsing the pre-Darwinian history of Western philosophy claims that "few words in our language foreshorten intellectual history as much as does the word species"—that is, the notion of *eidos* rendered "idea" or "form" in Plato, and "species" in Aristotle.[6] Unfortunately Dewey, like his mentor James, fails to take cultural differences into account when he universalizes the metaphysical realism that follows from this notion of *eidos* as a kind of *human* (rather than specifically a pre-Darwinian Western) common sense:

There are, indeed, but two alternative courses. We must either find the appropriate objects and organs of knowledge in the mutual interactions of changing things; or else, to escape the infection of change, we must seek them in some transcendent and supernal region. The *human mind*, deliberately as it were, exhausted the logic of the changeless, the final and the transcendent, before it essayed adventure on the pathless wastes of generation and transformation.[7]

Friedrich Nietzsche, more keenly aware that cultural specificity does make a difference in the formation and content of this deep stratum, describes it as a "philosophy of grammar" that is peculiar to different language groups. In reporting on the Indo-European languages, he observes:

> The strange family resemblance of all Indian, Greek, and German philosophizing is explained easily enough. Where there is an affinity of languages, it cannot fail, owing to the common philosophy of grammar—I mean, owing to the unconscious domination and guidance by similar grammatical functions—that everything is prepared at the outset for a similar development and sequence of philosophical systems; just as the way seems barred against certain other possibilities of world-interpretation.[8]

Such observations on the power of entrenched linguistic propensities such as these proffered by James, Dewey, and Nietzsche—soft versions of the Sapir-Whorf hypothesis that are resistant to any heavy notion of linguistic determinism—might occasion a reconsideration of our usual way of thinking about the originality of our own great philosophers. Without slighting their defining influence on their respective traditions, we might ask to what extent in the "history of thought" are a Plato, an Aristotle, and indeed a Confucius constructing their philosophical oeuvres out of whole cloth, and to what extent are they—with penetrating insight, certainly—only making explicit what is already implicated in the structure and function of the languages they have inherited from their antique predecessors? In what degree are they cultural archaeologists in the business of "recovering" and laying bare the legacy of "common sense" bequeathed to them by their progenitors? That is, to what extent are they reclaiming their own "philosophy of grammar"?

A corollary to the Nietzschean thesis that grammar in real degree promotes and constrains patterns of thought is the anticipation that

II · An Interpretive Context for Understanding Confucianism

disparate cultures are going to have different "philosophies of grammar." Indeed, the prescient Cambridge rhetorician, I. A. Richards, in reflecting on the difficulties of moving from one cultural "common sense" to another—in his case, from our own contemporary Western tradition to that of classical China—also worries that "analysis" as a methodology might well be smuggling in a worldview and way of thinking quite alien to the early Chinese corpus:

> Our Western tradition provides us with an elaborate apparatus of universals, particulars, substances, attributes, abstracts, concretes, generalities, specificities, properties, qualities, relations, complexes, accidents, essences, organic wholes, sums, classes, individuals, concrete universals, objects, events, forms, contents, etc. Mencius ... gets along without any of this and with nothing at all definite to take its place. Apart entirely from the metaphysics that we are only too likely to bring in with this machinery, the practical difficulty arises that by applying it we deform his thinking.... The danger to be guarded against is our tendency to force a structure, which our special kind of Western training (idealist, realist, positivist, Marxist, etc.) makes easiest for us to work with, upon modes of thinking which may very well not have any such structure at all—and which may not be capable of being analysed by means of this kind of logical machinery.[9]

Again, Richards identifies explicitly the familiar vocabulary of metaphysical realism assumed in those categories of "common sense" announced above by James—a common sense that privileges "analysis" as a methodology—as our own default apparatus, an apparatus that Richards worries we might unawares bring with us to our interpretation of the classical Chinese corpus. What then is the common sense—the deep cultural stratum, the uncommon assumptions—of the ancient Chinese worldview within which Confucianism emerges?

We might begin from the process sensibilities of early Chinese cosmology by recommending a holistic *narrative* account rather than an *analytic* understanding of this common sense.[10] That is, we might identify Confucianism historically with the always changing yet still persistent cultural core, or *daotong* 道統, of the Chinese population itself, and then by extension and in different degrees, as a significant aspect of the sinitic cultures of Korea, Japan, and Vietnam. Interestingly, a porous yet enduring "Confucianism" thus understood predates the historical figure of Confucius. But then Confucius himself allows as much, claiming that he is a cultural transmitter rather than an innovator who has inherited the substance of his philosophy from the legacy of the Zhou dynasty and earlier:

> The Master said, "Following the proper way, I do not forge new paths; with confidence I cherish the ancients—in these respects I would presume to compare myself with Old Peng."[11]

Confucius as he is remembered historically is a particularly good example of the combination of "flux and persistence" (*biantong* 變通) that marks the Chinese cultural narrative. With his reliance upon the core canons of the tradition, he is an effective transmitter of the abiding "common sense" while at the same time with his own contribution to the development of a specific philosophical vocabulary, he is a source of novel insight. Indeed, appreciating his modesty in demurring at the suggestion that he has been an innovator, we still have substantial evidence to comfortably assert that Confucius was both a transmitter and someone who sought to break new ground. In broad strokes Confucius does self-consciously continue a tradition that reaches back into the second millennium BCE:

> The Master said, "The Zhou dynasty looked back to the Xia and Shang dynasties. Such a wealth of culture! I follow the Zhou."[12]

But at the same time, Confucius also seems to have been responsible for introducing, redefining, and investing in such key notions as *ren* 仁 ("consummate person/conduct"), *junzi* 君子 ("exemplary person"), *yi* 義 ("optimizing appropriateness"), and *li* 禮 ("achieving propriety in one's roles and relations") as an authorized philosophical terminology. Again, it is Confucius who promotes personal cultivation as the defining Confucian project and who grounds Confucian role ethics and the vision of the consummate life in "family feeling" (*xiao* 孝). This being the case, it is not surprising that Zhu Xi 朱熹 canonizes the *Analects* as the second of the *Four Books* for the explicit reason that it not only provides the fundamental vocabulary of the tradition, but it also provides a narrative example of personal cultivation that is at the heart of the Confucian project described in the first of his *Four Books*, the *Great Learning* (*Daxue* 大學).

II · An Interpretive Context for Understanding Confucianism

David Keightley in his lifetime study of Shang-dynasty divination practices provides us with considerable insight into the substance of the cultural legacy that was transmitted to Confucius from earlier times. Keightley claims that "the origins of much that is thought to be characteristically Chinese may be identified in the ethos and world view of its Bronze Age diviners."[13] Indeed,

> ... it is possible for the modern historian to infer from the archaeological, artistic, and written records of the Shang some of the theoretical strategies and presuppositions by which the Bronze Age elite of the closing centuries of the second millennium BC ordered their existence.[14]

Keightley would insist that certain presuppositions of the Shang culture evolved to become further articulated in what we take to be the formative period of classical Chinese philosophy:

> The glimpse that the oracle-bones inscriptions affords us of metaphysical conceptions in the eleventh and tenth centuries B.C. suggests that the philosophical tensions that we associate primarily with the Taoism [Daoism] and Confucianism of Eastern Chou [Zhou] had already appeared, in different form, in the intellectual history of China, half a millennium earlier.[15]

Keightley, like Nietzsche before him, perceives the invested structure of language itself to be a resource that can be mined to reveal a vein of cultural assumptions and importances:

> Without necessarily invoking the Sapir-Whorf hypothesis of linguistic relativity, one can still imagine that the grammar of the Shang inscriptions has much to tell us about Shang conceptions of reality, particularly about the forces of nature.[16]

What then specifically are these underlying assumptions that Keightley and like-minded scholars have identified and recovered in this archaeology of Shang dynasty culture? What is the common sense—the deep cultural stratum—that persists and is being transmitted as the ancient Chinese worldview? In identifying these uncommon assumptions, Keightley contrasts a Chinese cosmology of ceaseless process with a classical Greek worldview in which a metaphysical transcendentalism guarantees an idealized reality:

Put crudely, we find in classical Greece a Platonic metaphysics of certainties, ideal forms, and right answers, accompanied by complex, tragic, and insoluble tensions in the realm of ethics. The metaphysical foundations being firm, the moral problems were intensely real, and as inexplicable as reality itself. To the early Chinese, however, if reality was forever changeable, man could not assume a position of tragic grandeur and maintain his footing for long. The moral heroism of the Confucians of Eastern Chou [Zhou] was not articulated in terms of any tragic flaw in the nature of the world or man. This lack of articulation, I believe, may be related to a significant indifference to the metaphysical foundation of Confucian ethics.[17]

Positively, Keightley ascribes to these divinatory sources what is today being described by many interpreters of classical China as a distinctively Chinese mode of "correlative thinking" that is made explicit and is further elaborated upon later in the interpretive portions of the *Yijing* 易經 or *Book of Changes*. According to Keightley's reading, oracle-bone divination subscribed to

> ... a theology and metaphysics that conceived of a world of alternating modes, pessimistic at times, optimistic at others, but with the germs of one mode always inherent in the other. Shang metaphysics, at least as revealed in the complementary forms of the Wu Ting [Ding] inscriptions, was a metaphysics of yin and yang.[18]

Keightley appeals to the *pien-hua* (*bianhua* 變化) understanding of this process of change as articulated in the *Great Tradition* (*Dazhuan* 大傳) on the *Book of Changes*—a rhythm of "alternation and transformation"—as a later expression of the modality of change already present in Shang dynasty metaphysics. This notion of change is articulated in the language of symbiotic bipolar opposites that entail each other, and together constitute the whole.[19]

The correlative thinking that permits insight into and productive participation in this world of alternations, with its origins dating back at least to the Shang dynasty, is a dominant modality of thinking that advances in both complexity and explanatory force through a proliferation and aggregation of productive dyadic associations, novel metaphors, suggestive images, and evocative patterns, all of which are weighed, measured, and tested in ordinary experience. And it is this persistent way of thinking inherited by Confucius and further articulated by him and his protégés, and then continued by the tradition following in their wake, that serves as ground for the vision of the consummate life we have come to call "Confucianism." We might cautiously call this broad interpretive context a "correlative cosmology" or a "correlative *qi* 氣 cosmology," while at the same time being cognizant of the fact that the research of scholars such as Nathan Sivin and Michael Nylan argues persuasively for the evolutionary change that this notion of *qi* undergoes throughout its early history.[20]

The *Book of Changes* (*Yijing* 易經) and Chinese Natural Cosmology

As important as the Daoist and Confucian canons have been in the articulation of Chinese intellectual history and as much as they can be appealed to as documented evidence for claims about early Chinese cosmology, perhaps no single text can compete with the *Yijing* 易經, or *Book of Changes*, in terms of the sustained interest it has garnered from succeeding generations of China's literati, and in terms of the sustained influence it has had on the Chinese self-understanding. The *Yijing* has been and still remains, in every sense, the first among the Chinese classics. Indeed, it is this open-ended document with its centuries of accruing commentaries that has set the terms of art for Chinese cosmology.

The *Yijing* is a complex text that includes both a manual used as an apparatus for making correlations, and seven appended commentaries. Since three of these commentaries are divided into two sections each, in sum they are often referred to as the "Ten Wings." The manual, used traditionally as a heuristic for pursuing productive associations, is of a much earlier vintage than the commentaries, and has come to be referred to independently as the *Zhouyi* 周易.

The commentaries are themselves composite and sometimes fragmentary, and even though they belong to a much later period than the manual itself, portions of these commentaries are still hugely important as a summary statement of an early Chinese cosmology that has had a persisting influence on the Chinese sense of its world. One of these commentaries, the *Appended Statements* or *Xici* 繫辭, also called the *Great Tradition* (*Dazhuan*), is perhaps the most important source we presently have for exploring early Chinese cosmology. Given that a silk manuscript version of it dating from 168 BCE was found at the Mawangdui site in Changsha in 1973, we have at least a *terminus ad quem* for its compilation.

Willard Peterson in analyzing this profound, protean, and frustratingly opaque document—the *Great Commentary* or *Great Tradition*—insists that it "has been for some two thousand years one of the most important statements in the Chinese tradition on knowing how the cosmos works and how humans might relate to that working. Especially from the Sung [Song] through the Ch'ing [Qing] periods, the 'Great Commentary' ('Ta chuan [Dazhuan]'), as it was called, provided the *locus classicus* for vocabulary and concepts in nearly every major abstract discussion of the physical world and man's place in it."[21]

Edward Shaughnessy, in his retranslation of the *Great Tradition* based on the Mawangdui materials, echoes Peterson's evaluation of its importance in observing that "the worldview of its *Xici* or *Appended Statements* Commentary—integrating man and nature through the medium of the *Yijing*—is arguably the most sophisticated (it is certainly the most subtle) statement of the correlative thought that has been so fundamental to all of China's philosophical systems."[22] Shaughnessy is not exaggerating when he says that "indeed, so central has the *Yijing* been to Chinese thought over these two millennia that a history of its exegetical traditions would require almost a history of Chinese thought."[23]

The *Yijing*, or *Book of Changes*, as a text is itself an object lesson in the worldview that it attempts to present. That is, when we reflect on the nature of particular "events" within this process worldview, the relationship between these particular foci and their fields lends itself to a holographic understanding of world systems. As Peterson suggests, the text of the *Yijing* itself as a particular focus "duplicates relationships and processes at work in the realm of heaven-and-earth," and thus provides those who understand it with a window on the workings of the cosmos. For it is the timely application of a knowledge of these same relationships and processes that "is the basis for efficacious action in the realm of human society."[24] As Peterson continues, "the *Change* [*Yijing*] is not separate from but equal to the cosmos, and it is in virtue of that relationship that it 'works.'"²⁵ This same claim is made explicitly in the *Great Tradition* itself:

> As a document, the *Yijing* is vast and far-ranging, and has everything complete within it. It contains the way of the heavens, the way of human beings, and the way of the earth.²⁶

There is a cluster of key philosophical terms around which the *Great Tradition* is constructed. The world as immediately experienced provides us with a seemingly endless vocabulary of correlated binary terms: the high and the low, the moving and the still, the hard and the soft, the full and the empty, the large and the small, the bright and the dark, the hot and the cold, and so on. The correlative, bipolar, and dynamic tensions inherent in a world so defined circumscribe the domain within which the processes of change take place. And it is these same tensions that are the source out of which the novelty that attends these processes is produced.²⁷

A familiar metaphor in the early corpus for the novel arising and subsiding of the always unique phenomena of the world are the "swinging gates of *tian*" (*tianmen* 天門):

> Thus the closing of the swinging gate is called *kun* 坤; the opening of it is called *qian* 乾. The ongoing alternation of openings and closings is called flux (*bian* 變), and the inexhaustibility of the comings and goings is called persistence (*tong* 通). When something is manifest, it is called an image (*xiang* 象), and taking on physical form it is called a phenomenon (*qi* 器). To fashion and make use of these things is called emulation (*fa* 法). Putting them to good use in everything that is done so that all of the people can take advantage of them is called inspiration (*shen* 神).²⁸

This passage, like so many in the *Great Tradition*, begins from an observation about the ongoing natural processes, and then concludes with advice on how an effective collaboration with the changing world can inspire the human experience:

> Thus, that which goes beyond form is called *dao*; those things that have form are called phenomena. The transforming and tailoring of things is called flux. The extending and applying of things is called continuity. To take up this understanding and bring it into the lives of the common people is called the grand undertaking.²⁹

The coordination of the relationship between the changing world and the human experience is the main axis of the *Yijing*. The purpose of this text is fundamentally normative and prescriptive. It purports to address life's most pressing question: What kind of participation in these natural processes can optimize the possibilities of a world in which natural and human events are two inseparable, mutually shaping aspects?

Confucian morality itself is a cosmic phenomenon that emerges from the synergistic transactions that take place between the operations of nature and human effort:

> The greatest excellence of the world (*dade* 大德) is said to be its giving of life. The greatest treasure of the sage is said to be the attainment of stature (*wei* 位). How one maintains one's stature is by being consummate in one's conduct (*ren*). How one attracts and gathers together other people is through the use of resources. To manage the available resources, to insure that language is used properly, and to prevent the people from doing wrong is called appropriateness (*yi*).[30]

Spirituality in the community arises from a penetrating understanding of the workings of change, and the quality of optimally appropriate conduct that such an understanding can inspire. Simply put, spirituality is the product of inspired living: of reading initial conditions while they are still inchoate, anticipating their possibilities, and then aspiring to make the most of them. The "intensive" conduct of the exemplary person becomes "extensive" as it serves as a model for, and is deferred to, by the community:

> Understanding the incipient (*ji* 幾) is inspiration (*shen*). That exemplary persons (*junzi*) are not obsequious in dealing with superiors or self-serving in dealing with subordinates is because they understand the incipient. The incipient is a hint of movement from which one can see in advance impending fortune. Exemplary persons having seen the incipient are aroused to action without waiting to see what happens.... Exemplary persons in their understanding of both the inchoate and the obvious, of both the soft and the hard, make of them a beacon for the myriad people.[31]

In fact, it is a spirituality emerging from always-appropriate and productive conduct that is the highest achievement humanity can seek after:

No one has yet to figure out how to go beyond this, because making the most of spirituality (*shen*) and understanding the process of transformation is the fullness of excellence (*de*).³²

This *Great Tradition* in telling the story of its own origins explains how a human responsiveness to context has in the past, and continues now, to enchant the cosmos. The remote ancestors Fu Xi 伏羲 and Shen Nong 神農 established a rhythm in the human experience, enabling them to chime in with the cadence of the "flux and persistence" (*biantong*) that they perceived as persistent characteristics of the world around them. Encouraged by the efficacy achieved in applying their insights into the workings of the cosmos to the human experience, they then represented their interpretation of life in the world in a hexagramic language of images, models, and patterns for the benefit of generations yet to come. Importantly, these antique sages were not natural scientists engaged in some disinterested interrogation of objective nature, but rather were fully occupied by a project of personal understanding and articulation.

> According to the *Yijing*, when things run their course, there is flux (*bian*), where there is flux, there is continuity (*tong*), and where there is such continuity, it is enduring.³³

By their efforts at *ars contextualis*—the art of effectively contextualizing and coordinating the experience of the human being within the processes of nature in an effort to optimize the creative possibilities of the cosmos—Fu Xi and Shen Nong cultivated a thick continuity between "nurture" and "nature" expressed in the evocative images that constitute the *Yijing*. This perceived resonance between the human experience and the natural and cultural forum in which it occurs is made explicit in expressions that have come to characterize the relationship, such as "the continuity between the religious, natural, and cultural context, and the human experience" (*tianren heyi* 天人合一), and the "mutual responsiveness of the numinous context and the human experience" (*tianren xiangying* 天人相應 or *tianren ganying* 天人感應). It is important to note that such expressions report on the continuing symbiotic mutuality of these dimensions of experience rather than on the reconciliation of two originally separate aspects of the world after the fact. Personal cultivation is *not* the bringing together and the "uniting" of the world and human experience, but is rather the deepening and intensifying of the productive continuities that conjoin two inseparable aspects of experience, that is, oneself and one's world.

Indeed, this assumed continuities between nature and nurture—between petroglyphs and the striations in stone, for example—is reflected in the fact that the same vocabulary is used to express the creative advance in both the human and the natural ecologies. For example, "the way of things" (*dao* 道), vital energies (*qi* 氣), "inscribed culture" (*wen* 文), "patternings" (*li* 理), *yinyang* 陰陽, and the perpetual interface between "flux and persistence" (*biantong* 變通) itself are all terms that reference both the human and the natural worlds.

In this co-creative relationship with the world around us, there is no initial and originative *logos*. Language and its significance emerge *pari passu* with a world that is continually being spoken into being. Imagination is anything but imaginary. That is, the process of making meaning within our world of experience, inspired by our imagination, becomes our *imaginaire*, our lived reality.

Building on this auspicious beginning, the sage kings who were descendents of Fu Xi and Shen Nong—that is, the Yellow Emperor, Yao, and Shun—continued to construct technologies, modes of transportation, social institutions, and customs that were evoked by particular hexagrams, each of the hexagrams providing a dynamic image of some natural process:

> The sages had the capacity to see the way the world operates, and perceiving the way things come together and commune, they put into practice their statutes and codes of propriety.[34]

It is this gradual and ongoing process of structuring and ritualizing the human experience thus remembered in and induced by the *Great Tradition* that has enchanted life in the world, and in so doing, continues to produce its spirituality:

> In comprehending the flux and flow of the world around them, the sage kings were able to save the people from exhausting themselves. With their spiritual insight (*shen*), they transformed the people, and enabled the people to find what was most fitting for them.[35]

The productive symbiosis that can be achieved between the human and the natural worlds is practical inspiration for effective human living.

In addition to enabling human beings to live moral and aesthetic lives, this understanding of the processes of change and productivity revealed by the *Yijing* allows them access to the very mysteries of the cosmos. Significant for our understanding of the role of religiousness in this evolving culture, the enchanted, numinous dimension of the human experience (*shen* 神) does not belong to another world. Far from it, such spirituality is the inexhaustible product of human efficacy and refinement in this one:

> The *Yijing* is the sage's means of probing what is profound to its very limits, and examining thoroughly what is still incipient (*ji* 幾). It is only through this profundity that the sages can discern the purposes of the world; it is only through the incipient that they can consummate the business of the world; it is only through insight into the spiritual they can be quick without haste and can arrive without even going.[36]

In the course of time, such high expectations of the human experience have produced what might be called an "a-theistic" human-centered religiousness—a religiousness without appeal to an independent, transcendent Deity as the source of order. Human beings, without reference to limiting assumptions about religious transcendentalism and supernaturalism, have become a source of profound meaning in their own world—indeed, the only world. It is the cosmic import of human co-creativity that moves the *Zhongyong*, the last of the *Four Books* that Zhu Xi takes to be the culminating statement of the Confucian project, to its religious crescendo:

> Only those in the world of utmost creativity (*zhicheng* 至誠) are able to separate out and braid together the many threads on the great loom of the world. Only they set the great root of the world and realize the transforming and nourishing processes of heaven and earth.
> How could there be anything on which they depend?
> So earnest, they are consummate (*ren* 仁);
> So profound, they are a bottomless abyss (*yuan* 淵);
> So pervasive, they are *tian* (*tian* 天).
> Only those whose own capacities of discernment and sagely wisdom extend to the powers of *tian* could possibly understand them.[37]

Correlative Cosmology and Traditional Chinese Medicine (TCM)

Another avenue that lends itself to an exploration of this correlative cosmology is Traditional Chinese Medicine (TCM). It is commonplace to observe that the standard curriculum of students of TCM begins from a sustained and substantial mining of classical Chinese philosophy to excavate the images and cultural metaphors that give the tradition its vocabulary and meaning.[38] Perhaps we students of Chinese philosophy would do well to repay this compliment by reflecting on the cosmological assumptions that ground Chinese medicine as touchstones for finding our bearing and retaining a secure footing in the fast flowing philosophical narrative.

In classical China, the totality of animating, transforming *qi* 氣 was conceptualized in terms of what in modern parlance we might call a "vital energy field." But just as we must be wary of ascribing an essential notion of human nature to the Confucian canons, we must also be careful to avoid collapsing this notion of *qi* into a monism or a homogeneous materialism. This vital field is not only pervasive as a shared condition of all things that makes them continuous with each other, and the medium from which all particular things emerge and out of which all things are constituted: it is also the *sui generis* configuration of relationships and connectivity of each thing that, having both a more subjective and a more objective aspect, differentiates it and guarantees its particularity and uniqueness.

Qi properly understood accounts at once for unity and plurality, for continuity and difference.[39] Indeed, specific "form" and "animating *qi*" are two nonanalytic aspects of the same trans-*form*-ing reality, where the "transitivity" and the "form" are both implicit ways of understanding the rhythm of a process. By nonanalytic, I mean that "form" and "animation" are simply two ways of looking at the same phenomenon, and that these perspectives are separable only by foregrounding one as opposed to the other. And by rhythm I mean that form attended by process yields a discernable cadence rather than a static structure. As such, "animating *qi*" and the various ways of saying "forming" are an explanatory rather than an ontological vocabulary. That is, we need both terms to give a fair account of the changing relations that locate us within our ongoing experience. Each of us is constituted by our manifold of relations, and in this sense we are continuous with each other. But again, the manifold of relations in which my life is embedded is specifically and uniquely me, and no one else.

Today we are most familiar with *qi* as a vital energy field in the areas of health, medicine, and exercises leading to bodily wellbeing. Understanding "body" as *qi* can be helpful. But in this classical correlative cosmology, the term "body," like any predication of *qi*, must of course be used advisedly; everything is a continuous field of *qi* manifesting itself at once as "lived body" and as "environs," as "physical" and as "spiritual," as "forming" (*ti* 體) and as "functioning" (*yong* 用), as "temporal" (*shi* 世) and as "spatial" (*jie* 界), as "persistent" (*tong* 通) and as "flux" (*bian* 變). It is because of just such assumptions about the "body" that traditional Chinese medicine can provide us with a useful explanatory window on *qi* cosmology and a significantly different way of understanding the myriad "things" that constitute this world. As medical anthropologist Judith Farquhar observes:

> *Qi* is both structural and functional, a unification of material and temporal forms that loses all coherence when reduced to one or the other "aspect."[40]

Thus physiological systemic functions have parity if not privilege over the more persistent anatomical structures in traditional Chinese medical sensibilities, and prescriptions must be holistic and inclusive rather than specific and exclusive. Pursuing her observation that structure and function are two aspects of the same thing, Farquhar searches for an appropriate language that will provide the necessary contrast between traditional Chinese medicine's very different processual understanding of the body and the formal anatomical assumptions of biomedicine:

> Chinese medicine most classically envisions embodiment as a dynamic complex of interwoven processes, as a physiology that must be understood in the living through analysis of signs, symptoms, and a subjective sensorium.[41]

This functional understanding of formal structures in correlative cosmology is radically contextual, locating "things" such as the "lived body" or "the body as experienced" within its ever-changing circumstances—thus forming a collaboration between an internal and an external landscape. Body is understood from the inside and from the outside, as more or less subjective and more or less objective. The irreducible complexity of the relationship between "forming" and "functioning" is captured in the graph *shen* 身, often translated generically and simplistically as "body," but which requires a much more nuanced understanding. *Shen* means not only particular and subjective "lived-body," but in its archaic oracle bones and bronze forms, *[i]* and *[ii]* respectively, the graph is clearly the profile of a "pregnant lived-body," underscoring its nested sense of inside and outside, its vital particularity, its procreative functionality, its sociality, and its fecund, generational continuity.[42]

Medical anthropologist Zhang Yanhua analyzes the irreducibly subjective and gerundive implications of the two characters that as a binomial are usually used to denote "body" (*shenti* 身體):

> If we have to make a distinction between *shen* and *ti* as bodies, we may say that *shen* implies a socially informed body-person or body-self, while *ti*, frequently used in or as a verb, emphasizes "embodying" as a process of knowing and acting. Both concepts resist dualistically positioned mind and body, subject and object.[43]

This verbal sense of *ti* is very much present in the expression *tihui* 體會: a kind of knowing that is vital, visceral, and unifying, a collaborative quality of knowing that draws upon concrete experience and that enables a participatory realization in the sense of "making something real." Farquhar cautions that if we are to overcome "our commonsense commitment to a materialism which must reduce phenomena to synchronically observable collections of objects," we must understand "things" as both existing in time, and as entailing a subjective, existential dimension. That is, the temporality and reflexivity of "things" must be considered in any and all attempts at understanding them. "Body" must be understood diachronically or "through time":

> [I]t is signs and symptoms, experiences and perceptions, which are the material foundation of medical perception. They are not less concrete than anatomical organs, but they are not conceivable outside of lived time.[44]

Thus, any tendency to treat "body" as simply a physical object would violate the vital, contextual, and processional sensibilities of the correlative cosmology in which traditional Chinese medicine is grounded. Unsurprisingly, the personal narrative as the reflexive aspect of corporality is of enormous importance in traditional Chinese medical practices:

> The evidence here suggests ... that Chinese medicine accords a certain importance to quotidian self-perception; while never denying the object-nature of bodies, it privileges processes of change that take place in personal time, which can only be entered into medical consideration via the patient's own narrative.[45]

The inseparability of the subjective "lived body" and the "body for others" in traditional Chinese medicine provides one way of making sense of ourselves as organisms. The body—at once the self-conscious "I" as the existential experience and the embedded "me" as "my living body for other subjects"—is an indissoluble continuity between self and world. Zhang insists that the vocabulary used for both the formal and the vital aspects of life must be understood as resolutely situated and transactional:

> Although *jingshen* 精神 is translated in English as "mind" or "spirit," it is very much part of *shenti*.... Primary *jing* provides the basis for the process of transforming the energy distilled from food and is enriched and strengthened by "acquired *jing*." Chinese medical theories view *jing* and *qi* 氣 (air, breath, vital energy) as the same life-giving energy. When it is concentrated, it is *jing*; when it is dispersed it turns into *qi*. If *jing* is the nurturing aspect of this energy, *qi* is the active configurational aspect of the same energy.... If *jing* and *qi* are the basis of life, then *shen* 神 is the manifestation of that life.... In other words, *shen* is the phenomenon of life activity itself.[46]

The flow of life energy requires coordination and direction. The heartmind (*xin* 心) provides the directive force negotiated in and guided by the efficacious possibilities inherent in the particular circumstances. In the human experience,

> ... *xin* is a system of functioning that forms a continuous process of being or becoming a person, involving the physiological, psychological, and sociological.... What is particular about this process-centered heartmind physiology is ... the commitment to an unobstructed process of

transformation in accordance with a given social context and natural environment.[47]

If "things" are constituted from their relations, in asking after the *what* and the *how* of anything we must begin from the whole complex of relations. In fact, the purpose of the self-cultivating regimens that have been the continuing focus of philosophical inquiry, whether predominantly physical or spiritual (and usually both), has been to achieve an equanimity and balance that allows for a productively continuous flow of *qi* throughout the whole organism and its various environments without it suffering stagnation or obstruction. We might use the heartmind as an illustration.

Isolated, decontextualized, and thus deprived of its vitality for little more than a minute, this organ called the heartmind would devolve into nothing more than a dead piece of meat. But understood physiologically as a ceaseless progression of "forming" and "functioning," it is a dense and vital focus of a continuing, symbiotic process in which the complex internal network of relations in the circulatory system is nourished through the appropriation of the boundless external environments—wind and water, sun and air, and all of the nutrients needed to support life. When the *xin* in all of these relations achieves and sustains a fluid equanimity and balance without obstruction or stagnation, we call it "health," or perhaps better, in respect of the continuing character of the process, we might call it "healthing." To evaluate *xin*, we need to locate it as a specific, concentrated vitality within its full matrix of relations. We need to begin from the whole and understand it as a concentrated focus within its evolving field.

But the *xin* also has a subjective and sociological dimension: it has an emotional, intellectual, and spiritual aspect. The *xin* is the dense locus of feeling and thinking that is invested and expressed in the broad field of roles and relations that constitutes each one of us. When we achieve an unobstructed harmony and balance in the events of our family and communal lives, we might call this quality of life a joyful wisdom.

There are three additional points worth making concerning the heartmind thus understood. First, to ask after the essence of the heartmind either physiologically or socially—that is, "what is the heartmind in itself?"—is a misguided question. The heartmind is dynamic and radically embedded, and is nothing more or less than what it does within its field of relations. Secondly, the membrane that we are inclined to take as the boundary of the heartmind is porous and fluid, serving as an indication of a nested, central focus of activity rather than an exclusive limit that demarcates the inside from the outside. Finally, in the next chapter we will turn to this image of the physical, intellectual, and affective heartmind as a way of thinking about relationally constituted persons—persons as an embodied locus of conduct in the roles and the relations that are defining of them.

The means and the goal of healthy living advocated by TCM that is captured in this heartmind image is an achieved equilibrium in which we are able to make the most of the transactional human experience by achieving proper measure in our social and natural activities. In so doing, we are able to avoid both excess and insufficiency in giving and getting, in doing and undergoing:

> Harmony defined here is related to the Chinese sense of *du* 度 (degree, extent, position).... In other words, in a dynamic interactive environment, harmony is brought about when each particular unfolds itself in its unique way and to an appropriate *du* such that "each shines more brilliantly in the other's company" (*xiangde-yizhang* 相得益彰).[48]

Correlative Cosmology as an Ecological Cosmology: From "Things" to "Gerunds" and "Vital Relations"

But how can we extend these insights from TCM to the correlative cosmology, and use them to understand the nature of "things" more generally? How can we extrapolate from the radically situated, lived, reflexive, and vital body to the world more broadly?

One consequence of the unwillingness in this processual cosmology to separate lived time from matter is that there is no warrant, in Aristotle's language, to distinguish an active, efficient cause from a passive material cause. This presupposition precludes any understanding of *qi* as some monistic stuff out of which everything is constructed. In fact, expressions such as *ziran* 自然 and *tiandi* 天地, conventionally translated "nature" and "the world" respectively, do not simply refer to *a* world or *the* world; they refer to an active, ongoing, autogenerative process *as experienced from within it*. It is for this reason that, following the primacy of the physiological in TCM, the modal, gerundive form of such expressions, were they not ungrammatical in English, would be a fairer expression of their entailments: *Ziran* is "naturing" and *tiandi* is "worlding."

A corollary to this notion of an invigorated world is the absence of any final boundary between the sentient and insentient, animate and inanimate, living and lifeless. It is a commonplace in classical Western interpretations of the vital and spiritual character of things to appeal to a physical and spiritual dichotomy, assuming that the animating principle is distinguishable from the things it animates. But with respect to the notion of *qi*, there are no separate things to be animated. This correlative *qi* cosmology is thus "hylozoistic": That is, life and matter are inseparable aspects of the same reality, two ways of looking at the same thing. There is only the field of *qi* and its many animated, focal manifestations. "Things" are one and many at the same time: a wife, a mother, a daughter (or better, "wifing," "mothering," "daughtering") each phase of her evolving identity embedded within her defining manifold of relations. Such "things" are persistent yet transitory perturbations of vital energy subject to the relentless process of flux, and ultimately, of transformation.

"Time" (*shi* 時) is to be understood as the quantum of transformation as it is lived by particular things. It is an abstracted and sometimes quantified description used to denote the active, processual, and lived quality of transactional experience that, when optimally productive from one perspective or another, evidences "good timing," and is indeed, for its collaborators, "timely." This *qi* energy is "vital" in the sense that the internal dynamic process is more primary than the persistent form, defying any severe or final dichotomy between the formal and the functional, the material and the spiritual, the subjective and the objective, this focus and its field.

Qi as energizing field is expressed as the unique and always changing foci of every "thing" that comes to constitute our experience. The resolute uniqueness of these always situated "things"—this "myriad of phenomena" (*wanwu* 萬物)—precludes the existence of forms or ideas or categories or principles or inviolate species that provide a ground for a doctrine of "natural kinds." Thus, "things" begin from their uniqueness, and are sorted, grouped, and generalized (*tuilei* 推類) as they are associated with each other by perceived qualitative resonances and analogies derived from specific conditions. Discriminations are made in terms of observed and conventionalized classifications associated with diurnal and seasonal changes, directions, deities, colors, tastes, sounds, numbers, smells, body parts and so forth. Marcel Granet puts it this way:

> Instead of observing successions of phenomena, the Chinese registered alternations of aspects. If two aspects seemed to them to be connected, it was not by means of a cause and effect relationship, but rather "paired" like the obverse and reverse of something, or to use a metaphor from the *Book of Changes*, like echo and sound, or shadow and light.[49]

Such dynamic, relational discriminations and mutually informing correlations, far from being final in any sense, are described by Joseph Needham as processive and diffusive, "patterns simultaneously appearing in a vast field of force, the dynamic structure of which we do not yet understand."[50] As Needham goes on to report, it is the aggregation and application of these productive correlations that enables us to act effectively:

> The sum of wisdom consisted in adding to the number of intuited analogical correspondences in the repertory of correlations.[51]

To take an example of such correspondences, an understanding of the correlation between emotions and physical well-being provides us with a wisdom that takes us beyond hypochondria as an adequate explanation of depression to a functional awareness of the centrality of feeling in the quality of one's health.

The division of the world not into kinds, but into "*yinyang*" qualities and correlations, while arguably implicit in the natural cosmology of a proto-Chinese worldview that can be documented as far back as the Shang dynasty, was in the course of time formalized, systematized, and made explicit in the complex Han dynasty cosmological charts and the "*yinyang* five phases" (*yinyang wuxing* 陰陽五行) doctrines.[52] As Wing-tsit Chan has pointed out, the interdependence and inseparability of structure (or formation) and function characteristic of this correlative *qi* cosmology—or more simply put, what things are "becoming" and what they are "doing"—is implicit in the correlative *yinyang* vocabulary of the early texts. Such associations are persistent in the tradition, and over the centuries they become an explanatory vocabulary expressed in a proliferation of correlative pairings such as "forming and functioning" (*tiyong* 體用), "knowing (or realizing) and doing" (*zhixing* 知行), and so on.[53]

In *Daodejing* 42 we read:

> Everything carries *yin* on its shoulders and *yang* in its arms and blends these vital energies (*qi*) together to make them harmonious (*he*).[54]

All things are constituted of contrastive relations that can be made most productive—that is, healthy and robust—through free-wheeling associations of an educated imagination and the process of correlation that such insight inspires. In the classical Daoistic literature we have sources such as the meditative "Inward Training" (*Neiye* 內業) chapter of the *Guanzi* 管子 that elaborate upon this "harmonizing" with techniques of correct posture, diet, and breath control aimed at bringing the internal landscape into harmony with its external conditions, thereby enabling the practitioner to achieve health and long life.[55]

Qi is an image that, like water, is deliberate and provocative, defying the Aristotelian categories that have come to structure and discipline our language and our thinking. That is, *qi* is at once one and many. When it accumulates and coagulates, it can have a formal coherence by taking on a shape inspired by its context that is persistent and yet changing too. Axiologically, *qi* is again both noble and base. It is conceived of through the analogy of water, where water is life-giving and purifying, irrigating our world and cleansing our bodies and spirits. At the same time, water is destructive and contaminating, working its way down through the bowels and into the sewers to offend against polite human sensibilities. Similarly the most refined spiritual aspects of the most elevated of things such as human beings themselves are constituted by the most refined *qi*, while the baser, more physical aspects of the same human being is of a baser *qi*. And just as water can be a "thing" (water) and an "action" (to water) and an "attribute" (moist) and a "modality" (cascading) all at the same time, so too *qi* will not be resolved into categories that would separate forming from functioning. Again, water is not simply an objective phenomenon, but constitutes the life and vitality that allows us to grow a world from within it. *Qi* too is not only what we are, but also the life force felt within that animates our most exquisite aesthetic accomplishments.

In the third-century commentary on the *Daodejing* by Wang Bi 王弼, he describes this notion of vital and persistent transformation as *tiyong* 體用, the inseparability of forming and functioning, an expression that from that time forward became a mainstay of Chinese cosmology. It is subsequently extended as an explanatory idea from Daoism to Confucian and Buddhist philosophy, and emerges as a fundamental expression of correlative cosmology.[56] *Tiyong* describes a nondual cosmos in which all experience must begin from locating it within the totality of relations, and in which all polar distinctions such as human nature and conduct, the body and the mind, and matter and life are thus simply alternative ways of looking at the same changing reality. "Forming" and "functioning"—the *what* and the *how*—are an explanatory, nonanalytical vocabulary used for describing the rhythm of the dramatic and ceaseless unfolding of our experience in both its formal and its animated aspects. *What* we think about, for example, and *how* we think about it, are two coterminous aspects of the same continuing process. There is no ontological disparity between the phenomenal world of experience and the living source of its ongoing transformations.

Significantly, this notion of ceaseless, vital transformation is pervasive in the tradition, and is the background against which the mainstream Confucian thinkers must be understood. Even the ever-practical Confucius has a speculative moment in which he uses the vitality of water to muse on the flux and flow of life:

> The Master was standing on the riverbank, and observed, "Is not life's passing just like this, never ceasing day or night!"[57]

Kwong-loi Shun in the preamble to his discussion of the references to *qi* found in the *Mencius,* rehearses passages from the classical anthologies of historical stories, the *Zuo Commentary to the Spring and Autumn Annals* (*Zuozhuan* 左傳) and the *Discourses on the States* (*Guoyu* 國語), that expound upon *qi* as the vital energies making up and activating human beings and the natural world around us.[58] In the several discourses in which Mencius himself invokes *qi,* he is not waxing mystical, as suggested by some interpreters.[59] On the contrary, I would suggest that he is simply making explicit the common sense of his own time and place in the intellectual life of early China. Indeed, to make sense of the *qi* worldview in our own epoch, we might consider it the classical Chinese analog of the now largely unconscious quantitative, genetic, and atomistic assumptions about natural kinds that began for Western culture in classical Greece, and that continue to shape our own common sense.

Correlative Cosmology as a Moral Cosmology: *This* Focus (*de* 德) and *Its* Field (*dao* 道)

But *qi* is not simply of cosmological significance as an underlying assumption about the nature of our experience. The proper existential coordination of *qi* brings with it a profoundly moral as well as its psycho-physiological aspect. In the next chapter I will use the seminal Confucian text, the *Great Learning* (*Daxue* 大學), to argue that the theme most persistent and pervasive in shaping the Chinese philosophical tradition broadly is the project of personal cultivation. Mencius himself offers advice on the attainment of human excellence in one's conduct, understanding the field of *qi* in terms of specifically moral energy. He speaks of his ability to nourish his "flood-like *qi*" (*haoran zhi qi* 浩然之氣), describing this *qi* as that which is "most vast" (*zhida* 至大) and "most firm" (*zhigang* 至剛):

> Mencius said: "... By the age of forty I was no longer perturbed in my heartmind." ...
>
> Gong-sun Chou asked: "Is there some way that one becomes unperturbed in one's heartmind? ... May I dare to ask after your success in this respect?"
>
> Mencius replied: "I understand discourse,[60] and I am adept at nurturing my flood-like *qi*."
>
> "May I ask what you mean by 'flood-like *qi*'?"
>
> Mencius replied: "It is difficult to express. It is the most extensive and the most intensive quality of *qi*. If one nurtures it faithfully and without respite, it will fill up all between the heavens and the earth. As a quality of *qi*, it is a piece with achieving optimal appropriateness in one's conduct (*yi* 義) and walking the proper way (*dao* 道). Without it, one is starved. It is what is born of an cumulative habit of appropriate conduct, and is not something that can be had through random acts of appropriateness."[61]

Restated in the cosmological language of focus and field, Mencius is saying that, when properly nurtured and cultivated, his "flood-like *qi*" achieves the greatest "extensive" (most vast) and "intensive" (most firm) magnitudes in his relations with his environs. This language of extensive field and intensive focus suggests that when one nourishes one's *qi* most successfully, one achieves the greatest degree of meaningful resolution (*yi* 義) within the most extensive field of *qi* (*dao* 道). In this manner, sustained excellence in one's conduct (*daode* 道德) is attained through acquiring the greatest degree of potency and effectiveness (*de* 德) in relation to the most far-ranging elements of one's environments (*dao* 道). In fact, this is the explicit message of *Mencius*:

> Everything is here in me. There is no joy greater than, on introspection, to find that one is truly sincere (*cheng* 誠). And there is nothing more immediate in striving to be consummatory in one's conduct (*ren* 仁) than making every effort to put oneself in the other's place (*shu* 恕).[62]

The character *cheng* in this passage is conventionally translated as "sincerity" or "integrity." In most occurrences in the classical corpus it does carry this meaning, and this *Mencius* passage is no exception. But in a processive and transactional world, sincerity is the bond that unites one in one's relations with others, and that makes the process of personal co-creativity possible. Under such circumstances, "integrity" is not simply retaining what you "have" or being who you "are": It is what you "do" and "become" in *integrating* effectively with family and community. *Cheng* is thus the ground of an *integrative and creative process* of becoming consummately human. It is not "being whole," but the process of "becoming whole" within the multilateral relations that constitute one's natural, social, and cultural environments.[63] This inseparability of integration and creativity is reinforced explicitly in this *Mencius* passage by appeal to *ren*, the correlative, consummatory notion of "person" in which the realizations of oneself and other persons are mutually entailing. The *Analects* defines the project of becoming *ren* in precisely these terms:

> Consummatory persons (*ren*) establish others in seeking to establish themselves and promote others in seeking to get there themselves. Correlating one's conduct with those close at hand can be said to be the method of becoming consummate in one's conduct (*ren*).[64]

When understood in light of this pervasive notion of *qi*, the phenomenal world is not only a site of process and becoming, but also has the existential possibility of deployed artistry in correlating relations and contextualizing things productively. In such a world, the human experience is a *field* both focused by and bringing into focus the myriad items and events comprising. Indeed, in addition to its *extensive* field of *qi*, the *Mencius* passage places equal emphasis upon the *intensive* "me"—*this* particular focus—as an active participant in the quality and meaning of the emerging world. There is no external vantage point outside of the ceaseless flow of *qi*. The vital world is necessarily entertained from one particular vantage point or another, and hence this insistently particular field of *qi* is always construed perspectivally—from a continuing "here" or from a continuing "there," from a persistent "me" or from a persistent "you." Further, each particular perspective is holographic in the sense that it contains within its own compass the extensive field of relations that contextualizes it—a field of relations that is made more or less meaningful by its own intensity of focus, its own resolution. As such, a meaningful life achieved amplifies the meaning of the cosmos.

Thus, recalling the meaning of *qi* as a continuous field, perhaps a more vernacular rendering of "everything is here in me" in the *Mencius* passage cited above might be: "The field of *qi* is focused by me, and thus in my extensive, boundless web of relations, all *qi* is implicated here in me." Indeed, this is precisely the way in which Zhu Xi reads this passage in his commentary upon it:

> This passage describes the basic character of relationality. The more complex patterns are those that obtain between ruler and subject and between father and son; the more simple patterns are those that obtain among things and events in their minutia. There is no aspect of these actual relations that do not reside within one's particular nature.[65]

Paraphrased in more familiar language, we might say that our lives have cosmic consequences. I am, in my ecological relations, continuous with the entire world as experienced, and to the extent that in the cultivation of my own person I have been able to construe my life in an intense and meaningful way, I am able to enhance the meaning of the cosmos as a whole. When understood in this way, it is not difficult to discern the ultimately religious dimension of this Confucian project of personal cultivation, both with respect to the human and the cosmic realms. If religiousness is to be understood as an intense sense of personal worth and unbounded belonging, then the achievement of a meaningful life in family, community, and cosmos is itself a warrant for just such a profound and gratifying feeling.

Correlative Cosmology as a Religious Cosmology: The Emergence of Cultural Exemplars

If we translate this pursuit of the most intensive focus within the most extensive field into the vocabulary of the human community, we might say that exemplary persons (*junzi* 君子) are communal resources that serve as an inspiration for others. What makes them "exemplary" for their community is the assiduous cultivation that has produced personal growth within their manifold of relations. By virtue of this personal intensity and its acknowledged worth, they are celebrated as objects of emulation within the community, thereby extending their influence through patterns of deference both within their own generational boundaries, and for generations yet to come. In the words of the *Mencius*, they have become "most vast" (*zhida* 至大) as persons of extensive and enduring influence, and "most firm" (*zhigang* 至剛) as resolute beacons that guide others toward human excellence.

Such particular exemplars provide the "heading" (*dao* 道) for the continuing community. This need for models to emulate, then, has required the Confucian philosopher to be a paradigmatic individual—a scout to reconnoiter and recommend a "way" for future generations. This analogical appeal to models is ideally bi-directional: a getting and a giving back. Personal cultivation entails the emulation of worthy exemplars available as cultural leaders within one's own world. At the same time, the personal growth made possible by such emulation allows one to aspire personally to a quality of conduct that will, in the fullness of time, make one a continuing inspiration for one's own family and community members, and that will ultimately add to the aggregating quantum of human culture.

In lieu of God or gods as a separate and independent order of being, from early on Chinese cosmology with its emphasis on this world has elevated ancestral figures, cultural heroes, and supreme personalities to cosmic status, and has continued to celebrate them over its long career. Although the veneration of cultural exemplars is profoundly religious in nature, such deference is human-centered, and is still better conceived of as reverence or veneration rather than worship. That is, perfection on the part of an object of worship places it in a relation of utter independence from those who would worship it. By contrast, the inspirational value of Confucius as a model life grows exponentially with the quality of the literati as they emerge to guide the culture across succeeding generations. The interdependent and recursive relationship between the exemplary model and the aspirant is one more example of the fact that a world of processes and events eschews any notion of final discreteness. It is because of this reflexivity between exemplary model and protégé, where they are what they are because of their interdependent and constitutive relationship with the other, that correlative *qi* cosmology requires the use of a focus/field rather than a part/whole vocabulary in its explication. Each model and aspirant is implicated in the other and is successful to the extent that each achieves maximum resolution in the relationship.

One of the implications of the shift from a part/whole to a focus/field sensibility involves the manner in which one characterizes the interactive dynamics of the human experience—one's transactions with the "ten thousand" processes and events that give one context. Familiar notions such as subject and object, action and reaction, cause and effect, grounded as they are in the assumption that things are externally related to each other, have little relevance. Essentialist ideas of some given potential and subsequent actualization and the notion of a linear causality driven by teleological assumptions do not apply. Instead, all such interactions are to be understood in terms of mutual growth and creative advance in the "doings and undergoings" of interdependent, transactional events. We shape and are shaped by the other participants in the shared, interdependent ecology in which we live our lives. All creativity is reflexive: In acting upon the world, we are acting upon ourselves; in cultivating ourselves, we are transforming the world.

In our discussion of *qi*, I have highlighted several differences between the dominant modes of Chinese cosmology and what Heidegger has called and has criticized as our own "theo-ontological" assumptions. In summary, the notion of *qi* entails the acceptance of a lived, phenomenal world that is a manifold of ever-changing processes and events without any reference to some putative permanent and substantial "reality" behind it. This is a world that is at once a vital process and its myriad contents as lived from within. Secondly, the worldview entailed by *qi* is one in which continuity is pervasive, both synchronically and diachronically, across both space and time. Such a world requires that one resort to a focus/field rather than a part/whole explanatory model in understanding the intrinsic relationships that obtain among insistent particulars and their contextualizing world. Thirdly, the wholeness of experience is primary. Thus, only through a process of conceptual abstraction can experience be understood as either subjective or objective, self or other. Fourthly, the cosmos is vital in that it is experienced from within and necessarily requires a uniquely subjective, lived dimension to explain it. Finally, in the absence of discrete, externally related "objects" or "things," causal interpretations must be replaced by the intuition of situated, interdependent, synergistic, and mutually creative processes. Because such processes are attended by the spontaneous emergence of novelty, they are reducible to a simple causal analysis. Change and novelty are both real, and neither will be denied.

The Collateral and Constitutive Nature of Relationality

In the next chapter we will have the occasion to reflect on the *Great Learning* which defines the radial Confucian project of personal cultivation. This seminal text begins from the ecological interconnectedness and interdependence of all of the many dimensions of the human experience within which this collaborative process of personal consummation is to be pursued. The Confucian project begins from a recognition of the wholeness of experience and the constitutive nature of relationality that is entailed by it. Moreover, because each person and event is constituted by an interdependent web of relations, what affects one thing affects all things in some degree or other. Meaningful relations within this family make the entire cosmos more meaningful; barren relations detract from it.

Said another way, within the correlative cosmology that serves as context for the development and the evolution of Confucianism, nothing happens on its own. Nothing happens unilaterally and in isolation. Physically, breathing is a symbiotic collaboration between lungs and air; seeing, between eyes and sun; running, between legs and ground; friendship, between friend and friend. All activity occurs within a context, and is thus necessarily collateral in nature. Unsurprisingly, we find that *all* of the terms of art defining of the Chinese natural cosmology are binomial rather than singular, reflecting this ubiquitous collaterality. The vocabulary is transactional and collaborative: "divinity and humanity" (*tianren* 天人), "the heavens and the earth" (*tiandi* 天地), "forming and functioning" (*tiyong* 體用), "flux and persistence" (*biantong* 變通), "the furthest reaches and beyond" (*taiji/wuji* 太極無極), the *yin* and the *yang* 陰陽, "this particular focus and its field" (*daode* 道德), "configuring and vital energy" (*liqi* 理氣), "determinacy and indeterminacy" (*wuyou* 無有), and so on. No term can stand alone as an independent, determinative principle. There can be no superordinate and independent "one" in this ecological cosmology, no single cause, no grounding, foundational standard, no one privileged order. Consonant with this observation, when in chapter five we ponder the religious implications of Chinese natural cosmology, we will have occasion to cite Marcel Granet who, like many other preeminent Chinese and Western sinologists, tells us that "Chinese wisdom has no need for the idea of God,"[66] no need for the One that explains the many.

If we begin our reflection on this always emergent cosmic order from the wholeness of the lived experience, we can view such experience in terms of both its dynamic continuities and its manifold multiplicities, as both a ceaseless processual flow and as distinct consummatory events. That is, any particular phenomenon in our field of experience can be focused in many different ways: On the one hand, it is a unique and persistent particular, and on the other, holographically, it has the entire cosmos and all that is happening implicated within its own unique and dynamic pattern of relationships. Each phenomenon is one unique way of construing the entire cosmos. Indeed, the mutual entailment of a thing and its context is yet one more example of the mutual implication of opposites that characterizes all phenomena in the Chinese natural cosmology—in this case, the particular and the unsummed totality.

If, as a heuristic for making such abstract cosmological assumptions more concrete, we take the notion of "persons" as our example, we can say that persons are "one" both in their unique individuality and in the unbroken continuity they have as they stand together with their environing others. And yet these same persons are "many" not only as a population of many unique individuals, but also with each of them being a divided and sometimes conflicted "multiplicity" of relations. That is, each person constitutes a veritable *field* of selves through which each of their many roles and personae is expressed: someone's parent and someone else's child, someone's colleague and someone else's adversary, someone's teacher and someone else's lover, someone's benefactor and someone else's nemesis.

This inseparability of one and many is the background for *li* 禮— an achieved propriety in our roles and relations. This notion of *li* expresses a dynamic social pattern within which we are each unique as a configuration of specific roles and relations, and at the same time collaborate as the many corporate persons who together define each particular role and relation as sons and mothers, grandparents and grandchildren. Each of us is uniquely one, and at the same time contributes to the definition of our generalized roles and relations. Below when we come to examine more closely the notion of *xing* 性—a term that has conventionally been translated as "human nature"—we will find that it too has to be understood in this same "one and many" way. There is no discrete, essential, innate, and reduplicated "nature" independent of a person's specific context; there are only unique yet analogically similar persons constituted by their always-specific roles and relationships. And we make generalizations about persons and humanity in general by correlating particular instances and qualities rather than by beginning retrospectively and causally from some essential formula.

In reflecting upon the common binomial, "natural tendencies and unfolding circumstances" (*xingqing* 性情) as it is meant to explain the human experience, the notion of *xing* 性 refers generally to the initial conditions that humans begin from within a family context, and the vitality expressed as growth in the pattern of relations that define these conditions. It is what one is and what one does for others. As we will see, *xing* also indicates the existential resources that are available to us in our quest to become consummately human; we understand the project from the inside. *Qing* 情, on the other hand, looks at personal growth morphologically, providing us with the dynamic, concrete circumstances that tell us what something really is for its context. Who someone really is (*qing*), for example, is determined by the qualitative growth of their initial conditions, and in the "extensiveness" (*zhida* 至大) and the "intensiveness" (*zhigang* 至剛) of what is achieved. *Qing* then is both the facticity of and the feeling that pervades any particular situation. Any perceived fact/value distinction between "circumstances" (*qingkuang* 情況) on the one hand, and "feelings that are responsive to circumstances" (*ganqing* 感情) on the other, collapses.

This inseparability of fact and value is no different from the interdependence of the qualitative and the quantitative. That is, what we might take to be "objectively" quantitative—being one's own person and expressing one's individuality, for example—is simply an abstraction from the quality of those deferential relations that are distinctive to this person and that distinguishes him or her as a unique individual. In the absence of such robust relations, one is quite literally a "nobody." Thus it is from the qualitative that the quantitative emerges. Individuality is not a given; it is the accomplishment of becoming distinctive and distinguished in one's relations with others. When we acknowledge that cosmological terms such as "natural tendencies and unfolding circumstances" (*xingqing* 性情) are collateral and as such, inform each other, we are really only allowing that the context of something must be always be taken into account as integral to its own evolving meaning.

When we turn to the human community and reference the social grammar of those roles and relations (*li*) that distinguish each of us and set us apart as unique persons, we have to acknowledge that it is the achievement of a shared, synchronizing musicality (*yue* 樂) in these same relations that brings us together as members of a harmonious family and community. When we reference the unique and yet incipient human tendencies (*xing* 性) that constitute our initial conditions as persons and the energy of growth, we again have to include the manifold of changing circumstances, both facticity and feelings (*qing*), in which these same tendencies will come to life. Such dyadic terms—in this case, communal roles and the playing of music (*liyue* 禮樂), and human tendencies and the unfolding of circumstances and feelings (*xingqing* 性情)—are invariably two nonanalytic ways of looking at the same phenomenon, the unique particular and its context. Everything needs to be understood both genetically and morphologically, both as this focus and this field. In this Chinese natural cosmology, it is this resolute collaterality of all things and events that requires that we begin reflection from the always-contextualized yet unique particular without assuming some appeal to essences and natural kinds.

Our familiar epistemic vocabulary—"comprehending, grasping, getting, understanding"—suggests a search for an objective, decontextualizing essence behind the accidents and appearances, thereby allowing us to categorize persons or things correctly by "calling them by their own names." By contrast, the vocabulary of "knowing" in this Chinese collateral cosmology—"unraveling the patterns" (*lijie* 理解 or *liaojie* 了解), "finding a way and knowing how to proceed" (*zhidao* 知道), or "penetrating through" (*tongda* 通達)—is directed at mapping the always evolving relational context, thereby enabling us to "call something or someone by another name." This always-conditional, paronomastic epistemology assumes that the source of meaning—the source of one's personal significance—is productive relationships, and hence that these always changing relationships must themselves be the substance of knowing. In order to know other people we must come to understand them in their relationships with others. Persons are properly known by calling them by the many collateral roles and relations they "live" within our community: someone is at once auntie, teacher, neighbor, cousin, coach, and so on. It is only by knowing how persons function in the dynamic patterns of the many roles and relationships with others that we really come to know them.

The principle of individuation in this cosmology is not a ready-made and replicable essential identity that constitutes us as natural kinds—a soul, a heavenly-endowed human nature, a rational mind, a virtuous character, a self-conscious self, an independent agency. Rather, it is a qualitatively achieved distinctiveness in the configuring of one's relations within family and community. In this Confucian model of the constitutive relations of role-bearing persons, then, we are not "individuals who associate in community," but rather because we associate effectively in community we become distinguished as relationally constituted individuals; we do not "have minds and therefore speak with one another," but rather because we speak effectively with one another we become like-minded and thrive as a family and community; we do not "have hearts and therefore are empathetic with one another," but rather because we feel effective empathy with one another we become a whole-hearted, self-regulating community. Indeed, paronomasia—defining and realizing a world through associated living—is the Confucian way of making meaning in a communicating community.

Confucian Creativity: "What Makes *This* Life Significant"

In traditional Chinese cosmology, with the *Book of Changes* (*Yijing*) being the first among the classics, the presumption has long been that knowledge is to be found in what John Dewey has described as "the mutual interactions of changing things"—the omnipresent processes of "generation and transformation."[67] Chinese cosmology subscribes to an assumption that Alfred North Whitehead has come to call "the ontological principle"—the notion of an ontological parity of finitude that give all things an equal claim on being real. We might alternatively term such a cosmology "a realistic pluralism."[68] This ontological principle is an affirmation of the reality of any thing as it is constituted by the manifold of its relations, whether it be each and every thing, each and every kind of thing, or the unsummed totality of things as experience itself. In the *Zhongyong* we read:

> The way of the world can be captured in one phrase: since events are never duplicated, their proliferation is unfathomable.[69]

Such a world of unique particulars is a *pluri*-verse rather than a universe in the sense that construals of order are unique and many, and that the totality of these orders is not dominated by any one particular pattern or any one thing. Rather, order is the emergent harmony achieved in the always-contingent relationships that obtain among this unsummed totality, "the myriad things and events" (*wanwu* 萬物). With no "One behind the many" as the ultimate source of meaning, there is no single-ordered world, no strict sense of *kosmos* that assumes an external orderer; there is only the ongoing evolving harmony expressed as the quality of life achieved by the insistent, co-creating particulars which together make a world for themselves.

In this world in which things are constituted by their conditioning relations, meaning does not arise *ex nihilo* from some independent and external source—from some conception of God or Natural Law or Platonic ideas or Muse, or from some audacious, reclusive genius.

Instead, increased significance is always situated and situational. Meaning arises *in situ* through the cultivation of deepening relations that we have expressed elsewhere as *ars contextualis*: "the art of finding optimal contextualization within one's roles and relations."⁷⁰ Of course, this absence of an assumed privileged order does not preclude meaningful generalizations that can be made among analogous particulars, and functional categories that can be established to facilitate our activities in this world. As we shall discover in the final chapter of this essay, we can be meaningfully generalized as "human beings." Indeed, it is the capacity and the responsibility of such creatures to be co-creators of the cosmos that establishes a direct line between Confucian role ethics and Confucian religiousness.

Tang Junyi 唐君毅 and Chinese Process Cosmology

As we have seen, the legacy of Chinese process cosmology certainly has ancient roots, but it has also persisted in many different forms across the centuries, and is alive in the world today. Tang Junyi was one of China's most distinguished contemporary philosophers who came to be described in the 1980s as a prominent member of the "New Confucians" (*xinruxuejia* 新儒學家). Still, decades after his death, Tang has something compelling to say in answer to the question: "How might we describe this persistent Chinese cosmology?" In my mind, Tang Junyi's foremost contribution to philosophy as a global phenomenon is his synoptic philosophy of culture. In his early writings he exhibits an uncanny ability to discern and to articulate, with truly penetrating acuity, as clear a contrast as can be established between the presuppositions grounding the metaphysical thinking that has had such prominent play in much of the pre-twentieth-century Western philosophical narrative, and those persistent cosmological assumptions that ground correlative thinking and that continue to shape an always changing Chinese worldview. Tang is able to argue effectively for a range of uncommon assumptions that, giving the lie to the homogenization of Enlightenment universalism, must be taken into account if we are to allow this Confucian cultural narrative its many unique and important contributions.

The contemporary philosopher Guo Qiyong 郭齊勇 in a seminal

article argues that Tang Junyi is typical of the other New Confucians in relying heavily upon the *Book of Changes* and its commentaries as one of his foremost resources, drawing upon this canonical literature to offer his own creative interpretation of its cosmology. These New Confucians explore the intersection between modern philosophical thinking and the far-ranging cosmology of the *Book of Changes*, affirming that the characteristics of Chinese philosophy that most distinguish it from its Western counterpart consist in a naturalistic view of the vital life forces that animate the cosmos wherein the goal of the consummate human being is to participate fully in optimizing the harmony of the totality.[71]

I will make another foray into establishing an interpretive context for exploring Confucian role ethics by appealing to several propositions that Tang Junyi offers us as a specifically comparative vocabulary for recovering the worldview within which the Confucian philosophical narrative has evolved—a vocabulary that in a different language inspired by the canonical texts rehearses the same correlative *qi* cosmology as that articulated in the *Great Tradition* of the *Book of Changes* sketched above, and that is implicit in the worldview that gives ground to Traditional Chinese Medicine.[72] In the several chapters that follow, I will have occasion to apply these propositions in exploring some of the defining Confucian terms of art that have been used over the centuries to promote Confucian philosophical thinking, and that have come to constitute the vocabulary of role ethics: that is, Confucianism's notions of "family reverence" (*xiao* 孝), "consummate person/conduct" (*ren* 仁), "exemplary person" (*junzi*), "achieved propriety in ritualized roles and relations" (*li*), "optimizing appropriateness" (*yi* 義), and so on.

In delineating the cosmological background of the Confucian tradition, Tang describes a holographic, interdependent, and productive relationship between "part" and "totality"—a conception of ecological relationality as *the* distinguishing feature and most vital contribution of Chinese culture. As the underlying character of this traditional culture, Tang endorses a philosophical holism that entails

> ... the spirit of symbiosis and mutuality of particular and totality. From the perspective of understanding this means an unwillingness to isolate the particular from the totality (this is most evident in the cosmology of the Chinese people), and from the perspective of ties of feeling and affection,

it means the commitment of the particular to do its utmost to realize the totality (this is most evident in the attitude of the Chinese people toward daily life).⁷³

We might appeal to the concrete image of "this person" constituted by "these family relations" to bring greater clarity to Tang's abstract description of the relationship that obtains between "particular" and "totality." That is, when this idea of optimizing the collaterality and interdependence of what Tang calls "particulars" and "totality" is translated into the more concrete social and political dynamics of the human community, it becomes the value of inclusive, consensual, and optimally productive cooperation that emerges from the well of family feeling. This symbiosis becomes the realization of a vital, productive harmony (*he* 和) within the family, and by extension, the community.

Tang uses a language that I have translated as "particulars" (*bufen* 部分) and "totality" (*quanti* 全體) here. But given the organic assumptions underlying this cosmology, such a characterization would perhaps be more apposite if it employed a vocabulary that expressed the intrinsic, constitutive nature of relations—"foci" and "fields," or perhaps "ecologically situated events" and their "environments"—to make the relationship between "part" and "totality" more clear. This organic interdependence of things and the processual nature of the human experience is captured and elaborated upon in the seven propositions Tang uses to characterize Chinese natural cosmology.

In framing this aesthetic holism, Tang begins with the Confucian affirmation of the reality and sufficiency of empirical experience without appeal to supernatural elements beyond the ordinary events of the day. In his first proposition—"the notion that there is no fixed substance" (*wudingti guan* 無定體觀)—he rejects outright the relevance of any notion of permanent substratum, of some metaphysical ground as an underlying reality, and in so doing, acknowledges the fluidity of *qi* 氣 and the ontological parity among events in their ceaseless flux and flow.⁷⁴

As we have seen, this correlative *qi* cosmology is not a reductionistic "One-behind-the-many," monistic ontology. Vital particulars and the specific relations that constitute them are real. In the absence of any essentializing substratum—that is, "what it means to be this kind of a thing"—and without any "things" that can be parsed as indivisibles into a taxonomy of natural kinds, the human experience is constituted by resolutely unique perturbations of *qi* often referred to collectively as the "myriad of things" (*wanwu* 萬物). The uniqueness of each particular as a nexus of specific relations attended by its own possibilities precludes any notion of strict identity among them—no two things are precisely the same. Further, given the intrinsic nature of relatedness, putative "things" that are constituted by their relationships stand in contrast to each other as currents in a stream of unique, mutually conditioning "events"—a manifold of happenings that have ontological parity within the unsummed totality of things. And the web of always shifting relationships that constitutes each "event" is itself a novel and unique construal of the totality—that is, it is "this" particular focus of "this" particular field of experience.

Importantly, the foci and their unfolding fields are an always-dynamic process. Indeed, the processual flow of experience without initial beginnings or putative end is what Tang, appealing specifically to language from the *Book of Changes*, describes as "the notion of ceaseless procreation" (*shengsheng buyi guan* 生生不已觀).[75] The human experience is persistent, historicist, and naturalistic in the sense of being autogenerative and emergent without appeal to any metaphysical or supernatural source, or to any predetermined end. The phenomenological world in classical China is an endless flow, evidencing its formal character only as "trans-*form*-ation."

In fact, the *Great Commentary* of the *Book of Changes* says explicitly "thus it is that spirituality is without squareness and change is without body."[76] Willard Peterson in interpreting this passage suggests that "to have no 'squareness' is to be not susceptible of being differentiated into parts and to be not adequately delimited by any conceptual bounds."[77] The processual and provisional nature of things makes them ultimately resistant to rationalization and predictability. And for change to have no body is another way of saying that within a process of ceaseless change, the formal must be understood as the determinate rhythms of change rather than as any fixed and recalcitrant structures. What we take to be "things" are in fact a ceaseless, processive flux of "events," where it is the intersticies among the shifting dispositionings of these events that is the fecund source of all life and growth.[78]

Tang's corollary to this "notion of ceaseless procreation" is the irrelevance of any kind of hard determinism or external agency for Confucian cosmology—what he terms "the notion of non-fatalism" (*feidingming guan* 非定命觀).⁷⁹ The ceaseless process of procreation has the energy of transformation within it, and evolves according to the changing dispositions of the events that constitute it. Fatalism by contrast would introduce a notion of necessity that violates the presumption of ceaseless procreation, and that renders creativity and real novelty null considerations. Rather, without any fixed pattern or guiding hand, experience is the bottomless unfolding of an emergent, contingent world according to the rhythm of its own internal creative processes.

Tang, keenly aware that a teleologically predetermined universe would preclude the possibility of any meaningful notion of temporality, sees time itself as inseparable from the emerging world of unique "things." Indeed, genuine change and growth—that is, life as the spontaneous emergence of novelty in the unique relations that are constitutive of things—is just another way of saying genuine time.

The penumbra of indeterminacy that honeycombs an always-provisional cosmic order means that the forming and functioning of things are symbiotic, an assumption that is captured in the cosmological vocabulary of "flux and persistence" (*biantong* 變通) and "forming and functioning" (*tiyong* 體用). Moreover, all form is constantly undergoing adjustment to maintain functional equilibrium, and is ultimately vulnerable to and outrun by the process itself. Although some things are more persistent than others, there is nothing that does not give way ultimately to trans-*form*-ation.

This transformative character of the Chinese cosmology that undergirds Confucianism is described by Tang with two additional propositions: "the notion that nothing advances but to return" (*wuwang bufu guan* 無往不復觀), and the "the notion that there is a continuity that obtains between determinacy and indeterminacy, motion and equilibrium" (*he youwu dongjing guan* 合有無動靜觀).⁸⁰ Tang in describing Chinese cosmology references "the world as such"—a unique and boundless world within which the observer is always reflexively embedded. In his own language:

> When Chinese philosophers speak of the world, they are thinking of the world that we are living in. There is no world beyond or outside of the one we are experiencing.... They are not referencing "*a* world" or "*the* world," but are simply saying "world as such" without putting any indefinite or definite article in front of it.[81]

Without an external standpoint for asserting objective truths, persons are always reflexively implicated in the way in which they organize their world. As a consequence, saying something about the world is always a matter of selected interest that also says something about one's own self-understanding. Any criticism of prevailing conditions is directed at "us" rather than "them": "We must all try to do better."

The absence of some ultimate basis for objective statements about the world makes fact and value interdependent and mutually entailing, and renders notions such as objective definition and simple description problematic. The values of the always-interested observers are implicated in their observations, and their description of what they see privileges some values over others. The line, then, that divides science from art, chemistry from alchemy, astronomy from astrology, geology from geomancy, and psychology from physiognomy, has always been somewhat tenuous. Indeed, the distance between description and prescription becomes a matter of the degree of one's own self-consciousness.

Again, in the absence of a Creator, there is no grand design or final purpose that would make change linear and directed. The mutual entailment of opposites—day becoming night, young becoming old, full becoming empty, contracted becoming outstretched, and so on—guarantees a spiraling explanation of change where the process although *sui generis* always comes back upon itself. As it says in the *Daodejing*, "Returning is how way-making (*dao*) moves,"[82] or giving it a more explicit interpretation, "Returning is how experience unfolds." In the rhythm of the year, spring becomes summer, summer becomes autumn, autumn becomes winter, and then the year turns back again to the always novel yet also familiar cadence of spring. This pattern of return is captured in the cycle of the sixty stems and branches used to designate the succeeding years in the sixty-year cycle (*huajia* 花甲).

The related proposition that underscores the contingent nature of emerging order is its underdeterminacy. That is, there is an indeterminate aspect entailed by the uniqueness of each participant in experience that qualifies its order, making any and every pattern of experience novel and site specific, irreversible, reflexive, and in degree, unpredictable. Human beings are similar enough to justify certain generalizations—a provisional conception of human nature (*xing* 性), for example—yet each person is at the same time unique, *one* of a kind. Each person is a dynamic manifold of specific relations that determine this person's trajectory through life. It is this uniqueness of each person that precludes the possibility of any logarithmic understanding of human conduct, and that keeps any definition of humanity open ended, conditional, and under construction.

This proposition—"the notion that there is a continuity that obtains between determinacy and indeterminacy, motion and equilibrium"—precludes the possibility of any absolute void in space and any eternality in time. Any reference to "emptiness" is a bounded "emptiness"; any reference to stillness is an achieved equilibrium within motion that requires constant adjustment. Cast more broadly, this proposition speaks to the collaterality and fluidity of order, where any predication of experience is always couched within and attended by the impending transformation into its opposite. Emptiness is only possible because of fullness, and vice versa; equilibrium is only possible because of movement, and vice versa.

From what Tang has said so far, his characterization of the cosmology that grounds Confucianism is resolutely hierarchical, historicist, particularist, and emergent. Tang takes as a further generic feature of the Chinese processual cosmology an expression that can be read many ways. *Yiduo bufen guan* 一多不分觀 is at once "the inseparability of the one and the many, of uniqueness and multivalence, of continuity and multiplicity, of integrity and integration."[83] Importantly, this notion of intrinsic, constitutive relationality—the assumption that the constitution of any "one" entails "many"—is an aspect of Chinese natural cosmology implicated in all of the other propositions described above.

Cosmologically, this proposition of the inseparability of one and many asserts that any phenomenon in our field of experience can be focused in many different ways. This person while uniquely "one" is some parent's daughter, some husband's lover, some child's mother, some candidate's American, and so on. On the one hand, she is a unique and persistent particular, and on the other, she has the entire cosmos and all that is happening implicated within her own intensive and extensive patterns of relationships. The consummatory goal for the unique individual in cultivating these many relationships is to optimize their possibilities—to make the most of the opportunities that circumstances allow.

Given that order is an invariably negotiated, emergent, and provisional harmony contingent upon those many elements that constitute it, it is neither rigidly linear nor disciplined toward some given end. The meaning of this family is not predetermined, but is negotiated out of the continuing needs and contributions of the members that belong to it, and is disclosed in the quality of meaningful relations they are able to achieve. Hence, Confucian harmony (*he*) although consummatory is not expressible in the language of conformity, completion, perfection, or closure. Rather, harmonious order is a continuing aesthetic achievement made possible through *ars contextualis*, "the art of opitimal contextualizing within one's roles and relations." Such achieved harmony is most appropriately expressible in the aesthetic language of elegance, complexity, intensity, balance, disclosure, efficacy, integrity, and so on. Without appeal to some originative principle and the linear teleology that comes with it, the world has no grand preassigned design; its governing purpose is a localized and temporalized self-sufficiency—a collaboration among the participating elements to make the most out of each situation. This then is the meaning of Confucian harmony (*he*).

In the chapter that follows, we will have the occasion to develop the last of Tang Junyi's seven cosmological presuppositions that seek to characterize the collaboration of cultivated human beings and their environments as a source of cosmic meaning. This proposition states specifically that "human nature is nothing but the unfolding of the natural and cultural processes themselves" (*xing ji tiandao guan* 性即天道觀).[84] Persons begin their careers inchoately as both one and many. That is, persons at their inception, although unique, have little to distinguish themselves as individuals. Yet such persons are born into a matrix of relations thick with culture and values made available to them initially through the care of a small circle of family intimates. The natural and cultural context provides the nourishment for persons who will, in the fullness of time, make their own contribution to the world that has sponsored their growth. Importantly, the relationship between person and environment is symbiotic and collaborative rather than unilateral and derivative. While Confucius can say: "It is the natural and cultural environment (*tian* 天) that has engendered the excellence in me," we can also say that it is Confucius who has made a substantial contribution to the character of Chinese culture.[85]

Using the Confucian vocabulary, we might describe the evolving careers of members of the community from beginning as mere persons (*ren* 人) to becoming exemplary in their conduct (*junzi*) for their community through achieving a consummate relational virtuosity (*ren* 仁) with other people. For only a few, by coordinating and embodying in themselves the values and the meaning that distinguish some historical epoch of human flourishing, they have the ultimate distinction of becoming sages (*shengren* 聖人), and as such, sources of enduring cosmic meaning. In Confucian philosophy, the expectation is that human beings and the natural, social, and cultural worlds they inhabit must be full collaborators in a flourishing cosmos.

At the very heart of Confucian role ethics, distinguishing it fundamentally from more familiar Western ethical "theories," is a concept of a relationally constituted person who realizes a vision of the consummate life through a kind of moral artistry. It is to an articulation of this notion of person as relational virtuosity that we now turn.

III

The Confucian Project: Attaining Relational Virtuosity

"Human *Beings*" or "Human *Becomings*"?

What is a human "being"? This was the perennial Greek question asked in Plato's *Phaedo* and in Aristotle's *De Anima*. And perhaps the most persistent answer from the time of Pythagoras was an ontological one: The "being" or essence of a human being is a permanent, ready-made, and self-sufficient soul. And "know thyself"—the signature exhortation of Socrates—is to know this soul. Each of us *is* a person, and from conception, has the integrity of *being* a person.

In what way does a person *become* consummately human? This was the perennial Confucian question asked explicitly in all of the *Four Books*: in the *Great Learning*, in the *Analects of Confucius*, in the *Mencius*, and again in the *Zhongyong*. And the answer from the time of Confucius was a moral, aesthetic, and ultimately religious one. One *becomes* human by cultivating those thick, intrinsic relations that constitute one's initial conditions and that locate the trajectory of one's life force within family, community, and cosmos.[1] "Cultivate your person" (*xiushen* 修身), the signature exhortation of the Confucian canons, is the ground of the Confucian project of becoming consummate as a person (*ren*): It is to cultivate one's conduct assiduously as it is expressed through those family, community, and cosmic roles and relations that one lives. In this Confucian tradition, we need each other. Becoming consummate in our conduct (*ren*) is something that we *do*, and that we either do together, or not at all.[2]

It will be the argument of this chapter that insufficient attention has been paid to this fundamental difference between ontologically constituted human "beings" and the Confucian project of "becoming" human. As a consequence, there is a real danger of inadvertently shoehorning the Confucian foot into a Greek sandal. The exciting documents recovered in recent archaeological finds have persuaded our present generation of scholars to go back and take another look at our received texts. In doing so, we have found some issues that we have overlooked, and other things that we have been able to clarify by reference to these new materials.

As an example, we have found that an epistemology of concrete "feelings" (*qing* 情) is fundamental to an emerging Confucian tradition that, after the death of Confucius himself, we associate with the lineage traced from Confucius's grandson, Zisizi 子思子, down through Mencius (*simengpai* 思孟派). As a consequence, we have had to rethink our more cognitive, conceptual, and theoretical interpretations of the early Confucian canons to make sure that we have given the affective dimension of personal cultivation appropriate consideration.

Further, I believe that these same archaeological documents provide us with additional textual evidence for clarifying the Confucian notion of relationally constituted "human becomings" and for distinguishing this notion of "person" fundamentally from an essentialist understanding of discrete human beings. The philosophical implications of this distinction between the Confucian *ren* and a foundational individualism that had its beginnings in classical Greece are pervasive and enduring, and unless and until we are clear on this difference, we will continue to theorize Confucian philosophy according to assumptions that are not its own.

How have contemporary scholars who are not inclined to distinguish *ren* from the notion of the discrete individual and who thus read it in an essentialistic way come by their interpretations? I will begin to address this question by examining one familiar passage from the *Analects*:

> Exemplary persons (*junzi* 君子) concentrate their efforts on the root, for the root having set, one's proper path in life (*dao* 道) will emerge therefrom. As for family reverence (*xiao* 孝) and fraternal deference (*ti* 弟), these are, I suspect, the root of becoming consummate in one's conduct (*ren* 仁).[3]

What does it mean to take the practical activities of revering family members (*xiao* 孝) and of deferring appropriately to elders (*ti* 弟) as the *root* (*ben* 本) of becoming consummate in one's conduct as a person (*ren* 仁)?[4] Should we not rather regard such *xiao* and *ti* activities as a practical expression of *ren* as human nature? In making what is taken to be "human nature" the product rather than the ultimate source of human conduct, are we not putting the cart before the horse?

Zhu Xi 朱熹, the Southern Song philosopher who compiled the *Four Books*, seems to worry over this possible inversion, and cites the interpretation of his philosophical predecessors, the Cheng brothers 二程, on this same *Analects* passage for clarification. The Cheng brothers argue that the problematic expression in this *Analects* passage "becoming *ren*" 為仁 should in fact be read as "practicing *ren*" 行仁:

> When reverence and deference are practiced within the family, a consummate love (*ren'ai* 仁愛) is extended in all we do. This is what is called expressing affection in kin relations (*qinqin* 親親) and dealing with the people in a consummate manner (*renmin* 仁民). It is in this sense that becoming consummate in one's conduct (*ren*) has its root in family reverence (*xiao*) and fraternal deference (*ti*). But in reference to human nature (*xing*), it is *ren* that is the root of *xiao* and *ti*. Some have wondered whether or not identifying *xiao* and *ti* as the root of *ren* is because *xiao* and *ti* can bring about *ren*. I think not. Saying that practicing *ren* commences from *xiao* and *ti* means that *xiao* and *ti* are expressions of *ren*; saying that they are the root of practicing *ren* is fine, but saying that they are the root of *ren* itself will not do. As for *ren*, it is human nature (*xing*); *xiao* and *ti* are its applications (*yong* 用). Within human nature, there are only the four components: *ren* 仁, *yi* 義, *li* 禮, *zhi* 智. How would *xiao* and *ti* factor into it? Now the main import of *ren* is love, and there is no love greater than that for one's kin. Hence the text reads: "As for family reverence (*xiao* 孝) and fraternal deference (*ti*), these are, I suspect, the root of becoming consummate in one's conduct (*ren*)."[5]

One familiar way of reading this Cheng commentary is to assume that classical Confucianism has a notion of human *beings*, and that the Cheng brothers are, by properly separating nature from nurture, simply clarifying the internal, essential, and exclusive status of human nature (*renxing* 人性) we associate with Mencius. A second way of reading the commentary here is to argue that the Cheng brothers, as neo-Confucian philosophers, influenced as they were by an originally Indo-European Buddhism, departed from a Mencian notion of "human *becoming*" by internalizing and essentializing human nature, taking it to be an original potential that is then actualized in what it means to become a human being. Yet another reading of this Cheng commentary would begin by allowing that by the Song dynasty, the Buddhism influencing these neo-Confucian thinkers had been so thoroughly sinicized that it would not have introduced such a major disjunction with the Mencian understanding of human nature. This interpretation would further argue that the notion of human nature at play here is consistent with Mencius' "four inklings or sprouts" (*siduan* 四端) in being described as the "root" (*ben*) that nourishes our human behavior—a root that cannot in any way be conceived as independent of the other elements that together constitute the organic process of becoming human. This third interpretation would take nature and nurture as interdependent and correlative categories, rendering them symbiotic and mutually entailing. Indeed, in the Mencius, *xing* is often used verbally as something that is done.⁶ In the ecological cosmology that gives this Cheng commentary context, one must understand the notion of root in its relation to the whole process of becoming a tree and must reflect on the nature of a person or any particular thing as the ongoing outcome of the total dynamic pattern of its relationships.

In contesting the first two of the possible interpretations of the Cheng commentary and arguing for this third reading suggested above, I will be seeking an interpretation of how one becomes consummately human that does not violate the basic and persistent assumptions of classical Chinese natural cosmology that we surveyed in chapter two. I want to attempt to make sense of this particular *Analects* passage and the Confucian canons broadly in such a way that it does not insinuate a Greek understanding of an essential human nature into the Confucian canons. By locating the notion of human nature within this relational *qi* cosmology, we will discover that what are sometimes taken to be unilateral and exclusive terms generally associated with human nature such as "root," "potential," "cause," and "source" have to be reconceived as collateral, transactional, and reflexive. The tree is an organic whole, and while the root may be thought to grow the tree, the tree in turn grows its roots. A poem by Tanya Storch comes to mind:

III · The Confucian Project: Attaining Relational Virtuosity

> Roots are branches
> underground.
> Branches—roots
> into the sky.[7]

This understanding of the root and the tree as a symbiotic whole as an alternative to thinking of the root as an independent, single source reflects cosmological assumptions that require a situated answer to one of our most fundamental and perennial philosophical questions: "Where does meaning come from?" In the Abrahamic traditions, the answer is simple: meaning comes from a Divine source beyond and independent of the individual: Yahweh, or God, or Allah provides us with life's purpose. For the Confucian project, on the other hand, without appeal to some independent principle, meaning arises *pari passu* from a network of meaningful relationships. A personal commitment to achieving relational virtuosity within one's own family relationships is both the starting point and the ultimate source of personal, social, and indeed, cosmic meaning. That is, in cultivating one's own person through achieving and extending robust relations in one's family and beyond, one enlarges the cosmos by adding meaning to it, and in turn, this increasingly meaningful cosmos provides a fertile context for the project of one's own personal cultivation.

Confucius is adamant that moral motivation is the motor of personal cultivation. While always self-effacing, Confucius not only allows but actually repeatedly endorses one description of himself—that he is a person who "cares deeply for learning" (*haoxue* 好學). And for Confucius, such learning means quite specifically having the unrelenting resolve to become consummate in one's conduct as a person (*ren*). Becoming consummate in one's conduct is a lifelong project that quite literally begins at home, and that is irreducibly collateral and transactional—the refined and elegant expression of a relational virtuosity. As Confucius is reported to have stated in the *Analects*: "Correlating one's conduct with those close at hand can be said to be the method of becoming consummate in one's conduct."[8] Again, he insists that "becoming consummate in one's conduct is self-originating—how could it originate with others?"[9] And further, Confucius has the highest expectations for the transformative outcome of such resolve: "I study what is near at hand and aspire to what is lofty."[10]

Indeed, in this Confucian tradition, there is a direct corridor from the achieved consummate life to a human-centered religiousness as the highest expression of personal cultivation. Confucian religiousness—the powerful sense of achieved worth and personal belonging that arises from the concerted growth of meaningful relations—is the *spirituality* achieved when members of family and community *aspire* to contribute themselves utterly in their relations with others, and thus live *inspired* lives. Such religiousness is itself the source and product of the flourishing family and community, and the quality of this religious life is a direct consequence of the quality of communal living. Said another way, religiosity is not only the root of the flourishing community and the seed from which it grows, but is most importantly its mature fruit, its radiant flower. The synergy between personal cultivation and the numinous is captured in the familiar mantra that is often appealed to by students of Chinese religiousness in distinguishing Confucian familial and communal reverence from Abrahamic God-inspired worship: That is, Confucian religiousness is characterized by "the symbiotic continuity between the natural and cultural context and the human experience" (*tianren heyi* 天人合一).

Setting the Project: The *Great Learning* (*Daxue* 大學)

The *Great Learning* 大學, the seminal, foundational canon that sets and anchors this Confucian project early in the tradition, describes the process of becoming human. It insists that it is only through committing oneself to a resolute regimen of personal cultivation that one can achieve the comprehensive intellectual and moral understanding that will make the most of the human experience. The central message of this terse yet comprehensive document is that while personal, familial, social, political, and indeed cosmic cultivation is ultimately coterminous and mutually entailing, it must always begin from a commitment to personal cultivation. In the language of the text itself:

> The way of achieving greatness through learning lies in demonstrating real personal excellence, in cherishing the common people, and in dedicating oneself to doing what is best. Such a course of learning can only be set once one has made this commitment. Only in having set such a course is one able to find equilibrium, only in having found equilibrium is one able

to become self-assured, only in having become self-assured is one able to be deliberate in what one does, and only in being deliberate in what one does is one able to get what one is after. There is the important and the incidental in things and a beginning and an end in what we do. It is in realizing what should have priority that one approaches the proper way (*dao*).[11]

Having endorsed the priority of making a commitment to personal cultivation, the text then continues by rehearsing the cosmic proportions the ancient sage-kings were able to achieve once they dedicated themselves to this project:

> The ancients who sought to demonstrate real excellence to the whole world first brought proper order to their states; in seeking to bring proper order to their states, they first set their families right; in seeking to set their families right, they first cultivated their own persons; in seeking to cultivate their persons, they first knew what is proper in their own heartminds; in seeking to know what is proper in their heartminds, they first became sincere in their purposes; in seeking to become sincere in their purposes, they first became comprehensive in their wisdom. And the highest wisdom lies in seeing how things fit together most productively.
>
> Once they saw how things fit together most productively, their wisdom reached its heights; once their wisdom reached its heights, their thoughts were sincere; once their thoughts were sincere, their heartminds knew what is proper; once their heartminds knew what is proper, their persons were cultivated; once their persons were cultivated, their families were set right; once their families were set right, their state was properly ordered; and once their states were properly ordered, there was peace in the world.[12]

Each person stands as a unique perspective on family, community, polity, and cosmos, and through a dedication to deliberate growth and articulation, everyone has the possibility of bringing the resolution of the relationships that locate and constitute them within family and community into clearer and more meaningful focus. The "learning" (*xue* 學) of the *Great Learning* is the cultivation of productive, transpersonal habits of conduct.[13]

As the *Great Learning* enjoins us, in the singularly important project of becoming consummate persons, we must get our priorities right:

> From the emperor down to the common folk, everything is rooted in personal cultivation. There can be no healthy canopy when the roots

are not properly set, and it would never do for priorities to be reversed between what should be invested with importance and what should be treated more lightly.[14]

The *Book of Rites* (*Liji* 禮記) version of the *Great Learning* concludes this text by declaring that giving priority to achieving personal excellence is wisdom at its best. In its own words:

> This commitment to personal cultivation is called both the root and the height of wisdom.[15]

Here again, the "root" and its product, wisdom, are to be perceived as an organic whole that grow together or not at all.

In appealing to an understanding of Chinese natural cosmology as the relevant interpretive context for this Confucian project, I have tried to provide a language that will distinguish this worldview from the reductive, single-ordered, "One-behind-the-many" ontological model that grounds classical Greek metaphysical thinking wherein one comes to "understand" the many by knowing retrospectively the foundational and causal ideal that lies behind them. Instead, we have found that in Chinese correlative cosmology there is a symbiotic and holistic focus-field model of order that is illustrated rather concisely here in the organic, ecological sensibilities of the *Great Learning*. The meaning of the family is implicated in and dependent upon the productive cultivation of each of its members, and by extension, the meaning of the entire cosmos is implicated in and dependent upon the productive cultivation of each person within family and community. Personal worth is the source of human culture, and human culture in turn is the aggregating resource that provides a context for each person's cultivation.

While certainly having important theoretical implications, the enduring power of this Confucian project is that it proceeds from a relatively straightforward account of the actual human experience. It is a pragmatic naturalism in the sense that, rather than relying upon metaphysical presuppositions or supernatural speculations, it focuses instead on the possibilities for enhancing personal worth available to us here and now through enchanting the ordinary affairs of the day. A grandmother's love for her grandson is at once the most ordinary of things, and the most extraordinary of things.

Confucius develops his insights around the most basic and enduring aspects of the ordinary human experience—family reverence, deference to others, friendship, a cultivated sense of shame, growth and education, life in community, and so on—and in so doing, he has guaranteed their continuing relevance. One characteristic of Confucianism prominent in the words of Confucius himself that has made his teachings so resilient in the Chinese tradition is its porousness and adaptability. His contribution was simply to take ownership of the cultural legacy of his time, to adapt the wisdom of the past to his own present historical moment, and then to recommend to future generations that they do the same.[16]

The personal model of Confucius that is remembered in the *Analects* does not purport to lay out some generic formula by which everyone should live their lives. Rather, the text recalls the narrative of one special person: how he in his relations with others cultivated his humanity, and how he lived a fulfilled and a fulfilling life, much to the admiration of those around him. We might take liberties and play with the title of the *Analects*, reading "discoursing" (*lunyu* 論語) more specifically as "role-based discoursing" (*lunyu* 倫語). Indeed, in reading the *Analects*, we encounter the relationally constituted Confucius making his way through life by living his many roles as best he can: as a caring family member (5.1, 5.2), as a strict teacher and mentor (16.13), as a scrupulous and incorruptible scholar-official (15.1), as a concerned neighbor and member of the community (9.10), as an always-critical political consultant (12.18), as the grateful progeny of his progenitors (7.5), as an enthusiastic heir to a specific cultural legacy (3.14, 9.5), indeed, as a member of a chorus of joyful boys and men singing their way home after a happy day on the river Yi (11.26). He offers us historical models rather than principles, and exhortations rather than imperatives. The power and lasting value of his insights lie in the fact that, as I will endeavor to show, these ideas are intuitively persuasive, and readily adaptable to the conditions of ensuing generations, including our own.

Indeed, in invoking the Chinese natural cosmology as context, what makes Confucianism more empirical than empiricism—that is, what makes Confucianism a *radical* empiricism—is the fact that it respects the uniqueness of the particular, and the need for a generative wisdom that takes this uniqueness into account in anticipating a productive future. Rather than advancing universal principles and assuming a taxonomy of natural kinds grounded in some notion of strict identity, Confucianism proceeds from always-provisional generalizations made from those *particular* historical instances of successful living, the specific events recounted in the narrative of Confucius himself being a case in point.

"Family" as the Governing Metaphor

The timelessness and broad appeal of the teachings of Confucius begins from the insight that the life of almost every human being, regardless of where or when, is played out within the context of his or her own particular family, for better or for worse. For Confucius and for generations of Chinese that have followed after him, the basic unit of humanity is *this* particular person in *this* particular family rather than either the solitary, discrete individual or the equally abstract and generic notion of family. In fact, in reading Confucius, there is no reference to some core human *being* as the site of who we *really* are and that remains once the particular layers of family and community relations are peeled away. That is, there is no "self," no "soul," no discrete "individual" behind our complex and dynamic habits of conduct. Each of us is irreducibly social as the sum of the roles we *live*—not *play*—in our relationships and transactions with others. The goal of living, then, is to achieve harmony and enjoyment for oneself and for others through behaving in an optimally appropriate way in those roles and relationships that make us uniquely who we are. The analogy with music here is irresistible. Harmony requires that each component maintain its own integrity and be itself while simultaneously joining in and integrating with the other participants to form an organic unity distinct from, and more than, the sum of its parts. The unity of each of us emerges as we pursue this inclusive harmony within the orchestra of our roles and relations.

Confucianism is grounded in the everyday lives of the people, and has as its source of animation the natural deference that pervades family living. For Confucianism, the meaning and value of family relations is not just the primary ground of social order; family relations have cosmological and religious implications as well. Family bonds properly observed are the point of departure for understanding that we each have moral responsibility for an expanding web of relations that reach far beyond our own localized selves.[17]

The profound influence of family on personal development begins from the utter dependency of the infant upon the family relations into which it is born. If infancy teaches us anything, and it teaches us much, its first lesson should be the inescapably interdependent nature of the human experience. Indeed, when Confucius's rather unremarkable student, Zaiwo, resists the burden and inconvenience of the traditional three-year mourning period for his parents, Confucius chides him by observing that parents quite literally give to infants three years of themselves, nourishing them and ensuring the continuing viability of their offspring as persons.[18]

The family is conceived as the center of all order, social and cosmic, and as we have seen in the *Great Learning*, all meaning ripples out in concentric circles from personal cultivation within family, and then returns again to nourish this primary source. In fact, if we ask after the meaning of personal "roles" (*lun* 倫) or perhaps a more primarily gerundive expression of them—"the living of one's roles and relations"—as this process is understood in the classical Chinese language, this character *lun* is one of a cluster of immediately cognate terms that offer various ways of characterizing radial order. We might begin from the notion of "a wheel, or taking turns" (*lun* 輪). And the notion of "bonding" in our roles is reinforced by cognates such as "selecting out" (*lun* 抡) and "twisting a cord, the woof" (*lun* 綸). This family of terms shares in the association of developing and strengthening a functional pattern of relations and of achieving a desired order. But the dynamic, articulate, and discursive aspects of living our roles are perhaps best captured in cognates such as "conversing, conversation" (*lun* 論), "rippling, ripples" (*lun* 淪), and the root character, "turning over in one's mind, thoughts, ordering, achieving coherence" (*lun* 侖). Indeed, this root character *lun* 侖 dates back to the oracle bones, and is constructed from an "opened mouth" and "an orderly bundle of bamboo written strips," *[iii]* suggesting a coherent exposition that elicits from and brings coherence to a particular written document.[19]

[iii]

When we bring these various associations of this family of characters together, the insight gleaned is that the perceived source of growing proper "relations" is fundamentally discursive: an aggregating "relating to" and "giving an account of oneself" within the compass of one's roles that define family, and by extension, community. Simply put, a thriving, family-based community derives from continuing familial patterns of effective communicating. Said another way, "speaking" family roles in the broadest sense of living them is the ultimate source of coherence and order within the human experience. Family roles as a strategy for getting the most out of relations are thus an inspiration for order more broadly construed—social, political, and cosmic order. We might say that Confucianism is nothing more than a sustained attempt "to family" the lived human experience. For Confucianism, it is through discursive living in a communicating family and community that we are able to enchant the ordinary, to ritualize the routine, to invigorate the familiar, to inspire the customary habits of life, and ultimately, to commune spiritually in the common and the everyday.

The Discursive Nature of Family Relations

When all is said and done, what is a family "relationship"? To begin with, we are not separate "I" entities that then come into "we" relationships. As relationally constituted persons, "we" is the starting point, and we grow our lives significantly only through the extension and amplification of those relations that we already share as mother and wife and neighbor. For the relationally constituted conception of person, a relationship is comprised of various levels and modalities of discourse sustained over time. We shape each other linguistically through a sustained discourse, and also through other discursive media such as body, touch, and gesture. Certainly *li*—an achieved propriety in one's roles and relations—is linguistic, but it is not just speaking to each other. It is also the language of body and gesture, of music and food, of deference and attentive respect in the roles and relationships that we live. For Confucius, the human being is a social achievement, an adaptive success made possible through the applications of social imagination and intelligence. Society is not derivative of individual properties, nor is the individual the product of social forces. Rather, it is from the ecological and organic "doings and undergoings" of always-unique persons in their communities that both society and individual emerge together.[20] Given the reality of change, any success is

III · *The Confucian Project: Attaining Relational Virtuosity*   99

always provisional, leaving us as incomplete creatures with the always new challenge of contingent circumstances. And yet this success is at the same time progressive, programmatic, and consummatory.

The community is nothing more or less than a sustained "conversation" among a population of people, and exemplary persons within community are those who are virtuosic in effective speech and action, and who are both relationally and contextually catalytic in bringing to fruition the thriving community. The efficacy of what exemplary persons say and do not only influences the immediate community, but can have a profound and lasting effect on the world broadly.

In this early and persistent Chinese cosmology, human becomings and the discoursing that constitutes them are the inside and the outside of the same event, where meaning is made through productive associations. Human becomings are their meaningful relations. Hence the flourishing family is the outcome of an increasingly "familiar" discourse, and the thriving community is the outcome of an increasingly robust "communicating" and "communion" among its members. Importantly, in this Confucian tradition, all relationships—even the cosmological relationships between the heavens and the earth—are construed in discursive familial terms.

In reflecting on the power and substance of language, Hans-Georg Gadamer observes:

> The "use" of words is not a "using" at all. Rather language is a medium, an element: language is the element in which we live, as fishes live in water.... In the exchange of words, the thing meant becomes more and more present. A language is truly a "natural language" when it binds us together in this way.[21]

The Chinese processual cosmology would perhaps take this Gadamerian insight into language one step further and claim that, in its broadest sense, "language," more than a medium, is constitutive of who we are as irreducibly relational people. The *Great Commentary* of the *Book of Changes* turns explicitly to the way in which communication functions to form persons discursively. The identity of a person, while certainly localized by "body" and "home," is in fact defined as a concentrated focus of patterns of deference established and fostered through effective discourses that entail body and gesture, but that also include the written and spoken language, music, ritualized roles and relationships, food, and so on. Throughout classical Confucianism, the contention is that the proper and effective use of language (*zhengming* 正名) is the substance of relationships, and is basic to the flourishing community in all of its overlapping dimensions. Using language properly is how we achieve what is most *appropriate* in our associations, and hence what is most *meaningful*. Indeed, both of these qualities of conduct—appropriateness and meaningfulness—are captured in the term *yi* 義, a central terminology in this Confucian vision of the consummate life. This power of language as the primary source for effecting social order is not lost on Confucius:

> "Were the Lord of Wey to turn the administration of his state over to you, what would be your first priority?" asked Zilu.
>
> "Without question it would be to insure that names are used properly (*zhengming*)," replied the Master.
> "Would you be as impractical as that?" responded Zilu. "What is it for names to be used properly anyway?"
>
> "How can you be so dense!" replied Confucius. "Exemplary persons defer on matters they do not understand. When names are not used properly, language will not be used effectively; when language is not used effectively, matters will not be taken care of; when matters are not taken care of, the achievement of a ritual propriety in roles and relations and the playing of music will not flourish; when the achievement of ritual propriety and the playing of music do not flourish, the application of laws and punishments will not be on the mark; when the application of laws and punishments is not on the mark, the people will not know what to do with themselves. Thus, when exemplary persons put a name to something, it can certainly be spoken, and when spoken it can certainly be acted upon. There is nothing careless in the attitude of exemplary persons toward what is said."[22]

This notion of *zhengming* has conventionally been translated as "the rectification of names," suggesting that in our conduct we need to satisfy the stipulated definition of names and ranks. And this requisite is certainly part of the story. For Confucius, there is an immediate association between using political titles of office strictly, and the integrity of the state. In the *Zuozhuan* commentary on the *Spring and Autumn Annals* there is an account of a person who in being rewarded for saving a prominent man's life declines the offer of a city and asks instead to be allowed to use the dress and accoutrements of a prince. On hearing of this, Confucius denounces this charade bitterly in language reminiscent of the *Analects* passage cited above:

> What a pity! It would have been better to give him many cities. It is insignias of office and titles alone that cannot be conceded to pretenders— they must be managed by the ruler. Proper titles give rise to confidence, and confidence is what protects the insignias of office. It is insignias in which the meaning of ritual propriety is invested, and it is ritual propriety that carries appropriate conduct (*yi*) into practice; appropriate conduct is what gives rise to benefit, and it is benefit that brings equanimity to the people. Such things are what structure government, and if you concede them to pretenders, you concede the government along with them. If the government is lost, the country will follow, and there can be no stopping it.[23]

A major theme that runs through the *Analects* is Confucius's insistence that unrelenting attention must be given to retaining a strict correspondence between formal ritual practices and the ranks of office, with the risk of political collapse being the consequence of doing otherwise.[24] More specifically, in his home state of Lu, Confucius was repeatedly chagrined at the powerful Ji family's usurpation of practices and privileges appropriate to the royal house.[25]

Certainly, living language is informed by a history of usage that allows for its content to be stipulated, and in this sense, is retrospective in its meaning. But the need to *zhengming* does not end here. It is also prospective. That is, it is a living language and has to be used in a way that is sensitive to the specifics of the always changing context and in a way that respects the uniqueness of the persons involved in the conversation. It is often remarked upon that on six different occasions in the *Analects*, Confucius is reported to have been asked by his protégés about the meaning of "consummate conduct" (*ren*), and on each of these occasions he gives each of these different students a different answer. This is because an impoverished, reticent, respectful, and conscientious Yan Hui would need a different understanding of what it means to become consummate in his conduct than a wealthy, self-possessed, assertive, and sometimes self-serving Zigong. We might reflect on the fact that language has syntactical and morphological implications as well as semantic force, and as such, requires a sensitivity to "positioning and place" (*wei* 位) as being integral to its meaning. It is not just what one says that conveys meaning, but where, when, and to whom one is speaking.[26]

Indeed, the efficacy of what the exemplary person has to say not only influences the immediate community, but also has a profound and lasting effect on the world broadly. The exemplary person as the source of effective speech and action has to be understood as catalytic within a configuration of circumstances in precipitating a certain course of events:

> If what the exemplary persons say even while remaining at home is felicitous, those in distant quarters will respond to it; how much more so those near at hand. If what is said is not felicitous, those in distant quarters will oppose it; how much more so those near at hand. What is said comes from one's person but has an effect on the people; actions arise near at hand but are seen from a distance. Words and actions are the hinge and trigger of exemplary persons. And the operations of hinge and trigger control honor and disgrace. Since it is with words and actions that exemplary persons move the heavens and the earth, how could they be but circumspect with respect to them?[27]

The quality of discourse is measured by its degree of appropriateness (*yi*), and this feeling of appropriateness is whence a sense of genuine commitment and of belonging within meaningful relations emerges. Indeed, it is the quality of genuineness within the discourse that is the ground of effective communication, and that distinguishes virtuosic orchestration from manipulation, ethical exhortation from propaganda, liberating intimacy from an invasion of privacy, and inspiration from sensationalism.

Achieving Personal Identity through Embodying (*ti* 體) Propriety (*li* 禮) in One's Roles and Relations

In attempting to explore the Confucian focal notion of personal identity, we might begin from the challenge that William James directs at the familiar "substance" understanding of the unity of "essence" and "attribute" in the notion of our foundational individuality. James uses the analogy of "climate" to illustrate the redundancy that a superordinate substance such as "soul" or "self" or "mind" introduces into an analysis of personal identity:

> The low thermometer to-day, for instance, is supposed to come from something called the "climate." Climate is really only the name for a certain group of days, but it is treated as if it lay *behind* the day, and in general we place the name, as if it were a being, behind the facts it is the name of. But the phenomenal properties of things ... do not inhere in anything. They adhere, or cohere, rather, with each other, and the notion of a substance inaccessible to us, which we think accounts for such cohesion by supporting it, as cement might support pieces of a mosaic, must be abandoned. The fact of the bare cohesion itself is all the notion of the substance signifies. Behind that fact is nothing.[28]

The Confucian alternative to locating personal identity in some superordinate soul or self or mind is to find this same coherence in the achieved coordination and integration of one's conduct expressed through one's embodied roles and relations. In the *Zhongyong*—a canonical text included along with the *Great Learning*, the *Analects* and the *Mencius* as the fourth and most inspirational of the *Four Books*—we are told explicitly that family feeling is the ultimate source of the civility and propriety that is fostered within our ritualized roles and institutions:

> Consummate conduct (*ren* 仁) means comporting oneself as a person (*ren* 人), wherein devotion to one's kin is most important. Appropriateness (*yi* 義) means doing what is fitting (*yi* 宜), wherein esteeming those of superior conduct is most important.[29] The degree of devotion due different kin and the degree of esteem accorded those who vary in excellence of conduct is what gives rise to the achievement of propriety in our roles and relations (*li* 禮).[30]

Qian Mu 錢穆 insists that these family-based ritualized roles and relationships (*li*) are a deep cultural identity that must be distinguished fundamentally from the highly variable local customs (*fengsu* 風俗) that separate region from region. For Qian Mu, it is shared *li* rather than different customs that constitute the resilient and enduring fabric of Chinese culture:

You might say that the *jia* [家], or "family," is the place in Chinese culture where *li* [禮] is transmitted. But it is important to distinguish between *jiating* [家庭], "the family living group," and *jiazu* [家族], the "family descent group." It is through the *jiazu* that the standards of social relationships extend beyond the family to relatives. The descent group, which includes the relatives on both sides of the family, can only exist if the standards of *li* are applied. So, when the *li* are extended, a family descent group is made, and when they are further extended, a "people's descent group," or *minzu* [民族] is made. The Chinese are a *minzu* because the *li* set the standards in social relations for all of the people.[31]

Coordinated family relations (*lun* 倫) then are quite literally the fabric (*lun* 綸) of the Chinese as a particular "people."

Tang Junyi like Qian Mu affirms the centrality of family feeling as the distinguishing Confucianism value. The centrality of family is for Tang one of the most profound differences separating Western and Chinese values. He establishes a contrast with the Western philosophical narrative in which "family" as an institution has not been a significant inspiration for order within the broad sweep of the evolution of Western philosophy and culture.[32] Indeed, we are unable to find any family-centered philosophical notion that is comparable to and that has had the vital importance that "family reverence" (*xiao* 孝) holds for Confucian philosophy. The key characters cognate with the term "family reverence" (*xiao*) are revealing of its invested cultural value. This "intergenerational reverence" (*xiao* 孝) that binds families together through the "respect and emulation" (*xiao* 效) of family models and cultural exemplars is one of two elements that constitutes the Chinese graph for "teachings" (*jiao* 教) broadly.

Using Qian Mu's language, just as the "family living group" (*jiating* 家庭), the "family descent group" (*jiazu* 家族), and the "people's descent group" (*minzu* 民族) are radial extensions outward from the conduct of particular family members, it is the coherence in the conduct within these embodied roles and relations that constitutes the identity of the particular members themselves. We might use a traditional expression that continues in the modern Chinese language as a heuristic for explicating the fundamental importance of family as ground for the achieved identity of Confucian persons. In the English language we might say "*everybody* (or *everyone*), please stand up," using the "body" and a presumed discreteness ("one") as indices for "person," thereby reinforcing linguistically an assumption that the "indivisible" individual is the lowest unit in our social organization. By extension we refer to "anybody," "nobody," and "somebody" (or "anyone," "no one," and "someone").

In vernacular Chinese, however, we would say "*dajia qing zhanqilai*" 大家請站起來—literally, "*big family*, please stand up," suggesting that family relations are perceived as constitutive of our persons, and that indeed it is life together within our specific familial roles rather than any single individual that is the lowest social unit. Implicit in this usually unconscious but rather stark contrast between the expressions "everyone" and "big family" (*dajia* 大家) is a fundamental, default distinction between individuated, self-sufficient, and thus discrete human *beings*, and situated, relational human *becomings* who grow and realize themselves as distinctive persons through a sustained commitment to their always-collaborative, transactional roles within the nexus of family and community.

Applying this Confucian perspective to an understanding of my own person, I might reason that I am certainly incarnate and live my life as an embodied individual, and that my somaticity is integral to my "big family" identity. At the same time I must allow that I am D. C. Lau's student, and Bonnie's husband, and Jason and Austin's father, and Sor-hoon's old teacher, and Tze-wan and Chan-fai's friend and colleague, and David and Henry's long-time collaborator, and so on—and that these roles and relationships as we have grown them together over a lifetime weigh heavily in any adequate understanding of personal identity. After all, these wonderfully satisfying roles and intimate relations are complex and enduring, and are truly the inspiration that animates my always-embodied conduct. In considering personal identity from a Confucian perspective, we must appreciate fully the way in which both our somaticity and our complex manifold of relations with others enable us to achieve and sustain our coherence as a person, a coherence that is best understood as a dynamic focus of identity rather than as something separate and discrete. We might recall the focal and functioning understanding of the psychophysical and spiritual heartmind (*xin* 心) as an apposite analogy for the Confucian notion of person. At the same time, just as "what is the heartmind in itself?" is a meaningless question, so we must resist the familiar, uncritical assumption that being embodied and being "enroled" necessarily commits us to the notion of superordinate, individual "selves."

The character for "body" (*ti* 體) that has "bones" (*gu* 骨) as its classifier emerges relatively late in antiquity.[33] Although by the time of the silk manuscripts dating from 168 BCE that were recovered at Mawangdui *ti* does occur in this present form, it appears earlier on the Zhou dynasty bronzes with a "lived body" (*shen* 身) signifier as *[iv]*, and then on the bamboo strip manuscripts with a "flesh" (*rou* 肉) signifier as *[v]*.[34] We can use these three alternative classifiers that constitute the varient forms of this character *ti—gu* 骨, *shen* 身, and *rou* 肉—as a heuristic for parsing *ti*'s range of meaning. We must allow that *ti* with the "bones" (*gu* 骨) classifier references the "discursive body" as a process of "structuring," "configuring," "embodying," and thus "knowing" the world not only cognitively and affectively, but also viscerally. Each of us collaborates with the world to discriminate, conceptualize, and theorize the human experience, embodying and giving form to our culture, our language, our habitat. Above I cited Hilary Putnam who in *Realism with a Human Face* insists that our "language" and our "minds," together with the values that attend them, penetrate so deeply into human experience that it would be a nonsense to try to separate out some reality that stands independent of them.[35] The more holisitic Confucian philosophy would take Putnam's claim further in arguing that it is not just language, mind, or indeed, a human face, that penetrates our reality, but our persons in their entirety.

[iv]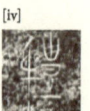
[v]

Ti with the "lived body" (*shen*) classifier highlights another dimension of embodying experience by referencing the vital, existentially aware lived-body in its dynamic social relations with others. Experience always has a subjective dimension, an inside as well as an outside. And *ti* with the "flesh" (*rou*) classifier references the carnal body—the body as flesh and bone. At the most primordial level, the body via these three mutually entailing modalities serves as the bond that conjoins our subjectivity with our environments and that mediates the processes of thinking and feeling with our patterns of conduct.

Zhang Yanhua describes the active and intentional nature of the term *shenti* 身體 in precisely these terms:

> *Shenti* is both physical and extraphysical, capable of feeling, perceiving, creating, and reasoning or embodying changes and transformation on the social world as well as in the natural world. It is the world: at the same time, emotive, moral, aesthetic, and visceral.... In other words, the domains of body, mind, and emotion are mutually penetrating and activating.... Its practical logic involves a language of "bodies" in dynamic process and constant transformation and a language of relations.[36]

The idea that the entire world is brought into focus by and implicated in each of our embodied persons is captured in the expression "valuing one's person" (*guishen* 貴身) that appears as a strong theme in the *Daodejing*. That is, attending to one's own relationally constituted person is by extension treasuring the world:

> Thus those who value the care of their own persons more than the care of the world can be entrusted with the world. And those who begrudge their persons as though they were the world can be put in charge of the world.[37]

In the Confucian tradition, the body is an inheritance we receive from our families, and as a current in a genealogical stream that reaches back to our most remote ancestors, brings with it a sense of continuity and belonging, and the religious significance that such feelings bring with them. To respect one's own body is to show reverence for one's ancestors and one's relationship to them, while disregard for one's body is to bring shame upon one's lineage. As it states in the opening chapter of the *Classic of Family Reverence* (*Xiaojing* 孝經):

> Your physical person with its hair and skin is received from your parents. Vigilance in not allowing anything to do injury to your person is where family reverence begins ...[38]

This responsibility to preserve one's body intact is a major theme throughout the Confucian canons. In the *Book of Rites*, it says:

> Among those things born of the heavens and nurtured by the earth, nothing is grander than the human being. For the parents to give birth to your whole person, and for one to return oneself to them whole is what can be called family reverence. To avoid desecrating your body or bringing disgrace to your person is what can be called keeping your person whole.[39]

Confucius's protégé, Master Zeng, is a name often associated with family reverence (*xiao* 孝) in the canonical literature, and in the *Analects* it is recorded that on his deathbed he said the following:

> Master Zeng was ill, and summoned his students to him, saying, "Look at my feet! Look at my hands! The *Book of Odes* says:
>> Fearful! Trembling!
>> As if peering over a deep abyss,
>> As if walking across thin ice.[40]
>
> It is only from this moment hence that I can be sure I have avoided desecration of my body, my young friends."[41]

This relationship between the responsibility one has for keeping one's body intact and the appropriate attention to family reverence (*xiao*) works in the opposite direction as well. Traditionally, in the application of penal law (*xing* 刑) as is captured with the knife element (*dao* 刀) in the character itself, amputory and branding punishments were often meted out for serious crimes. Such punishments are a deliberate strategy for not only alerting the community to the presence of a ne'er-do-well in its midst, but also as a way of assuring that such felons wear their shame before their ancestors in the world beyond.

Nathan Sivin has explored the correlations between body, cosmos, and state in the pre-Qin and early Han dynasties, arguing that "the ideas of Nature, state, and the body were so interdependent that they are best considered a single complex."[42] Perhaps the writings traditionally ascribed to the Han dynasty Confucian, Dong Zhongshu 董仲舒, are the *locus classicus* for describing the many correspondences between the human person and the cosmos—between microcosm and macrocosm.[43] Therein Dong describes not only associations between the changing seasons of the year and the rise and fall of the human passions, but also explores the many ostensive correlations between the anatomy and physiology of the human body and the structure of the material cosmos.[44] Further, early in the tradition, an elaborate vocabulary evolved that associates specific family relations with different parts of the body: the "living person" (*shengshen* 生身) is a metaphor used to refer to one's parents, "bones and flesh" (*gurou* 骨肉) for one's children, "hands and feet" (*shouzu* 手足) for one's brothers, "stomach and heartmind" (*fuxin* 腹心) for one's friends, and "of the same womb" (*tongbao* 同胞) for one's countrymen.[45]

In the *Book of Rites* (*Liji*) and several other canonical texts, there is a further correlation pursued in associating the proper structure of the cosmos (*li* 理) as a whole with propriety in human roles and relations (*li* 禮), suggesting that human morality has its counterpart in the harmonious workings of the cosmos. What is significant in this reflection on our embodied persons is that physically, socially, and religiously, our bodies are a specific matrix of nested relations and functions, and are invariably a collaboration between our persons and our many environments. "Nobody" and no "body"—not the vital, the social, or the carnal bodies—do anything by themselves.

In this Confucian tradition, we might correlate "body" (*ti* 體) and its cognate character "achieved propriety in one's roles and relations" (*li* 禮) by arguing that they express two ways of looking at the same phenomenon: That is, they reference "a living body" and "embodied living" respectively. If we use the vocabulary of contemporary medical anthropology to capture the nonanalytical relationship between living and embodying, we might cite Zhang Yanhua who concludes that "*jingshen* 精神 is not perceived in opposition to *shenti* 身體 but constitutive of it"—that is, our animated life activities are not distinct from our embodiment, but are integral to and an expression of it.[46]

Ti and *li* are further correlated in the *Book of Rites* as a "corpus" or a "body" of ritual proprieties:

> Now the great corpus of ritual proprieties (*li zhi dati* 禮之大體) is embodied (*ti*) in the heavens and the earth, emulates the four seasons, takes *yin* and *yang* as its standard, comports with human feeling, and is thus called "ritual proprieties" (*li*). As for those who would denigrate these proprieties, they have no idea where such things come from.[47]

Peter Boodberg in searching for the common ground shared by these two cognate terms, *ti* 體 and *li* 禮, allows that "form, that is, organic form ... appears to be the link between the two words, as evidenced by the ancient Chinese scholiasts who repeatedly used *t'i* [*ti*] to define *li* in their glosses."[48] Deborah Sommer goes back to the usages of *ti* in the *Book of Odes* to quite literally dig out its earliest connotations. *Ti* is associated in the early literature with vegetable propagation that is "accomplished not with seeds but by dividing the roots, stems, tubers or other fleshy parts of plants into segments that are then replanted to develop into 'new plants.'"⁴⁹ Sommer observes that "for people of an agriculturally based society, the notion that plants can be multiplied through vegetative division would have been a commonplace."⁵⁰ There is both continuity and origination in the process of sprouting tubers being dissected and grown again and of the unusable roots of defoliated herbs generating a new harvest of leaves and stems. From these early references, Sommer offers an abstracted understanding of the *ti* body as

> ... a polysemous corpus of indeterminate extent that can be partitioned into subtler units, each of which is often analogous to the whole and shares a fundamental consubstantiality and common identity with that whole.... When a *ti* body is fragmented into parts (literally or conceptually), each part retains, in certain aspects, a kind of wholeness or becomes a simulacra of the larger entity of which it is a constituent.⁵¹

Although in Sommer's survey of this early literature she concludes that "*ti* bodies often act more like plants than like humans,"⁵² I would hesitate in making such a sharp distinction between these two categories. Indeed I would want to press her analysis a step further as providing real insight into the early Chinese way of thinking specifically about human genealogical continuity, and in so doing, provide an opportunity to extrapolate from horticulture to human culture. In chapter two above we rehearsed Tang Junyi's proposition, "the inseparability of the one and the many, of uniqueness and multivalence, of continuity and multiplicity, of integrity and integration" (*yiduo bufen guan* 一多不分觀). If we take human procreativity as an illustration of this proposition, such a characterization is another way of affirming *paisheng* 派生, the birthing of a distinctive and unique person from those who are genealogically prior. At the same time, within the ongoing, ceaseless process of shaping and being shaped called *huasheng* 化生, the "many" prior progenitors persist and live on in this process of transforming into someone else. That is, while persons emerge to become specifically who they are as individuals, the parents and grandparents of such individuals continue to live on in them, just as they too will live on in their future progeny. The focus-field language that we have proposed as a way of thinking about the relationship between particulars and the totality seems immediately relevant to the kind of holography Sommer alludes to when she says that "each new plant in some sense is still the parent plant, and there exists a material continuity of identity from one life form to the next.... Mother and daughter plants are at once autonomous and yet consubstantial."[53]

We might take an elaboration of this *ti* genealogy a step further. This process of division, diffusion, and derivation can provide additional illumination if we reflect upon the complex transmission of always-embodied knowledge from generation to succeeding generation. The body is the site of a conveyance of the cultural corpus of knowledge—linguistic facility and proficiency, religious rituals and mythologies, the aesthetics of cooking, song, and dance, the modeling of mores and values, instruction and apprenticeship in cognitive technologies, and so on—as a continuing, intergenerational process through which a living civilization itself is perpetuated.[54]

The communal *shen* body is diffused in the dynamic family and communal roles and relations that constitutes it, and just as the *ti* body does not carry with it a superordinate notion of "self" or "soul"—some ghost in the machine—likewise, achieved propriety in living one's roles and relations (*li*) that complements this body in constituting one's person is also primordial. That is, the quality of one's conduct is not mediated by or reduplicated in some notion of a discrete "agent" or "character" that would isolate and locate persons outside of the concrete pattern of their social and natural relations. Instead, the identity of persons lies in the achieved amalgamation, the integration, and the sustained coherence of their continuing habits of conduct within the embodied roles that constitute them.

These roles have their beginnings in "family reverence" (*xiao*), and are then extended in a process that quite literally brings the community home through surrogate family relations. As we perform our various roles, so we are in turn formed as persons. Tang Junyi describes the function of *li* in the following terms:

> When the "Ritualizing Experience" (*liyun* 禮運) chapter of the *Book of Rites* discusses the ideal of the era of Great Harmony (*datong* 大同), what is intended is simply that everyone should get what they deserve. Herein the concepts of propriety (*li*) and appropriateness (*yi*) are subsumed under the concept of person. As such, persons in the course of realizing this purpose must participate fully and appropriately in their symbiotic ritualized roles and relations before each person can get what they should get out of these relationships.[55]

Tang is here rehearsing a proposition that is also found in the *Analects* where it insists that any genuine harmony must be mediated through a robust sense of propriety in the roles and relations that situate us within family and community (*Analects* 1.12). Confucian "harmony" is much more than merely an absence of discord that could be maintained by indiscriminately enforcing social order. The ultimate achievement of an orchestrated harmony grounded in family feeling is to bring into focus and resolution the persons who make up a community in which everyone has developed a sense of shame and responsibility (*Analects* 2.3).

We find the Latin *proprius*—literally, "making something one's own"—as the root in words such as "proper," "appropriate," "propriety," and "property." This root provides us with a series of cognate expressions that are felicitous in translating those key Confucian philosophical terms defining of personal identity because such translations locate one as an active participant committed to personalizing one's various life forms—physical and social—and thus making them one's own. This always-reflexive personalization of one's roles—I am this son to this mother—has immediate consequence in the search for effective renderings of this philosophical vocabulary. For example, if we acknowledge the persistence of a relational rather than essential understanding of the Confucian person, *yi* 義 cannot be "righteousness"—putatively an individual's compliance with some external divine directive. Rather, *yi* must be an inclusive "conducting oneself appropriately" in those relations within one's particular family and community. That is, *yi* is doing what is most fitting within the specific circumstances, as opposed to simply following some external principle or rule in doing what is deemed correct. Similarly, *zheng* 正 cannot be simply "correct" or "rectified" conduct or language—again, an appeal to some external standard. Rather *zheng* must be an inclusive "conducting oneself properly" or "using language properly" as negotiated by a particular person within a particular social context. Relatedly, *zheng* 政 is not simply "government" but a reflexive "governing properly" that necessarily begins at home in the life of the family and then extends radially outward in the community and polity.[56] And *li* ("ritual propriety") is not just "performing formal observances flawlessly," but is the quality of propriety achieved by *personally and consistently* doing what is most appropriate in the roles and relations that define one. As is recounted in the *Analects*:

The expression "sacrifice as though present" is taken to mean "sacrifice to the spirits as though the spirits are present." But the Master said, "If I myself do not participate in the sacrifice, it is as though I have not sacrificed at all."[57]

On the informal and uniquely personal side, full participation in a ritually constituted community requires the appropriation and reauthorization of the prevailing institutions and values that are defining of a culture. What makes the mechanism of achieving ritual propriety in one's roles and relations profoundly different from merely comporting with law or rule is the sense of shame one develops in the ongoing process of making the tradition one's own. As we will see in the next chapter, shame looms large as a key element in ethical motivation because shame is an earned awareness that we live together interdependently in family and community, and that each of us is responsible in our conduct for the well-being of the world that we share.

A careful reading of the classical Confucian literature uncovers a way of life carefully choreographed down to appropriate facial expressions and physical gestures, a world in which a life is an embodied performance requiring concentrated and unrelenting attention to detail. Importantly, this *li*-constituted performance begins from the insight that personal refinement is only possible through the discipline provided by formalized roles and behaviors. But form alone without sustained personalization is coercive and dehumanizing law. On the other extreme, creative personal expression in the absence of form is randomness at best, and license at worst. It is only with the appropriate combination of and balance between formality and functional personalization that family and community can become elegant, refined, and self-regulating.

Zhang Yanhua appeals to "an aesthetics of relationships" in her attempt to take full cognizance of the powerful emotional dimension of family flourishing that is instrumental in fostering an immediate sense of both intra- and inter-generational continuity and belonging:

> The cultural aesthetics of *renhe* 人和 (harmonious interpersonal relationships) finds its full expression in Chinese family ethics that guide the way the family members care for and interact with each other according to their places within the family. The harmonious family also includes a vertical dimension. This concern for harmonious family relationships extends to the deceased

members of the family, that is, the spiritual world.... This is also related to the Chinese sensibility of *tong* 通 (connection and flowing).... For the Chinese, harmony presupposes a healthy process of connecting and extending.[58]

In addition to the vertical concern for ancestors that reinforces the continuity of family identity, there is an important horizontal dimension of interdependent family relations that expands outward through the vital role of friendship in the Confucian project. As Zhang Yanhua reports:

> It is also important that the cultural aesthetics of *renhe* (harmonious interpersonal relations) extend beyond one's immediate circle of family members and relatives through extensive networks of "human emotions" (*renqing* 人情) created and maintained diligently by all forms of social exchanges, of gifts, labor, services, respect, and so on.[59]

The Liberating Role of Friendship

Zhang Yanhua's observation about cultural aesthetics leads us to a reflection on the vital importance of the notion of friendship in Confucian role ethics. Within the web of Confucian relations, intimate friendships take on a transformative force that can only be adequately explained by understanding them as an extension and amplification of the family itself. As a dimension of a Confucian family-centered ethic, friendship serves as a definite, sometimes compensatory source of meaning and value. While immediate family relations are usually a matter of birth and blood, developed friendships are contingent, and entail diversity and deliberate choice. We might describe the role of friendship as a doorway through which erstwhile outsiders enter to join and add a remarkable depth to the ranks of family relations.

The vital importance of friendship for Confucianism lies in its function as an open conduit that leads from the security and stability of one's own family out into the more uncertain and sometimes taxing social, political, and cultural realm. When Zilu asks after the makings of a scholar-official, Confucius says plainly:

> Persons who are critical and demanding, yet amicable can be called scholar-officials. Persons need to be critical and demanding with their friends, and amicable and acquiescent with their older and younger brothers.[60]

Confucius thus anticipates that friendships can in some ways be more challenging than intimate family relations. One can fairly take for granted the love and protection of one's immediate family, while successful life in the public sphere requires a higher degree of discrimination and a more critical sense of engagement. But then again the dividends to be reaped from enduring friendships over a lifetime are truly substantial, introducing into the project of personal growth resources that provide a deeper degree of difference. In this Confucian tradition, to "make" friends is quite literally to participate in the "making" of each other to the extent that it is the friendship itself that becomes what is most concrete, while the "individuals" who participate in the growth of the relationship become increasingly an abstraction from it.

In choosing one's friends, Confucius is emphatic: "Exemplary persons ... do not have as a friend anyone who is not as good as they are."[61] This declaration is a clear acknowledgment of his understanding that personal growth and diminution are a function of associated living. It prompts us to ask again: For Confucius, where does the meaning in a "meaningful" friendship come from? In a Platonic-come-Christian world wherein meaning has a transcendent reference, friendship is instrumentalized as a commitment to a common end. The conclusion of the reflection on friendship in the *Phaedrus* is that friends hold all things in common. And when what they hold in common is an *eros* directed toward the transcendent Good, they are *true* friends. Similarly, for the Christian, *philia* as the love among friends and family members is subordinated to *agape*, the love of a transcendent God channeled through His creatures as their love for one another.

Aristotle, like Plato, takes commonality as the basis for friendship. In both cases, there is a high value invested in self-sufficiency. For Aristotle, there is a lower level of incidental friendship that seeks utility and pleasure. But *true* friends by contrast are "another self" or "a second self" because they mirror one's own virtuous character and the intellectual activity of *nous* that is identical in all people. Indeed, Aristotle appeals to the mirror metaphor to illustrate how the real friend in being similarly virtuous is a source of self-knowledge.[62] He allows that "contemplative friendships" are higher than the practical kind, and that such virtue friendships are rare; they are only available to an elite circle of equally virtuous people.[63] There is a superiority of the theoretical life over the practical, and of the speculative vision over daily moral activities. Thus, for Aristotle, the eternal truth that can be grasped by *nous* must be given priority over friendship, even when it means turning one's back on one's own teacher—in his case, Plato:

> We had perhaps better consider the universal good and discuss thoroughly what is meant by it, although such an inquiry is made an uphill one by the fact that the Forms have been introduced by friends of our own.... [W]hile both are dear, piety requires us to honor truth above our friends.[64]

For Confucius, like his Greek cousins, friendships are in some ways a matter of common cause:

> Master Zeng said, "Exemplary persons attract friends through their refinement, and through these friends promote consummate conduct (*ren*)."[65]

May Sim has identified many resonances between the Confucian and Aristotelian models of friendship, taking careful account of their important similarities.[66] But beyond these commonalities, it must be allowed that there is significant distance between the accounts of friendship we find in Aristotle and Confucius. We must take into account the metaphysical and biological uniformities in Aristotle's foundational individualism, the self-sufficiency of final and unchanging first principles and causes that are the object of contemplation, and the centrality of rationality as the ground in making moral decisions. For Confucius, *contra* Plato and Aristotle, the ultimate source of meaning is not external, but emerges through the nurturing process of the friendship itself. And it is the ways in which friends are qualitatively superior to and different from each other that provides the opportunity for a collaborative advancement. Confucian friendship is a classic illustration of the mantra: "Exemplary persons seek harmony not conformity; petty persons are the opposite."[67] When Zigong was asked who Confucius had as his teacher, his reply is inclusive:

> The moral vision (*dao*) of Kings Wen and Wu has not collapsed utterly— it lives on in the people. Those of superior character have grasped the greater part of it, while those of lesser quality have grasped a bit. Everyone has something of Wen and Wu's way in them. Who then did the Master not learn from? Again, how could there have been a single constant teacher for him?[68]

The message here is that since each person is different, Confucius had something—sometimes more, sometimes less—to learn from everyone. This generous appreciation of both the positive and negative possibilities that most relations with other people provide us for moral development is made abundantly clear:

> The Master said, "In strolling together with just two other persons, I am bound to find a teacher in their company. Identifying their strengths, I follow them, and identifying their weaknesses, I reform myself accordingly."[69]

Personal growth is a function of the quality of the specific productive relations achieved among family and friends. In seeking out and developing meaningful friendships, we have latitude and a degree of freedom that is not characteristic of our relations with blood relatives. Confucius is keenly aware that broadening and expansive friendships, compensating to an important degree for family constraints, can serve as a real opportunity for personal growth. Poorly chosen, however, these erstwhile friendships can also be a source of personal diminution. He observes:

> Having three kinds of friends will be a source of personal improvement; having three other kinds of friends will be a source of personal injury. One stands to be improved by friends who are true, who make good on their word, and who are broadly informed; one stands to be injured by friends who are ingratiating, who feign compliance, and who are glib talkers.[70]

Confucius's point here is that friendship provides a porous border on the institution of family that allows for a more deliberate and purposeful shaping of one's own personal relations, and hence, one's own person. These voluntarily chosen relations are still to be construed as familial, and yet they have a potential to provide a degree of growth and complexity that can often go beyond our more formal family bonds.

Commonality and overlap is covered in the vocabulary of friendship by the term *peng* 朋. In the oracle bone script this character originally identified a denomination of two strings of cowry shell currency as *[vi]* and later came to mean "peer" or "comrade" in the specific sense of being students of the same master. Although the power of the role of "classmate" (*tongxue* 同學) and "student older brother/sister"

[vi]

(*xuexiong/jie* 學兄/姐) continues down to the present day, the emphasis in Confucian friendship is on interdependence and difference rather than on sameness and self-sufficiency. Friendship as an opportunity for creative growth is built into the associations that the more frequently used term for "friend"—*you* 友—evokes. The oracle bone version of this character has "two hands" *[vii]* that are sometimes joined together *[viii]*, suggesting a common bond of friendship.[71] *You* is first cognate with *you* 右, "the right hand," and by extension, with what is to be honored and revered. It is further cognate with *you* 佑 "to assist," and *you* 祐 "a blessing." Combining these several associations, we might observe that a true friend is an object of deference to be honored and esteemed as a blessing that assists in one's personal growth.

A second philological correlation for "friend" (*you* 友) is its cognate and homophonous relationship with *you* 有, "to have, to be around (= wealth)," a term that also appears as a loan character for it. *You* 有 is depicted suggestively on the bronzes specifically as the honored right hand grasping a piece of meat, a scarce, valuable, and sometimes sacred commodity in an agrarian community: **[ix]**.[72] Again, the implication is that a true friend is a matter of proximity—someone who is there for you—and a resource whence to garner increased meaning in one's life.

That Confucius insists upon this restricted and specific use of "friend" (*you*) is suggested in a disagreement on the meaning of "establishing relations with others" (*jiao* 交) that involves two of his closest protégés, Zixia and Zizhang. In the years following the death of the Master, these two disciples matured into patriarchs in their own right and had their own interpretations of what Confucius had said and what he had meant by it:

> The disciples of Zixia asked Zizhang about establishing relations with others. Zizhang queried, "What has Zixia told you?" They replied, "Associate with those who are worthy of your efforts; spurn those who are not."

It would seem from Zixia's definition of "establishing relations with others" that he is retaining the strictness and the discrimination with which Confucius himself approaches friendship. But such a narrow reading does not go unchallenged. Zizhang counters:

> This is different from what I have learned. Exemplary persons exalt those of superior character and are accommodating of everyone, praise those who are truly efficacious, and are sympathetic with those who are less so. If in

comparison with others, I am truly superior in character, who am I not able to accommodate? If I am not superior in the comparison, and people are thus going to spurn me, what basis do I have to spurn others?[73]

In evaluating these two very different interpretations of Confucius's attitude to establishing relationships, it is helpful to recall the profile of these two students that emerges from frequent reference in the *Analects* and elsewhere.

Zizhang with his free-wheeling altruism is repeatedly rebuked by Confucius for paying more attention to appearances than to substance, and for using language without due care.[74] In one telling passage,

> Zizhang asked about the way of the truly efficacious person (*shanren* 善人). The Master replied, "Not following in the footsteps of others, one does not gain entrance to the inner sanctum."[75]

Confucius is here criticizing Zizhang specifically for not deferring sufficiently to moral exemplars—those who would be *true* friends—thereby precluding the possibility of his ever having access to those relations that open the door to real personal worth.

Zixia, on the other hand, is a man of letters, and being credited more than any other of Confucius's protégés for his scholarship, he is remembered by tradition as having played a major role in the transmission of the Confucian classics. Zixia has a central place in the last five chapters of the *Analects* where he underscores the importance of learning. Trying to compensate for his image as a pendent, Zixia insists that virtuosity in one's personal relationships is what learning is all about. Indeed, Confucius allows that he himself has gained a great deal from his conversations with Zixia. With these two profiles in mind, then, we can speculate that while many of us might admire the logic of Zizhang and prefer his seemingly more egalitarian and inclusive sentiments on the proper expression of what it means to be a friend, it is probably Zixia who, in underscoring the vital function of friendship for the possibility of personal growth, is transmitting the more genuine understanding of what Confucius himself expected from friendship.

But if Confucius has learned a great deal from Zixia, he has on his own admission learned much more from his favorite disciple, Yan Hui. Throughout the *Analects*, Confucius repeatedly singles out Yan Hui for high praise, according this one exceptional student alone the description of being consummate in his conduct (*ren*)[76] and of being truly fond of learning (*haoxue*).[77] Indeed, he places Yan Hui far above himself and everyone else in his capacity for learning:

> The Master remarked to Zigong, "Comparing yourself with Yan Hui, who is the better person?" Zigong replied, "How dare I have such expectations. With Yan Hui, learning one thing he will know ten; with me, learning one thing I will know two." The Master said, "You are not his match. Neither you nor I are a match for Yan Hui."[78]

Of course, "learning" here has an immediate moral and religious reference to personal growth achieved through assiduous cultivation and a demonstrated relational virtuosity in family and community. Confucius himself, far from being mysterious and aloof with his students, is candid about the limits of the mentorship that he can offer them:

> The Master said, "My young friends, you think that I have something hidden away, but I do not. There is nothing I do that I do not share with you—this is the person I am."[79]

At the same time, Confucius insists that it is one's contribution to the community rather than one's seniority that is deserving of deference. And he encourages an appropriate respect for the as-yet undisclosed potential and possibilities that might well attend the next generation:

> The Master said, "The young should be held in high esteem. After all, how do we know that those yet to come will not surpass our contemporaries? It is only when one reaches forty or fifty years of age and yet has done nothing of note that we should withhold our esteem."[80]

Given Confucius's critical attitude toward his contemporaries and his judicious admiration for the ways in which his students excel, we can surmise that his strict understanding of a mentoring friendship is more a matter of substantial difference than it is of hierarchical superiority. After all, since good teachers learn much from good students, we would have to conclude that on his own premises, Confucius would allow that students too can be a source of meaningful friendship. This would certainly seem to have been the case in his fervent admiration for Yan Hui:

When Yan Hui died, the Master grieved for him with sheer abandon. His followers cautioned, "Sir, you grieve with such abandon." The Master replied, "I grieve with abandon? If I don't grieve with abandon for him, then for whom?"[81]

The Embeddedness and Growth of "Human Becomings"

As we have seen, in this Confucian model of what I have called a "human becoming," one's personal realization is irreducibly "other-entailing" and all relations are inclusively familial. Friends too become family. The flourishing of one's person and the thriving of one's family and community are isomorphic and co-terminus. We might bring this distinction between the "human being" and the "human becoming" into clearer focus by reflecting on Aristotle's understanding of the human being. The extent to which the contrasting understandings of person constitute a fundamental disjunction between Aristotle and Confucius is not lost on the comparative philosopher, May Sim:

> Confucius appeals to no entity that we call the "self" (in several meanings of that term), much less a metaphysical *psychê*.... When Aristotle asks about human well-being, he quickly turns to questions about human *being*. The focus and source of this being is the *psychê*—even more precisely the rational "part" of the *psychê* that marks what is distinctive to humankind. The well-functioning of this part of ourselves is the best thing in us and most to be prized, Aristotle argues. Although it is formally identical in every member of the species and thus what underwrites our talk of shared human nature and common basic virtues (and according to later Aristotelians, the moral equality of persons), an actual *psychê* is always *this-psychê* and hence individual.[82]

In what follows I will contend that the classical Confucian texts, taken on their own terms rather than on Aristotle's, appeal to a relatively straightforward account of our actual life experience rather than to abstract entities, and in so doing, provide a justification for reinstating the intimacy of family feeling as the concrete ground of an always-emergent moral order. I will further argue that there is a difference between Western ethical theories that are directed at enabling people to think and to talk about ethics more cogently, and a Confucian vision of a consummate life that seeks to inspire people to be better persons.

Following Henry Rosemont in referring to this Confucian vision as a *role ethics*, we do not intend to advance it as an alternative moral *theory* so much as a vision of human flourishing, one that integrates the social, political, economic, aesthetic, moral *and* the *religious* dimensions of our lives. In this view, we are not individuals in the discrete sense of an Aristotelian *psyche*, but rather are interrelated persons living a multiplicity of roles that constitute who we are, and that allow us to pursue a unique distinctiveness and virtuosity in our conduct. We are, in other words, the sum of the roles we live in consonance with our fellows.

From the Confucian perspective of the relational human *becoming*, we are inclined to make the same miscalculation in thinking about ethical principles and virtues as we do in thinking about human nature as the ground of "being" human. Principles, virtues, and human nature too are all abstractions from concrete instances of continuing conduct. With human nature, as with principles and virtue, we are inclined to default to a retrospective causal or a teleological explanation rather than provide a more holistic, prospective, contextual, and processive account of what it means to *become* human—a *human becoming*, as it were. In so doing, we come to presuppose that human nature is either a given potential to be actualized or some pre-existing ideal to be attained. It is believed by some scholars that free agency and moral responsibility require the isolation of individuals from their relationships by positing such a definition of what it *is* to be human, a ready-made definition of human *being* or a guiding teleological hand that in fact truncates any robust existential notion of agency or responsibility.[83]

Negative freedom as the absence of constraint is not, in and of itself, productive. As Dewey observes: "No man and no mind was ever emancipated by being left alone."[84] In the Confucian tradition, real freedom is concrete: It is the opportunity to realize oneself fully within the roles and relations that constitute one first in the family, and then by extension within the world more broadly construed. Freedom is maximizing personal growth as it is determined by full participation in and enjoyment of one's family and community relations.

Similarly, equality, rather than being quantitative and entailing some essential shared identity, is an equitable getting and giving. It is having available to one's person everything that is needed to pursue one's own unique trajectory as an increasingly consummate person through the various phases of one's life, and in the process, making full return on this investment by enhancing the worth of the family and community. Such equality allows for the optimizing of resources in the successive stages of beneficiary, benefactor, and again beneficiary in the living of the many roles that make up the process of a normal human life. For always-unique persons, such equality means having all the assets necessary to accomplish what in the fullness of time will allow them to become their own best thoughts.

And the notion of justice—rather than being an appeal to abstract principles to enforce a blind impartiality that requires all particular differences to be set aside and all persons be treated equally—references the complex, creative process of achieving what is most appropriate in the specific, usually inequitable relations and situations that locate us within family and community. The resolutely hierarchical and dynamic pattern of the human experience that begins in family relations is going to have to be included in the equation that expresses a Confucian notion of justice. Such a Confucian understanding of freedom, equality, and justice, without deploying such terms specifically, is nested in the concrete project of achieving consummate conduct (*ren*) by being optimally appropriate (*yi*) in one's proper roles and relations (*li*).

We might rehearse an anecdote from the later Confucian text, the *Xunzi* 荀子, that gives us a starting point for clarifying the enormous difference between the unilateral integrity of *psyche*-invested, discrete "human beings" who aspire to a self-sufficient autonomy, and the multilateral integrity of "human becomings" as they are embedded in and emerge from the "big family." Indeed, integrity for the "human becoming" is not "being resolutely who you already are," but is rather a continuing process of "becoming one together."

It is because Confucius himself introduces and develops the neologism, "consummate person or conduct" (*ren* 仁), as a key philosophical idea that his students ask him repeatedly to clarify what he means by this term. And he in turn provides each of them with an explanation—indeed, as we have seen, an explanation that is tailored to the different needs of different students. One day, recounts the *Xunzi*, the Master is holding court with his protégés, and quizzes each of them to evaluate their current understanding of his new term, *ren*.

The first, a passionate but less-capable student, Zilu, demonstrates some degree of insight in his response. He insists that *ren* means raising the self-esteem of others by making them feel good about themselves—that is, "causing others to love themselves" (*shiren aiji* 使人愛己). Indeed such persons, says Confucius, have achieved a degree of refinement, and might be called scholar-officials (*shi* 士). His more imaginative student, Zigong, in replying to Confucius's question about the meaning of *ren*, reverses the direction and asserts that *ren* is a kind of altruism—"loving others" (*airen* 愛人). Confucius allows that such persons in loving others have indeed attained a higher degree of refinement, and might be called not only scholar-officials but also exemplary in their persons (*shijunzi* 士君子).

Then Confucius's favorite student, Yan Hui steps up to take his turn, stating flatly that *ren* means "self-loving" (*ziai* 自愛). Confucius is delighted with what he takes to be a most concise and penetrating understanding of *ren*, describing such a self-regarding person as being a truly enlightened, exemplary person (*mingjunzi* 明君子).[85]

Of course, among discrete "human beings," it would be hard to see how "self-loving" would lead to consummatory conduct. Indeed, *ren* so defined might be misconstrued as a self-regarding narcissism that would hardly lead to excellence in one's relations. The difference that makes a difference for the "human becoming" lies in an alternative understanding of "self" as an evolving configuration of relationships. Yan Hui's point in this passage is that given the collaterality of the "human becoming," "self-loving" is neither the self-directed egoism assumed when one encourages others to love themselves nor the other-directed altruism of loving other people. Indeed, for the person comprised of intrinsic rather than extrinsic relations in constitutive rather than contingent roles, such a self-regarding love with its embedded sense of "we" is bi-directional; it is at once reflexive and inclusive.

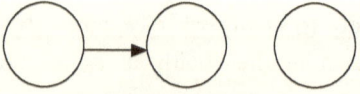
Extrinsically related, discrete human "beings"

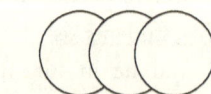
Constitutively related, collateral human "becomings"

That is, "self-loving" would mean to cherish those specific roles and relationships that I am committed to nourishing as the very source and substance of my own personal realization—it is loving me in my relationship with my spouse, my children, my students, my colleagues, and so on.

This use of a reflexive binomial such as "self-loving" (*ziai* 自愛) found in this passage from the *Xunzi* that defines one within one's relationships is quite common in the early Confucian texts. Indeed, Herbert Fingarette suggests that, in translating the Confucian philosophical literature that includes terms such as *zixing* 自省, we do better to use the reflexive prefix form of "self-" as in "self-examining" or the postfix "-self" as in "examining myself" as a deliberate strategy for avoiding the entification of a substantial, superordinate self. That is, he would have us avoid altogether the independent noun "self" as in "examining the self."[86] I quote Fingarette at some length here:

> Why should we reify "self" by giving it the independent noun form in English, and thus impute to Confucius the notion of some inner entity, some core of one's being—whether egoistic or ideal.... [W]e ought to make it a point to avoid speaking of "the self" in Confucius. We ought to speak of a person as acting, but not suggesting by "person" this notion of an Actor who somehow embraces inwardly a moral or psychic core which is then expressed in action. On the contrary, the fundamental moral-human reality is ... the social nexus, and persons along with many other things received their specific, humanly relevant nature, as well as their humanly relevant location, by reference to and as a result of the communal life-forms. "Person" is an abstraction, a set of complex attributes conceptually abstracted from the social reality; social reality on the other hand is not an abstraction but is the concrete reality.[87]

This claim by Fingarette has been frequently misunderstood. He is not denying a vital subjective dimension to the human experience, but is rather insisting that such a subjective aspect is never independent of our communal life-forms, our social reality. Said another way, he is unwilling to abstract and reify the Confucian notion of person and locate it outside of the wholeness of the personal experience itself that is lived through the roles and relations with others as constituting our concrete social reality.

"Human Becomings" as *Creatio in Situ*

When Hellmut Wilhelm observes that "the division of the creative process into two aspects is an idea frequently found in early Chinese writings," he is remarking upon this relational and contextual nature of the personal, social and cosmic reality that makes all creativity a matter of "co-creativity."[88] Wilhelm's insight is borne out by the description that is offered repeatedly in the *Analects* of how we create ourselves as persons by modeling ourselves on others:

> Consummate persons establish others in seeking to establish themselves, and promote others in seeking to get there themselves.[89]

When Confucius says that consummate persons promote both themselves and others in what they do, he means that they accrue dividends of significance from their meaningful relationships that enhance the worth of both themselves and others as persons. Using Fingarette's language, their persons are situated in and constitute a configuration of relations within the social reality, and any notion of a discrete and independent "self" is an abstraction from and in fact a distortion of this same reality. Thick and robust relations are a source of growth in the world, enriching the family, the community, and the cosmos. It is thus that in the vocabulary of personal realization in Confucian philosophy, the negative example of "the morally deficient person" (*xiaoren* 小人)—literally "a small, petty, or mean person"—is contrasted with those who are characterized in a language of personal growth and extension: "personal excellence" (*de* 德), for example, is defined paronomastically as "getting" (*de* 得), "spirituality" (*shen* 神) is a "stretching and extending" (*shen* 伸), "becoming exemplary" (*jun* 君) is a "gathering in of others" (*qun* 群), "becoming human" (*ren* 人) is a "becoming relationally virtuosic" (*ren* 仁), and so on. Indeed, the cosmos grows bigger and better because contemporary encounters with Confucius continue to produce meaningful people.

A reflection on the Confucian notion *cheng* 誠—conventionally rendered "sincerely," "honestly," or "with integrity"—is revealing of this sense of relational growth. First, etymologically the character *cheng* is comprised of "completing" (*cheng* 成) and "discoursing" (*yan* 言)—

suggesting an accomplishment achieved through the various modalities of communicating effectively with one another. Beginning with the *Shuowen* 説文 as the earliest lexicon, in the traditional dictionaries *cheng* 誠 and *xin* 信 as "living up to one's word" are most frequently glossed by appeal to each other. *Xin* 信 denotes the situational rather than agency-centered combination of perceived "credibility" and the concomitant "trust" that such credibility inspires; it describes a situation in which its participants conduct themselves sincerely and honestly with mutual regard. The cultivation of these honest relationships entails integrity not only in the sense of the persistent particularity of persons, but also in the integrative sense of becoming one together in their concrete, social relationships. And the spontaneous emergence of significance in these relationships is the very meaning of this collaborative personal creativity. Indeed, the prefix "co-" is made redundant by the fact that it is *only* this kind of situated co-creativity— at once cognitive and affective, aesthetic and intensely religious—that can legitimately be called "creativity." Or stated negatively, *creatio ex nihilo* as creativity without context is incoherent because there is nothing that does anything in isolation and by itself.

Again, "self-loving" (*ziai* 自愛) gives primacy to immediate feelings, suggesting as it does that the dominant site of personal growth lies in the exercise of the thinking and feeling that we associate with the "heartmind" (*xin* 心). The activities of the mind cannot be divorced from the feelings of the heart; the cognitive is inseparable from the affective. There are no rational thoughts devoid of feeling, nor any raw feelings lacking cognitive content. As we observed in chapter two above, in the classical Chinese worldview in which process and change have priority over form and stasis, it is frequently observed that, in TCM, physiology has priority over anatomy, and function takes precedence over site. This being the case, it might well be argued that *xin* means "thinking and feeling" first, and then derivatively and metaphorically, the specific organ with which these experiences are to be associated. *Xin* is only metaphorically an organ because it is in fact an unbounded center or focus of activity. And the site of realizing a trusting relationship with each other is the reservoir of thoughtful feelings that fill our hearts and minds. This is only to say that the creative personal transactions—the doings and undergoings among persons that disclose their feelings for one another—are the source and the substance of meaningful relations.

Tang Junyi 唐君毅 on "Human Nature" (*renxing* 人性) as Conduct

In Tang Junyi's general discussion of the Confucian understanding of the "nature" (*xing* 性) of things, he quite appropriately begins from the etymology of the term by allowing for its immediate association with "life" (*sheng* 生) itself. Expanding upon this connection, he acknowledges the irreducibly relational and contextual character of the content of the human experience, and notes that for this reason, the *xing* of anything including human beings necessarily has two referents: *Xing* denotes the continuing life and function of a particular thing itself, and also refers to that whereby a thing continues and contributes to the life of other things. The "nature" of the earth, for example, lies not only in its own conditions—something that has various mineral properties or something that is stable and firm. The "nature" of earth also lies in its propensity to grow and give life to other things—the way in which earth provides sustenance for plants and by extension, animals, and the way in which it provides a foundation on which suitable human habitation can be built.[90] Analogously, Confucian persons are defined relationally and collaterally—not only by what they "are," but more importantly, by what they "do" with and for other persons and things in the world.

In the concluding portion of chapter two, we rehearsed a series of propositions that Tang Junyi offers as generalizations that are defining of a persistent yet always changing Chinese natural cosmology. These propositions proffered by Tang Junyi have provided us with an alternative vocabulary for reiterating and reinforcing the characterization of Chinese cosmology we were able to abstract from the *Great Tradition* 大傳 commentary on the *Book of Changes* 易經. Tang in one final proposition invokes yet another feature of Chinese cosmology that provides insight into the vectoral yet always contingent nature of the human experience. For Tang Junyi, as a Confucian, "nature" (*xing*) is a provisional, generalized disposition that is at once persistent and yet always under revision in its interactions with other things. In

Tang's own words, Chinese cosmology entails the notion that "'human nature' is nothing but the unfolding of the natural and cultural processes themselves" (*xing ji tiandao guan* 性即天道觀).[91] He further clarifies what he means by this proposition:

> Within Chinese natural cosmology what is held in general is not some first principle. The root pattern or coherence (*genben zhi li* 根本之理) of anything is its "life force" (*shengli* 生理), and this life force is its "natural tendencies" (*xing* 性). Anything's natural tendencies are expressed in the quality of its interactions with other things and events. "Natural tendencies" or "life force" then entailing spontaneity and transformation have nothing to do with necessity…. The emergence of any particular phenomenon is a function of the interaction between its prior conditions and other things and events as external influences. So how something interacts with other things and events and the form of this interaction is not determined by the thing in itself…. Thus the basic "nature" of anything includes this transformability in response to whatever it encounters.[92]

For Tang Junyi, any teleological or genetic assumptions we might have about being human have to be qualified by the spontaneous emergence of novelty within any specific context, and by a creative advance in the continuing present of any situation. "Human nature," then, is a generalization regarding the aggregating, purposeful yet open-ended disposition of human beings over time, and is nothing more or less than an expression of the ongoing attainment of relational virtuosity (*ren* 仁) within our inherited natural and cultural legacy (*tiandao* 天道). That is, the nature of each person must be recovered from and understood in terms of the continuous unfolding of the entire cosmos. In fact, rather than referencing some fixed endowment, for Tang it is precisely the indeterminate possibility for deliberate, creative change that is the most salient feature of the human *xing*. What is given in the *xing* of persons—that is, in their initial conditions—is most importantly the propensity for growth, cultivation, and refinement.

To illustrate this notion of contingent emergence, Tang provides a gloss on the opening passage of the *Zhongyong*. In his commentary on this text, Tang seeks to preclude any theistic interpretation of *tian* 天 (conventionally translated "Heaven") and any essentialistic interpretation of human nature. In explanation of the phrase "what *tian* commands is called natural tendencies" (*tianming zhi wei xing* 天命之謂性), he states explicitly:

> What is meant by this claim is not that *tian* according to some fixed fate determines the conduct and progress of human beings. On the contrary, *tian* endows humans with a natural disposition that, being more or less free of the mechanical control of their established habits and of external intervening forces, undergoes a creative advance within their context that is expressive of this spontaneity.[93]

Tang then goes on to identify what he takes to be distinctively human, where it is the degree of self-conscious freedom and creativity that distinguishes humans from other things:

> It is only in having more interactions with other things that something increases its creative impulse.... The quality of something is a function of what novelty emerges and is manifested in its interactions with other things and events. It is also a function of the ongoing tendency toward expansiveness that comes with being self-consciously able to constantly seek out more and better interactions, and being able to abandon the mechanical control of one's own past habits and those mechanical habits from external intervening forces. But this is not something that the ordinary run of things can do—it is only we humans who can do it.[94]

It is in this sense that the *Book of Rites* can claim that "humans are the heartmind of the world."[95] It is through an irreducible intersubjectivity that persons become reflexive and self-conscious in their conduct, and thus have the freedom and creativity to strive after optimal relations.

In Tang Junyi's extensive work on "human nature" (*renxing*), he demonstrates a great sensitivity to the existential coloring of the classical Confucian conception of what it means to become human. For Tang, "since any particular existent has life, in saying that it has a *xing*, what is important is not in saying what the nature and character of this entity is, but in saying what the direction of its life's existence is."[96] It is only in that existing things have life, growth, and purpose that they have *xing*. And among things, as we have seen, humans are a special case. The *xing* of humans cannot be approached in the same way as our understanding of the *xing* of other phenomena because humans have an internal existential perspective on their own evolving constitution that is not available to them in the investigation of other things. In reflecting on the relationships between experience and conceptualization, Tang asserts that:

> It is not certain that human realization can exhaust human possibilities; if one wants to understand human possibilities it is not like seeking to know the possibilities of other things that can, on the basis of inference and hypothesis, be known objectively. Rather it comes from the way in which persons realize their internal aspirations and how they then come to know them. Once we have an understanding of this human *xing*, we will of our own accord surely have the linguistic concepts through which to express it. Such linguistic conceptualization follows upon what is known, and is formed continuously as the opportunity presents itself.[97]

Tang thus emphasizes the primacy of the actual existential realization of human aspirations as they emerge in an ever-changing context over the conceptualization and articulation of these pursuits, giving full notice to the personal locus of that realization. He disassociates the conversation among classical Chinese philosophers over the meaning of *xing* from the contemporary science of psychology to the extent that in the latter case, there is a desire to treat the human "being" as an objective phenomenon. For Tang, it is the reflexive and self-conscious existential project that is the fundamental distinguishing characteristic of the classical Confucian conception of *xing*. In fact, it is precisely the indeterminate possibilities for inspired, creative change that Tang identifies as the most significant feature of the human *xing*:

> Usually what is meant by "nature" as quality or character, as when Westerners refer to it in the language of "property, characteristics, propensity, and essence" is a fixed quality, disposition, or directionality. But when we reflect upon what nature is from the perspective of the experience of the inner aspirations that we as humans have in relation to our world, there is a real question as to whether or not we can say that humans have any fixed nature. This is because the world that humans encounter and the aspirations they bring to it both entail limitless change.... For the most part, the discussion of human nature in Chinese thought has had as its one common feature a reference to this capacity for boundless change as wherein the special nature of the human lies. This then is the human's spiritual nature (*lingxing* 靈性) that differs from the fixity and lack of spirituality in the nature of other things.[98]

What is an initial condition in the nature of human beings is most importantly the propensity for purposeful growth, cultivation, and refinement—a human capacity for radical changeability. Thus throughout Tang's analysis, and especially in reference to the human phenomenon, he underscores the fundamental relationality and collaterality of *xing*:

> It is my opinion that in looking at the beginnings of a theory of human nature in China's early philosophers, the basic idea was not to take humans or their *xing* as some objective thing that can be looked at and discussed in terms of its universal nature or its special nature or its possibilities. As humans encountered the myriad things and heaven and earth, and as they encountered the inner experience of their own aspirations, what was important for them was to reflect on what the *xing* of this human is, and what the *xing* of heaven and earth and the myriad things is. The way the human was perceived within the mainstream of Chinese thought was as a kind of thing amidst and among the myriad things, and not just as one kind of the myriad things.[99]

If we were to summarize the notion of "human becoming" that follows from Tang Junyi's description of "human nature" (*renxing*), taking the notion of "growing and living" (*sheng* 生) within its contextualizing relations as its defining feature, we would have to allow that such an irreducibly complex notion of person is vital and inherently active, and is not only responsive to its environments, but is further characterized by the freedom of purpose and the creativity to be self-defining and self-aware. This reflexive, gerundive "self-" has to be understood as irreducibly transactional: shaping and being shaped in its contextualizing relations. This process of person-making is first and foremost a striving and a "doing" that expresses its life and growth, and that in the production of enhanced meaning, brings with it aspiration, frustration, and hopefully sometimes, satisfaction. Such an understanding of person is wholly naturalistic in that it makes no appeal to a metaphysics of self or to any unifying substratum such as soul or mind, and thus is more of a centered, concentrated vitality than a bounded unity. This process of becoming a person is always embodied and embodying as a porous membrane that strives to achieve meaning and coherence in the changing configuration of its relations. It is hylozoistic—that is, at once psychic and physical. It offers a revisionist and emergent understanding of person that is animated and projective, and that, having developed its own inflected and reflexive sense of itself out of its intersubjective relations with others, becomes increasing enculturated through the semiotic processes and symbolic competencies that come to shape it in these associations. It is radically embedded, and can only be understood by moving from field to focus, from the totality to the particular, taking into account the full compass of its contextualizing relations. Against the background of its *creatio in situ* cosmology, becoming a person is the creative and always-unique process of aggregating and integrating relations in the world over the span of a human narrative. Indeed this understanding of person in the Confucian terms of art is an expression of the ongoing attainment of relational virtuosity (*ren* 仁) within our inherited cultural legacy (*tiandao* 天道), allowing Tang to insist that "human nature is nothing but the unfolding of the natural and cultural processes themselves" (*xing ji tiandao guan* 性即天道觀). It is this sense of growth in its achieved personal uniqueness and its intimate continuity with the totality through family and community relations that provides a direct line from the self-conscious deference, veneration, and gratitude of the consummate life to the spirituality we associate with an increasingly religious sensitivity. This notion of human becoming breathes life into the Confucian vocabulary, transforming terms such as "excellence" (*de* 德) into striving after and "realizing oneself" (*zide* 自得) and "appropriateness" (*yi* 義) into a self-conscious sense of responsibility and accountability in one's relations with others.

I want to argue further that, with respect to this notion of human nature, Tang Junyi's "New Confucianism" is not so new. Indeed, this collateral and multilateral understanding of person-making is in fact consistent with the Confucianism espoused in the *Great Learning* that sets the Confucian project. And I have described this Confucian project as a radical empiricism that is directed at achieving the highest integrated cultural, moral, and spiritual growth for the person-in-community. For Confucius, communal harmony begins here in indefatigable personal cultivation. And through growth in familial, communal, and natural relations, the aspirant to sagehood seeks ultimately to ascend to cosmic consequence in spiraling radial circles. The Confucian sages are no more than ordinary persons who, through their resolute commitment and assiduous discipline in family and communal relations, learn to do the most ordinary of things in the most extraordinary of ways. As it states in the *Zhongyong*:

> The vision of the consummate life (*dao*) is not at all remote. If someone considers this consummate life to be something that is distant and inaccessible, they have taken a wrong turn.[100]

This idea that the inspired life is nothing more than the transformation of immediate human relations is a familiar theme in the Confucian canons:

> The Master said, "How could consummate conduct (*ren*) be at all remote? No sooner do I seek it than it has arrived."[101]

The Confucian claim that "everyone can become a sage" is often read essentialistically as an assertion that the sage is some universally given potential in human nature that if actualized provides a person with those extraordinary talents through which to shape the world in some incomparable way. Some interpreters in searching for democratic elements in classical Confucianism have latched on to this claim as a ground for an ostensive egalitarianism. We have seen that Tang's processual and provisional understanding of "human nature" precludes the possibility of such a familiar, default interpretation. Indeed, for him this same claim that "everyone can become a sage" is an assertion that the spontaneous emergence of real significance in the ordinary business of the day is itself the meaning and content of sagely virtuosity. Those ordinary persons who in their own lives achieve *real* significance in so doing are sages. And given our initial conditions and our cultural resources, all of us have the opportunity to live such significant lives. The potential for sagehood lies not *within* individuals exclusive of their worlds, but through a process of transformation that includes their worlds in the fullest sense. When sages do appear, they have emerged *pari passu* from their radically situated, collaborative, and transactional careers as human becomings.

Our Uncommon Assumptions

The *Mencius* has been definitive in the articulation of a distinctively Confucian conception of what it means to become a consummate person. And Tang Junyi has provided us with a nuanced and unfamiliar understanding of "human nature" that requires us to look again at the prevailing interpretations of what in the *Mencius* has been conventionally translated as "human nature" (*renxing*). We should begin our investigation of Mencius by first registering the unadvertised presuppositions that we might inadvertently bring to this text in our best attempts to interpret it. Michael Sandel, in his *Liberalism and the Limits of Justice*, reflects on the variety of names we use to express our self-understanding, one of them being "human nature." He observes that:

> To speak of human nature is often to suggest a classical teleological conception, associated with the notion of a universal human essence, invariant in all times and places.[102]

John Stuart Mill is a fair example of such an assumption, insisting as he does that all social activity can be traced back to a fixed an invariant human nature:

> The laws of the phenomena of society are, and can be, nothing but the laws of the actions and passions of human beings united together in the social state. Men, however, in a state of society are still men; their actions and passions are obedient to the laws of individual human nature.[103]

The familiar vocabulary of our liberal self-understanding—individualism, autonomy, equality, and freedom—often entails the humanistic assumption that the liberating of ready-made and omnicompetent individuals from numbing political strictures to pursue their own self-interest will guarantee a functional democracy. Freedom from constraint will allow unencumbered individuals, if left alone in their untrammeled state of nature, to "manifest" themselves as full-blown participants in a healthy political life. The language of spontaneity, originality, and genius belongs to the belief that an unconstricted humanity has the inborn assets to flower of its own accord.

These assumptions have a long history. As the sometimes reluctant heirs to metaphysical realism as our shared common sense, we find that sedimented into our language is the unannounced and unremarkable notion of repeatable universals subsisting in particular things that individuate things as individual "members" of a kind. And our logic of knowing has been to identify and grasp the intelligible universal as it is instantiated in the particular, and thus to be able to call the objects of knowledge by their own name: individually, specifically, and generically. While we seldom perform such an analysis self-consciously, we certainly entertain such assumptions as a matter of course in the way in which we operate in our ordinary experience. It is this long-established habit of thought that makes the quantitative "individuality" of human beings obvious and commonsensical.[104]

Persistent and powerful philosophical ideas promoted largely by classical liberal Enlightenment thinkers such as Kant, Locke, and Mill have become the common currency of political philosophy, and have influenced the way in which many sinologists, Chinese as well as Western, have come to their interpretation of the Mencian notion of *renxing*.

The *Mencius* (*Mengzi* 孟子) and "Human Becomings"

Broadly speaking, in the current literature Mencius has come to be widely understood as forwarding an *a priori* conception of an abstract, innate, essential human nature, a given, inborn potential that is then actualized in the life experience.[105] As the interpretation in this literature stands, Mencius offers a clear explanation of what we are as "human *beings*."

What is at issue here in saving Mencius from essentialism is the question: How do we define what it means to be human?—by a speculative and reductive assumption about innate, isolatable causes that locate persons outside of their roles and relations, or alternatively, by taking account of the initial conditions and context of persons, and then by assaying the full aggregation of consequent action? How do we explain growth?—by reduplicative causal accounts (the child is a ready-made adult), by teleological accounts (the child is simply preliminary to the actualization of the existing ideal), or by a contextual, narrative account available to us through a phenomenology of personal action? We must ask whether the metaphysical way of thinking about "human beings" is consistent with the Confucian project of becoming consummately human within a natural correlative cosmology, a project that seems to demand not only motivation and real effort, but also imagination and a creative responsiveness to ever changing circumstances. If, as it is so often assumed, Mencius is proffering a superordinate and substantial conception of human nature, how do we square this assumption with his own minimalist claim that initially "what distinguishes people from the brutes is infinitesimal"?[106] And again, why would he use the minimalist metaphorical language of *duan* 端—the first inklings or signs, the tips, the sprouts—if he is indeed describing a substantial facticity?[107]

To make the case for a processual understanding of "human nature" (*renxing*), we might take one of these "beginnings" as an example: "achieved propriety in our roles and relationships" (*li*). On the side of the infant, born within the context of its familial life forms, there is certainly a predisposition and a propensity to develop over time into a responsive and thus responsible member of this social unit. But a distorting limitation in our thinking arises when we locate the discussion of *renxing* exclusively within the abstracted individual infant rather than within the inclusive and concrete web of family relations. Regardless of how we describe a human nativity and its initial responsiveness to the institutions and structures of communal living, it is the family as the articulated social and cultural locus of otherwise inchoate persons—an invested and meaningful concentration of beliefs, skills, interests, values, occupations, and so on—that is the predominant creative source out of which persons grow, and to which grown persons ultimately contribute their particular meanings.

Infants have a predisposition to communicate, but it is the world of cultural meanings into which they are born that provide them with the communicative resources necessary to participate effectively in their specific families and communities. If there is proof needed that the weight of "human nature" as defining of what it means to become distinctively human lies in the concrete social situation of which the individual is a part, rather than exclusively in inchoate individuals themselves, we have simply to reference the staggering diversity of ways of thinking and living within the vastly disparate human cultures. On the other hand, proof that the initial conditions are not the substance of what it means to become human might be the phenomenon of remarkably similar feral children who seem to be the ineluctable consequence of disconnected and dislocated "human beings" living out their animality without the resource of family life.

Indeed, I will argue in what follows that the *Mencius* is positing the notion of a relationally constituted "human becoming," a notion of person that requires an understanding fundamentally different from any retrospective, essentialistic conception of the human being. I am further persuaded that the recently recovered Confucian document, *Five Modes of Proper Conduct* (*Wuxingpian* 五行篇), resonates in many ways with the *Mencius* and corroborates this interpretation of the Mencian *renxing* as a prospective, processual, transactional, and radically contextual understanding of what it means to become human.

As I have argued elsewhere, a first step in understanding *renxing* 人性 in the *Mencius* is to distinguish it clearly from a second notion that also has an important role in the cluster of terms through which Mencius explicates the project of personal cultivation, that is, the "heartmind" (*xin* 心).[108] There has been a decided tendency on the part of scholars in interpreting Mencius to elide *xing* and *xin* without respecting their important differences. This confusion emerges because the *xing* as a creative process is rooted in the heartmind (*xin*), and human beings in general do have certain determinative propensities as a function of their initial natural conditions. But it is precisely over and against these determinate propensities that we are able to observe the creative process of change, growth, and refinement that constitutes *xing*.

We are told explicitly in the *Mencius* that persons all have heartminds (*xin*), and that these heartminds share a given incipient propensity for moral conduct that is metaphorically described as "the four inklings" (*siduan* 四端):

> The heartmind in feeling pity at suffering has the first inkling of consummate conduct; the heartmind in feeling shame at crudeness has the first inkling of appropriate conduct; the heartmind in feeling a sense of modesty and deference has the first inkling of propriety in conduct; the heartmind in feeling a sense of approval and disapproval has the first inkling of wise conduct. Persons having these four inklings (*siduan*) is like their having four limbs.... Now acknowledging these four inklings in me, the process of realizing the development and fruition of them all is like a fire beginning to burn or a spring of water beginning to break through. Persons who are able to bring them fully to fruition can sustain all within the four seas; persons unable to do so cannot even serve their own parents.[109]

This passage describes the initial conditions of the heartmind, but we have to remember that the graph for *xing* 性 is comprised of both "heartmind" (*xin*) and "to be born, to grow, to live" (*sheng* 生). Taking this verbal "growth" (*sheng* 生) complement to heartmind as an important further consideration, in the *Mencius* we are again told explicitly that:

> Consummatory conduct (*ren*), a sense of appropriateness (*yi*), an achieved propriety in roles and relations (*li*), and a capacity to live wisely (*zhi*) that exemplary persons engender and grow (*xing*) as their habits of conduct is rooted in their heartminds, and grows in their countenance. The luster of this conduct is manifest in their faces, is discernible in their posture, and extends throughout their bodies. They do not need to explain what they are doing to be understood by others.[110]

If we couple this passage with the analogical claim in the 2A6 passage cited above that "persons having these four inklings (*siduan*) is like their having four limbs," we can appreciate that the four inklings and the body are both incipient sites of growth.[111] Indeed, it is only through this assiduous process of cultivation that the *xing* can be fully developed:

> Those who exhaust their heartminds (*xin*) realize their *xing*, and to realize their *xing* is to realize *tian*. Preserving their *xin* and nurturing their *xing* is the way to serve *tian*.[112]

As one example of this problem of conflating *xin* and *xing*, Zhang Dainian suggests that "since the sage is also a man, the *xing* that the sage has is the *xing* that all people have."[113] On a careful reading of the *Mencius*, Zhang could certainly assert that the sage has a *xin* that is similar to that of all people. In fact, the *Mencius* describes the *xin* as an organ (*guan* 官) on a plane with the organs of sight and hearing.[114] But Zhang's assumption would seem to be that *xing* like *xin* is a given potential shared by all, and the sage is simply the one who successfully actualizes it. However, as Tang Junyi has argued, the possibility of *xing* does not lie within *xing* itself; *xing* is a creative collaboration between something and its various environments. Being a person does not make one a sage; becoming a sage makes one most fully a person. There is an important difference between saying that everyone has the nature of a sage and saying that everyone who conducts themselves as a sage is a sage. The potential for becoming a sage emerges *pari passu* in the transactional events that constitute the substance of a human life. Mencius makes this point explicitly:

> Cao Jiao inquired: "Is it the case that we can all become Yaos and Shuns?"
>
> Mencius replied: "... The way of Yao and Shun is nothing but family reverence and fraternal deference. If you wear Yao's clothes, speak his words, and do what he does, then you *are* a Yao."[115]

The passage that is generally cited from the *Mencius* as defining of his understanding that human nature is essentially good (*xingshan* 性善) is the following:

> As respects one's actual circumstances that one can act efficaciously is what is meant by *shan*. As respects one acting ineptly, this is not the fault of one's native ability. All people have a heartmind that feels pity at suffering, that feels shame at crudeness, that feels a sense of modesty and deference, and that feels a sense of approval and disapproval. The feeling of pity at suffering leads to consummate conduct; the feeling of shame at crudeness leads to appropriate conduct; the feeling of a sense of modesty and deference leads to propriety in conduct; the feeling of sense of approval and disapproval leads to wisdom in conduct. These four inklings in conduct do not illuminate me from without. They are tendencies that I have but have simply failed to acknowledge. It is for this reason that it is said: "If you seek it you will get it; if you don't you will lose it." That some people are twice, five times, and indeed infinitely better than others is because there are those who fail to make the most of their native ability.[116]

I would argue that the basic misreading of this passage arises from interpreting the distinction between inside and outside as exclusive and essential rather than as correlative, experiential, and a function of circumstances. It is the same misreading that is possible when Yan Hui's definition of *ren* as "self-loving" (*ziai* 自愛) is understood to be exclusive of others rather than relational. The point is that these inclinations in conduct locate relationally constituted persons within experience in which their subjective dispositions as well as their objective behavior must both be acknowledged. Moral conduct is a collaboration between persons and their worlds rather than being a pattern of behavior derived solely from the outside, or solely from the inside.

Perhaps the key to understanding this passage is defining efficacy (*shan*) as something we are inclined to do rather than something that we essentially are: *keyi weishanyi* 可以為善矣 ("one can act/become/do *shan*)." This active understanding of *shan* suggests that efficacy is a quality of activity that one is disposed to achieve by virtue of one's situation, rather than as the expression of some innate quality of character irrespective of one's circumstances.[117]

That efficacy (*shan*) is an inclination that must be developed and brought to fruition is made clear in a more careful reading of another frequently cited passage that D. C. Lau has translated as:

> It is certainly the case ... that water does not show any preference for either east or west, but does it show the same indifference to high and low? Human nature is good just as water seeks low ground. There is no man who is not good; there is no water that does not flow downwards.[118]

The problem with this translation is that in saying that "human nature *is* good, just as water *seeks* low ground," it fails to respect the symmetry of the sentence. Observing the parallel structure, we might translate it as:

> Water certainly has no inclination to flow eastward as opposed to westward, but does the same hold true in its flowing downwards or upwards? Human *xing* seeks efficacy (*shan*) just as water seeks to flow downwards. There is no person who does not seek efficacy; there is no water that does not flow downwards.

Important here is that the text is saying that *xing* entails an inclination in personal growth in which one *seeks to* become *shan*, not that *xing* in itself "is" *shan*.

A second important consideration is the difference that human effort makes in the cultivation of one's native tendencies—native inclinations that if not acted upon can even be lost utterly. That some people become so much better than others speaks to the vital role that disciplined, habituated conduct has in growing what, after all, are only one's initial conditions. Mencius reiterates the point that the initial conditions can only become productive if they are actively engaged, and that it is this deliberate conduct itself that makes all the difference—indeed, a quantum difference—in the quality of one's person:

> Gongduzi asked Mencius: "Since they are equally human, how is it that some persons become exemplary while others are wholly deficient?"
>
> "Those who follow their superior parts (*dati* 大體) become superior; those who follow their inferior parts (*xiaoti* 小體) become inferior," replied Mencius.
>
> "Since they are equally human, how is it that some would follow their superior parts while others would follow their inferior parts?" he asked.
>
> "Our physical senses such as sight and hearing are not reflective, and can be deceived by external things. When one thing is engaged by another, it is simply distracted by it. The function of the heartmind on the other hand is thinking, but it will only accomplish something if it actually thinks. We have been given this as our native ability. If one begins by attending to the superior parts, the inferior parts will not be able to take their place. This is how one becomes a superior person."[119]

The *Mencius* allows that certain tendencies are native to us by virtue of our initial circumstances. Mencius however wants to reserve the category of *xing* to include only those among such tendencies that when fully cultivated make us distinctively human. While we have bodily senses such as taste, sight, hearing, and smell—a physical sensorium, as it were—these senses are not exclusively human, and so Mencius chooses to call them basic conditions (*ming* 命) rather than natural tendencies (*xing*):

> The mouth's propensity for tastes, the eye's for colors, the ear's for sounds, the nose's for smells, and the four limbs' for comfort—these are native tendencies (*xing*), and yet because basic conditions (*ming*) also have a role in these capacities, exemplary persons are not given to referring to them as *xing*. A propensity for consummate conduct in the father-son relation, for appropriateness in the ruler-subject relation, for ritual propriety in the guest-host relation, for wisdom on the part of superior persons, and to have sages for the way of *tian*, are basic conditions (*ming*), yet because *xing* also has a role in these capacities, exemplary persons are not given to referring to them as basic conditions.[120]

We as persons are born into a manifold of family and community roles and relations, and by virtue of these thick initial conditions, we have feelings of pity at suffering, feelings of modesty and deference, a sense of propriety and a sense of approval and disapproval—indeed, an ethical sensorium. The ethical sensorium is rooted in the heartmind (*xin* 心) as a generalization of the conditions which obtain when a person is born, and it is this sensorium that is then articulated across the particular narrative of a distinctively human life as a collaboration between person and world to become one's *xing* 性. Mencius says that:

> Context alters one's vital energies just as what one eats alters one's body. Huge indeed is the function of context. Would we not otherwise just be anybody's son?[121]

It is in this sense that we might claim that relatively speaking, persons are less importantly similar and more importantly distinctive and unique cultural achievements, and that what it means to become human is a generalization made from the collective history of our narratives and our accomplishments. It is for this reason that Mencius claims "the various doctrines on *xing* that have been discussed in the world are all nothing but a matter of invoking historical precedents."[122]

The *Five Modes of Proper Conduct* (*Wuxingpian* 五行篇)[123] as a Window on the *Mencius*

I will use the *Wuxingpian* document recently recovered in archaeological finds first at Mawangdui near Changsha in Hunan province (1973) and then more recently at Guodian near Jingmen in Hubei (1993) to affirm that the Mencian "four inklings" (*siduan* 四端) are certainly the initial conditions for becoming human, and to agree that in this sense they are native. Yet at the same time I will use this same text to argue that these "four inklings," like the first four modes of proper conduct (*sixing* 四行) described in the *Wuxingpian*, are informed by the primarily acquired conditions of radically contextualized, relational, and emergent persons where most of the active force and meaning of this conduct in the first years of life derives not from the "person" exclusive of family relations, but on the contrary, from the already matured family-side of one's collateral roles and relationships. I will thus be arguing for a genealogical and historical understanding of the Mencian notion of human inclinations rather than for one based upon metaphysical speculation.

By collateral roles and relationships that define persons, I mean that generally speaking there are no children without mothers, no brothers without siblings, and certainly no viable babies born without a family circle that, in loving them, enables them to survive and to thrive. Indeed, the acquired habits of the family are primary in preserving and educating the life of the infant, and the native conditions of the infant are secondary as largely dependent upon the stimulation and interpretation of the family. The "four inklings" of *renxing* are anchored deeply in family relations, and initially the growth in meaning and value of these relationships derives largely from family intimates as their immediate source. It is such relations that are the entry point for humans to develop and to become distinctive as individuals, and in the fullness of time, to become distinctively human.

The always-unique persons in this collateral sense—this daughter to this mother—do not "have" relationships, or "come into" relationships, but rather are constituted as irreducibly relational by those bonds that locate them as foci within the field of the big family. They begin as "we" rather than "I." As Mencius claims, "all things are here in me," and most immediately and importantly among all things are one's family relations.[124] Indeed, any putative "individuality" must be understood as either an abstraction from these concrete, native, and primarily acquired conditions, or an achieved distinctiveness cultivated in one's relations with others that makes one an identifiable object of deference.[125] Similarly, any notion of "family" is an abstraction from these specific, particular persons who collectively and organically constitute a human nexus. Both particular persons and particular families are concrete configurations of particular relationships, and stand in a dynamic focus-field relationship with one another.

From its content we might surmise that the document entitled *Wuxingpian* preceded the *Mencius* chronologically, and has identifiable resonances with the *Mencius* that might bespeak of some influence, direct or otherwise, upon the content of this later text.[126] *Wuxingpian* describes how "five modes of proper conduct" (*wuxing* 五行)—that is, "conducting oneself consummately" (*ren* 仁), "acting with optimal appropriateness" (*yi* 義), "achieving propriety in one's roles and relations" (*li* 禮), "acting wisely" (*zhi* 知), and "behaving sagaciously" (*sheng* 聖)—aggregate over time to become a unified excellence that informs future action. These

III · *The Confucian Project: Attaining Relational Virtuosity* 145

are five acquired habits that need to be cultivated for interacting most productively in family and community. Importantly, there is an explicit connection between both the specific order and the substance of these "five modes of proper conduct" and the Mencian notion of the "four inklings" (*siduan*) as the positive initial conditions of the human heartmind (*xin* 心) that prompt and inform our growth (*xing* 性) to emerge as fully moral humans.[127] How do we put these two lists of desired conduct together?

A major contribution of the *Wuxingpian* from its opening paragraph lies in pressing the idea that it is compounding proper conduct itself that is the primary source and substance of our moral habits. In large measure, we become what we do. Mencius's conception of "natural tendencies" (*renxing*) likewise is best understood as a process of moral growth that begins with initial conditions within the context of family, and results in a dynamic pattern of always-contextualized and evolving moral habits. That is, *this* family is the point of entry and initial source that makes the cultivation of *this* distinguished person possible, and it is the emergence of *this* distinguished person that in turn enhances the meaning of *this* family.

The *Wuxingpian*'s description of the "five modes of proper conduct" as "moral excellences" (*de* 德) rather than as the "four inklings" (*siduan*) of our "natural tendencies" (*xing* 性) is significant in this argument. As the *Wuxingpian* explains from the opening passage, the five moral excellences (*de* 德) are something acquired (*de* 得) and harmonized (*he* 和) through an ongoing process of habituation:

> Consummatory conduct (*ren* 仁) taking shape within is called acting upon excellent habits (*de* 德); where it does not take shape within, it is called merely doing what is deemed consummate. Appropriate acting (*yi* 義) taking shape within is called acting upon excellent habits (*de*); where it does not take shape within, it is called merely doing what is deemed appropriate. A sense of ritual propriety (*li* 禮) taking shape within is called acting upon excellent habits (*de*); where it does not take shape within, it is called merely doing what is deemed proper.[128] Acting wisely (*zhi* 智) taking shape within is called acting on excellent habits (*de*); where it does not take shape within, it is called merely doing what is deemed wise. Acting in a sagely way (*sheng* 聖) taking shape within is called acting upon excellent habits (*de*); where it does not take shape within, it is called merely doing what is deemed sagacious.[129]

When harmony (*he*) is achieved among these five modes of proper conduct, it is called moral excellence (*de*). Achieving harmony among the first four of these modes of proper conduct is called efficacy (*shan* 善). Efficacy is the human way (*rendao* 人道); moral excellence is the way of *tian* (*tiandao* 天道).[130]

This first passage of the *Wuxingpian*, with its emphasis on the nurturing of our moral excellences, might be associated with a similar distinction between the habituation of moral excellence in conduct and mere conduct that is made in *Mencius* 4B19:

> Mencius said, "What distinguishes people from the brutes is ever so slight, and where the common run of people are apt to lose this quality, exemplary persons dwell on it and preserve it. Shun was wise to the way of all things and had real insight into human roles and relationships. He acted upon his moral habits to be consummatory and appropriate in his conduct rather than merely doing what is deemed consummatory and appropriate."[131]

The last two lines of this *Wuxingpian* passage that distinguish between the way of human beings and the way of *tian* further suggest a collaborative rather than an exclusive understanding of the relationship between *tian* and human beings. After all, this is not a theism wherein an independent creator deity unilaterally endows human beings with an essential nature. The *Analects* 7.23 passage observes: "*Tian* has given life to and nourished moral excellence in me,"[132] a phrase that has its counterpart in *Mencius* 6A15 cited previously: "The function of the heartmind on the other hand is thinking, but it will only accomplish something if it actually thinks. We have been given this as our native ability."[133] If in our interpretation of these passages we consider the symbiotic and interdependent relationship assumed to obtain between *tian* and *ren*—that is, between the natural and cultural context and the human—we might read it as saying that *tian* provides not only the initial conditions, but also a legacy and the context in which the project of personal cultivation can take place efficaciously (*shan* 善). But importantly, it is the human habituation of moral excellence (*de*) in conduct that extends and gives articulation to the way of *tian* (*tiandao* 天道). For *ren* 人 and *tian* 天, we know them collaterally by what they mean for each other as the ultimate source of aggregating meaning and as the meaningful context that facilitates continuing human growth.

The Pragmatic Notion of Relational Person: An Associative and Contrastive Analogy

In the introductory chapter, I argued that analogy is not only crucial to cultural translation, but unavoidable. Further, I maintained that these selected correlations can serve understanding as either associative or contrastive analogies, and that in pursuing these connections, we need to think retail rather than wholesale. In thinking through and seeking to clarify the Confucian notion of the radically embedded, relationally constituted, and always-emergent person, we might take John Dewey's notion of "individuality" as a potentially productive example of an associative analogy. Indeed, Dewey's individuality can perhaps serve as both an associative and a contrastive analogy in bringing this Confucian version of relationally constituted person into clearer resolution. Dewey, in his phenomenology of human conduct, combines the process psychology of William James and the social psychology of George Herbert Mead to locate persons within their natural and social relations. As Mead insists, "self" is coterminous with the world:

> The self cannot arise in experience except as there are others there. The child experiences sounds, etc., before it has experience of its own body; there is nothing in the child that arises as his own experience and then is referred to the outside things.... Only a superficial philosophy demands the old view that we start with ourselves.... There is no self before there is a world, and no world before the self. The process of the formation of the self is social.[134]

These pragmatists are revolutionary within the Western narrative in dispensing with the "old psychology" that begins from assumptions about a superordinate and discrete *psyche*. In *Human Nature and Conduct*, Dewey echoes many of the ideas proffered by Tang Junyi on "human nature" that were cited above, with both philosophers calling into question the separation of "human nature" and "conduct" by disputing the very distinction between them. Indeed, both Tang and Dewey shave with Ockham's razor by dispensing with the superordinate "person, soul, self" and insisting that cultivated moral dispositions as habits of conduct are themselves the substance of what it means to become a consummate person. There is no need felt to appeal to some reduplicative notion of a discrete "agent" or "character" that would isolate and locate persons as a motive force outside of the pattern of their social and natural relations.

While Tang focuses on an always-situated and contextual meaning of *xing* in the transactional and collateral nature of human conduct, Dewey must struggle to overcome the default assumptions that have become entrenched within his own tradition:

> The doctrine of a single, simple and indissoluble soul was the cause and the effect of failure to recognize that concrete habits are the means of knowledge and thought. Many who think themselves scientifically emancipated and who freely advertise the soul for a superstition, perpetuate a false notion of what knows, that is, of a separate knower.[135]

Instead, Dewey, in a different language but still analogous in many ways to the Confucian notion of a relationally constituted person, arrives at an understanding of the human being as a dynamic combination of habit and impulse:

> Now it is dogmatically stated that no such conceptions of the seat, agent or vehicle will go psychologically at the present time. Concrete habits do all the perceiving, recognizing, imagining, recalling, judging, conceiving and reasoning that is done. "Consciousness," whether as a stream or as special sensations and images, expresses the functions of habits, phenomena of their formation, operation, their interruption and reorganization.... A certain delicate combination of habit and impulse is requisite for observation, memory and judgment.[136]

Dewey further insists that, whatever we have as the initial conditions situating us within community, these conditions must be attended by a substantial process of nurturance and growth: "We are born organic beings associated with others, but we are not born members of a community."[137] For Dewey, "individuality" is not quantitative: it is neither a pre-social potential nor a kind of isolating discreteness. Rather, it is qualitative, arising through distinctive service to one's community. Individuality is "the realization of what we specifically are as distinct from others,"[138] a realization that can only take place within the context

III · The Confucian Project: Attaining Relational Virtuosity 149

of a flourishing communal life. "Individuality cannot be opposed to association," says Dewey. "It is through association that man has acquired his individuality, and it is through association that he exercises it."[139] An individual so construed is not a "thing" but a "patterned event," describable in the language of uniqueness, integrity, social activity, relationality, and qualitative achievement.

We might appeal to some Deweyan observations on habits of personal growth as an alternative vocabulary that provides us with an associative analogy for this Confucian relational, situational, and transactional notion of personal conduct. First, Dewey is critical of the hypostatization of conduct as a notion of a discrete agency that locates instincts within isolated individuals:

> A combination of traditional individualism with the recent interest in progress explains why the discovery of the scope and force of instincts has led many psychologists to think of them as the fountain head of all conduct, as occupying a place before instead of after that of habits. The orthodox tradition in psychology is built upon isolation of individuals from their surroundings. The soul or mind or consciousness was thought of as self-contained and self-enclosed.[140]

Dewey appeals to the actual situated human experience as we live it in rejecting the priority of an ostensive autonomous "self" over that of an organic configuration of relations, and in questioning the priority of instincts to shared cultural life forms. He argues that any infant isolated from its dependent relations would quickly become a dead infant; that is, infants left to their own devices without access to or intervention by culturally informed relations could not survive for a single day. Even the meaning of the actions and gestures of infants is derived from the mature communal context within which they reside:

> The inchoate and scattered impulses of an infant do not coordinate into serviceable powers except through social dependencies and companionships. His impulses are merely starting points for assimilation of the knowledge and skill of the more matured beings upon whom he depends. They are tentacles sent out to gather that nutrition from customs which will in time render the infant capable of independent action. They are agencies for transfer of existing social power into personal ability; they are means of reconstructive growth.[141]

Dewey is, in his own tradition, a flat-out revolutionary in insisting upon the primacy of the relationally constituted, concrete situation as the garden of social intelligence and the locus for the pursuit of the consummate life. The optimally appropriate response to our ever-present uncertainties and any confident resolution of these uncertainties can only be negotiated within the actual circumstances themselves, with individual agency itself being an abstraction from them:

> The primary significance of the unique and morally ultimate character of the concrete situation is to transfer the weight and burden of morality to intelligence. It does not destroy responsibility; it only locates it. A moral situation is one in which judgment and choice are required antecedently to overt action. The practical meaning of the situation ... the action needed to satisfy it—is not self-evident. It has to be searched for.[142]

Dewey is radical in this social construction of the person. He certainly rejects the idea that the human being is in any way complete outside of the association one has with other people. Indeed, he would claim that "apart from the ties which bind him [the human being] to others, he is nothing."[143] As James Campbell observes, this passage is easily and often misunderstood as a negation of the individual.[144] But as we have seen with Dewey's notion of emergent "individuality," to say that persons are irreducibly social is not to deny the integrity, uniqueness, and diversity of human beings; on the contrary, it is precisely to affirm these conditions.

In commenting on Dewey and the social processes in which persons are created, Campbell avers Aristotle's vocabulary of "potential" and "actual":

> Dewey's point is not just that what was potential becomes actual when provided with the proper conditions, as, for example, the growth of a seed into a plant is sometimes understood (Cf. LW 9:195-96). His point is rather that persons are incomplete without a social component and develop into what they are—individual members of groups, socially grounded selves—in the ongoing process of living in a social environment.[145]

Similarly, we can argue that the Mencian "inklings" (*siduan*) of the heartmind are not inborn and essential qualities that in and of themselves make us human "beings." These "inklings" are certainly native

III · *The Confucian Project: Attaining Relational Virtuosity* 151

and incipient as the initial relational conditions that bind us into our families. But they are only the largely dependent beginnings of a process of growth in associated living that need to be nourished to make us full, active participants in family and community. The *siduan* describe the particular ethical, aesthetic, cognitive, and religious beginnings whence human beings emerge. The Confucian project, then, is to incorporate inchoate yet organically interdependent persons within the family nexus and to transform them into eager participants in a flourishing and thus spiritual community.

Dewey invests enormously in the centrality of language and other modes of communicative discourse (including signs, symbols, gestures, and social institutions) in explaining how the community grows its persons:

> Through speech a person dramatically identifies himself with potential acts and deeds; he plays many roles, not in successive stages of life but in a contemporaneously enacted drama. Thus mind emerges.[146]

For Dewey, mind is "an added property assumed by a feeling creature, when it reaches that organized interaction with other living creatures which is language, communication."[147] For Dewey, then, what we might call "heartmind" is created in the process of realizing a world. Heartmind, like world, is *becoming* rather than *being*, and the question is how productive and enjoyable are we able to make this creative process. The way in which heartmind and world are changed is not simply in terms of human attitude, but in real growth and productivity, and in the efficiency and pleasure that attends this process. The alternative—for a community to fail to communicate effectively—is for the community to wither, leaving it vulnerable to the "mindless" violence and "heartless" atrocities of creatures that have failed to become human.

In Confucianism, as in Deweyan pragmatism, the process of personal and communal development is driven by effective communication. To cite Dewey:

> Everything which is distinctively human is learned, not native, even though it could not be learned without native structures which mark man off from other animals. To learn in a human way and to human effect is not just to acquire added skill through refinement of original capacities. To learn to be human is to develop through the give-and-take of communication an

effective sense of being an individually distinctive member of a community; one who understands its beliefs, desires, and methods, and who contributes to a further conversion of organic powers into human resources and values.[148]

Dewey's position expressed here might on the surface seem to contradict that voiced in the *Mencius* when the latter claims:

> The capacities that people have without having learned them are the root of their capacities; the wisdom that people have without having reflected upon it is the root of their wisdom. There are no young children who do not know to love their parents, and on coming of age, there are none who do not know to respect their elders. Loving one's parents is being consummate; respecting one's elders is being appropriate. There is no other reason that these habits can prevail in the world.[149]

But neither Dewey nor Mencius would dispute the fact that all activity is a collaboration between persons and their environments, and this being so, that persons bring significant capacities with them in their various activities that are a function of their initial conditions. Dewey is focusing on the transactional nature of all human conduct that invariably entails a "doing and an undergoing," while Mencius is insisting that all action invariably has a subjective dimension to it, and that becoming moral is not entirely derived from some external source. The key lies in understanding that when Mencius rejects the claim that virtuosic conduct is derived from something "external" (*wai* 外), he is not alternatively claiming that such conduct is entirely a matter of actualizing and manifesting some internal nature independent of the external circumstances of one's roles and relations.[150] Rather, he is asserting, like Dewey after him, that person and personal growth are both a collaboration between an emerging subject and a more-or-less objective world.

Dewey is helpful in providing insight into the inseparability of person and context, but in spite of the development of his relationally constituted person as a radical departure from an entrenched foundational individualism, in spite of his sustained commitment to the ultimacy and the complexity of the concrete situation in his rejection of an abstract moral idealism, and most importantly, in spite of his awareness of the vital role of early childhood education and his own intense personal experience as a much-engaged parent, he still does not develop the seemingly obvious implication that the generalizable site of associated growth for most people is going to be their families. Indeed, the uniquely Confucian perception of how we become persons departs fundamentally from the Deweyan conception of personal cultivation in its stress upon our immediate family roles and relations as the entry point and the ground for acquiring moral competence.[151]

Where Confucian role ethics departs from and stands in plain contrast to the pragmatists is in requiring that certain basic moral considerations be located within the arena of family life. For example, while the pragmatists within their own tradition have to develop a revised understanding of the familiar liberal vocabulary of freedom, equality, and justice, these terms do not appear in the Confucian texts because such abstractions, along with the notions of moral principles, values, and virtues, are located in and derived from actual life experience within one's specific roles and relations in family and community.

As noted above, if we rehearse the important contributions of what are acknowledged to be the most prominent Western philosophers across the centuries, with few exceptions we are hard-pressed to find any significant thinker who invokes family as a productive model for organizing and optimizing the human experience. Plato's rejection of the family in the *Republic* and Aristotle's denigration of the "household" (*oikis*) as a source of privation are fairly representative.[152] Even John Dewey, whose relational cosmology and emphasis on the great community offers frequent analogy with Confucian assumptions, is true to the mainstream of his own tradition, opining that China has to get beyond its traditional family system as a precondition for democratization.[153]

Undoubtedly this persisting indifference to the importance of the perceived "partial" relations that emerge from family feeling is closely aligned with the assumed centrality of impartiality as a necessary condition for ethical conduct pervasive among those philosophers who would look to universal principles, objective procedures, impersonal teleological uniformities, and moral reasoning as the ultimate source of and warrant for moral order. Such a disinterest in family as a measure of moral order in the Western philosophical narrative contrasts starkly with the Confucian worldview in which family is *the* governing metaphor, and in which in fact *all* relationships are familial.[154] It is the uniqueness of this Confucian moral sensibility that has led Henry Rosemont and me to describe it as "Confucian role ethics" in an effort to distinguish it from other more familiar ethical theories.[155] The signature of Confucian role ethics that will be further developed in the next chapter is that immediate family feeling is not only the entry point for an educated moral competence, but is also an inspiration and model for optimizing order in all of the dimensions of human life. Indeed, family feeling is the foundational moral epistemology of Confucian philosophy. We know each other primarily through our empathetic feelings for each other.

Making Better Sense of the Notions of "Root," "Source," "Potential," and "Cause"

In the *Mencius* and other canonical Confucian texts, the familiar appeal to the horticultural and husbanding metaphors—knowing the "root," for example—is often construed as reinforcing the idea that specific plants and animals grow to become what they essentially are: They simply actualize their inherent potential. But in fact what makes horticulture and husbanding apposite analogies for relationally constituted "human becomings" is the acute dependence that farming and raising animals has upon a contrived environment and upon concentrated human effort. Without sustained intervention, most seeds, far from becoming what they "are," become anything and everything else. Without the benefit of intensive intervention and cultivation on behalf of what we think they will "naturally" become, most acorns become squirrels, most corn becomes cows, and most eggs become omelets. The "root" or "seed" of anything and what it will become is as much a function of the contingencies of circumstances as it is of the initial conditions from which it "begins."

Turning to the notion of "source," *dao* 道 is often described as a "source" and might shed light on how "source" is to be understood when ascribed to "human nature." The conventional understanding of "source" is that it is the point of origin exclusive of what is derived from that point. Geographically, the source of the Yangtze river is the Himalayas. When we introduce the idea of efficient cause, the source becomes something analytically independent of the product that it causes, creates, initiates. It is the maker from which whatever is made is derived. Such notions of "source" have no relevance to *dao*. *Dao*, far from standing independent of the world we experience, is in fact the unsummed totality of all that is happening. *Dao* is the process of the world in its entirety.

To understand the notion of *dao* as "source" we might cite the *Daodejing* that states "*dao* emulates what is spontaneously so of itself."[156] The energy of growth and transformation resides within the world itself, wherein the entire field of what is happening is implicated in each relationally constituted event.

Bringing this rather abstract reflection to bear on how we are to understand "human nature" as the "source" of what we become as humans, we would have to allow that human nature is a provisional generalization made with respect to the totality of human lives as they have been lived within their natural and social relations. The contingency in the ongoing process of what humans have become is no less relevant to this notion of source than where they have come from so far. The source is the collaborative, open-ended nature of human relations themselves *and* what is produced in this collaboration. In becoming human, as in making friends, there is no separation between maker and made, between means and end, between cause and effect, between source and product.

Further, we might clarify the notion of "potential" to underscore the inseparability of person and context in this Confucian conception of persons. The "potential" for becoming human is not simply the first inklings, something inborn "within" the person that is exclusive of family relations. In the first place, there is no such person. Since persons are constituted by their relations, the "potential" of a person in fact emerges from the specific, contingent transactions that, in the fullness of time, eventuate in this particular person in this particular family. Thus, the best sense we can make of "potential" here is that rather than being antecedent and ready-made, it evolves *pari passu* with the ever-changing circumstances; rather than being generic or universal, it is always unique to the career of the relational person; and rather than existing as an inherent and defining endowment, it can only be known *post hoc* after the unfolding of the particular narrative.[157] The argument, then, is that the preponderance of the content of "human nature" (*renxing* 人性) as it is expressed in the habitude of "consummatory conduct" (*ren* 仁),

"acting optimally appropriate in meaningful relations" (*yi*), "achieving propriety in roles and relations" (*li* 禮), and "acting with intelligence and wisdom" (*zhi* 智) is acquired. "Natural tendencies" (*xing* 性) are no more an essential and inborn given than is "consummatory conduct" (*ren*). Both are a source and a product. That is, they are the articulation of tentative native conditions in the consequent process of habituation. "Acting with wisdom" is not applying an antecedent wisdom to a situation, but an informed quality of acting that arises with the efficacy of one's actions.

What makes "human nature" most profoundly variable is the quality of the families and cultures into which we are born. If the family is a morally strong and thriving association of significant persons within a mature culture, much is available for investment in and growth for the incipient person. If the family is barren and troubled within only a thinly cultured environment, it is a more difficult road for the emerging person. But even when the legendary Shun is born into the family of the morally deficient Blind Man, the model of Emperor Yao is still available as part of a rich cultural resource that enables Shun, through the assiduous cultivation of habits of conduct, to become a sage himself. Shun's circumstances are a fair demonstration that there are cultural assets available for everyone to draw upon in aspiring to become sagely in their conduct.

The basic significance of the mantra, "the continuity between the natural and cultural context, and the human experience" (*tianren heyi* 天人合一) that is invoked to describe the Confucian religious sensibility is making this same point about potential. It is the person nourished by culture who becomes consummately human, and it is the life of the consummate human who contributes to the cultural resources that make a consummate humanity possible. Potentiality emerges in these collaborations between aspiring persons and an inspired world.

Turning to causality then, given the constitutive nature of relations, causality is not some agency outside and prior to the perceived configuration of things happening—it is not some independent "first cause"—but rather is a function of the creative and thus causal nature of the relations themselves. The originally militarist notion of causality captured in the term *shi* 勢 comes immediately to mind. *Shi* describes the always-particular and inclusive manifold of spatial, temporal, and existential factors as they unfold in an emerging situation. *Shi* is a calculus of differentials in configuration, momentum, timing, terrain, morale, equipment, logistics, and so on, that constitute the propensity of circumstances, and that can be calibrated and adjusted to produce welcome outcomes.

There is a fallacy in taking human nature as causal in the sense that it reduplicates itself in action—that is, the idea that our conduct is *ren* because we are potentially *ren*. Rather, habits of moral conduct and native conditions should be understood as symbiotic and mutually determining. When we ask "Which comes first, the chicken or the egg?" we have to allow that they come together or not at all. From the perspective of classical Western metaphysics, we might say that Chinese cosmology shaves with Ockham's razor not once, but twice. Chinese cosmology does not appeal to the notion of a transcendent and independent God as the independent causal source of the world, but begins from what is happening in the autogenerative world itself (*ziran* 自然). And Chinese cosmology does not appeal to an independent nature or soul as the source of human conduct, but begins from a phenomenology of what unfolds and aggregates as moral habits within human conduct itself. It is with this understanding of the Confucian relationally constituted person as a "human becoming" that we now turn to Confucian role ethics as concrete familial and communal guidelines for achieving consummatory habits of conduct, and to the alternative understanding of religiousness that emerges from them.

IV

Confucian Role Ethics

On the Source of "Principles" and "Virtues": Value as Growth in Relations

In guiding our actions, we are inclined to presume uncritically perhaps that because we have a word, we have a "thing": Not only does "courage" or "justice" have an immediate referent, but this referent is somehow independent of our actions, and thus has either causal status as a given antecedent to what we do, or a teleological status as a predetermined goal for our actions.[1] To the extent that we think of courage or justice as *principles*, there is a strong sense of antecedence, generality of application, and derivation. Indeed the idea of principle carries just such connotations: a basic source, an essence or determining characteristic, an original faculty or endowment, an originating or actuating or determining force, a higher-order norm from which lower and more specific rules of behavior are derived, a fixed or predetermined mode of action, an axiom of conduct.

But in fact, on reflection we can argue from a Confucian perspective that if courage or justice do have a referent, it is primarily as a generalization derived from acting courageously or justly within our family and community relations. Courage is an abstracted characterization of the unrelenting tenacity of this mother protecting her child from danger, and justice is the deliberate, circumspect evaluation of the applications of these students by this teacher. Rather than being fixed and retrospective, such principles point most concretely to the unfolding of complex configurations of always-unique, specific relations as they are informed by analogy with past experience. Putative "virtues" are in fact a virtuosity—a quality of conduct itself when it is informed by our best efforts at cultivation and personal growth, thereby making our actions efficacious and qualitatively productive.

As we saw earlier in chapter two, Tang Junyi takes a commitment to optimizing the interdependent and potentially productive relationships among "parts" and "totality"—better yet, among foci and their fields, or among ecologically situated "events" and their environments—as *the* distinguishing and most vital contribution of Chinese culture broadly. When this holistic, aesthetic vision of the mutuality and synergistic relations of particulars and totality that grounds Chinese cosmology is translated into the more concrete social and political arena of the human family and community, it becomes a celebration of the value of inclusive, consensual, and optimally productive cooperation as the ultimate source of personal, political, and religious satisfaction.

Value itself so construed is nothing more or less than enhanced worth in relations. The situated, situational, and prospective nature of values in the Confucian vision of the consummate life (*dao* 道) becomes apparent when we recognize that, rather than being grounded in and derived from antecedent principles, values are in fact simply characterizations made from everyday modalities of acting well. The ongoing refinement and enhanced worth of relationally constituted persons can only occur within the context of their shared activities and experience. And such conduct achieves greatest significance when it has been inspired by optimum consideration for relational growth.

In developing his version of a pragmatic ethics, John Dewey suggests that we use adverbs rather than nouns to express particular values as modalities of action. He would recommend that it is best to avoid describing values with substantive nouns such as "health" or "justice" or "courage" for example, where using nouns would tend to reify these values and invest them with an antecedent and causal status as an object of discourse. Instead he suggests that we use the adverbial form to return the discussion back to our continuing, concrete, and familiar life processes. For Dewey, to say that persons seek health or justice or courage is only to say that they are doing their best to live healthily or justly or courageously. While Dewey's suggestion has the merit of remaining within the constraints of English syntax, we might presume to take his observation one step further (and risk taking the grammar one step back) by recommending that the active and programmatic nature of values can best be expressed gerundively as "health-ing" and "justice-ing." By using a verbal noun that allows at once for the fluidity of action and the stability of personal dispositions or habits, we avoid the unwarranted implication that some notion of discrete agency can be separated from the shared actions we perform, and instead suggests that agency and action are simply two ways of looking at the same phenomenon. A corollary point to be made with respect to values that further refines Dewey's observation is that just as putative agents are an abstraction from an evolving matrix of active relations, the isolation and individuation of the values themselves as they become evident in the actions of persons also entails a process of abstraction from an always-complex and changing situation in which at any one time a broad field of such values is at play.

When we turn to Confucian role ethics, it certainly offers guidelines for conduct, but more than appealing to *abstract* principles or values or virtues, it looks primarily to the contours of our concrete familial and social roles for guidance, roles that are existentially more instructive than such abstractions. We have real intuitive insight into the role of brother or daughter from our lived experience. Role ethics offers guidance on how to behave most productively, and provides an explanation for proper conduct that allows for the inevitable complexity of human activities. By comparison with abstract principles, there is a vital sense of propriety in our concrete roles and relations that suggests to us quite specifically what we ought to do next.

As Confucius remarks:

The Master said, "Zilu, have you heard of the six problems that can attend the six ways of behaving properly?"

"No, I have not," replied Zilu.

"Sit down," said the Master, "and I will tell you about them. The problem with being fond of acting consummately (*ren* 仁) without due regard for learning and personal growth (*xue* 學) is that you will be easily duped; the problem with being fond of acting wisely (*zhi* 知) without due regard for such personal growth is that it leads to self-indulgence; the problem with being fond of making good on one's word (*xin* 信) without due regard for such personal growth is that it leads you into harm's way; the problem with being fond of being straightforward (*zhi* 直) in one's conduct without due regard for such personal growth is that it leads to rudeness; the problem with being fond of acting courageously (*yong* 勇) without due regard for such personal growth is that it leads to unruliness; the problem with being fond of acting firmly (*gang* 剛) without due regard for such personal growth is that it leads to rashness.²

We must understand that Confucius as he is portrayed in the *Analects* takes *xue* 學 to mean not just "learning," but more importantly, "learning as personal growth." Confucius is explicit in making a distinction between such personal growth and the more cognitive exercises we generally associated with learning in a passage that evidences the characteristically radial nature of such personal articulation from family relations to community more broadly:

> As a son and a younger brother, be reverent in familial relations at home and be deferential to elders in the community; be cautious in what you say and then make good on your word; love the multitude broadly and be intimate with those who are consummate in their conduct. If in so behaving you still have energy left, use it to improve yourself through more academic pursuits (*xuewen* 學文).³

Xue on the oracle bones is written as *[x]*, and is understood quite literally as joining hands to construct a house. The bronze script introduces the element "youth" (*zi* 子) as *[xi]*, both the locus of and the most critical time for such growth.⁴ The *Shuowen* lexicon associates *xue* 學 paronomastically with *jue* 覺: a cultivated and focused awareness. The process of *xue* requires the deepening of one's awareness as one lives one's network of relations, thereby enabling one to become an increasingly sensitive and responsive member of family and community. This being the case, we can see that any particular "virtue" such as wisdom or courage is a quality of conduct achieved within the specific transactions of enlightened and intelligent social living. In fact, respecting the specific and complex configuration of relations involved, such conduct might be more clearly and accurately referenced as this concerned parent "parent-ing," or this deferential son "son-ing" or this devoted friend "friend-ing." Principles and virtues and values are the abstract designators we give to the evolving significance of ongoing relations as they are achieved and embodied in our specific activities. Indeed, it is our lived roles and relations that are primary as those composite activities from which we abstract, generalize, and indeed simplify their otherwise complex content as principles, virtues, and values.

A Son Covers for His Father: And Being "True" Lies in Doing So

In order to illustrate the concrete locus of values in Confucian ethics, there is a much-cited passage from the *Analects* that suggests a clear contrast between a *post hoc* appeal to principle as a basis for adjudicating proper conduct, and the pressing need to continue to cultivate virtuosity in family relations as the ultimate ground of all familial, communal, and political morality. While on tour late in his life, Confucius travels from the state of Cai to visit the region of She in the state of Chu. The governor of the local county, knowing Confucius's reputation as a distinguished moralist and teacher, and wanting to impress him with the high ethical standards of the people under his jurisdiction, relates an incident that involves one particularly upright young man in his district known revealingly as "True Goody":[5]

> The Governor of She[6] in conversation with Confucius said, "In our village there is this 'True Goody.' When his father took a sheep on the sly,[7] he reported his father to the authorities."
>
> Confucius replied, "Those who are 'true' (*zhi* 直) in my village conduct themselves differently. A father will cover for his son, and a son will cover for his father. And being 'true' lies in doing so."[8]

The position that Confucius is advocating here is that a true and trusting relationship among members of a family is the fabric from which the norms of community, society, and ultimately polity draw their tensile strength.[9] He perceives quite plausibly that calling in the police is *not* what we would do in response to such a lapse on the part of a family member, but is something we would only do if at all as a last resort; initially at least we would almost surely try other means to remedy the problem. As far as our family is concerned, and very probably our neighbors and friends as well, there are priorities in our response to situations that require ingenuity and imagination.

What sheds light on this case while at the same time making the situation somewhat more complex, is the internal demand in Confucian role ethics to make the situation right by achieving optimal appropriateness in the particular situation (*yi*). To this end, "remonstrance" (*jian* 諫)—that is, the obligation that a child has to protest against and to rectify the conduct of an erring parent—has a prominent and crucial role in the Confucian literature on family reverence (*xiao* 孝). With this in mind, we would have to assume that the expectation of Confucius in his evaluation of this case would be that the concerned son in "covering for his father" would necessarily do his best to set the ledger right with any members of the community who had suffered loss on account of the conduct of his parent, and further, would do what is needed to return his father to the straight and narrow.

Confucian role ethics is not an abstract theory that provides principled moral judgments for those particular problematic situations we might encounter along the way, nor does it give primacy to developing a deliberate, rational means to achieve some moral end. In characterizing those general assumptions behind much ethical theorizing that preclude the consideration of family roles as relevant factors, Henry Rosemont and I have observed:

> If the dignity of *everyone* is derived from the (highly valued) qualities associated with this individualism—autonomy, equality, rationality, freedom—then it is just these qualities we must respect at all times, and hence gender, age, ethnic background, religion, skin color, and so on, should play no significant role in our decisions about how to interact with others. On this orientation it is thus incumbent upon us to seek universal principles and values applicable to all peoples at all times.... Only by divesting persons of any uniquely individuating characteristics can we begin to think of developing a theory of moral principles that will hold in all instances. With respect to family, this is precisely what we cannot do if we are even to attempt to formulate the relevant moral questions about loyalties and obligations coherently, for as soon as we use the expression "my mother" in a moral question, we are not dealing with an abstract, autonomous individual, but one who carried us, brought us into this world, nurtured and comforted us, giving of herself extraordinarily for our benefit. Thus to search for a universalistic principle of some sort in the Confucian writings is to try to square the circle, for Confucianism is paradigmatically

particularistic—resolutely particularistic—just as Kant, Bentham, and Mill endeavor to be universalistic. To seek a principled ground for moral judgments in the classical Chinese texts is, to our minds, like expecting a Kantian to take specific cultural differences into account as conditions that qualify his Categorical Imperative, when in fact the Categorical Imperative is the very test for principle as unconditional universal law. Stated succinctly, we cannot appeal to Western moral theory to adjudicate the decidedly Confucian problem of family loyalty versus loyalty to the state.[10]

Rather than appeal to some set of objective principles, then, Confucianism offers a way of trying to live consummately in family and community through achieving relational virtuosity (*ren* 仁) in one's conduct. Such a holistic vision of life within relationships requires the ongoing cultivation of an aesthetic, moral, and religious imagination that will enable one to pursue an optimal appropriateness in all that one does (*yi*). It is an attempt to use personal artistry in one's roles and relations to live the most significant life possible.

This being so, the Confucian problem in this passage is not a legal one that places an individual's conduct in tension with the laws of the state as a case of harboring a criminal or obstructing justice. The Confucian question is not "Is it just for a son to cover for a father who has committed a crime?" Rather, what is at issue is a matter of determining and acting upon those priorities that conduce to optimal social and political harmony. The question is: In the search for optimal social and political harmony, does loyalty to the family trump loyalty to the state? This concern is what the *Great Learning* has described metaphorically as setting the roots as a precondition for growing a luxurious canopy. Indeed, the focus is not upon the father as a discrete, autonomous individual perpetrating a crime against the state, but rather on what adjustments are necessary to "true" (*zhi*) the mutually constitutive father-son relationship when warped by such untoward circumstances. What should be done under the circumstances to redirect action and to ensure that the family, the community, and ultimately the state can continue to rely upon and "trust" this foundational relationship?

For the son, to "true" his relationship with his father requires the imagination necessary to be prospective and prescient in the thinking that informs his conduct. The character "true" *zhi* 直 occurs on the oracle bones as *[xii]* and on the bronzes as *[xiii]*, where the centrality of the "eye" element suggests the need for both insight and foresight in finding one's way. Indeed, the *Shuowen* lexicon defines *zhi* as "seeing properly" (*zhengjian* 正見). In addition, the character *zhi* carries with it a decidedly moral aspect in its immediate association with "moral excellence" (*de* 德), a character that on the Mawangdui bamboo strips is in fact written as 惪, constituted in this alternative graph of "true" (*zhi* 直) with "heartmind" (*xin* 心) beneath it. Again the moral connotation of *zhi* is apparent from its frequent use as a loan character for the cognate character "value" (*zhi* 值).[11] The assumption on the part of Confucius here would be that endorsing a litigious course of action on the part of a son as the most appropriate way to behave would not only be anathema to the interests of familial and communal harmony, but ultimately it would be detrimental to the prospects of a prosperous state. With *zhi* invoking the metaphor of being true to the moral "path or way" (*dao* 道) that allows the family to find its bearing, being "true" is the taxing job of accruing and exercising sufficient imagination to discern the best way to adjust the situation and to hold one's course.

We might take an analogous case perhaps more familiar in our modern world. If parents discover that their child has been shoplifting, what is the most efficacious response? One possible course of action in the service of justice would be for the parents to dial 911 and summon the police to apprehend the felon. They might then contact the local newspaper's city desk to cover the story. In so doing, they maintain their own innocence, and allow the proper authorities and the public to resolve the unfortunate situation by trying the offending child in the courts and in the press. This is certainly the best way to bring the criminal quickly and publicly to justice for all to see and to learn from. Surely there are laws against stealing. But what parent would really do this?

A more imaginative approach might be to rely upon shame rather than retribution to redirect the situation. More enlightened parents— parents who "see properly"—might accompany a wayward but otherwise good child who has done a bad thing back to the scene of the crime, and allow the child to negotiate the situation directly with the shopkeeper whose property has been stolen, with both parent and shopkeeper taking full advantage of the power of shame to reform the child's conduct. The outcome presumably would be to remedy the situation for the short term by restoring the property to its rightful owner and to secure their family and their community for the long term by not only educating the child, but also by reinforcing the communal solidarity of all of those concerned. Such a scenario is not only more creative; it has the huge virtue of approximating what we would actually do. It is in everyone's interest—the parent's, the child's, the shopkeeper's, and indeed the state's—that this case be resolved with the ingenuity necessary to make the best of a bad situation. And it is in no one's interest, because of a lack of foresight, to abandon a child to a slippery slope that might well lead ultimately to a lifetime of crime.

This more imaginative course of action would be a "father covering for a son." And from a Confucian point of view, given the always-collateral responsibilities of "family reverence" (*xiao*) and the obligation of the young to remonstrate (*jian*) with an erring elder, a son in "covering for a father" has no less a responsibility for securing an imaginative and appropriate remedy for a moral lapse than does the parent.

Since family feeling is the ground of Confucian role ethics, and since polity in this tradition is a direct extension of the family as quite literally "country-family" (*guojia* 國家), Confucius can further claim that being a responsible and productive member of one's family is tantamount to governing the country. This is the claim that Confucius intends when some mean-spirited person, aware of Confucius's life-long frustration at never having been appointed to any important political office, feigns surprise at Confucius's failure to secure a station appropriate to his gifts:

> Someone asked Confucius, "Why are you not employed in governing?"
> The Master replied, "*The Book of Documents* says: 'It is all in family reverence! Just being reverent to your parents and a friend to your brothers is carrying out the work of government.' In doing this I am engaged in governing. Why must I be employed in governing?"[12]

This passage can be easily misunderstood as minimalist—that is, each one of us in our families makes our own small contribution to the greater political order. I believe, however, that Confucius's point is quite the opposite. Most of the real significance of our political lives (and our religious lives too) transpires close to home. If we ask after the relative importance of the state and the family in effecting cosmic harmony, we must allow that family is the ultimate source and ground of political order, and in the absence of the flourishing family and the thriving community it enables, political order is a sham or worse. It is for this reason that any formal pretence to be a strong state independent of the thriving community is an empty abstraction: what Whitehead would call "misplaced concreteness."

Let me be clear on what Confucian role ethics asserts. Confucian role ethics would contend that those family roles and the extended relations we associate with community that designate a specific configuration of activity—the roles of father, mother, son, daughter, teacher, friend, and neighbor, for example—are themselves a normative vocabulary more compelling than abstract injunctions. Such roles recommend in the most concrete of terms an existentially informed disposition and the search for a course of conduct that is the ground of family and community life. In Confucian role ethics, "to mother" and "to neighbor" are not merely descriptive; they serve as ethical injunctions, and unlike abstract principles, they serve as concrete guidelines that help us to determine what to do next.

> Duke Jing of Qi asked Confucius about governing effectively. Confucius replied, "The ruler must rule, the minister minister, the father father, and the son son."
>
> "Excellent!" exclaimed the Duke. "Indeed, if the ruler does not rule, the minister not minister, the father not father, and the son not son, even if there were grain, would I get to eat of it?"[13]

Family and community relations as guidelines for conduct are a normative language that in application usually bring with them a degree of clarity and insight greater than that provided through an appeal to those simple norms or principles which in fact have been abstracted from the complexities of some prior concrete experience.

A Flourishing Harmony (*he* 和)

This is not to say that Confucian role ethics is without assets to deal with order at a more abstract level. But here again, in addition to sometimes appealing to the language of abstracted norms, we also find the Confucian texts invoking socially and aesthetically determined terms of art. The vocabulary that is most frequently used to express the more general, aggregated sense of human flourishing orchestrated out of these interpenetrating values are "harmonizing, harmony" (*he* 和) and "centering, equilibrium, focus, balance" (*zhong* 中). The kind of achieved "harmony" referenced by the term *he* 和 is not simply the mutual accommodation of difference that attenuates discord, but more importantly, the creative and productive outcome when such differences are coordinated to optimum effect. Indeed, the original character for "harmony" suggests that the desired outcome is to achieve and sustain a human and a cosmic "musicality." The composition of the earlier, more complex character for "harmony" (*he* 和) found on the oracle bones is *[xiv]* and on the bronzes is *[xv]*. This earlier graph 龢 is composed of a *yue* 龠 wind instrument constructed out of reed pipes, making the playing of music available as metaphor for understanding this sense of harmony.

The character *zhong* 中 meaning "centering, equilibrium" appears on the oracle bones as *[xvi]* and *[xvii]*, and on the bronzes as *[xviii]*. These graphs reference perhaps the two most common ways of assembling the people and of rallying the troops: The first way is by sight and the second is by sound. The *zhong* character depicts a banner or standard that would be hoisted in the market place as a visual signal for the people or for the troops to gather together. Another way of calling assembly for the people or the military implicated within the graph would be to sound a drum. The mouth of the drum 口 suspended on a stand is thus visually represented with the graph for *zhong* 中. As with "harmony" (*he* 龢) constructed with the *yue* wind instrument, *zhong* 中 in including a visual reference to the drum also has an immediate musical association.[14]

The *Zhongyong* appeals directly to "harmony" and "equilibrium" in its own iteration of the holistic and aspirational Confucian project of coordinating human relations with immediate repercussions for the natural world. The opening passage of this text traces cosmic flourishing back to the achieved harmony of human feelings:

> The condition when the feelings of joy and anger, grief and pleasure have yet to arise is called a nascent equilibrium (*zhong* 中); having arisen, that these feelings are then coordinated and brought into proper measure is called harmony (*he* 和). This notion of equilibrium is the great root of the world; harmony then is the advancing of the proper way (*dadao* 達道) in

the world. When equilibrium and focus are sustained and harmony is fully realized, the heavens and the earth maintain their proper places and all things flourish in the world.[15]

Stated more simply, when the expression of human feelings as the ultimate resource for achieving moral competence is orchestrated into a productive harmony, the Confucian vision of the consummate life is advanced, and all things in the world flourish. What needs to be emphasized here is the Confucian assumption that such human flourishing must be mediated through familial roles and relations for it to be genuine. It is the family that is the ultimate source and indispensable ground of an achieved propriety (*li*) in all of our roles and relations. As it states in the *Analects*:

> Achieving harmony (*he*) is the most valuable function of observing propriety in our roles and relations (*li*). In the ways of the Former Kings, this achievement of harmony by observing propriety in our roles and relations made them elegant, and was a guiding standard in all things large and small. But when things are not going well, to realize harmony just for its own sake without regulating the situation through observing propriety in our roles and relations will not work.[16]

Morality so understood describes that quality of conduct that makes relations stronger and thicker and more enduring. Without being properly situated within these roles and relations, actions are meaningless or worse. That is, a "harmony" that is effected by simply imposing external constraints as a means of enforcing order—the application of laws, edicts, principles, or rules—is dehumanizing to the degree that it precludes personal participation and confirmation. For example, thin dispositions that would otherwise be quite properly deemed lethargy, timidity, rowdiness, or rudeness by mediating them through appropriate relations can be elevated and transformed to express the important social values of deference, caution, bravery, and candor:

> The Master said, "Deference unmediated by observing propriety in our roles and relations (*li*) is lethargy; caution unmediated by observing propriety in our roles and relations is timidity; bravery unmediated by observing propriety in our roles and relations is rowdiness; candor unmediated by observing propriety in our roles and relations is rudeness.

Where exemplary persons are earnestly committed to their parents, the people will aspire to consummate conduct; where they do not neglect their old friends, the people will not be indifferent to each other."[17]

It is the proper mediation of conduct through the roles and relations of family and through the responsiveness such exemplary behavior inspires that invests these actions—deference, caution, bravery, and candor—with their socially redeeming significance and value.

Propriety in Roles and Relations (*li* 禮) as a Source of Face and of a Sense of Shame

Another way to identify the distance between Confucian role ethics and the more formalized and reductionistic principled- or virtue-based theories is to give an account of how in this holistic Confucian moral vision the particular, the informal, and the contextualizing aspects of experience, far from being discounted or marginalized, in fact take on a central importance. First, there is the aesthetic dimension that comes with a holistic understanding of human conduct in which all factors have more or less relevance in determining the moral worth of a course of action. It is because the vision of Confucian role ethics is concerned with coordinating the contribution of each aspect of experience in achieving the total harmonious effect that the language it appeals to is fundamentally aesthetic. As an example of this aestheticism, there is the perceived inseparable relationship between elegance and morality, and conversely, between vulgarity and immorality. On being asking about family reverence (*xiao*), Confucius insists that it cannot be captured by some set of prescribed activities. Indeed, he gives primacy to the manner and attitude with which actions are carried out rather than to the specific, formal actions themselves:

> The Master said, "Family reverence (*xiao*) lies primarily in showing the proper countenance. As for the young contributing their energies when there is work to be done, and deferring to their elders when there is wine and food to be had—how can merely doing these things be considered showing proper family reverence?"[18]

Conversely, since morality itself is nothing more than those modalities of acting that conduce to enhancing relations, any kind of conduct that has a disintegrative effect on the fabric of family or community is perceived to be fundamentally immoral. Lifestyle takes on crucial import when we consider the corrosive consequences to the community of those persons who live lives without style. Carelessness becomes of major concern when we have to worry about those persons who couldn't care less. And graciousness has gravity when we reflect on the relevance that charm and deportment have for an overall sense of fittingness and propriety. Morality is associated more with poise and deportment in our transactions with other people than it is with any formal correctness:

> Master Zeng said: "... There are three things that exemplary persons consider of utmost importance in their vision of the consummate life (*dao*): By maintaining a dignified demeanor, they keep violent and rancorous conduct at a distance; by maintaining a proper countenance, they keep trust and confidence near at hand; by taking care in their choice of language and their mode of expression, they keep vulgarity and impropriety at a distance. As for the details in the arrangement of ritual vessels, there are minor officers to take care of such things."[19]

The integrative nature of the moral experience means that a socially responsive "sense of shame" (*chi* 恥) is of high value in Confucian culture. As we have seen, shame is such a powerful expression of moral awareness that, when properly nurtured, can become a pervasive value that enables the community to be both inclusive and self-regulating (*Analects* 2.3). Shamelessness on the other hand is poison in the well, unleashing aberrant individuals to roam freely and to act arbitrarily without reference to the roles and relations that would properly locate them within their families and community. Such selfish individuals diminish in a dramatic way the communal solidarity on which the consummate life depends.

Confucius himself had a much-developed sense of shame. In reading the *Analects*, there is a tendency to give short shrift to the middle books nine through eleven that are comprised primarily of a series of intimate snapshots depicting the historical person, Confucius. If such personal information is taken into consideration at all, there is the tendency to deem it insufficiently philosophical to be relevant to his vision of the consummate life. In fact, in overlooking these very details we are in danger of missing the substance of Confucius's aspirations. At a general level, it is precisely these passages, remembering as they do the concrete moments in the life lived by Confucius himself, that are most revealing of the extent to which the appropriate conduct of a scholar-official participating in the daily activities of the court was at once formalized and intensely personal: the cut of his robes, the cadence of his stride, his keen sense of context and proprieties, his posture and facial demeanor, his profound expression of reverent attention, his tone of voice, his gestures of deference, even the rhythm of his breathing. We must not lose sight of the fact that Confucian role ethics ultimately and invariably has to do with specific persons in specific situations. This being the case, the deferential yet authoritative life habits of Confucius himself and the appropriation of this model by succeeding generations has immediate relevance as an object lesson in understanding the real workings of his role ethics:

> On passing through the entrance way to the Duke's court, Confucius would bow forward from the waist as though the gateway were not high enough. While in attendance, he would not stand in the middle of the entranceway; on passing through, he would not step on the raised threshold. On passing by the empty throne, his countenance would change visibly, his legs would bend, and in his speech he would seem to be breathless. He would lift the hem of his skirts in ascending the hall, bow forward from the waist, and hold in his breath as though having difficulty with his breathing. On leaving and descending the first steps, he would relax his expression and regain his composure. He would glide briskly from the bottom of the steps, and returning to his place, he would resume a reverent posture.[20]

From this passage and many others like it, it should be clear that achieving propriety in one's roles and relations does not reduce to generic, formally prescribed "rites" or "rituals" performed at stipulated times to announce status and to punctuate the seasons of one's life. The *li*—the expression of propriety through one's roles and relations—is more, much more.

The graph for *li* 禮 is found in a simpler form on the oracle bones as *[xix]* and on the bronzes as *[xx]*: the displaying of a ritual vessel containing two pieces of jade to seek blessings and good fortune.[21] Although clearly having a formal and a religious side that we will

[xix]

[xx]

explore in the final chapter of this book, still the preponderant weight of significance in the *li* as they came to define social life lies in their personal, informal, and particular aspects. They have a somatic dimension whereby body is often more effective than language in communicating the deference necessary to strengthen the bonds among the participants in the various communal life forms. Witness the way in which Confucius's body expresses *li* in his appearance at court recounted in the passage above. *Li* have a profoundly affective aspect wherein feelings suffuse and fortify the relational activities, providing the communal fabric a tensile strength that resists rupture. Refinement through the performance of *li* must be understood in light of the uniqueness of each participant engaged in the profoundly aesthetic project of becoming consummate as a person. *Li* is a process of personal articulation—the cultivation and expression of an elegant disposition, an attitude, a posture, a signature style, an identity. *Li* is a resolutely personal performance revealing one's worth to both oneself and to one's community, a public discourse through which one constitutes and discloses oneself qualitatively as a unique individual, a whole person, to the benefit of all.

Importantly, there is no respite; *li* requires the utmost and unrelenting attention in every detail of what one does at every moment that one is doing it, from the drama of the high court to the posture one assumes in going to sleep, from the reception of honored guests to the proper way to comport oneself when alone, from how one behaves in formal dining situations to appropriate extemporaneous gestures. One compelling image of Confucius is the display of his dedication to official duties even from his sick bed:

> When Confucius was ill, and his lord came to see him, he reclined with his head facing east, and had his court robes draped over him with his sash drawn.[22]

Indeed the studied image revealed in these middle pages of the *Analects* is of one person aspiring in the conduct of the largely routine events of daily life to express a virtuosity in his roles and relations that is sufficiently robust to transform and indeed to enchant the ordinary experiences of a life lived together with others.

Gerundive Persons as Evolving Configurations of Roles (*ren* 仁)

Chapter three above was devoted to the search for an appropriate language to express the Confucian notion of the relationally constituted "human becoming." Confucianism offers a holistic conception of cultivated personal conduct that requires a fundamentally aesthetic understanding of the family-grounded human experience as the artistry of finding optimally productive contextualization within one's roles and relations. We found that this Confucian notion of radically embedded and situationally responsive persons requires a focus-field rather than the more familiar individual-society, part-whole *gestalt* as its default language. The focus-field image, although perhaps not sufficiently vital and fluid to capture the Confucian personal dynamic, does at least allude to the holographic foregrounding-backgrounding activity required as we continuously adjust and consolidate ourselves as unique foci of dispositional relations within the extended field of this family and this community.

In exploring this Confucian conception of person as a configuration of relational activity, we were able to discover a degree of felicitous analogy with the Deweyan notion of "individuality"—the emergence of distinctive and distinguished persons through effective associated living. But while Dewey offers us this analog of a relationally constituted person, what makes the Confucian person profoundly different from Deweyan individuality is the pervasive force of family relations in Confucian role ethics. Foregrounding the family, we can say that the unity, integrity, and value of the family is a function of achieving the appropriate patterns of deference among the members that constitute the family. And foregrounding individual members of the family, we can say that the unity, integrity, and worth of particular persons is a function of coordinating effectively all of the various roles and relations that they live within family and by extension, community. One lives all of these roles and relations in every moment of one's life, and each role is present in the activities that are defining of every other role. In being a son to my mother and father, I am simultaneously making adjustments and growing in my relation as a brother to my younger sister and to my older brother. Indeed, it is an adaptive correlation of the demands and the rewards of these roles, even when conflicted and in tension, that gives me an increasingly focused, persistent identity as a person: a stability that others might regard as my personality and my character.

The Confucian moral vision is fundamentally one of personal growth: that is, becoming a consummate person (*ren* 仁), becoming a great person (*daren* 大人), becoming an efficacious person (*shanren* 善人), becoming a mature and complete person (*chengren* 成人), becoming an exemplary person (*junzi* 君子). As we have seen in chapter three, in the Confucian vocabulary itself, the primary locus and ground for the articulation of this relationally virtuosic person is expressed as *ren* 仁, and the root whence *ren* conduct develops is familial deference and respect for elders (*Analects* 1.2).

The reason I take the *Analects* as the primary reference and ultimate source for this definition of *ren* as consummate personal conduct is because the term is associated most closely with Confucius himself. The fact that Confucius is asked so often what is meant by the expression *ren* reflects the fact that he is reauthoring a previously obscure term for his own purposes, and that those protégés in conversation with him are not comfortable in their understanding of his neologism. Confucius's creative investment of new meaning in *ren* is borne out by a survey of its infrequent and relatively insignificant appearances in the earlier corpus. *Ren* does not occur in the earliest portions of the ancient canons at all, and only three times in the later parts. This unexceptional usage compares with 105 occurrences in the *Analects* alone in 58 of the 499 sections. The centrality of the notion of "consummate personal conduct" that begins with Confucius bears witness to first the qualitative, and only then the quantitative, understanding of person. That is, it is only through the cultivation of robust relations and a concomitant increase in self-esteem that an initially inchoate and unfocused manifold of relations can emerge over time as a distinct and distinguished individual.

[xxi]

[xxii]

Much is made of the relational implications of the character for *ren* 仁, constituted as it is by "person" (*ren* 人) and the number "two" (*er* 二). As remarked, prior to Confucius *ren* is relatively insignificant in the canonical literature, and it appears only rarely on the oracle bones and bronzes as *[xxi]* and *[xxii]* respectively. For the composition of this character, interesting speculations are being made on its form in the recent archaeological finds at Guodian where *ren* is constructed with the graphs *shen* 身, an impregnated body, with the heartmind radical *xin* 心 beneath it. Scholars have opined that such a graphic representation in expressing the kind of concern one would extend to a pregnant woman captures the soft, gentle, and intimate feelings—*ru* 儒—that are to be presumed as defining of the consummately human conduct we associate with the "gentrified literati learning" (*ruxue* 儒學) tradition.[23]

Ren is perhaps most commonly translated in the philosophical literature as "benevolence," and "humaneness." What might make "humaneness" seem a better translation than "benevolence" is that *ren* references one's entire personal behavior: one's cultivated cognitive, aesthetic, moral, and religious sensibilities as they are expressed through the conduct of the roles and relationships that in aggregate are defining of one's person. It is this "field of selves"—a matrix of significant relationships—that constitutes one as an irreducibly social person. *Ren* is not only intellectual and spiritual, but physical as well: one's posture and comportment, one's gestures and bodily communication. It can be argued that to translate *ren* as "benevolence" is to narrowly "psychologize" a much broader idea in a tradition that has had no need of the notion of *psyche* in its efforts to understand and refine the human experience. Although some notion of "benevolence" is certainly an important aspect of *ren*, taken as a standard translation it impoverishes the term by isolating one out of many moral dispositions at the expense of so much more that comes together in the complexity of becoming human.

But then again, "humaneness" has its own limitations as a rendering for *ren*. "Humaneness" might suggest a shared, essential, and precultural condition of being human owned by all members of the species—a given human nature. Yet *ren* does not come so easily. Far from being an essentially endowed potential, *ren* is what one is able to make of oneself given the interface between one's native, initial conditions and one's natural, social, and cultural environments. While we can all commit ourselves to *ren*, to actually become consummately *ren* is something rarely achieved. For Confucius, it is the hard-won culmination of an aesthetic project, and an unusual and most considerable accomplishment.[24] Certainly the human being at birth is an incipient locus and focus of constitutive familial relationships, and as such, has an initial disposition. But *ren* is first and foremost the process of "growing" (*sheng* 生) these relationships to become a vital, robust, and healthy participant in the human community. It is for this reason that Confucius—ever focused on discipline and education—would say that "human beings are similar in their initial dispositions (*xing*), but vary greatly by virtue of their habits."[25] Confucius is more interested in what we do concretely in aspiring after the consummate life than he is in grand metaphysical speculation directed at isolating some putative source of human morality in our initial conditions (*xing* 性) or in the numinous context within which we live our lives (*tiandao* 天道).[26]

There is another problem with "humaneness" as a translation of *ren*. Given that *ren* is generalized from the qualitative transformation of *particular* persons, it is made further ambiguous because it must be understood relative to the specific concrete conditions of those persons. *Ren* for this person is going to be different from *ren* for that person. This particularity of *ren* is further amplified when we consider that it is achieved through an appeal to and collaboration with environing models, and not through a compliance with principles as such (*Analects* 6.30, 13.1, 13.2, 13.4). There is no template, no formula, no ideal. Like a specific work of art, *ren* is a process of disclosure rather than closure, resisting fixed definition and replication. At the end of the day, recalling Tang Junyi's insistence that our understanding of what it means to become human is profoundly subjective and existential, *ren* for each of us is the challenge to aspire to become our own best thoughts.

Having emphasized its particularity, we must allow that there is certainly a more "objective" dimension to *ren*. *Ren* entails the "authority" that persons come to occupy in community by embodying in themselves a particular interpretation of the values and institutions of their tradition through aspiring to an optimal and elegant propriety in their roles and relations. Certainly achieving a robust propriety in one's roles is, by definition, a conservative process of appropriating and internalizing the tradition—that is, "of making the tradition one's own." But *li* as the institutionalized horizon of moral conduct is also whence alternative possibilities begin. In this sense *ren* is profoundly creative. The way of becoming human (*dao*), although passed on from generation to generation within the tradition, is by no means a given; *ren* conduct is "road-building," and requires continuous participation in a resourceful "authoring" of the culture for one's own place and time (*Analects* 15.29).

A contrast between top-down and impositional "authoritarian" order and the bottom-up, deferential sense of becoming "authoritative" in one's conduct is also salutary. Authoritative persons are models that inspire others who, in responding to this opportunity for growth, gladly and without coercion defer to such exemplars in the shaping of their own conduct. The prominence and visibility of *ren* conduct is captured in the *Analects* with the metaphor of the mountain: still, stately, enduring, a sacred and spiritual beacon, an iconic landmark for the local culture and community.[27]

Although remaining persuaded that the search for inevitably disappointing English translations of the central Confucian vocabulary must stand as a distant second priority to urging the student of Chinese philosophy to learn the original Chinese terminology, I am inclined to use "consummate person or conduct" as a tentative translation for *ren*. This is a deliberate choice. "Consummate" has the virtue of using the collective and intensive prefix "con-," denoting the sense of "together, jointly" that does justice to the irreducible relationality and thus particularity of *ren*. In addition, *summa* is that form of "completion" that suggests disclosure more than closure, a transactional maturation and fruition more than the actualization of some given potential. *Summa* is the highest efficacy in some particular achievement and not merely a replication of something previously accomplished, and as such, is high praise by the community for someone's particular attainment (*summa cum laude*).

Ren 仁 as the Expedient in the Way of Acting

We might claim that *ren* is what is most expedient by way of conduct—what is most appropriate to the purposes of one's actions. After all, "to expedite" is to facilitate an activity so that it can be performed most efficiently. And if the activity is becoming a person, then cultivating a *ren* disposition in one's actions is precisely what enables one to get the most out of one's experience. But the use of this word "expedience" prompted an avalanche of criticism when William James claimed that his pragmatic understanding of truth amounted to "the expedient in the way of thinking."[28]

Subsequently, "mere" expedience and "bald" expedience have been invoked frequently by critics to caricature James's pragmatism. Perhaps something can be learned about how *ren* assumptions differ from those that ground a foundational individualism if we ask: Whence arises the decidedly negative connotations that "expedience" has in reference to conduct?

The problem with the term "expedience" in common parlance is that it generally references one side of an exclusive self-other, means-end dualism. It is understood as promoting one's own interest at the expense of others, and as being driven by a concern for self-interest rather than for principle. Further, expedience is often assumed to advocate any means to a desired end that serves the urgency of one's needs.

But the "self-other" and "means-end" distinctions that would qualify the use of "expedience in conduct" have little relevance for the Confucian notion of *ren*. From the Confucian perspective in which persons are constituted by their relations and in which the goal of becoming a person is to become consummately so, these self-other and means-end distinctions have no purchase. That is, if the other who is constitutive of my own person does better, I do better as well. The teacher and the student become consummate teacher and student together, or not at all. And further, the Confucian would claim that "principles" are guiding cultural generalizations drawn from efficacious actions rather than antecedent, self-sufficient rules that can be applied as regulative standards to adjudicate conduct. This being so, expedient conduct is itself the ultimate and continuing source of principles rather than an offense against them. With respect to means and ends, in the Confucian tradition in which both the method and the ultimate purpose is consummatory personal conduct (*ren*), means and ends are inseparable and mutually entailing. We seek to act consummately (*ren*) in order to act consummately (*ren*). With these Confucian qualifications in hand, we can thus fairly claim that *ren* is indeed the expedient in the way of acting.

"Virtues" as "Virtuosity": The Optimizing of Meaning in Roles and Relations

Looking at our conventional discourse from a Confucian perspective, the main problem in the way we have come to think about virtues is the tendency to reify and "metaphysicalize" them and give them a life of their own, thus rendering them as one more iteration of what John Dewey has dubbed "*the* philosophical fallacy." In so doing, we take the fixed and final to come before experience (in our appeal to moral principles), we mistakenly take kinds and categories as an adequate expression of what are complex, relationally defined, social situations (in our appeal to virtuous individuals), and we think because we have abstract names we also have "things" that match up with them (in our appeal to virtues such as "courage" and "justice").

Given that Confucianism is fundamentally an aestheticism, it is not surprising to find that it uses language such as the "beautiful" (*mei* 美) and the "coarse and unseemly" (*e* 惡) to denote modes of conduct.[29] But *mei* 美 in classical Chinese means "beautiful" rather than "beauty" in referring to how certain relations come together within a specific context; it is not nominalized and entified to mean "beauty-in-itself." So too human actions become "virtuous" by reference to how they come together within a specific dynamic context rather than by being "virtues-in-themselves." Whatever we call virtue, then, is nothing more or less than a vibrant, situated, practical, and productive virtuosity.

What this means is that *ren* is not a specific virtue that can be named and analytically isolated as being defining of one's character any more than what it means to behave in a consummately humane way can be stipulated and replicated without reference to a specific situation. Rather, *ren* is generic as a cultivated virtuosity in role-specific dispositions that conduce to making any particular action optimally elegant and appropriate (*yi* 義), and thus rendering such an action a source of significance (*yi* 義) for all concerned. Hence, in one conversation, Confucius says: "Being firm, resolute, honest, and deliberate in speech is getting close to consummate conduct (*ren*)."[30] And in another encounter, he allows:

> A person who is able to carry five dispositions into practice in the world can be considered consummate (*ren*).... Deference, accommodation, making good on your word, diligence, and generosity. If you are deferential, you will not suffer insult; if accommodating, you will win over the many; if you make good on your word, others will rely upon you; if you are diligent, you will get results; if you are generous, you will have the goodwill to employ others effectively.[31]

What is telling in these alternative descriptions of *ren* conduct is the extent to which they characterize virtuosity in terms of effective relations. *Ren* is not *a* "good" but an efficacious "good at, good in, good to, good for, good with" that describes a relational dexterity within the unfolding of social experience. As "right" conduct, *ren* is "right on"—timely, and conducive to strengthening relations, and appropriate to a purpose. As "correct" behavior, it is a corrective—making those adjustments in relationships needed to maximize the shared possibilities available in the circumstances. *Ren* is not primarily a retrospective "what" but a prospective "how." And *ren* is not one's "intrinsic" worth alone, but necessarily includes what one means to and for others. By requiring that the quality of action be determined and evaluated relationally—that is, by asking after what persons do with their interdependence and mutuality both in terms of motivation and consequences—*ren* is the difference between efficacy and waste, between elegance and ugliness, between healthy relations and those that are injurious.

This relational responsiveness is what Confucius is referring to when he claims that "where one's purposes are set on consummate conduct, one can do no wrong," and that "the consummate person (*ren*) alone has the wherewithal to properly discriminate the better person from the worse."[32] He is observing that relationally aware and responsive persons are the foremost resource for and the best judges of consummate conduct because they are committed to doing what is most appropriate for everyone in the situation (*yi* 義) rather than just doing what is more narrowly to their own personal advantage (*li* 利).[33]

Ren is both antecedent and an outcome. As a transformative virtuosity, *ren* is antecedent to and evokes those specific actions that will satisfy the quality aspired to in concrete situations. It is not any specific kind of action; the situation is primary and will itself determine the most appropriate response. But *ren* requires a certain quality of action to satisfy it. For example, what would transform an act of boldness into one deemed courageous would be the way in which the action is situated relationally and how it plays out in terms of both motivations and consequences: Whose interest is the action on the behest of, whose interest does it serve, and what is the quality of relatedness it enhances? Its moral value arises from the situated appropriateness and achieved significance of the action (*yi*):

Zilu asked, "Does the exemplary person give first priority to being bold (*yong* 勇)?"

"In fact," the Master replied, "the exemplary person gives first priority to appropriate conduct (*yi* 義). An exemplary person who is bold yet lacking in a sense of appropriateness will be unruly, while a petty person of the same cut will be a thief."[34]

The Beginnings of Moral Competence: Family Roles as Ethical Injunctions

In the *Analects* we find repeatedly the same radial structure of personal cultivation that is expressed in the *Great Learning*, where the vision of the consummate life emerges from immediate family relations and is then, as a direct extension of family roles, extrapolated to inform one's dealings within the community more broadly. Indeed, just as family is the pervasive metaphor in the Confucian worldview, familial reverence (*xiao*) is both the means and the end as well as the inspiration for and the consequence of Confucian learning. Just as one acts consummately in order to become consummate, one *xiao*'s in order to be *xiao*. Given the central role of the family in Confucianism, appropriate family feelings are the ground from which our pathways through life emerge. The expectation repeated several times in the *Analects* is that one embarks on this journey with one's parents, and never during their lifetime ventures far from them either in person or in spirit.[35] The Confucian life is a family life lived together.

The *Xiaojing*, or *Classic of Family Reverence*, like the *Analects*, begins by establishing the centrality of familial reverence in the project of becoming consummately human. The opening passage that seeks to set the theme for this canonical document states clearly that family feeling is the ground of both personal worth and education: "'It is familial reverence (*xiao*),' said the Master, 'that is the root of excellence (*de*), and whence education (*jiao*) itself is born.'"[36]

The character translated "familial reverence" (*xiao* 孝) is constituted by the graph for "elders" (*lao* 老) and that for "son, daughter, child" (*zi* 子), encouraging an existential understanding of what this particular combination of images would convey. Like *ren*, which requires us to access and to build upon our own existential sense of what it would mean to become consummate as a "person" in our relations with others, *xiao* too has immediate reference to our lived experience. In fact, if we examine the earliest form of the character "elders" (*lao* 老) found on the oracle bones, it depicts a old person with long hair leaning on a walking stick as *[xxiii]* that later in the Small Seal script becomes stylized as *[xxiv]* . In comparing this character for "elders" with the earliest form of the character for "family reverence" (*xiao*) found on the oracle bones as *[xxv]* , the image of a youth has taken the place of the walking stick as the source of support for the elders.

In the *Xiaojing* passage cited here, Confucius in correlating family reverence and education is taking advantage of the cognate relationship between the character for "education" (*jiao* 教) and that for "familial reverence" (*xiao* 孝), where the graph for "education" (*jiao* 教) simply adds on the "branch or stick" (*zhi* 支) radical to *xiao*. This character *jiao [xxvi]* as it appears on the oracle bones seems to depict a familiar if no longer popular image of education as being best promoted through a timely correlation between hand, stick, and pupil.[37] The classical *Shuowen* lexicon defines "education" (*jiao*) transactionally and generationally as "that which those above disseminate and those below emulate."[38] Importantly the character for education (*jiao*) itself underscores the perceived centrality of familial reverence to the actual content and purposes of education, just as the cognate relationship that both of these characters share with the term "emulating" (*xiao* 效) emphasizes the modeling role that the older generation has in instructing its progeny.

In this first chapter of the *Classic of Family Reverence*, the content of "family reverence" is again defined in a way that recalls the radial and aspirational structure of the *Great Learning* by beginning most concretely from attention to one's own physical well-being and then extending this concern outward to achieving distinction for one's progenitors:

> Vigilance in not allowing anything to do injury to your person is where family reverence begins; distinguishing yourself and walking the proper way (*dao*) in the world; raising your name high for posterity and thereby bringing esteem to your father and mother—it is in these things that family reverence finds its consummation. This family reverence then begins in

service to your parents, continues in service to your lord, and culminates in distinguishing yourself in the world.[39]

The vocabulary surrounding this central notion of "family reverence" provides concrete guidelines for moral conduct by acknowledging the practical, situated, interpenetrating, and dispositional nature of all goods, values, and virtues. While we do have a compelling sense of how to act as mothers to our sons and uncles to our nieces, including acting courageously to defend them and treating them justly, we must struggle to find our way when we try to act on "courage" or "justice" as abstract virtues. In seeking directives for moral conduct, the ambiguity that invariably attends our practical understanding of complex family relations is somewhat offset when we attempt to identify, stipulate, and apply moral principles that,while seeming to be more straightforward, are in actual deployment anything but clear.

A persistent obstacle to a deeper understanding of *xiao* arises from a common and simplistic equation between filial reverence and obedience.[40] It is important to note that in promoting the family as the pervasive model of order, the Confucian worldview does not accept that hierarchical social institutions are necessarily pernicious, or that simple egalitarianism should have an uncritical value. As a moral vision drawn from the unfolding of the actual lived human experience, Confucianism has to allow for persistent disparities among generations within the structure of family life. Indeed, Confucianism in fact relies upon hierarchy and the appropriate patterns of deference that define it as a necessary condition for achieving family solidarity. After all, it is not the inevitability of hierarchy that compromises relationships, but coercion within that hierarchical structure. Relations suffer from a diminution in their significance when, from whatever source, a disintegrating coerciveness and oppressive unilaterality contaminate them.

Xiao that is grounded in the bottom-up deference and respect children owe to their elders must be distinguished clearly from *paterfamilias* and the *patria potestas*—the paternal top-down, unilateral power and privilege that we associate with Roman culture. Indeed family relations, like all relations within a Chinese ecological cosmology, are collateral. The elderly, having taught the subsequent generation by their own example, in their own time certainly bask in the deference of the younger generation, but the expectation is that members of the younger generation also derive considerable pleasure from attending to the needs and feelings of their seniors from whom they have learned so much:

> Expressing propriety in one's roles and relations is simply a matter of attentive respect (*jing* 敬). Thus, the son finds pleasure (*yue* 悦) in respecting his father; the younger brother finds pleasure in respecting his elder brother; the minister finds pleasure in respecting his lord; and all of the people find pleasure in respecting the Emperor. Those who are respected are few, but those who find pleasure in showing this respect are legion. This is what is called the vital way (*dao*).[41]

Existentially we can understand that the thoughtful daughter in caring for her aged mother is more likely to construe this obligation as an opportunity rather than as a burden.

An important consideration in understanding the workings of family reverence is that instruction is to be conducted through modeling rather than by fiat. The elder generation teaches their children appropriate deference most effectively by demonstrating the same quality of respect in their interactions with the grandparents of their children, and in the remembrances offered to the ancestors of their children as well. Children come to emulate what transpires among their more senior relatives within the home and community.

But deference is only the more obvious part of the equation, having as it does a sometimes overlooked complement. At times being truly filial within the family, like being a loyal minister within the court, requires remonstrance (*jian* 諫) rather than compliance. And this remonstrance, far from being discretionary or optional, is considered a stern obligation. In the *Classic of Family Reverence*, for example, Confucius responds impatiently to his student's suggestion that family reverence can be reduced to simple obedience:

> Zeng asks: "I would presume to ask whether children can be deemed filial simply by obeying every command of their father?"

> "What on earth are you saying? What on earth are you saying?" said the Master. "... If confronted by reprehensible behavior on his father's part, a son has no choice but to remonstrate with his father, and if confronted by reprehensible behavior on his ruler's part, a minister has no choice but to

remonstrate with his ruler. Hence, remonstrance is the only response to immorality. How could simply obeying the commands of one's father be deemed filial?"[42]

In the *Xunzi* too, much of an entire chapter is devoted to the complexity of these relations, challenging any simple reading of family reverence or loyalty to one's lord as blind obedience. It provides many ready examples of where it is in fact *un*filial and *dis*loyal to comply uncritically with the demands of one's senior or superior.[43]

Remonstrance is an inclusive and reflexive concern; it is focused on the "we" in enjoining us to ask "How can *we* do better?" As such, it must be distinguished from the kind of protest that is exclusive and dialectical—an objection directed at "you" alone. Of course, to be effective in altering patterns of behavior, such remonstrance must be pursued with enormous sensitivity and tact, and with considerable imagination as well. Yet such an obligation to question authority also has its limits, and is never a warrant to pit one's own judgment stubbornly against that of one's elders. Just because a child has the responsibility to remonstrate with the parent, it does not follow that the child invariably has on offer advice that should be heeded. As Confucius remarks:

> In serving your father and mother, remonstrate with them gently. On seeing that they do not heed your suggestions, remain respectful and do not act contrary. Although concerned, voice no resentment.[44]

A second important stratum of familial bonding is captured in the expression, "fraternal deference" (*ti* 悌): that is, the respect expressed within the same generation by younger brothers for their elder siblings. Indeed, similar to *xiao* as the appropriate relationship between elders and children, this fraternal attitude is thought to be so natural and obvious that the original graph expressing it is composed of nothing more than "younger brother" (*di* 弟), with the later, more complex graph combining younger brother with "thoughts and feelings" (*xin* 心) as *ti* 悌. The expectation is that these patterns of fraternal deference first nourished within the immediate family will overflow such initial boundaries and ripple out into the extended community to consolidate it as a super-family:

Since exemplary persons are respectful and impeccable in their conduct, and are deferential to others and observe propriety in their roles and relations, everyone in the world is a brother. Why would exemplary persons worry over having no brothers?[45]

A third stratum of family reverence that is itself an extension of both family reverence (*xiao*) and fraternal deference (*ti*) is a devotion to a circle of friends (*you* 友) that range across generational bounds, and that require responses analogous to those of family members.

The family is the point of embarkation; a prosperous and thriving world is the goal. The use of roles as an existentially informed and morally invested vocabulary bridges the divide between family, community, and state. The expectation in this radial and organic conception of relational order is that flourishing families are the direct and immediate source of the flourishing state, and, as Confucius makes clear, the state is dependent upon these families as its resource for maintaining its strength and equilibrium (*Analects* 2.21, see also 2.20). In the *Classic of Family Reverence*, so much is made of the direct line between family reverence and political loyalty (*zhong* 忠) that many contemporary commentators from their perspective of having lived though several generations of Marxist and Maoist ideology have argued (wrongly I would suggest) that the primary although oblique purpose of this text has been to indoctrinate the population in its proper submission to its rulers.[46]

As we have seen, the ultimate source of consummate conduct (*ren* 仁) is immediate family relations. When the quality of these relations is pursued broadly within the social and political forum, consummate conduct becomes exemplary for those in the community who would defer to it. Consummate conduct (*ren*) is thus perceived as a necessary condition for exemplary persons (*junzi*).[47] And becoming exemplary as a person, like becoming consummate, is irreducibly collaborative, dependent as it is upon a correlation with effective models rather than with compliance with abstract principles:

The Master remarked about Zijian, "He is truly an exemplary person (*junzi*). If Lu had not other exemplary persons, where could he have gotten this from?"[48]

A Preemptive Vision of the Consummate Life

There are of course different ways of conceiving the consummate life. A traditional occupation of moral philosophy has been to discover some ostensible fixed point of morality, some bottom line—a self-evident and irrecusable principle, or an ideal pattern of life, or a faculty of will or reason or both, or a natural law under which all other criteria can be subsumed. The next step is to clarify this precept, to defend it against all comers, and then to proceed to apply it to particular cases for their resolution. In this familiar idealization of the consummate life, the principle precedes the application to particular cases, and comes into play to solve moral issues as they arise. Principle must thus wait upon moral problems for its proper function.

Confucian role ethics does not start from an attempt to isolate, identify, and explain some causal factor in moral action: some originative principle or agency or faculty. Rather, Confucian role ethics begins by considering what is happening, and ends by trying to make what is happening happen better. In Confucian role ethics, the moral excellence of consummate conduct (*ren*), like a work of art, is a specific expression of virtuosity and imagination assessed as a quantum of satisfaction, and it is only in that sense and against that measure that it can be evaluated in some degree by applying the general terms of right or wrong, correct or incorrect. At the same time, far from entailing a strict application of some predetermined and self-sufficient moral principle to difficult situations, *ren* accumulates as a reservoir of moral meaning that is embodied in people and that elevates and transforms the human experience. Confucius is explicit in identifying this achieved sense of belonging as the vital difference between a deference-patterned community with its self-regulating, non-coercive structure and an authoritarian society governed by the rule of law:

> The Master said, "Lead the people with policies and keep them orderly with penal law, and they will avoid punishments but will not develop a sense of shame. Lead them with excellence and promote social order through the attainment of propriety in their roles and relations and they will develop a sense of shame, and moreover, will order themselves."[49]

Ren is a moral artistry that enhances the quality of the community as a whole. By disposing persons in community to develop a shared elegance in their various undertakings, *ren*'s function is specifically to preempt the emergence of morally deficient situations. Ideally, with *ren* as a communal aspiration, only occasionally and incidentally when such habits of conduct fail to prevail does a situation arise that requires deliberation on specific problems. In service to such an ideal, Confucius looks to a community that aspires to rise above any appeal to the rule of law:

> The Master said, "In hearing cases, I am the same as anyone. What we must strive to do is to rid the courts of cases altogether."[50]

We might extrapolate from this passage to infer that appeal to the application of a creed of moral rules like the appeal to law is in itself an admission of communal failure—too little too late. There is more justice to be found in creating a social fabric that precludes abusive situations than in punishing perpetrators for what is deemed their unjust actions.

Of course, *ren* understood as relational virtuosity has an immediate correlation with living wisely (*zhi* 知), and so it ought to come as no surprise that these two terms, like the rain water that shapes the mountains and the mountains that occasion the rain, are never far apart in the Confucian vocabulary:

> The Master said, "The wise (*zhi* 知) enjoy water; those consummate in their conduct (*ren* 仁) enjoy mountains. The wise are active; the consummate are still. The wise find enjoyment; the consummate are long-enduring."[51]

For Confucius, "Consummate persons (*ren*) find satisfaction in acting consummately; wise (*zhi*) persons flourish in it."[52]

The character *zhi* 知, with or without the "speaking" (*yue* 曰) or "sun, day" (*ri* 日) signifier[53] beneath it as *zhi* 智, is usually translated as "knowing, knowledge, wisdom." *Zhi* 知 also means "an intimate or friend," thus putting a human face on what it means to know as "a pattern of relations one can trust in" that allows the community to live wisely together. In analyzing the etymology of the character *zhi* 智 as it appears on the oracle bones *[xxvii]*, one version has been interpreted as a big person handing wisdom down to the younger generation both orally and on written documents. On other oracle bones *[xxviii]* and some of the later bronzes *[xxix]*, 智/知 is composed of an arrow (*shi* 矢)

and a mouth (*kou* 口).⁵⁴ This "mouth" element and other related ways of indicating communicating such as "speaking" (*yan* 言), "showing" (*shi* 示), "listening" (*er* 耳), and "thinking and feeling" (*xin* 心) appear in many, if not most, of the key philosophical terminologies in classical Chinese philosophy. Together with the "speaking" (*yue* 曰) semantic indicator in "wisdom" (*zhi* 智), this association with speaking reflects the importance of the social, communicative aspect of knowing. In fact, the distinguished philologist, Bernhard Karlgren, perhaps persuaded by some of the oracle bone variants, speculates that the "arrow" element in the character *zhi* was originally "persons" (*ren* 人), which if true reinforces the sense that *zhi* entails a sociology of knowledge rather than any solitary knower.⁵⁵ Given the irreducibly social character of the Confucian person, the locus of knowing is not the individual knower, but a knowing community wherein knowledge as an applied wisdom is perceived as an immediate resource for communal happiness.

This social aspect of *zhi* leads to a second observation: *Zhi* is meliorative—it seeks to make the world better. Confucius observes:

> Cherishing it is better than just knowing it, and finding enjoyment in it is better than just cherishing it.⁵⁶

As suggested here, *zhi* certainly has a cognitive dimension. But the expectation is that this cognitive capacity must be extended and cultivated into a quality of communing that is productive of human happiness. The kind of knowledge that is directed and purposeful has privilege over simple cognition, and that kind of knowledge that actually conduces to communal enjoyment is better yet. If we were to take liberties with the last proposition of Spinoza's *Ethics* that reads: "Blessedness is not the reward of virtue, but is virtue itself," we might say that happiness is not the reward of living wisely, but is wisdom itself. Said perhaps more clearly, rather than taking happiness to be the goal of living wisely, we might say that happiness is the affective character of wise living.

The classical Chinese language does not distinguish between "knowledge" and "wisdom." In the absence of a severe theory/praxis and self/other dichotomy, the assumption is that "knowledge" must be authenticated in communal action for it to qualify as knowledge. It must be practically efficacious. Since *zhi* has this important pragmatic entailment, we might understand this kind of "wisdom" more fully as "intelligent social practice." And since *zhi* involves practice, it is always a localized knowledge, a situated wisdom. There is no putative "view from nowhere," no "God's eye view" that would provide a strictly "objective" perspective. This being the case, knowing a world is reflexive and evaluative: It is to recommend this world from this point of view.

We can say that "knowing" thus understood as intelligent social practice is not only informative, but also has performative force. "Knowing" does something; it changes the world. In this sense, *zhi* might also be translated as "realizing" in order to highlight this sense of "making the desired outcome real"—that is, bringing a particular world into being. Knowing is a normative world-making. Again, *zhi* has a perlocutionary force: It entails an epistemology of feeling. "Knowing" has a direct and significant effect on the feelings, beliefs, and the mood of those who come to know each other empathetically. Such knowledge quite literally changes their hearts as well as their minds.[57]

As we have seen, the Chinese epistemic vocabulary suggests "mapping out" and "making one's way" (*dao*) as its dominant image. The language of knowing is to read the signposts as we walk together in the proper direction. This sense of mapping carries over into modern Chinese in which the expression for "I know" is quite literally "I know the way" or "I am walking the way" (*wo zhidao* 我知道), suggesting both a specific bearing and how best to get there. To know is to be cognizant of prevailing conditions, to have the imagination to see their possibilities, and through relational virtuosity (*ren* 仁) within one's own community, to have achieved the deference necessary to rally support behind and enthusiasm for a chosen future. "To know" in this classical Confucian world is indeed a source of a joyful wisdom. And the assumption is that such social intelligence, broadly diffused, will in important measure preclude the hard cases that require ethical deliberation and its attendant appeal to regulative ideals.

Importantly, in the transitive "I know the way" (*wo zhidao*), "the way" (*dao*) is not the "object" of knowledge as such, but has a real subjective dimension. It is a term like "life" or "history" or "experience" that does not resolve into dualisms. *Dao* is a qualitative way of conducting one's life in the world that entails both subject and object, and the attributes of the subject as well as the modality of the actions being carried out. *Dao* defies Aristotle's categories, having as much to do with the conditions of the subject as with the object, and having as much to do with the quality of understanding as it does with the conditions of the world as understood. Knowing tells us as much about the *ren* quality of the person who "knows" as it does about something known, as much about a particular disposition to act as it does about the modality of acting itself.

An Explanatory Vocabulary for Confucian Role Ethics

We have seen that *ren* 仁 is a cultivated disposition to seek optimal meaning within the manifold of family-grounded relations defining of any situation, and as such, is frequently associated with a socially productive wisdom (*zhi* 知). The *Analects* provides us with an explanatory vocabulary for understanding how *ren* eventuates in the moral growth of persons and their communities, and how the aggregating growth over time produces an *ethos*—a persistent communal ethic and cultural identity. At issue in the Confucian literature is how we might best proceed to make the most of a situation. How do we use the human resources that can guide conduct wisely to get the most out of our conditions? And what are the long-term outcomes of personal growth for the community and for the culture?

We begin from the moral uncertainty that attends all of the human experience. There is truly a "momentousness" to the vision of a consummate life both in the sense of the need for an unrelenting awareness in every moment of experience, and of the tranformative significance that such an awareness engenders. As Confucius says:

> There is nothing that I can do for people who are not constantly asking themselves: "What to do? What to do?"[58]

Each actual situation presents its own configuration of relations and conditions that need to be inventoried and assessed with discernment. But beyond the given facticity of any state of affairs, the actual situation also offers a range of possibilities for further growth, the scope of which is dependent upon the degree of imagination available to conjure forth what might be optimally appropriate, and upon our quality of responsiveness. Each encounter is unique, and requires a quantum of moral intelligence to be brought to bear in order to maximize its possibilities. The centrality of moral imagination is vital because some responses are always going to be better than others. This graduated differential among possibilities means that, as a counterweight to merely habituated responses, every moment requires keen attention to alternative possibilities, the exercise of an informed judgment that secures the best among them, and sufficient moral motivation to realize this optimum possibility.

Confucius's holistic vision of the consummate life requires unremitting attention in all of our concrete situations in order to find the most productive way forward. The demands of the consummate life are unrelenting. There are no moral holidays for *ren* conduct. Indeed, it is because of Yan Hui's capacity to sustain this attention to achieving *ren* in all of his activities that Confucius lavishes praise on his favorite student:

> With my student, Yan Hui, he could go for several months without departing from consummate thoughts and feelings; as for the others, only every once in a while might consummate thoughts and feelings make an appearance.[59]

Whatever compass and capacity one is able to achieve in one's fondness for learning, *ren* conduct requires that such learning be made relevant to what is immediately at hand:

> Learn broadly yet be focused in your purposes; inquire with urgency yet reflect closely on the question at hand—consummate conduct (*ren*) lies simply in this.[60]

Shu 恕: "Putting Oneself in the Other's Place"

On an occasion when Confucius claims that the conditions of his "way" (*dao*)—his vision of the consummate life—are bound together on a single, continuous strand, one of his senior protégées, Master Zeng, then defines this thread for the other students in attendance:

> The moral vision of the Master is doing your utmost (*zhong* 忠) and putting yourself in the other's place (*shu* 恕), nothing more.[61]

On another occasion, making *shu* even more primary, Confucius identifies *shu* as "the one expression that can be acted upon until the end of one's days."[62]

There can be no question about the central importance of *shu* in the Confucian ethical vocabulary. *Shu* expresses both moral perplexity and the creative search for the most appropriate response. *Shu* is defined frequently in the classical texts and in the *Shuowen* lexicon by reference to *ren*, "consummate conduct," as the desired outcome of *shu*. The association between *shu* and *ren* is one of function. Just as *ren* is analogical—a coordination of both similarity and difference in one's roles and relations—so too is *shu* a matter of correlating one's own conduct with the behavior of others.

The centrality given to *shu* respects the unparalleled importance that imagination plays in the productive correlating of one's conduct and in the refining of one's moral judgment. Imagination is not invoked as supplemental or subsidiary or remedial, but as an empathetic capacity drawing on all of one's resources that require education and nurturance. Like any aesthetic judgment, imagination is an attempt to correlate specific details with the totality of the effect achieved within the circumstances as a whole, and in so doing, to broaden the context for and depth of moral consideration.

Shu has the meaning of "generous" and "indulgent," and has been translated within the philosophical literature variously as "altruism" (Wing-tsit Chan), as "reciprocity" (Tu Wei-ming and Raymond Dawson), as "consideration" (Waley), as "mutuality in human relations" (Fingarette), as "understanding" (Slingerland), and as "using oneself as a measure in gauging the wishes of others" (Lau).[63] That *shu* 恕 is an "other-regarding" generosity that entails analogical projection is clearly borne out by the etymology of the character, constituted by the cognate character, *ru* 如, meaning "as to, like, as if, to resemble" and *xin* 心, "heartmind." *Ru* 如 occurs in the oracle bones as *[xxx]*, interpreted as one person being questioned by another.[64] That is, *shu* is consideration: a thoughtful and heartfelt deference to others in what we do. This notion of analogical deference is also suggested in the cognate *ru* 汝—"you."

Shu contrasts sharply with more abstract and calculative analytic or theoretical strategies for determining moral conduct. Understood as "putting oneself in the other's place," it is the most fundamental gesture of a concrete, contextualizing moral disposition. It entails a recognition of the importance of "deference" both in the sense of deferring action until we overcome uncertainty in our moral inquiry, and in the sense of taking under consideration the interests of others in that process.

Shu is a fundamentally aesthetic disposition initially shaped within the *xiao-* 孝 and *ti-* 悌 governed family bonds where one's "person" emerges in the process of striving to optimize concrete roles and relations—this grandson responding to this grandmother, taking her both as an object of his deference and as a resource for his own personal growth. In the fullness of time, *shu* is then extended as a quality of responsiveness in shaping and deepening relations outside of the home. "Putting oneself in the other's place" (*shu*) is thus an omnipresent and indispensable disposition for living life responsively and thoughtfully.

Shu is prompted by uncertainty—a perplexity in how to respond in a particular situation. It then requires a conjuring forth of how the alternative possibilities one can imaginatively construct might play themselves out. Finally it eventuates in crafting what one determines to be the most appropriate disposition for conduct. One shapes a response through a process of analogical thinking, taking the present situation and associating it with other remembered or imagined correlates. We might summarize this process by saying that *shu* is a contextualized doubt in search of a guiding idea to stabilize one's actions. *Shu* at its best requires a keen memory that recalls analogous situations, a penetrating intelligence that is able to make the most felicitous correlations, and a creative imagination that can provide a serial rehearsal of possible scenarios in anticipation of their consequences. This analogical process is captured in a much-cited passage in the *Analects*:

> Correlating one's conduct with what is near at hand can be said to be the way of becoming consummate in one's conduct.[65]

There is a role for cognition and deliberation in *shu* certainly, but we do not want to overly rationalize this process. *Shu* requires a holistic responsiveness. With *shu* there is perhaps an even more central role for an affective inquiry—a knowing through feeling—that requires a weighing of the circumstances with empathy and concern. Just as a critical skepticism can become a matter of intelligent habit, so too can an empathetic responsiveness to others become a sedimented, spontaneous pattern of compassionate conduct. In fact, the evolution of a *shu* habitude lies in its potential to grow from a more deliberative exercise to become a kind of extemporaneous, unselfconscious moral artistry in one's interpersonal activities.

Certainly one of the most revealing passages in the canonical literature that stresses the central place of artistry and imagination in Confucian role ethics is the *Zhongyong* elaboration on this notion of *shu*:

> The Master said, "The vision of the consummate life (*dao*) is not at all remote. If someone considers this consummate life to be something that is distant and inaccessible, they have taken a wrong turn. In the *Book of Odes* it says:
>
> > In hewing an axe handle, in hewing an axe handle—
> > The model is not far away.[66]
>
> But in grasping one axe handle to hew another, if one only looks obliquely at the axe handle in one's hand, the two handles still seem far apart. Exemplary persons (*junzi*) in taking one person to work upon another relent only after having improved upon them. Putting oneself in the place of others (*shu*) and doing one's best on their behalf (*zhong*) is not straying far from the proper way. 'Do not treat others as you yourself would not wish to be treated.'"[67]

The vision of the consummate life (*dao*), far from referencing something distant and obscure, emerges out of the exercise of *shu* and *zhong* in the ordinary business of the day. This passage and its image of the process of shaping an axe handle is hugely instructive. First, the proper way of conducting oneself always emerges analogically from those resources close at hand—from what is immediately available in the particular, concrete circumstances. Still, there is nothing casual about this process. Although the pattern of the axe handle is close, the critical distance between the model and the product, between the established pattern and the particular axe handle that is presently being fashioned, can only be closed through painstaking scrutiny and resolve. The existing axe handle is both exemplar and instrument. The new and always-unique axe handle is not only hewn on the model of the existing one, but further, the existing axe handle itself is the means that is used to shape the emerging product, only to produce an instrument that will itself serve as a model for others. In this example of crafting an axe handle, the formal and efficient causes are one and the same, collapsing the familiar distinction between means and ends. Consummate conduct effects the desired end of consummate conduct by itself being consummate.

The dynamics of analogizing between the existing pattern and the newly fashioned article when applied to the irreducibly social way of becoming human is captured conceptually by *shu*. First, in our interactions, we must not look askance at each other (*ni* 睨). We must get beyond viewing each other obliquely and with distrust. In the mutual shaping that occurs through both patterns of deference and the modeling that such patterns entail, we require the utmost focus and concentration and the fullest application of all of our resources: our memory and our intelligence as well as our imagination. In the human world, the conduct of one person serves as a model that shapes the conduct of others, where that process of being shaped eventuates in consummate persons who will in their turn shape others. In all of this, the means and the ends are the same. We act consummately in order to act consummately.

There is a further point with regard to deference that can be inferred from this *Zhongyong* text. In this passage and in the *Analects* too, *shu*, "putting oneself in the other's place," is given an alternative characterization: *Shu* is defined negatively as "do not impose on others what you yourself do not want." This "negative" version of the Golden Rule is modest; it does not presuppose that one has access to some objective and universal standard that would serve as warrant for "doing unto others as you would have them do unto you." Just as the hewing of the axe handle uses a model rather than a template, so the shaping of one person in relation to another is directed at an accommodating harmony rather than an imposed uniformity. Rather than mere replication, an important degree of artistry is needed. Indeed, what is required in "putting oneself in the other's place" is the awareness that these are different places. Stated conversely, in the absence of some assumed universal standard, to begin from the presumption that one already knows what is most appropriate for someone else is disrespectful and condescending. Instead, one needs to be open and provisional, and to assume that deliberation on how to best grow a relationship can only be pursued through a careful consideration of the needs of this specific person and the possibilities of these specific circumstances. Even so, in our search for a way to optimize the possibilities in this relationship, to refrain from doing to someone else what we do not want done to us would at the very least be a good place to start. Beyond this rather obvious beginning, however, there is a world of contingencies that require thoughtful and imaginative exploration.

But this same *Zhongyong* passage has more to say. As in the section cited above, here again in what follows, the locus of the discussion is identified as the "everyday" (*yong* 庸): the concrete consummate life as it is lived. And here again this text associates the cultivation of a capacity to *shu* and to *zhong* with immediate family roles and relations:

> Of the four requirements of the exemplary person's consummate vision, I am not yet able to satisfy even one of them. I am not yet able to serve my father as I would expect my son to serve me; I am not yet able to serve my lord as I would expect my minister to serve me; I am not yet able to serve my elder brother as I would expect my younger brother to serve me; I am not yet able to be first in treating my friends as I myself would wish them to treat me.
>
> Where there are deficiencies in my everyday moral conduct and in my everyday speech, I must make every effort to address them; where there are excesses, I must make every effort to constrain myself. Speech that is accountable to conduct; conduct that is accountable to what is said—how could the exemplary person do other than earnestly aspire to such behavior?[68]

At issue here is one's cultivated propensity for appropriate deference in one's most immediate family and community relations. There are many examples in the *Analects* of Confucius himself exhibiting proper deference to others. One consideration in each novel situation is the specific people involved. As I have noted above, on several different occasions puzzled students ask Confucius what he means by the expression *ren*, and each time he acts on his *shu* disposition by being responsive to the specific profile of the individual student in giving an answer he deems appropriate to that student.[69]

This need to tailor one's responses to the concrete situation is again captured nicely in the conflicting advice Confucius gives to Ranyou and Zilu when they ask him about acting on what they have learned. On being queried by a third party about what are clearly contradictory answers to the same question, Confucius simply references their different needs: "Ranyou is reticent, and so I urged him on. But Zilu has the energy of two, and so I sought to rein him in."[70]

In fact, it is because *shu* must be understood as the evolving patterns of deference necessary for a flourishing community that Confucius invests such singular importance in it. In a world constituted of unique individuals located within a dynamic matrix of roles and relationships, the performance of these roles and relationships can only be effectively driven by the giving and the receiving of deference. When students in the classroom defer to the wisdom of their teacher, it activates the possibilities of their learning. When the teacher defers to important interventions on the part of the students, the class is further motivated, and everyone including the teacher is the beneficiary.

Zhong 忠: "Doing One's Utmost"

An important phrase in this *Zhongyong* passage cited above is that exemplary persons "relent" only after having improved upon other people. In addition to "putting oneself in the other's place" (*shu*), another related term that Confucius takes as critical to his moral vision is *zhong* 忠: "doing one's utmost." This indefatigable commitment to a positive outcome brings moral motivation into the discussion. D. C. Lau provides us with a significant corrective for the popular understanding of *zhong* as simply "loyalty" by insisting upon its more primitive meaning as "doing one's best":

> Translators tend to use "loyal" as the sole equivalent for *chung* [*zhong* 忠] even when translating the early texts. This is a mistake and is due to a failure to appreciate that the meaning of the word changed in the course of time.... *Chung* [*zhong*] is the doing of one's best and it is through *chung* [*zhong*] that one puts into effect what one has found out by the method of *shu*.[71]

Lau's interpretation of *zhong* is reinforced by the *Shuowen* lexicon that defines *zhong* as being "respectfully attentive" (*jing* 敬). Later commentary on the *Analects* defines *zhong* explicitly as "giving of oneself utterly" (*jinji* 盡己).

The character *zhong* 忠 appears on the bronzes as *[xxxi]*, constituted by the components "centering, into, interior, focus" (*zhong* 中) and "heartmind" (*xin* 心).⁷² The character *zhong* 中 was analyzed earlier in this chapter as suggesting ways of assembling the people visually and aurally with banners and drums respectively. The second element is the "heartmind" (*xin*), or perhaps better, "thinking and feeling." In combination, the graph means "doing one's best" or "giving oneself fully" to the task at hand—quite literally putting one's whole heart and mind into what one is doing. It is easy to see that when *zhong* comes to be used in the context of the political relationship between ruler and subject, "doing one's best" becomes more narrowly focused as "loyalty," but even here, an intelligent as opposed to a blind loyalty.

[xxxi]

Zhong, "doing one's utmost," is thus a conscientiousness in one's deliberations and actions. We have seen that an otherwise demurring Confucius is not shy about being described as "caring deeply for learning" (*haoxue* 好學). Confucius in his exhortations is given to recommending the more modal *how* to live morally because the *what* of one's specific actions is a complex variable that will always need to be qualified by the uniqueness and exigencies of the circumstances. Moral actions are thus resistant to general prescription.

Yi 義: "Optimal Appropriateness"

The vocabulary of *shu* and *zhong*—putting oneself in the others place and then doing one's utmost—resonates immediately with *yi* 義, a third term in this Confucian moral vocabulary. *Yi* is "achieving an optimal appropriateness in one's relations"—that is, the satisfaction of moral uncertainty through an acquired sense of what is most fitting in the situation. *Shu* can be thought of as rehearsing the possibilities for what would be most appropriate in a relationship, where the emphasis is on careful deliberation in identifying what the best course of action might be. *Shu* entails "other-directed" deference in the sense that one's action is shaped only after a full consideration of the needs and interests of others. And *zhong* then is giving this process of moral inquiry and the initiation of one's subsequent action the utmost in one's efforts.

Yi, on the other hand, reflects one's best judgment on how one might dispose oneself in one's relation to others in order to accomplish the recommended action, and confidence that what one is doing is appropriate in the circumstances. The emphasis is on following one's own sense of what is right in being responsive to the concerns of others. It entails a "self-including" sense of how best to interact with others. The searching *shu*, the modality of action, *zhong*, and the consequent *yi* are at play in situations that require ethical consideration.

Yi as an "optimizing appropriateness" locates present action both synchronically and diachronically. Synchronically *yi* action attempts to extend the context as broadly as possible, attending to the full range of possibilities involved, and taking under consideration the sometimes competing yet still legitimate interests of all concerned. Diachronically *yi* action in the present moment locates the immediate circumstances within the continuities it has with both past and future activity, making a comprehensive consideration of the continuing present the best way to make full use of those resources inherited out of past experience and the most productive way of anticipating what is yet to come.

Yi occurs in the oracle bones as *[xxxii]* and on the bronzes as *[xxxiii]*. Etymologically the graph is a stylized picture of a sheep (*yang* 羊) in combination with the first-person pronoun for "I, we, me, us," (*wo* 我).[73] The sheep signifier, carrying an association with sacrifice, is usually understood to suggest propitiousness. It occurs in characters such as "efficacy" (*shan* 善), "beautiful" (*mei* 美), "auspicious" (*xiang* 祥), and so on. Revealing here is that in a tradition in which persons are irreducibly social, the distinction between the singular "I" and the plural "we" is not marked. Perhaps even more telling, the distinction between the more independent, nominative "I" and the socially embedded, accusative "me" or the nominative "we" and the socially embedded accusative "us" is not indicated in the language.

But scholars of the classical language such as the Qing-dynasty philologist Duan Yucai 段玉裁 warn against making too much of the contemporary meanings of the two elements that constitute this character. This pronoun *wo*, as attested in the oracle bones and bronzes, depicts a dagger-axe (*ge* 戈): *[xxxiv]*. On the basis of this information, it has been argued that the *wo* character references a long-handled weapon with serrated, saw-like teeth. At some point, for phonological reasons, it came to be used as a lone character for its homophone, the first person pronoun *wo*. When it is remembered that sheep were periodically sacrificed at large communal gatherings, we may gloss *yi* as the solemn, dignified attitude one assumes and the proper social stance one takes when preparing the lamb for the ritual slaughter. This association of *wo* 我 and *yi* 義 with sacrifice is consistent with its cognate *xi* 犧, "to sacrifice, sacrificial animal," in that in its original form on the oracle bones and bronzes was written as *xi* 羲.[74] Again, *yi* is defined in the *Shuowen* lexicon as "dignity, majesty" (*weiyi* 威儀), where the connotation of assuming a proper demeanor can be attested by this cognate character 儀—"an *yi* person"—meaning specifically "a person with dignity, decorum, courtesy, graciousness." The propriety of this stance and its deferential attitude not only makes one a sacred representative of the community, but also purifies and consecrates the sacrificial animal.[75]

Above we found a correlation of *ren* 仁 with concern for a pregnant women in the Guodian version of the graph that is composed of *shen* 身 over *xin* 心, associating *ren* with a kind of pliant and gentle attitude. Similarly, there is a correlation between *yi* 義 as "the solemn and dignified demeanor of a person using a dagger-axe to prepare a sacrifice" with a kind of firmness and resolve. This contrast is remarked upon explicitly in the recently recovered document, *Five Modes of Proper Conduct*:

> To treat resolutely is how to be optimally appropriate (*yi* 義); to treat leniently is how to be consummate in one's conduct (*ren* 仁). Standing firm is how to be optimally appropriate (*yi*); being flexible is how to be consummate in one's conduct (*ren*).[76]

Yi has conventionally been translated into English as "righteousness" and "meaning," and less commonly as "rightness" and "morality." The decidedly biblical associations that attend the word "righteousness" as obedience to the will of God introduces an independent, objective, and divinely-sanctioned standard of what is right or "moral" into the equation that has little relevance for *yi*. While a sense of justice and fairness requires that one be resolved and stand firm, *yi* is still the outcome of a negotiation between self and the specific context that requires broadmindedness, flexibility, and accommodation. For

Confucius, we cannot enter an always-novel situation with the best outcome ready to hand. It is for this reason that he is stanch in respecting the particularity of the circumstances:

> Exemplary persons (*junzi* 君子) in making their way in the world are neither bent on nor against anything; rather, they go with what is most appropriate (*yi* 義).[77]

This search for an optimal appropriateness is consistent with how Confucius himself is frequently described:

> There were four things the Master abstained from entirely; he did not speculate, he did not claim or demand certainty, he was not inflexible, and he was not self-absorbed.[78]

Such an attitude of flexibility and accommodation in determining a course of action does not preclude firmness and resolve in acting upon it. As Confucius remarks, "Failing to act on what one deems appropriate (*yi*) is a want of courage."[79] Indeed, such resolve is a major theme in the *Analects*:

> To fail to cultivate excellence (*de*), to fail to practice what I have learned, to be unable to follow through on what has been deemed to be the most appropriate course of action (*yi*), and to be unable to reform conduct that is not efficacious—these are the things I worry about.[80]

Confucius summarizes this combination of flexibility and resolve in describing the process that the exemplary person goes through in determining and acting upon *yi*:

> Having a sense of appropriate conduct (*yi*) as one's basic disposition, putting such conduct into practice by aspiring to propriety in one's roles and relations (*li*), carrying it out with modesty, and attaining it by making good on one's word (*xin* 信): this then is the exemplary person (*junzi*).[81]

In looking for a tentative translation for *yi*, the contextually inclusive "appropriateness" and "fittingness" are perhaps the closest English equivalents. Such a translation is reinforced by the frequent paronomastic association of *yi* 義 with its near homophone, *yi* 宜, that like *yi* 義 has a primary religious reference in meaning "to sacrifice to the deity of the soil," and derivatively, to adjust to what is "right, proper, fitting." "Appropriate" as a translation for *yi* should be understood not only with its aesthetic and ethical connotations, but also with this sacred and religious import in mind. Optimally appropriate relations are not only meaningful; as we will explore in the next chapter, such relations are also the source of the intense sense of worth and belonging we associate with religious communion.

Yi, then, is an achieved sense of appropriateness that enables one to act in a proper and fitting manner, given the specifics of a situation. By extension, since appropriateness in relations is the ultimate source of meaning itself, it should not be surprising that *yi* also has the import of "meaning" as it is expressed and comes to reside in one's personal relations and conduct. Over time, *yi* becomes the aggregating significance invested by a living tradition in the observance of the various gestures of propriety; it is a sense of what is optimally appropriate as expressed in those roles and institutions that come to be defining of what is truly proper. And *yi* is the cultural authority that can be appropriated by persons as they become enculturated in the performance of these same roles and rituals. It is this invested significance that one appropriates from the social form that makes a salute, a handshake, and a marriage ceremony meaningful, and it is the sense of achieved and invested appropriateness in the performance of these ritualized activities that makes their observance profoundly personal.

Yi is the fittingness in relations that over time galvanizes the trust and credibility of the fiduciary community and the feelings of mutual confidence and reliability that give members a true sense of belonging within that community. Confucius is reported to have made just this connection in the following passage:

> That making good on one's word (*xin* 信) gets one close to appropriateness (*yi* 義) is because then what one says will bear repeating.[82]

Xin 信: "Making Good on One's Word"

This passage from the *Analects* serves as a segue for bringing attention to yet another term that is central to the Confucian vision of the consummate life. I usually translate *xin* 信 as "making good on one's word." It is also often rendered as "trust" and "credibility," but we need to be clear that *xin* is more than just good intentions; it requires practical results. Simply being sincere in what one says and does is not enough to be deemed *xin*; one must have the resources, human and otherwise, to follow through and make good on what one proposes to do. It is because of these practical demands of *xin* that there are few themes more pervasive in the classical Confucian literature than a reticence to speak for fear of not being able to live up to what one has said.[83]

Interestingly, as with many if not most classical Chinese terms, in understanding *xin* we must appreciate the priority of situation over agency. That is, *xin* in describing the situation of persons making good on their word goes in both directions, connoting both the increased credibility of the benefactor and the increased confidence and trust of the beneficiary. *Xin*, then, like friendship, is the consummation of a fiduciary relationship with agency being an abstraction from the concrete situation itself.

The fact that the *Shuowen* lexicon glosses *xin* 信 as *cheng* 誠, "acting sincerely and with integrity," and vice versa, glosses *cheng* as *xin*, suggests some considerable overlap in meaning. Indeed, as was discussed in chapter three, for the Confucian notion of the relationally constituted person, *cheng* is an essential affective ground for deepening one's relations with others, and in so doing, for achieving real personal growth. It is through this "integrative" sense of integrity that increasingly meaningful relations are a creative "becoming one together." *Xin* as a habit of making good on one's word is a specific and concrete way to promote the credibility and trust that must ground all personal growth.

De 德: "Excelling Morally"

A final term we need to register in this vocabulary that is used to capture the Confucian vision of the consummate life is *de* 德: "excelling morally," conventionally rendered nominally as "virtue" or "excellence." On the oracle bones, *de* appears as *[xxxv]*, depicting a person walking on a road with eyes focused on moving straight ahead.[84] This association provides a correlation between the metaphor of the "proper way" (*dao* 道) and walking straight ahead that has both the physical and the moral connotations of "straight" or "true." On the bronzes, the heartmind (*xin* 心) signific is added as an additional element in the character *[xxxvi]*,

underscoring the intellectual and affective dimension of the idea of walking the straight and narrow.[85] As noted above, in several of the recently recovered archaeological texts, the character *de* 德 is written using an alternative graph, 悳, with a heartmind radical *xin* 心 placed underneath the character *zhi* 直 that means "honestly, straight, true, upright, forthright." There is a cognate relationship between the two characters *de* 德 and *zhi* 直, and in the archaic language where the latter occasionally appears as a loan character for the former they have a similar pronunciation.

It should be clear by now that the several terms that constitute the explanatory vocabulary for Confucian role ethics are organic and overlapping in meaning. Each of these terms is a perspective on the same event, and functions to highlight a particular phase or dimension in achieving the consummate life. There is a sense in which *de* is used as the more general term for expressing the desired cumulative outcome of coordinating the shared experience effectively—both the achieved quality of the conduct of the particular person and the achieved *ethos* of the collective culture. Hence, the other terms we have explored above are all implicated in excelling morally (*de*):

> Zizhang inquired about accumulating excellence (*de* 德).... The Master replied, "To take doing one's utmost (*zhong* 忠), making good on one's word (*xin* 信), and seeking out what is most appropriate (*yi* 義) as one's main concerns, is to accumulate excellence."[86]

As we have seen in chapter two, Chinese cosmology begins from respecting the uniqueness and the integrity of the particular, where the cosmos is not more or less than the unsummed totality of the myriad things, the *wanwu* 萬物, as they accommodate each other. This means that our world of experience is a *kosmoi* rather than a *kosmos*, a "pluri-verse" rather than a "uni-verse," without any single order being privileged above all others, and with each thing having its own distinctive direction. In the early philosophical literature—the *Daodejing*, for example—*de* has strong cosmological implications, connoting this insistent particularity of things. It is for this reason that in this text *de* is conventionally translated as "virtue" or "power" or "potency," suggesting a forward momentum, or to use a Heideggerian vocabulary, *dasein* in the sense of a presencing, a "being-here," a directed pointing. *De* is most often but not exclusively positive, and because it is the human being more than any other phenomenon that has a penchant for growth and refinement, it is most often but not exclusively used to describe the acquired excellence of human beings and the attendant influence that such an achievement brings with it.

In Daoist philosophy, *dao* and *de* are related as field and focus respectively. The particular relational focus of an item establishes its unique perspective, and the totality as a noncoherent sum of all possible orders is implicated in each item. *De* is thus "holographic," meaning that each element in the totality of things contains and expresses the totality in some adumbrated form, with the greater degree of resolution that is achieved in any particular focus expressing the greater degree of significance. Distinguished persons, constituted as they are by a web of robust relationships, focus the world in profoundly meaningful ways; small persons who are deficient and diffused in their relations are neither intensive nor extensive in the resolution they express.

The earliest literature that we associate with Confucius is not speculative, tending to limit its concerns to the ordinary human experience where *de* more nearly suggests "excelling morally." *De* is what we can truly *do* and *become* if in living wisely we "realize" (*zhi* 知) satisfying personal lives as members of a flourishing community. Like "consummate conduct" (*ren* 仁), *de* can certainly be generalized from particular instances—we can speak of "human excellence" (*rende* 人德)—but it is a generalization that always begins from particular exemplars.

The extension of *de* entails both an act of intending and the attraction of the support necessary to effect what is intended. As artist, as communal leader, as teacher, one is able to organize one's natural, social and cultural environments and disclose their possibilities for a productive harmony. One is able to manifest, interpret, and display the local culture in one's own person. Such a person is thus a configuration of patterns of deference within a community and world, where the direction and volition of the contextualizing "others" are integrated into one's own field of interpretation, giving one influence and charisma.

There is both a political and a cosmic dimension to *de*. When referenced within the political realm, *de* describes the most appropriate relationship between a ruler and the people. To the extent that the ruler reaches out to become coextensive with the prevailing cultural propensities of the people, the ruler embodies the values of that community. To the extent that the ruler through superior leadership educes patterns of deference from the people, the people come to share the ruler's values and moral insights as they are won over to them.

Because *de* is what we accrue through a life of service to others, Confucius defines the accumulation of excellence (*chongde* 崇德) explicitly as "what one gets only after having given of oneself."[87] In this context, *de* has a range of meaning that reflects the priority of situation over agency, characterizing both giving and getting. That is, *de* is both the "beneficence" extended to the people in response to their perceived worth, and the deference and "gratitude" of a people expressed in response to the largesse of a worthy ruler. *De* is the disposition of both benefactor and beneficiary through productive, noncoercive communal relations.

It is for this reason that we must be careful not to give priority to agency in understanding *de*, thereby making the ruler and people exclusive categories, and making the ruler active and the people passive.[88] As the *de* of the people is manifest within the ruler's *de*, the ruler's potency is enhanced, becoming the wind that bends the grass (12.19), the north star around which the other stars revolve (2.1), the maker and transmitter of culture to which other persons subscribe (3.14). It is in this sense, as a focus of productive relations, that the emperor *is* the empire. *De* is the character or ethos of the polity as a whole as it is embodied in the ruler. On this basis, we might suggest "virtuality" as another possible translation of *de* in its archaic sense of "having inherent virtue or power to produce effects."

There is a coextensiveness of ruler and people in the sense that the ruler expresses the people through a government that accommodates their cultural proclivities, thus orchestrating an interpretation of culture that is both the ruler's and the people's. There is always, in this conception of *de*, a tension between attempting to maximize the possibilities for harmony provided by the attending conditions, and the need to do justice to one's own uniqueness and sense of appropriateness. It is the sensitive balancing of these forces that produces harmony within all of the human environments.

As we have seen, the *Daodejing*, literally "the classic of this *de* and its *dao*," is a text expressly dedicated to an exposition of this focus-field cosmology. Its central theme is optimizing the relationships between particular and totality—how this particular item can be most effective in bringing its perspectival field into focus. It is this process of focusing *de* that, for the human being, is productive of cognitive, moral, aesthetic, and spiritual meaning. The *Daodejing*, recognizing the meaning-creating and meaning-disclosing power of the cultivated human being, emphasizes the way in which this personal articulation extends beyond the human community to appreciate the cosmos itself. Those paragons of "highest excellence" (*shangde* 上德) have cosmological significance in maximizing the symbiotic relationship between the human experience and the environment within which that drama is set.

In the Confucian tradition, perhaps as a response to the more explicit cosmological speculation of the early Daoist works, the *Zhongyong* expands upon the human-centered focus of the classical Confucian texts and takes as its main theme the possibilities of the cultivated person as a full partner in cosmic harmony and creativity. Such a partnership begins as the cultivation of *de* is pursued through one's full participation in the ritualized community, where achieved excellence in the roles and relationships makes one an object of the deference of others. It is the extension of and participation in these patterns of deference that establishes a shared world of cultural values. Across time and space, it is the *de* of a corporate Confucius that serves to unify and perpetuate a shared Chinese identity, and it is the inclusive totality that is, sometimes more and sometimes less, an ongoing moral and indeed religious achievement (*daode*). And it is to this Confucian human-centered religiousness that we now turn.

V

Confucian Human-Centered Religiousness

Getting Past Transcendence: Distinguishing Process Cosmology from Substance Ontology

The distinguished French sinologist Marcel Granet observes rather starkly that "Chinese wisdom has no need of the idea of God."[1] Albeit in different formulations, this same characterization of classical Chinese philosophy has had many iterations by some of our most prominent sinologists and comparative philosophers. Tang Junyi for example states unequivocally:

> The Chinese as a people have not embraced a concept of "Heaven" (*tian* 天) that has transcendent meaning. The pervasive idea among Chinese with respect to *tian* is that it is inseparable from the world.[2]

Joseph Needham would also disassociate Chinese cosmology from assumptions about some underlying permanent structure when he claims that:

> Chinese ideals involved neither God nor Law.... Thus the mechanical and the quantitative, the forced and the externally imposed, were all absent. The notion of Order excluded the notion of Law.[3]

Indeed, our best interpreters of classical Chinese philosophy, Chinese and Western alike, are explicit in rejecting the idea that Chinese cosmology begins from some independent, transcendent principle.[4]

One important consequence of taking Granet's insight into Chinese cosmology seriously is that it might enable us to identify some of those equivocations that emerge when we willy-nilly elide classical Greek ontological assumptions with those natural cosmological presuppositions indigenous to the classical Chinese worldview. The real challenge is to disambiguate some of the central philosophical vocabulary of classical Chinese philosophy in order to allow the tradition to speak for itself. Indeed, Angus Graham encourages Western interpreters to be wary about such equivocations because a failure to take them into account can compromise our understanding of Chinese vocabulary:

> In the Chinese cosmos all things are interdependent, without transcendent principles by which to explain them or a transcendent origin from which they derive.... A novelty in this position which greatly impresses me is that it exposes a preconception of Western interpreters that such concepts as *Tian* "Heaven" and *Dao* "Way" must have the transcendence of our own ultimate principles; it is hard for us to grasp that even the Way is interdependent with man.[5]

Although it seems to be a widely accepted claim that strict transcendence is irrelevant for an understanding of classical Chinese cosmology, it still behooves us at the outset to be as unambiguous as we can as to what is being meant here by transcendence—that is, strict philosophical transcendence—because the philosophical implications of such a commitment are legion. I and my collaborators have perhaps not been as clear as we might have been in defining such transcendence, and as a consequence, we have inadvertently encouraged some scholars to first attribute to us a position that we do not hold, and then to criticize their own misunderstanding of what we do mean.[6]

To be clear, strict philosophical or theological transcendence is to assert that an independent and superordinate principle A originates, determines, and sustains B, where the reverse is not the case. This is the definition we first stipulated in *Thinking Through Confucius* in 1987, and we have continued to endorse this understanding of transcendence in all subsequent publications.[7] The notion of *eidos* that is both found and foundational in Plato and Aristotle as "ideals" and "immutable species" respectively, or the notion of an independent, perfect, and hence unchanging creator God—that is, the self-sufficiency or aseity of God—that emerges in mainstream Christian theology, would be familiar examples of such strict transcendence. If, as dominant classical Greek views that go back at least to Parmenides would have it, unity and permanence are fundamental, then the phenomenal world experienced as unbounded change cannot be finally real and cannot be the object of knowledge. In this received classical Greek ontology, "reality" must refer to that which *grounds* the world of appearances, while changing phenomena as *mere appearances* are at best misleading and illusory. Metaphysical realism (Plato) and substance ontology (Aristotle) both entail this strict sense of transcendence by postulating self-sufficient principles that exist in themselves as the ultimate objects of knowledge and of predication.[8]

In what follows, we will see that the philosophical implications of Granet's seemingly off-hand observation that China did not need the idea of a transcendent God in its various guises are fundamental and pervasive, entailing that China had no need for the plethora of dualistic categories that follow from such an ontological disparity. In chapter two of this present work I reconstructed a persistent Chinese process cosmology as an alternative interpretive context for exploring and evaluating Confucian philosophy, and in chapter three I argued that the familiar dualisms such as subject/object, agent/action, mind/body, nature/nurture, and so on, that arise from substance ontology have little relevance for the Confucian notion of relationally constituted persons. Indeed, this Confucian conception of person makes no appeal to superordinate, substantive categories such as "soul," "self," "will," "faculties," "nature," "mind," "character," and so on, but instead locates person gerundively as the embodied, social activity of thinking and feeling within the manifold of relations that constitutes family, community, and the natural environment. "Person" thus understood is a complex event rather than a discrete "thing," a process of "becoming" rather than an essential "being," an on-going "doing" rather than an autonomous "is," a configuration of concrete, dynamic, and constitutive relations rather than an individuated substance defined by some subsisting agency.

We can now carry this relational understanding of person over to shed some light on what I would call a Confucian understanding of human-centered religiousness. In the familiar language of substance ontology, "God" is to be understood as the imperceptible human "soul" writ large as a subsisting "world soul." Analogous to the soul as the invisible, immutable essence that makes us human "beings," the creator

God is the essential Being behind these beings—the one coherent invisible design standing behind and sustaining our "*uni*-verse," our "single-ordered cosmos." William James worries over this "inveterate human trick of turning names into things"—what we do here when we attribute this notion of "soul" as a substance that provides discrete agency to either human beings or to God:

> A group of attributes is what each substance here is known-as, they form its sole cash-value for our actual experience.... The name we then treat as in a way supporting the group of phenomena.... But the phenomenal properties of things ... surely do not inhere in names, and if not in names then they do not inhere in anything. They *ad*here, or *co*here, rather, *with each other*, and the notion of a substance inaccessible to us, which we think accounts for such cohesion by supporting it, as cement might support pieces of mosaic, must be abandoned.[9]

When we turn to Confucian religiousness, we find that it does not appeal to an independent, retrospective, and substantive Divine Agency as the reality behind appearance and as the ultimate source of all cosmic significance. The world is instead an autogenerative, "self-so-ing" process (*ziran er ran* 自然而然) that has the energy of self-transformation within the manifold of relationships that constitutes it. And human religious feelings themselves are the motor of religious meaning, understood prospectively as an unfolding and inclusive spirituality achieved within the qualitatively inspired activities of the family, the community, and the natural world. Human beings are both a source of and contributors to the numinosity that inspires the world in which we live.

Nathan Sivin has made a singularly important contribution in his efforts to distinguish Greek and Chinese cosmological assumptions. On the one hand he insists that cultures are too subtle and complex to allow for heavy-handed assertions, and has prudently cautioned us against a wholesale "rather than" approach to cultural comparisons.[10] With just such a caution in mind, Sivin in his essay "Comparing Greek and Chinese Philosophy and Science" is still given to making some fundamental generalizations that establish a framework and a helpful vocabulary for both associative and contrastive analogies. Indeed, in this regard, Sivin's work, while yielding substantial historical dividends, has important implications for philosophical interpretation as well.[11] For example, Sivin is consonant with his fellow sinologists in asserting that the reality-appearance distinction prevalent in early Greek philosophy "has no counterpart in China."[12] The philosophical entailments of the claim that the putative ontological disparity captured by the reality/appearance distinction has little relevance for early Chinese cosmology are numerous, several of which Sivin himself goes on to delineate in his summary reflections on a comparison between Greek and Chinese philosophy.

For starters, Sivin registers the relative absence of logic as a privileged field of study in early China while at the same time noting the pervasive importance of semantics and pragmatics in the evolving Chinese cultural narrative. This contrast between logic and pragmatics is another way of saying that the Chinese tradition does not privilege some fixed formal aspect—in this case, logic as the "form" of thinking—as being more "real" than what is otherwise in flux (that is, semantics). Relatedly, Sivin's observation regarding the ubiquitousness in the Chinese tradition of variations on the "using names properly" theme (*zhengming* 正名) suggests that the function of language used in a Chinese processual cosmology must itself reflect the flux and flow of that cosmos.[13] That is, Chinese cosmology accepts the processual, fluid, and hence provisional character of language without appeal to some ostensive literal ground that would describe and guarantee some underlying reality.

Sivin makes another important distinction between the dialectical versus the consensual expectations of philosophical engagement in the classical Greek and Chinese worlds respectively:

> Greek culture in the period that concerns us encouraged disagreement and disputation in natural philosophy and science as in every other field; in China the emphasis remained on consensus.[14]

The contrast noted here is between Greek dialogue with its assumption that rational analysis will provide access to some exclusive *logos*, and a Chinese conversation that requires the ongoing negotiation of an inclusive consensus. The epistemic quest for "apodictic" truth drove the Greek dialogue—that is, the search for an absolute and unconditioned quality of knowledge promised by its mathematical avatar. In China, the continuing need to negotiate order within the assumed processual cosmology had far-reaching ramifications for Chinese philosophy. Such ongoing, inclusive negotiation within the Chinese narrative would explain why achieved consensus in its many forms was regarded as having high value in the classical Chinese world. That is, there is a high value invested in the attainment of an inclusive harmony, in the intergenerational reauthorization of a moral orthodoxy, in the continuing commentary on a shared canonical core, in "the art of accommodation" (*jianshu* 兼術) in philosophical deliberation, in the didactic function that the sage has as virtuosic communicator and consolidator, in a recognition of a continuity between the human and its religious, natural, and cultural context, in the priority given to reflexive ritual propriety over objective rule or law, in the privileging of appropriate models as an inspiration for proper conduct over an appeal to moral principles, and so on.[15] Angus Graham echoes Sivin in developing the same contrast between dialectical and consensual engagement when he observes that dialectical dispute is characteristic of a people who would ask "what is the Truth?" as opposed to the promotion of consensus among those who would ask "where is the Way?"[16]

In the absence of a concept of "God," there seems to be some general agreement among sinologists that there is little recourse to anything like a "two-world," reality/appearance distinction to be found in classical Chinese thought.[17] There is little evidence that early Chinese thinkers were interested in the search for and the articulation of an ontological ground for phenomena—some Being behind the beings, some One behind the many, some ideal world behind the world of change. The notion of the real as *objective* is an immediate implication of the reality/appearance distinction and the dualistic worldview it entails. It is this ostensive ability to make an object of the world—that is, to make it *a* world or *the* world—that allows philosophers to think they can assume a view from nowhere, thereby decontextualizing themselves and stepping outside of the human experience. And it is indeed this "view from nowhere" that stands as guarantor for the possibility of objective description, the truth that would attend such description, and the quality of certainty such description would carry with it.

In the Chinese narrative, without this assumed notion of *objectivity*, there can only be the flux of passing circumstances. Without *objectivity*, erstwhile objects, rather than "objecting" to change and transformation, instead dissolve into the flux and flow, into the changefulness of their surround. Indeed, they are not *objects*, but *events,* continuous with all other events as currents in a stream. What are perceived as persistent "things" that ostensibly sustain an identity across time from birth, maturation, and eventual decline are in fact loci of relative yet transitory stability within a manifold of constant change. The identity of any "thing" thus conceived, though persistent, is fundamentally analogic in the sense of being constituted by and being a function of a range of dynamic associations. It is a deobjectified, defactualized, gerundive discourse that is the language of process, and to speak and to hear that language is to experience the flow of things. We have seen that such a cosmology stands behind the approach of Traditional Chinese Medicine:

> In traditional Chinese cosmology objects do not simply populate the world. Instead, the world consists of interrelating processes. The processes arise and are maintained by *qi* (energy flow). What in Western terms we refer to as "objects" are in Chinese terms, stabilized patterns of a flow.... Each entity is a process within a process, a flow within a flow, and within each entity are processes that constitute it. Nothing exists in the absence of the flow of energy.... Of course, for some purposes it may be useful to isolate individual phenomena. But this analysis is only a useful fiction.[18]

In this persistent cosmology, "things" are best understood as dissipative structures animated by a quantum of energy within an ongoing processual flow:

> The patterns exhibited by a dissipative structure are self-organized: That is, they emerge from the system's components' response to energy flow giving rise to new constraints reconfiguring internal interrelations within the system. So long as the energy gradient is maintained, the internal dynamics of the system maintains spatial and temporal structure.[19]

The notion of the real as *objective* fuels the analytic and dialectical mode of engagement that Sivin ascribes to the classical Greek thinkers, a dialectic promising a single truth that allows discrete parties to "protest" in the sense of "objecting," taking exception, and dissenting on behalf of this truth. As we have seen, the alternative, consensual mode of engagement reflects the more positive and inclusive sense of protest captured in the expression "I protest my innocence." That is, to protest is to "testify for": to affirm the content of one's remonstrance with solemnity under the assumption that we are all implicated in whatever decision we might make together, and in the consequences that follow from that decision.

Remembering Granet's notion of "God," the most fundamental difference between these two contrasting classical traditions is thus the prominence of some notion of permanent "substance" as ontological ground in the classical Greek tradition, and the fluid "process" orientation of the classical Chinese narrative. A corollary to the privileging of a formal, unchanging and substantial reality over the flux of appearances in the dominant classical Greek worldview is the tendency to give priority to the discrete and quantitative over the qualitative and continuous, to privilege nouns over gerunds, things over events.[20] The identities of "things" tend to be discrete and atomistic: a function of quantitative discreteness that parses identity in terms of essential and accidental properties, and thus ultimately external rather than internal relations. Wholes are constructed out of discrete yet coherent parts. Communities are a collection of individual persons, each of whom has his or her own integrity, like spoons in a drawer, like pennies in a jar. Each person in the community is defined by some self-same identical characteristic, and thus has some pre-social, pre-cultural, and enduring warrant for membership in a natural kind that locates them in an external relationship to every other person. There is some defining essence that lies outside of their contingent relationships with other things, and that provides them with their pesisting integrity. This priority of discreteness and quantity follows from the privileging of the substantial over the processual, of permanence and stasis over change. Further, this priority given to discreteness and quantity in turn disposes toward a persisting concern for the clarity of formally defined concepts and the necessity of unchanging truths—both conditions that are more congenial to a quantitatively discrete and measurable world.

Privileging Gerundive Language: Knowing *How*

We will find that an important corollary to this disinterest in positing a notion of "God" in Chinese process cosmology is the need for a different language in thinking about issues as basic as cosmic origins, the source of meaning and value in the world, and the nature of creativity itself. But it is not simply a different vocabulary, but more fundamentally a different way of thinking about what language does. We must be self-conscious about the cultural assumptions that we bring willy-nilly to our attempt to translate and understand the Chinese philosophical tradition, and about the interpretive danger of eliding the less-familiar Chinese cosmological sensibilities by superimposing those Greek ontological presuppositions on them built into the way in which we use language.

This worry over language and how it functions raises an important issue: Does the familiar distinction between a literal and metaphorical language have application to Chinese natural cosmology? If by "literal" we mean to accord with the exact or primary meanings of terms without context or embellishment, we can see that to conventionally translate *dao* 道 as "the Way" or *tian* 天 as "Heaven," far from being "literal" as many would claim, is a case of naïve exposition of the most egregious kind. After all, we must allow that "the Way" and "Heaven," as understood within our own linguistic universe, immediately infer and are indeed metonymic for the Abrahamic conception of "God" and all that it entails, a theological framework that has little relevance for traditional Chinese cosmology.[21]

In the classical Greek philosophical narrative, what is "literal" is what agrees with reality and hence is true. Such a conception of truth has commonly been understood as a correspondence between *what* is real—the Being behind the beings—and *what* is representational—a mental mirroring of what really is. Angus Graham warns us explicitly about importing this same problematic into the Chinese worldview:

> In seeking the One behind the many, as also in seeking the constant behind the changing, *Lao-tzu* [*Laozi*] is using concepts that seem fully identifiable with our own. There is however an important difference from the Western tradition, that no Chinese thinker conceives the One and the constant as Being or Reality behind the veil of appearance.... If we ourselves would prefer to think of it as absolute Reality that is because our philosophy in general has been a search for being, reality, truth, while for the Chinese the question was always "Where is the Way?" Chinese thinkers want to know how to live, how to organise community, and at the very end of the pre-Han period, how to relate community to the cosmos.[22]

On the side of Chinese process cosmology, then, with this "how-priority" attitude, comprehension in the human experience takes on a different shape, and comes at the cost of the priority given to definition and precision. With no separation between phenomena and their putative ontological foundations, "reality" is nothing more or less than that complex pattern of always-changing relationships that in sum constitute the myriad things of the world. Knowledge, then, is not abstractive in a formal sense, but in a selective sense: That is, knowledge has to do with *these* particular, concrete factors that are most relevant to *this* evolving situation as entertained from *this* perspective. And a more passive cognitive understanding of knowledge is transformed into wisdom through virtuosity in correlating this manifold of relevant factors into the most productive results. Knowledge is not so much representational as presentational: Knowing is a performative and participatory wisdom directed at achieving efficacy within these particular, concrete circumstances. While such knowledge, being at once productive and consummatory, certainly involves closure, it is more importantly a source of disclosure: the contributing of one's own capacities fully to enhance the possibilities of these particular, concrete circumstances. Such knowledge is not only cognitive and discursive, but is also a kind of know-*how*—a practicable doing. It entails both a realizing *how* and an *acting upon* such a realization. That is, it is a knowing how to apply one's best insights and feelings to get the most out of the existing possibilities.

This peculiar orientation to the "how?" question has the broadest of possible implications for the Chinese correlative mode of thinking, privileging the gerundive rather than the nominal in the use of language because both the organs and the objects of knowing require constant adjustment. As an example, this aspiration for a *how* over a *what* understanding of *tian* is announced by Tang Junyi in his explanation of *tianming* 天命—"the command or mandate of *tian*"—that he gleans from a survey of the early philosophical literature:

> The term "*ming*" represents the interrelationship or mutual relatedness of Heaven and man.... [W]e can say that it exists neither externally in Heaven only, nor internally in man only; it exists, rather, in the mutuality of Heaven and man, i.e., in their mutual influence and response, their mutual giving and receiving.[23]

Tang's point is that *ming* 命 is relational in the sense that "commanding" is collateral and bidirectional: The "command" of *tian* is a response to the respect "commanded" by the achieved excellence of the ruler. By knowing *how* to govern, and by governing effectively, the ruler establishes a relationship of trust and credibility first with the people, and then by extension, with *tian*.

Abjuring Clarity on *tian* 天 and *di* 帝

There are two specific Chinese terms that were appropriated from the classical Chinese language by Western missionaries to denote the Christian conception of transcendent deity: *tian* 天 (or *tianzhu* 天主) and *di* 帝 (or *shangdi* 上帝). In recent years, especially following the encounter between indigenous Chinese religiousness and Western "God-centered" religion, scholars seeking to better understand Chinese religiousness have spilled much ink in trying to bring these notions of *tian* and *di* into sharper focus. But perhaps this effort to stipulate precisely *what* these terms mean is asking something from the tradition that runs contrary to its own sensibilities.

The notion of *tian* that we generally associate with Zhou dynasty religiousness occurs in the oracle bones as the graphs *[xxxvii]* and *[xxxviii]*. Scholars have read this character as an ideogram depicting what is "above" the human head: certainly referencing the pedestrian sky, but also perhaps pointing to the sublime splendor of that same sky writ large as the humbling and unfathomable heavens. On the bronzes, *tian* is somewhat more stylized and closer to the modern character: *[xxxix]*.[24] The *Shuowen* lexicon bears out those speculations that would define *tian* in relationship to the human world by glossing *tian* paronomastically as *dian* 顛, meaning "top of the head," and then defining it in terms of the graphic components from which the character is constructed: the number "one" (*yi* 一) and the character for "greatest" (*da* 大) combine to mean "the highest, the most grand." Importantly, *tian* is to be understood in its relationship to life as it unfolds in the human world.

[xxxvii]

[xxxviii]

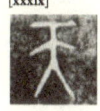
[xxxix]

One way in which the Confucian canons do invest the notion of *tian* with meaning and do make it determinate in degree for their readers is by putting a human face on what would otherwise remain an anonymous and recondite referent. Just as persons of stature and accomplishment in traditional Chinese paintings are depicted as proportionately larger than their retinue, so in the canonical description of consummate persons there is a tendency to present them hyperbolically in celestial terms. We might take a general example from Book 19 of the *Analects* as an illustration of this trope:

> Zigong said, "The missteps of exemplary persons (*junzi* 君子) are like an eclipse of the sun and moon. When they stray, everyone sees it, and when they correct their course, everyone looks up to them."[25]

There are several such examples again in the last sections of the *Zhongyong*:

> Only those in the world of utmost creativity (*zhicheng* 至誠) are able to separate out and braid together the many threads on the great loom of the world. Only they set the great root of the world and realize the transforming and nourishing processes of heaven and earth.
> How could there be anything on which they depend?
> So earnest, they are consummate (*ren* 仁);
> So profound, they are a bottomless abyss (*yuan* 淵);
> So pervasive, they are *tian* (*tian* 天).
> Only those whose own capacities of discernment and sagely wisdom extend to the powers of *tian* could possibly understand them.[26]

In these same texts, the human face given to *tian* becomes more specific and personal when they elevate cultural heroes such as Confucius himself to cosmic proportions:

> Shusun Wushu spoke disparagingly of Confucius. Zigong responded, "Do not do this! Confucius cannot be disparaged. The superior worth of other people is like a mound or a hill that can still be scaled, but Confucius is the sun and moon that no one can climb beyond. Were persons to cut themselves off from the sun and moon, what damage would this do to the sun and moon? It would only demonstrate that such persons do not know their own limits."[27]

Again in the last sections of the *Zhongyong* that celebrate the human capacity to be a co-creator with the cosmos, Confucius has a celestial profile:

> Confucius revered Yao and Shun as his ancestors and carried on their ways; he emulated and made illustrious the ways of Kings Wen and Wu. He modeled himself above on the rhythm of the turning seasons, and below

he was attuned to the patterns of water and earth. He is comparable to the heavens and the earth, sheltering and supporting everything that is. He is comparable to the progress of the four seasons, and the alternating illumination of the sun and the moon.[28]

Turning to the term *di* 帝 that is usually associated with the earlier Shang dynasty religiousness, it occurs on the oracle bones as *[xl]*, on the bronzes as *[xli]*, and on the silk and bamboo manuscripts as *[xlii]*. The literary theorist Wang Guowei 王國維 interprets this character as an early depiction of the stem of a flower or fruit (*di* 蒂). The philologist Xu Zhongshu 徐中舒 reads it as a ceremonial pyre on which to make sacrifices to *tian*, and by extension, as the earlier graphic form for what came to be designated as the grand *di* sacrifice 禘.[29] We learn in the *Analects* that Confucius had great reverence for this *di* sacrifice:

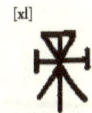

[xl]

[xli]

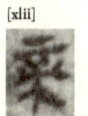

[xlii]

> Someone asked the Master for an explanation of the *di* imperial ancestral sacrifice, and he replied: "I don't have one. Anyone who did know how to explain it could rule the empire as easily as having it here." And he pointed to the palm of his hand.[30]

Although such definitions of *di* 帝 offered by earlier scholars are speculative and uncertain, we do know that this term was also used as a posthumous title for the Shang-dynasty kings, again putting a human face on an otherwise rather obscure designator for the numinous.

John Major alludes to this fluidity between the human space and that of the divine in his attempt to provide an appropriate equivalent for this term *di* in his translations of the Chinese canons into the English language:

> I translate *di* [帝] as "thearch"—a felicitous word first used, I believe, by Edward Schafer—when it refers to specific personage such as the Supreme Thearch (*shangdi* [上帝]) or the Yellow Thearch (*huangdi* [黃帝]), or to idealized rulers ("emperors"). Thearch captures well the character of ancient Chinese thought wherein divinities might be (simultaneously and without internal contradiction) high gods, mythical/divine rulers, or deified royal ancestors: beings of enormous import, straddling the numinous and the mundane.[31]

As we saw above, the graph depicting *tian* provides little semantic information other than an association with what is above the human head, not only physically, but perhaps conceptually as well. To cite Zhang Dongsun 張東蓀:

> The Chinese attitude toward the demands of *tian* 天 are simply the desire to know its purposes in order to secure good fortune and avoid misfortune. As to what kind of "thing" *tian* is, they are indifferent. This is because the Chinese people do not consider *tian* to be the ontological ground of the myriad things, and thus do not apply the category of ontology to it.[32]

It is certainly the case that philosophical notions such as *tian* and *di* are profoundly abstruse in the Chinese classics, with words such as "distant" (*yuan* 遠) and "dark" (*xuan* 玄) being frequently invoked to describe them.

The fact that the Chinese tradition itself does not pursue any real precision in its understanding of some of the vocabulary of Chinese religiousness has introduced a vagueness into this language that has occasioned a sustained misreading of its general import by some Western interpreters. It has become a commonplace to acknowledge that, in the process of Western humanists attempting to make sense of the classical Chinese philosophical literature, many unannounced Western assumptions have been inadvertently insinuated into the readings of these texts, and have colored the vocabulary through which this understanding has been articulated. This is nowhere more true than in the language appealed to in interpreting Chinese religiousness.

Indeed, as I have remarked upon in chapter one, over the last several centuries, the vocabulary established for the translation of classical Chinese texts into Western languages has been freighted by an often unconscious Christian framework, and the effects of this "Christianization" of Chinese texts are still very much with us. There are numerous examples of grossly inappropriate language having become the standard equivalents in the Chinese/English dictionaries that we use to perpetuate our understanding of Chinese culture: "the Way" (*dao* 道), "Heaven" (*tian* 天), "benevolence" (*ren* 仁), "rites" (*li* 禮), "virtue" (*de* 德), "filial piety" (*xiao* 孝), "righteousness" (*yi* 義), "principle" (*li* 理), and so on. A familiar theistic worldview is prompted by such a vocabulary, complete with intimations of God, church, and human obedience to the Divine Will. But in continuing to use such translations, we must ask: Although *li* can sometimes have a formal and ceremonial aspect, in what sense does its immediate reference to family life and to behavior that is appropriate as someone's son or daughter denote a "rite" or "ritual?" When and in what context would a native English speaker ever utter the word "righteousness" other than in describing compliance with the Will of God? Can a Western student of a Chinese text read the capitalized "Heaven," or "*the* Way" preceded by a definite article, as anything other than a metonym for the familiar notion of a transcendent God and His Way respectively? Does the idea of "principle" (or Lat. *principium* used to translate the Greek *arche*)—"the beginning, the ultimate underlying substance, the ultimate undemonstrable principle"—that locates *li* 理 squarely within classical Greek "One-behind-the-many" metaphysical thinking have anything to do with Chinese natural cosmology?[33]

Cosmic Origins: Genealogical Cosmogony and Its "Epistemogony"

This disinterest in positing an independent, transcendent source of the world in Chinese cosmology must be factored into the way in which cosmic origins has been understood. Summarizing cosmological speculations from a significantly earlier period, the second-century BCE "cosmology" section of the early Han dynasty text, the *Huainanzi* 淮南子, contains this passage:

> Before the heavens and the earth had yet to take shape,
> There was a soaring, gliding, plunging, sinking.
> This is known as the Great Natal Beginning.
> *Dao* was born out of the empty and remote,
> The empty and remote gave birth to space-time,
> And space-time gave birth to primordial *qi*.[34]

The "cosmogony" offered here is a natal and historical account that occurs within the unfolding process of "world as such" as opposed to describing a metaphysical intervention from outside of the world. It describes a birthing from an inchoate, incipient life-form that presupposes genealogy and progenitors rather than originative principles or divine design, and a pattern of always-situated and cultivated growth in significance rather than the linear actualization of some predetermined potential. This is what Frederick Mote means when he argues:

> The genuine Chinese cosmology is that of organismic process, meaning that all parts of the entire cosmos belong to one organic whole and that they all interact as participants in one spontaneously self-generating life process.[35]

Benjamin Schwartz also perceives this important generative feature of Chinese cosmogony when he is prompted to ask:

> Does the fact that in later Chinese high-cultural accounts of the origins of mankind or of the cosmos, the dominant metaphor is that of procreation or "giving birth," rather than that of fashioning or creating, have anything to do with the centrality of ancestor worship with its dominance on the biological metaphor?[36]

There is a clear contrast between metaphysical *creatio ex nihilo* assumptions defining of some Greek and Abrahamic interpretations of origins or beginnings, and the contextualized *creatio in situ* process that is characteristic of Chinese natural cosmology.

In the process cosmology of early China, continuity, particularism, change, context, and novelty are all conditions of a continuing present. This means that, in the fullness of time, whether viewing the cosmos retrospectively or prospectively, any rationalizing vocabulary that we might appeal to as an interpretive grid for explaining our experience is outrun by the never-ending generative process. Hence the language of interpretation offered in this *Huainanzi* passage such as "the heavens and the earth" (*tiandi* 天墜[地]), *dao* 道, "space-time" (*yuzhou* 宇宙), "primordial *qi*" (*yuanqi* 元氣), "empty and remote" (*xuguo* 虛霩), and so on, discloses our competence in explaining cosmic order in the present moment. But these same terms of art were "born" as insights into the nature of a changing reality, and their explanatory force will necessarily, in the passage of time, expire. That is, the cosmogonic account is also an "epistemogonic" narrative that at once recounts an emerging interpretation of world order, and sets historical limits on this interpretation. Our relatively clear understanding of our present, always-provisional situation cannot be universalized and relied upon to explain all situations. The cosmogonic narrative takes us back to an earlier set of conditions that, requiring its own terms of understanding, cannot be explained by the application of our present philosophical vocabulary. As the cosmos changes, so must the language of its explanation. The procreative process is traced back to a dark chaos that resists description in our familiar cosmological language, rather than to the increasing illumination provided by uncovering some ultimate source of design and cosmic meaning. Hence, unlike some traditional Western cosmogonies that usher us back to the source of an intelligibility that overcomes chaos, Chinese natural cosmogonies direct us back to what, from our present perspective, is a world wherein the further back we go, the more dark, amorphous, and remote it becomes for us.

Often *dao* 道 is described in the language of a cosmological "source," the "origins" of the world as we know it. But as I have argued above, this cosmological *dao* far from being a superordinated metaphysical principle that stands independent of its creatures is in fact the ongoing living processes that include them all. It is the generative and always contingent genealogical unfolding of the world itself as our field of experience. As we have seen, if order is truly inherent and emergent rather than existing as an independent principle, then the language that describes all aspects of this "world-ing" must be historicized as a provisional, sometimes poetic and sometimes metaphorical vocabulary for the world order *as we know it*.

Again, the sense of "beginning" in such cosmogonic narratives is expressed as *shi* 始—a natal beginning associated with a fetus (*tai* 胎) that inherits a world "bequeathed" (*yi* 詒) to it and "passed on" (*yi* 貽) from progenitors who have come before. The language is pervasively genealogical and ancestral (*zong* 宗), including within this vocabulary the rather vague expressions we have explored above such as "lord" (*di* 帝) and the often anthropomorphic *tian* that straddle the human and the numinous realms.

The "empty" (*xu* 虛) as it is used in this *Huainanzi* passage is to be understood contextually as a positive emptiness within shaped, determinate things that makes things functional: for example, the emptiness of a cup that anticipates the process of filling it up. In this instance, the natal is the "empty," indeterminate source that honeycombs the phenomenal world out of which a cosmos is constantly being born. This space is the fecund life source of the as yet unmanifested, but soon to be determinant phenomena that emerge to make our next moment different from this one. *Xu* has often and unfortunately been elided with the primordial Chaos as a gaping emptiness, a dark formless void, familiar in some classical Western cosmogonies. However, there is no decontextualized void as such in the classical Chinese cosmology, and thus no final emptiness. Both shaped and unshaped things have, by default, only a phenomenological reference to the interface between determinacy and indeterminancy that defines our experience. The absence of transcendence in Chinese cosmology precludes an ontology of Being as what really *is*, and of Non-Being (or Not-Being) as a putative absence of existing things.

Let me take this distinction between natal or genealogical birthings, and metaphysical beginnings a step further. Many scholars have noted that cosmogonic myths did not feature in classical Chinese cosmology, and only begin to appear in China in the literature of the Han period.[37] For example, Angus Graham states:

> The past to which Confucius looks back is not the beginning of things; there is no cosmogonic myth in pre-Han literature, merely a blank of prehistory before the first Emperors, who for Confucius are the pre-dynastic sages Yao and Shun.[38]

This position is contested by other scholars such as Paul Goldin, who is confident that the appearance of cosmogonies in China is not only of an earlier provenance, but that they are pervasive, and are similar in kind to those found in our classical Western sources.[39] This ostensive debate, however, really misses the point. The crux of the matter lies not in whether or not there is cosmogony in classical Chinese cosmology. This question is easily answered: Natural cosmology is procreative, and is cosmogonic in entailing continuing natal beginnings, whether such birthings are remembered by existing mythologies or not. The nub of the issue lies in distinguishing between a genealogical and a metaphysical cosmogony, the implications of this difference being profound. This fundamental distinction is not lost on Norman Girardot:

> There is no doubt that there are significant differences in the ancient Chinese world view in comparison with other traditions, but the notion that the cosmological gulf consists in the nonexistence of myth, creation myth, or mythological thought is an issue that deserves to be put to rest

V · Confucian Human-Centered Religiousness

with all possible dispatch. It is not the absence of creation mythology that accounts for the cosmological differences but the manner and nature of the Chinese interpretation of traditional mythological creation tales. The real "gulf" has to do with how different early civilizations fathomed the mythological gap of chaos.... The Chinese twist that is given to this archetypal plot is that creation as well as cosmological and soteriological meaning, do not ordinarily involve the epic idea of a final and permanent conquest of some existential chaotic foe.[40]

John Major in his interpretation of the technical chapters of the *Huainanzi* discusses in some detail the various accounts of cosmogony that are to be found in this work. Indeed we might join the conversation between John Major and Hal Roth when they compare a passage that first appears in the second chapter of *Zhuangzi* 莊子—probably of pre-Han vintage—with a similar account found in the second chapter of the early Han-dynasty text, the *Huainanzi* 淮南子. Indeed, these two passages, while being almost identical in content, make almost antithetical philosophical points—one questioning the very possibility of initial beginnings, and the other trying to describe the various stages of the gradual process of birthing as they unfold.[41] Here I will first translate the *Huainanzi* 2 version:

> There is that which had a beginning.[42] There is that which has not yet begun to have "that which had a beginning." And there is that which has not yet begun to have "that which has not yet begun to have that which had a beginning." There is "that which is something"; there is "that which is nothing." And there is "that which has not yet begun to be either something or nothing."[43]

The older *Zhuangzi* version seems very similar, although unlike the *Huainanzi* that references a concrete phenomenon as "something that had a beginning," the *Zhuangzi*'s focus is on the very conception of "beginning" itself:

> There is: a "beginning." There is: "not yet begun to have a beginning." There is: "not yet begun to have 'not yet begun to have a beginning.'" There is: "something." There is: "nothing." There is: "not yet begun to be nothing." There is: "not yet having begun to have 'not yet have begun to have nothing.'"[44]

While the intent of the author in the *Zhuangzi* passage is to reject *conceptually* and *logically* the possibility of an initial beginning by appealing to an inescapable infinite regress, the author of the *Huainanzi* version wants instead to describe *historically* the increasingly obscure stages as we move backward through the evolving birthing process of the phenomenal world that we presently know.

While the point being made in these two passages is clearly different, the *Zhuangzi* and the *Huainanzi* still share an important assumption that distinguishes both of them from what might otherwise be taken to be similar cosmogonic descriptions in classical Western sources: the cosmogonies to be found in *Genesis*, the *Timaeus*, and *Theogony*, for example. That is, we must resist the eliding of genealogical cosmogonies with metaphysical cosmogonies in which chaos is overcome by some external principle. Chaos as formlessness, as confusion, and as separation is overcome by command (will) (*Genesis*), by reason (*Timaeus*), or by unity (passion) (*Theogony*) respectively. Such "etiological tales"—stories of origins—introduce notions of agency and construal that give rise to causal thinking and rationality. To reason is to construe or uncover order; it is to think *causally*.

Both the *Zhuangzi* and the *Huainanzi*, as different as they are, come down on the genealogical side. In interpreting them, we must distinguish between a transforming world that *emerges* historically and genealogically in the classical Chinese texts where the generative energy of its birthing comes from within the world itself, and a world order *derived* from some transcendent principle familiar in some classical Western accounts.

Consistent with this historical cosmogony, we find that *tian* and *di* on the oracle bones and in the early canons often have an anthropomorphic reference, prompting some of the early interpreters of Chinese culture (and some contemporary scholars as well) to assume a correspondence between the sometimes anthropomorphic Abrahamic God and these Chinese terms.[45] But on the Chinese side, anthropomorphism is a natural extension of a human-centered religiousness, where the object of reverence is genealogical and ancestral. Indeed, the historicist anthropomorphism we find in Chinese cosmology that allows for the intervention of ancestors on behalf of their progeny is profoundly different in kind from a transcendentalism that depends upon divine revelation as its source of knowledge.

In a transcendental or metaphysical cosmogony, the originative and determinative principle—the Abrahamic God or Plato's Forms—stands independent of its creature and, as an external source, imposes a preassigned design on chaos. Even Aristotle's attempt to make form "immanent" does not alter its transcendental status as immutable in its relationship to matter, and his self-sufficient Prime Mover contemplating itself as the content of its own thought secures its independence from anything beyond it. Natural change is then driven by a linear teleology that takes us from origination to the realization of the given design. There is a plan, a beginning, and an end. Some ahistorical, acultural Agent—some Being behind the beings, some Creator behind the creatures—must be posited in order to explain why things *are* rather than *are not*, and *why* they are *what* they are. Metaphysical cosmogony is very ambitious: It promises us that if we are able to trace "the many" back to the ordering One, all will be known.

Meaning and Value: Confucian A-Theistic Religiousness

If classical Chinese cosmogonies do not take us back to some transcendent source of design, where then does meaning come from? It is the answer to this question that establishes a direct line between Confucian role ethics and Confucian human-centered religiousness.

A generation ago Herbert Fingarette chose the title *Confucius: The Secular as Sacred* for a small book that came to have an enormous impact on the understanding of Confucian philosophy within the Western academy. In this monograph and other seminal papers that followed from it, Fingarette argues forcefully that in the Confucian world the "ritualization" and refinement of the roles and relationships that structure family and community enchant the human experience, and stand as the ultimate source of what is sacred.[46] In chapter three above I have argued that one way of conceiving the Confucian relationally constituted person is to appeal to the cognate terms, "embodying" (*ti* 體) and "achieving propriety in one's roles and relations" (*li* 禮), as the progression through which we become human. And in chapter four I again rehearsed the meaning of this central, polysemous notion of "achieving propriety in ritualized roles and relations" (*li*) as the term of art in Confucian philosophy that describes this transforming and refining of the human experience as the ground for Confucian role ethics. It can be fairly argued again in this chapter that it is this same notion of *li* that can be used to bring Confucian religiosity into clearer focus.

It is often remarked that "religion" as a term might be derived from the Latin *religare* meaning "to bind tightly." One can see how *li* as a family and communal grammar locating persons in their proper place relative to each other would bind them together, thereby strengthening the fabric of society and encouraging a robust sense of shared meaning and belonging. Although within the Confucian context, *li* has not been broadly institutionalized as a formal "religion" per se, it still functions to foster a religious quality in the human experience in fortifying our family and communal bonds. A powerful argument has been made by philosophers such as Ralph Waldo Emerson, John Dewey, and most recently, Richard Rorty and Gianni Vattimo, that real religiousness, free from the sometimes suffocating uniformities enforced by formal religious institutions, can only be achieved by giving full expression to our own personal uniqueness, a process that in fact allows for the open informality and the distinctive personalization that are the defining features of *li*.[47]

The family ground of *li* allows for an immediate extension from "family" (*jia* 家) to "ancestor, ancestral temple, clan" (*zong* 宗), a character that occurs in the oracle bones as *[xliii]*, and that is explained by philologists as "the temple in which the ancestral tablets are displayed."[48] This association accounts for the pre-modern Japanese coinage of the term for "religion" as *shūkyō* 宗教 (Ch. *zongjiao*), literally "the teachings of the ancestral temple and the extended family" in which this family locus of religiousness is its primary reference.[49]

Li is defined in the *Shuowen* lexicon paronomastically—that is, by phonetic and semantic association—as *lü* 履 meaning "treading a path," and hence the continuing narrative of one's conduct or behavior. *Li* has been conventionally translated as "ritual," "rites," "customs," "etiquette," "propriety," "morals," "rules of proper behavior," "achieved propriety in ritualized roles and relations," and "reverence." Properly contextualized, each of these English terms can render *li* on occasion. In classical Chinese, however, the character carries *all* of these meanings, albeit with differing degrees of emphasis, on every occasion of its use. As we saw above, the compound character *li* 禮 is an ideograph connoting the presentation (*shi* 示) of sacrifices to the primarily ancestral spirits at an altar to them (*li* 豊), suggesting the profoundly religious significance that this term entails.

Parsed in its narrower but both formal and informal senses, *li* is how personally to serve the family and communal spirits, both living and dead, to bring about a thriving family and community, with its emphasis being clearly upon human flourishing in this world rather than in the next. This understanding of *li* as being processional, eventful, and family- and community-centered is a signature of classical Confucian religiousness in which the focus is on reverence for the continuity of one's lineage expressed through sincere family feeling and concern (*xiao* 孝). In its ceremonial form, it is the celebration of people who are now dead rather than any preoccupation with the "worship" of dead people. As Confucius says:

> To devote yourself to what is appropriate for the people, and to show respect for the ghosts and spirits while keeping them at a distance can be called wisdom.[50]

One possible interpretation of this passage would suggest the Confucian philosophy is a kind of secular humanism that resists more elevated religious practices. A better reading I believe would allow that for Confucius, spirituality as a human value arises in striving to do what is optimally appropriate for others within family and community, and that formal religious functions are properly instrumental in reinforcing this end. Confucius seems to be making this same point when he responds to his student, Zilu, explaining that the appropriate site for cultivating and expressing our religious feelings is the living world of family and friends:

> Zilu asked how to serve the spirits and the gods. The Master replied, "Not yet being able to serve other people, how would you be able to serve the spirits?" He said, "May I ask about death?" The Master replied, "Not yet understanding life, how could you understand death?"[51]

We have chosen to translate *li* in its broadest compass as "striving for propriety in one's roles and relations." Again, this rendering is a considered choice. On the formal side, *li* are those meaning-invested roles, relationships, and institutions that facilitate communication, and foster a sense of community. Most formal and conventionalized conduct that makes social living in our specific roles and relations meaningful constitutes *li*, including table manners, patterns of greeting and leave-taking, graduations, weddings, funerals, gestures of deference, ancestral sacrifices, and so on. *Li* are a social syntax that at any one time provides each member with a defined place and status within the family, community, and polity. Just as grammar as a felicitous arrangement of words functions to produce semantic meaning, so *li* as the attentive coordination of roles and relations conduces to the attainment of social meaning. *Li* are a hermeneutics of life-forms transmitted from generation to generation as repositories of emerging and compounding meaning, enabling individuals to appropriate persisting values and to make these values appropriate to their own, always unique, situations. While we perform the *li* in the present, much of their efficacy stems from their being a link to the past, and thereby, to the future as well.

Li is nothing less than "discourse" in its broadest sense where, in its most refined and religious applications, it can be the source of a communal poetry and a cosmic musicality that is so movingly expressed in the latter books of the *Zhongyong*. In the discursive community, meaning emerges out of the relational virtuosity made possible by effective communication in all of its forms. Given the speciousness of any "literal" metanarrative that would promise to give us access to some foundational truth, all we have is discourse as a currency for productively renegotiating situations as they arise—what Richard Rorty calls our possibility to generate infinite "redescriptions" (or perhaps better in the Confucian case, "re*pre*scriptions")—so that the conversation might continue.[52] Indeed, language becomes poetry in which the text emerges in its full autonomy as what the world really is. As Hans-Georg Gadamer observes, "Here language just stands for itself, it brings itself to stand before us."[53] What Gadamer means, I think, is that language commands a world into being, and cannot be treated instrumentally and reductively as mere representation of some given reality. Poetic language is presentational more than representational, is inciteful (and sometimes "insightful") more than referential, is perlocutionary and inspiring more than descriptive. It is in the poetry and in the song occasioned by *li* that we most immediately and dramatically experience the collaboration between human feeling and its contextualizing horizons as together we create our world.

Using the Confucian vocabulary itself to reiterate this opportunity for shared communicative growth, Confucius regularly contrasts his notion of socially and politically constituted "exemplary persons" (*junzi*) with those who fail to cultivate the roles and relationships that locate them in community—what he calls "small or petty persons" (*xiaoren* 小人). Not only do such "small persons" contribute little to the flourishing of their worlds, but further, their failure to develop the sense of shame and belonging that makes them responsive to others, and thus responsible members of community, can constitute a very real threat to social order.

Indeed, Vrinda Dalmiya makes a case that "'not doings' can be as violent as some doings."[54] The magnitude of this violence is underscored in Hannah Arendt's rather thin description of Adolf Eichmann as having been "thoughtless" and "banal" rather than evil, a seemingly mild indictment for a genocidal monster. But Arendt's point is that Eichmann's "carelessness"—the tyranny of a shameless individual who "couldn't care less"—emerges from the empowerment of the actions of a morally retarded person who perpetrates a maelstrom of violence that arises in the absence of thinking and feeling. In a Confucian world, there is a very real sense in which the disintegrative conduct of rude, thoughtless, and shameless persons is the ultimate source of immorality.

On the informal and uniquely personal side, full participation in a ritually constituted community requires the personalization of prevailing customs, institutions, and values. What makes ritually constituted order profoundly different from law or rule is this hermeneutical process of participating, confirming, and ultimately, reauthorizing the tradition as one's own. Ritual propriety, like most things Confucian, begins at home, and through radial patterns of deference, becomes cosmic in its reach. The performance of *li*, thus understood, sediments into the human community, defining the appropriate relationships between the present population and its forbearers, and the proper relationships between those who would exercise social and political authority and those who are governed by it.

Confucian Religiousness: The Flower of Inspired Living

Elsewhere I have argued that classical Confucianism is at once nontheistic, and profoundly religious.[55] It is a religious tradition certainly with "ghosts and spirits" in the sense of ancestors and cultural heroes and who knows what else, but without a God; it is a religious sensibility that affirms a shared spirituality that emerges out of the inspired human experience itself. There is no parish (except for the extended family), no altars (except for perhaps the dining room table), and no clergy (except for those exemplary models deferred to as the living center of one's family and community). Confucianism celebrates the way in which the process of human growth and extension is shaped by, and contributes to, the meaning of the totality—a notion of *creatio in situ* that stands in stark contrast to *creatio ex nihilo* traditions.[56]

We have encountered the *Zhongyong*, or *Focusing the Familiar*, earlier. It is a short yet seminal text that from Han-dynasty times had a prominence as both a chapter in the *Book of Rites* (*Liji*) and as an independently circulating text—a stature that was much magnified from the thirteenth century onward when, as one of the *Four Books* designated by Zhu Xi, it would have been known by heart certainly by every aspirant to civil office and by most Chinese intellectuals as well. It is because the *Zhongyong* is among the *Four Books* the most powerful statement of Confucian religiousness that Zhu Xi singles it out as the highest expression of the Confucian project.

In many ways the *Zhongyong* is an object lesson in the aggregating radial expression of Confucian religiousness that begins modestly with personal cultivation and culminates in a cosmic transformation. Following Zhu Xi in taking the *Zhongyong* as a linear and coherent document, we might observe that the cadence of this text in the early sections moves rather listlessly with an expressed concern over the continuing failure of human beings to forge their way effectively in the world. Indeed, an exasperated Confucius laments, "Alas, this proper way is not being traveled at all!"[57] But once under way, the *Zhongyong* gradually gathers speed, celebrating both our human capacity and our ultimate responsibility to step up as co-creators with the heavens and the earth in shaping the emergent order of the cosmos. As the text continues, the pace quickens dramatically, declaring that by participating fully in the transforming and nourishing activities of heaven and earth "human beings can take their places as members of this triad,"[58] and in so doing, "can become the complement of *tian*."[59] With a final burst of energy, then, the *Zhongyong* hastens toward its crescendo—its own "Ode to Joy"—in which it quite literally breaks into song, rejoicing in the capacity of consummatory human beings to create meaning and to realize their world.

In the Chinese cosmology expressed in the *Zhongyong*, the lived world is the bottomless unfolding of an always-provisional world order according to the rhythm of its own internal creative processes without any fixed pattern or guiding hand. And in the absence of any creator "God," this Confucian cosmology lifts the bar rather significantly with respect to the degree of creativity expected from the human collaborator. A meaningful world can only be achieved through concerted human effort.

There are several profound differences between this Confucian religiousness and those Abrahamic traditions that have largely defined the meaning of religion in the Anglo-European cultural narratives and beyond. I would argue that, unlike the "worship" model that defers to the ultimate meaning of some temporally prior, independent, external agency—what F. D. E. Schleiermacher has called religions of "absolute dependence"—Confucian religious experience is itself a *product* of the flourishing community where the quality of the religious life is a direct consequence of the quality of communal living. And the sacred in Confucianism is not only the root of the flourishing community as it is inherited from past generations, not only the foundation on which the culture is built, but it is also the ongoing achieved quality of inspired living—the blossom and the fruit of human flourishing. It is a human-centered, rather than a God-centered, religiousness that emerges through conscientious attention to refining the human experience through achieved propriety in our roles and relations.

A second way in which Confucian religiousness is distinct from the Abrahamic traditions is that Confucian religiousness is neither salvific nor eschatological. While it does entail a kind of conversion, it is specifically a transformation of the quality of human life in the ordinary business of the day that not only elevates and inspires our daily transactions, but further extends outward radially from the family and community to enchant the world. The cosmos is wider and deeper and richer when human foraging is elevated to *haute cuisine*, when stick markings are disciplined into fine calligraphy and breathtaking bronze designs, when coarse gestures are refined to become the sober cadence of ceremony and the exhilaration of the dance, when grunting interventions are amplified into a sublime and haunting melody, when the heat of random copulation becomes the constant and reassuring warmth of hearth and family. It is this transformation—the ordinary and everyday made elegant—that seems at least in part to provide the mystery other expressions of religious feeling find in some transcendent, supernatural appeal.

There are surely those who would regard a Confucian human-centered religiousness that makes no appeal to a transcendent deity as a much-impoverished sense of religion. They might remain unconvinced that such an alternative human-centered and naturalistic religious sensibility is sufficiently robust to be legitimately labeled "religious" in the first place, lowering the bar so dramatically that it might be better described as a kind of secular humanism. They might dispute my claim that the centrality of the religious aspect of Confucian philosophy with its focus on ritualized living is a viable "a-theistic" religiousness that warrants a vocabulary importantly different from that of theism.

But a Confucian response to such incredulity might join John Dewey in his critique on more conventional, institutionalized religion, suggesting that a transcendental appeal offers little respite or real relief to the vicissitudes of the human experience:

> Were it a thousand times dialectically demonstrated that life as a whole is regulated by a transcendent principle to a final inclusive goal, nonetheless truth and error, health and disease, good and evil, hope and fear in the concrete, would remain just what and where they are now.[60]

Dewey is asserting here that claims about a transcendent source do not make any real difference to the world we actually experience. But perhaps he is not going far enough. Might not the Confucian press Dewey's critique further to insist that there is, in fact, a real cost to transcendence—indeed, a "religious" cost—in that it takes a toll on the possibilities for the disclosure of personal meaning in one's actual relationships? That is, the power of the family to function as the radial locus for human growth in spirituality might be diminished when natural family and communal relations are perceived as being in competition with, a distraction from, or dependent upon some higher supernatural relations. Said another way, when human relations are subordinated to a personal relationship with a transcendent object of worship, whatever the benefits of such subordination might be, such dividends might well come at a cost to the fabric of family and community. In the Confucian case, it is persons themselves who emerge as objects of profound communal, cultural, and ultimately religious deference. Beyond the achievement of an intense religious quality felt in the everyday experience of their lives, these exemplary persons continue as venerated ancestors for their families and communities, and as contributors to the ancestral legacy—to *tian* 天—that defines Chinese culture more broadly construed. It is the cumulative investment of ancestors and traditional heroes over time that makes the cultural and the religious legacy determinate and meaningful.

We have seen that, for the Confucian, it is the creative possibility within the inspired human life to enchant the cosmos that is the more important meaning of "religiousness." This enchantment in the "thoughtful" feelings of family and friends emerges in their mutual and reciprocated sensitivity and awareness. Indeed such appreciation spills over to become "value-added"—quite literally raising the value of the cosmos in which these meaningful relationships mature. Our shared cosmos is much appreciated, becoming a more magnificent time and place because of the profound, indeed, the inspired feelings we come to have for each other.

Ironically, what might be interpreted as a Confucian challenge to conventional religious institutions and practices might also be read as serving to liberate religiousness in a way not unknown within American revisionist theology. We might be inspired by the early twentieth-century theologian, Henry Leuba, who insists that:

> Does God really exist? How does he exist? What is he? Are so many irrelevant questions. Not God, but life, more life, a larger, richer, more satisfying life, is, in the last analysis, the end of religion. The love of life, at any and every level of development, is the religious impulse.[61]

We might also appeal to Emerson's scandalous, yet wholly inspiring, "Divinity School Address" when he laments that we human beings have lost sight of our own divine capacity:

> The doctrine of the divine nature being forgotten, a sickness infects and dwarfs the constitution. Once man was all; now he is an appendage, a nuisance. And because the indwelling Supreme Spirit cannot wholly be gotten rid of, the doctrine of it suffers this perversion, that the divine nature is attributed to one or two persons, and denied to all the rest, and denied with fury.[62]

Emerson insists that the real message of Jesus is that he is a man, not a god, and that he "saw with an open eye the mystery of the soul":

> Drawn by its severe harmony, ravished with its beauty, he lived in it, and had his being there. Alone in all history, he estimated the greatness of man. One man was true to what is in you and me.... Thus was he a true man. Having seen that the law in us is commanding, he would not suffer it to be commanded. Boldly, with hand, and heart, and life, he declared it was God. Thus was he a true man. Thus is he, as I think, the only soul in history who has appreciated the worth of a man.[63]

Dewey too celebrates the human potential, being adamant that the ultimate religious and moral meaning of democracy itself arises from its capacity to conduce to the fullest expression of personal worth:

> Government, business, art, religion, all social institutions have a meaning, a purpose. That purpose is to set free and develop the capacities of human individuals without respect to race, sex, class or economic status. And this is all one with saying that the test of their value is the extent to which they educate every individual into the full stature of his possibility.[64]

Leuba and Emerson before him would both interpret real religiousness as persons achieving the fullest disclosure of their own uniqueness in contributing to cosmic significance and hence to an earned sense of belonging most meaningfully to this same cosmos. In thus creating themselves, they create their world.

The Nature of Creativity: Confucian Religiousness as Co-Creativity

I will argue that Confucian religiousness is precisely this sense of co-creativity of self and world, and in fact that such co-creativity is the only kind of real creativity. Indeed, in this Confucian cosmology, nothing happens by itself. To make this argument, I want to explore this notion of co-creativity at several different levels, beginning from the Confucian claim that in our own personal collaborations—in my case, in the delightful intellectual and emotional journeys that I have enjoyed with D. C. Lau, David Hall, and Henry Rosemont—we have done much to create each other. Ascending to a more general level, I want to suggest that in Confucian religiousness, the focus of creativity is the transactional process of human beings shaping and being shaped by their fellow human beings in family and community.[65] And finally, at the highest and most pervasive level, I will invoke the Confucian notion of the "three capacities" (*sancai* 三才) and the claim that human creativity is an ingredient integral and necessary to further inspire the heavens and the earth in the evolving process of generating cosmic spirituality.

The several questions that will guide our exploration of our own assumptions about the nature of creativity itself and that will enable us to develop a clearer understanding of how this seminal idea functions within the Confucian tradition are: 1) To what areas of the human experience do we usually apply the notion of creativity? 2) Is there an equivocation when we use creativity and originality, and if so, why? 3) How are the notions of integrity, genuineness, sincerity, and creativity interrelated? 4) What are the roles of feeling and thinking in creativity? and 5) How is "creativity" expressed in a Chinese philosophical vocabulary?

Let me draw on our translation and interpretation of the *Zhongyong* to try to respond to these concerns about the nature of creativity. The standard English rendering of the *Zhongyong* is the 1861 translation of the Scottish missionary, James Legge. It references the earlier Jesuit translations, and has had and continues to have a profound influence on most subsequent European-language interpretations of this text. For Legge, the opening passage provides him with a familiar and uncontroversial account of cosmic order:

> What Heaven has conferred is called THE NATURE; an accordance with this nature is called THE PATH *of duty*; the regulation of this path is called INSTRUCTION.

On Legge's reading of the *Zhongyong*, this wholly-credible theistic beginning gives way to an unfortunate rambling, and indeed, blasphemous exaltation of human creativity that subverts the very ground of Christian worship. Upon having completed his translation, Legge is prompted to challenge the high estimate that the Chinese tradition has lavished on this text with his own pious reservations concerning its content and its influence. Legge laments:

> It begins sufficiently well, but the author has hardly enunciated his preliminary apophthegms, when he conducts into an obscurity where we can hardly grope our way, and when we emerge from that, it is to be bewildered by his gorgeous but unsubstantial pictures of sagely perfection. He has eminently contributed to nourish the pride of his countrymen. He has exalted their sages above all that is called God or is worshipped, and taught the masses of the people that with them they have need of nothing from without. In the meantime it is antagonistic to Christianity. By-and-by, when Christianity has prevailed in China, men will refer to it as a striking proof how their fathers by their wisdom knew neither God nor themselves.[66]

What is particularly telling about Legge's honest if scathing evaluation of the *Zhongyong* is that he is wholly aware of the incongruency between his own theistic interpretation of the opening passage and the celebration of the cosmic magnitude of human creativity conveyed in the remainder of the text, a human creativity that challenges scriptural authority on human dependence upon a Creator God. Legge's understanding of the thrust of the *Zhongyong*, whilst wishing it were otherwise, is that human beings led by their sages have in their world everything necessary to achieve their own realization without reference to some transcendent deity, and moreover, that these exemplars so inspire the world around them with human creativity that the heavens and the earth too have no appeal beyond themselves to some more ultimate reality. Cosmic creativity is fully a collaboration between human beings and their world, a cosmology that is consistent with what John Berthrong calls "the world-dependent nature of divine reality."[67]

And as we have seen, Legge is not without good textual evidence for this human-centered interpretation of the *Zhongyong*. The opening passage of the *Zhongyong* emphasizes the capacity and the responsibility of the human world to achieve a creative harmony and balance in the expression of its feelings, and gives an account of how this human achievement conduces to a flourishing cosmos in which all things find their proper place. This radically situated, multilateral creative process is described unambiguously in this text by investing the Confucian term *cheng* 誠 with cosmic meaning. *Cheng* is a familiar term usually translated as "sincerity," "honesty," or "integrity," but herein it is used with an unfamiliar cosmological application that has prompted us along with other commentators to consider "creativity" as a possible rendering for it that captures this capacity:[68]

> Creativity (*cheng*) is self-realizing (*zicheng* 自成), and its way (*dao* 道) is self-advancing (*zidao* 自道). Creativity references things and events (*wu* 物) taken from their beginning to their end, and without this creativity, there would be nothing happening. It is thus that, for exemplary persons (*junzi*), it is creativity that is prized. But creativity is not simply the self-realizing of one's own person; it is also what realizes other things and events. Realizing oneself is becoming consummate in one's conduct (*ren* 仁); realizing the world is wisdom (*zhi* 知). This is an achieved excellence (*de* 德) in one's natural tendencies (*xing* 性) and is the way of integrating what is more internal with what is more external. Thus, when and wherever one applies such excellence, it is fitting.[69]

There are other passages in the *Zhongyong* that celebrate this human capacity to create meaning and to realize a world, characterizing the human being quite literally as a co-creator with the heavens and the earth. The text describes the collaboration between human beings and their social and natural environments in world-making, asserting that there is a profound symbiosis between human and natural creativity:

> Only those of utmost creativity (*zhicheng* 至誠) in the world are able to get the most out of their natural tendencies (*xing* 性). Only if one is able to get the most out one's own natural tendencies is one able to get the most out of the natural tendencies of others; only if one is able to get the most out of the natural tendencies of others is one able to get the most out of the natural tendencies of things and events (*wu* 物); only if one is able to get

the most out of the natural tendencies of things and events can one assist in the transforming and nourishing activities of heaven and earth; and only if one can assist in the transforming and nourishing activities of heaven and earth can human beings take their place as a member of this triad.[70]

The *Zhongyong* continues, taking this celebration one step further to identify optimum human creativity with sagacity. The virtuosic human being is not only a source of meaning, but of cosmic enchantment. It describes the process and the value of human world-making in full celestial hyperbole:

> Only those of utmost sagacity (*zhisheng* 至聖) in the world have the acuity and quickness of mind needed to oversee the empire; have the tolerance and flexibility needed to win them the forbearance of others; have the energy and fortitude needed to maintain their grasp; have the poise and impeccability needed to command respect; have the culture and discernment needed to be discriminating. So broad, expansive, and profoundly deep, they demonstrate these several qualities whenever needed. So broad and expansive like the heavens themselves; so profoundly deep like a bottomless abyss: they appear and all defer to them; they speak and all have confidence in what they say; they act and all find pleasure in what they do.
>
> It is for this reason that their fame spreads out over the Central States, extending to the Man and Mo barbarians in the south and north. Everywhere that boats and carriages ply, everywhere that human strength penetrates, everywhere that is sheltered by the heavens and is borne up by the earth, everywhere that is illumined by sun and moon, everywhere that the frosts and dew settle—all creatures that have breath and blood revere and love them. Thus it is said that they are the complement of *tian* 天.[71]

As I argued above, the familiar Confucian claim that "everyone can become a sage" is often read essentialistically as an assertion that sagacity is some universally given potential in human nature that if actualized provides any person with those extraordinary talents through which to affect the world in some incomparable way. But we have seen that, given the Confucian conception of the relationally constituted person, this same claim might alternatively be read as a recognition that optimizing the human experience within the broad social, natural, and cultural context of this processual world described here in the *Zhongyong* is truly creative and consummatory, and that the spontaneous emergence of real significance in a continuing present within the ordinary business of the day is itself the meaning and content of sagely virtuosity. The potential to become a sage emerges over time within the successful narratives of those persons who become most authoritatively human.

One might attribute Legge's outrage at what he interprets as unbridled hubris that challenges the very role of the Creator God to his stodgy Scottish "common sensism," a philosophical movement in Legge's nineteenth-century Britain. "Common sensism" provided a staunch and steadfast defense of the Christian religious and moral status quo that it took to be the anchor of common sense against a corrosive Humean skepticism. Whatever the source of Legge's displeasure, this reticence to allow the human being full partnership in cosmic creativity seems to be a common sense that is still very much with us today, and continues to be reflected in more contemporary translations of the *Zhongyong*. Translators of this text continue to follow Legge in presenting their readers with an unabashedly theistic understanding of the opening passage of the text. But unlike Legge, who is keenly aware of his own Christian assumptions and who thus recognizes the clear disjunction that the *Zhongyong* has with any theistic understanding of creativity, these interpreters insinuate a familiar conception of Divine creativity into the text, and in so doing, deny any real status to the human collaboration in producing cosmic order.[72]

I will take the recent Penguin translation of the *Zhongyong* by Andrew Plaks as an example. Because Plaks as translator is not convinced that locating the text within its own interpretive context is a necessary guard against cultural reductionism, his rendering of the *Zhongyong* comes to be invested with a transcendentalism not its own.[73] In his analysis of the first chapter, Plaks introduces the ontological assumptions of a two-world theory and "two separate orders of being" into the *Zhongyong*, distinguishing the pursuit of a compensatory harmony possible within the human sphere from "the static totality of the 'great foundation' of the universe." Plaks observes:

> For here we are told that the Confucian act of moral instruction, the other side of the coin of self-cultivation, is to be understood as a process of perfecting (literally, "repairing" or "restoring") the Way—as if the Tao [*dao*],

> the "Way" that has been defined immediately before this as *immanent* in the very nature of things imparted by the "ordinance" of Heaven, could be in need of any such repair. This is our first indication that the *Chung Yung* [*Zhongyong*] will not be concerned with the ineffable substance of the cosmic Way—important as this may be for the ontological grounding of the Confucian ethical system—but, instead, with the concerted efforts required on the part of man to attain a more accessible kind of "Tao," that is, to perfect his own *way* in the world.[74]

In this opening passage of the *Zhongyong*, Plaks finds the logic that he sees as governing the text as a whole and that gives the sometimes seemingly incongruent chapters a sustained integrity and coherence:

> The key to integrating the disparate elements of the text lies in grasping and consistently applying the reasoning implied at the very outset and reinforced in each of the subsequent contexts of discussion. This is the essential distinction between the cosmic and the sublunar planes of being and the assigning of primary significance to the concerted acts of human striving required for the ordering and perfecting of the latter realm.[75]

Beginning with chapter twenty, the *Zhongyong* develops an explicit distinction between the way of human beings and the way of *tian* (what Plaks translates as "the Way of Heaven"). Plaks reads this distinction in a familiar way, contrasting an independent, exclusive, and perfect cosmic order with the struggle that such perfection makes possible for the human experience:

> In accordance with this logic, a vital distinction is drawn between the "Way of Heaven" and the "Way of Man," such that—as we saw in the treatment of the parallel concepts of the mean and harmony in Chapter I—a state of unqualified perfection is attributed to the cosmic order alone, leaving in the hands of man the arduous pursuit of a lesser degree of integral wholeness.[76]

Plaks joins Legge in registering his reservations about the language of the *Zhongyong* that exalts human creativity as being on a par with "Heaven," (*tian* 天), offending as it does against our own theological common sense. But unlike Legge who indicts the text for what he takes to be its unrestrained hubris, Plaks instead finds ways to "sanitize" the language (his own term):

> This enunciation of the supreme metaphysical consequences of the most

perfect degree of cultivation—already hinted at toward the close of Chapter I—hinges upon the conspicuous use of two uncommon verbal expressions. The first, *tsan* 贊 ("to assist in"), introduces the idea of participation—presumably as more than a peripheral observer—in the continuous creation of the cosmic order. We can only speculate about how literally our author wishes us to understand these words.... The second unfamiliar usage is even more striking: it takes the numeral "three" (in a stylized classical written form) and turns it into an intransitive verb meaning something like "to join as a third term." In this way, the previous implication of potential "participation" in the cosmic process are raised to an even higher power, making man a full partner, so to speak, in the dynamic structure of the universe.[77]

Plaks exercises himself in finding a possible way to read the text that maintains the appropriate hierarchical disconnect between the divine creative source and the ostensive human partner:

The insertion of the comparative preposition *ju* 如 [*ru*] ("as," "as if") before the term *shen* ("god," "spirit") immediately softens the blow, allowing us to maintain that the Confucian "sage" only *appears* to embody divine attributes.... Moreover, there are good grounds for arguing that the term *shen* in early texts refers as often to divine *attributes*, notably prescience or perspicacity, as it does to divine beings. In this light, one could sanitize the present line and have it mean something as innocuous as: "he appears to be endowed with a god-like capacity."[78]

But, as we have seen in sections 22, 25, and 31 cited above, the *Zhongyong* is just too explicit and unambiguous about exalting the vital role of human creativity in the unfolding of the cosmos. Still, for Plaks, the "essential distinction between the cosmic and the sublunar planes of being" limits the human role to an historical instantiation of a transcendent ideal: that is, "the translation of an abstract universal ideal into concrete realization."[79] This ontological reading of the text that renders "the great root of the world" (*tianxia zhi daben* 天下之大本) in the first chapter as "the all-inclusive ground of being" is on Plaks's reading reinforced by traditional Chinese commentators who are themselves aware that the endowment received from this perfect source requires nothing further from its human recipient:

The traditional commentators agree that the universal Way, the Way that is immanent in all men and things by their intrinsic natures, requires no further *cultivation* on the part of man. That which man does need to cultivate through the discipline of "moral instruction" is, rather, the correct Confucian way of ordering the self and world.[80]

On Plaks's interpretation, if human beings are supposedly full partners in cosmic creativity, they still quite literally add nothing to what is really real.

Plaks is ascribing to the Confucian worldview what William James describes as a term of abject criticism, a "block universe." Far from entailing real change and the possibility of difference, such absolutism gives us what he in *A Pluralistic Universe* derides as "the rationalistic block universe, entire, unmitigated, complete."[81] Dewey, in explaining this expression as used by his mentor, states:

> Mechanism and idealism were abhorrent to him [William James] because they both hold to a closed universe in which there is no room for novelty and adventure. Both sacrifice individuality and all the values, moral and aesthetic, which hang upon individuality, for according to absolute idealism, as to mechanistic materialism, the individual is simply a part determined by the whole of which he is a part. Only a philosophy of pluralism, of genuine indetermination, and of change that is real and intrinsic gives significance to individuality. It alone justifies struggle in creative activity and gives opportunity for the emergence of the genuinely new.[82]

But at the same time, we can say that Plaks is providing his English-language readers with a common sense understanding of the *Zhongyong*—that is, a reading that appeals to *their* common sense. Indeed, if we reflect for a moment on our own common-sense use of the notion of "creativity" in ordinary language, we can see how the God-centered value of creativity that both Legge and Plaks are assuming in their interpretations of the *Zhongyong* is still inherent in the way in which we think and speak.

When we ask the first of the questions guiding our exploration of creativity—To what areas of the human experience do we usually apply the notion of creativity?—we see that it is invoked most comfortably with reference to the disciplines of the arts and literature, that is, with respect to the entertaining occupations of producing artifice and fiction. But when we turn to the serious business of the day—morality, theology, science, and even "business" itself—"creativity" becomes suspect. If I were to learn that a friend is morally "creative," while I might properly stand in admiration of his rakish charms, I would also be concerned about his having anything but a passing acquaintance with my comely wife or my innocent children. If our religious neighbors are known to be theologically "creative," the Pope perhaps more than me is going to be worried about the status of their immortal souls. If a scientific colleague is described publicly as having been "creative" in his experiments with the cloning of human organs, his multi-million dollar grants might well be put at risk. And if my financial advisors have been "creative" in their accounting and I have become unseemly rich as a consequence, I am likely to be audited by the IRS if not jailed first. In the discipline of philosophy itself, one can argue that Gadamerian "play" is philosophically intriguing because it challenges the Aristotelian seriousness and rigor that we have traditionally ascribed to philosophical inquiry. Indeed, what was perceived by many as Richard Rorty's grinning assault on our discipline banished him beyond the walls of philosophy proper to Stanford's Department of Comparative Literature and earned him all but excommunication from our professional society.

Further, while we generally associate "creativity" with our literary and artistic adventures, we do not seem to see these creative areas of the human experience as causal or linear, and thus progressive. Compare, for example, our sense of art history to other historiographies: Christian, Marxist, Hegelian, scientific. The strong commitment to teleology that is assumed in our common-sense understanding of the rationalized human experience drives cosmic progress without need for an appeal to any real human contribution.

A problem parallel to this truncated value of creativity seems to attend our common yet paradoxical use of the word "spontaneity." As Brian Bruya has observed:

> We can see the inception of what I call the Paradox of Spontaneity in the interpretations that Epicurus and Chrysippus give to natural human action. The Aristotelian internal teleology of natural objects, including humans, according to Chrysippus, allows us to say that all movement is spontaneous, that is, that there is no unmoved mover outside the natural order. For Epicurus, however, humans must remove

themselves from the determinacy of nature and choose freely, thus spontaneously. This paradox—that movement is spontaneous as determined and spontaneous as free—persists even into present everyday speech (e.g. we may say that grass grows spontaneously, or that so-and-so spontaneously broke into song). Although the Greeks did not have an equivalent for "spontaneity" as a term of art, they clearly wrestled with this tension and were the foundation of all later thought on the subject.[83]

Synonyms for spontaneity are on one side of the paradox "impulsive," that suggests randomness and disconnect, and on the other side "automatic," referencing something that is "predetermined." Both meanings preclude the role of agency. The term spontaneity, rather than referencing a cultivated virtuosity, has come to connote either random, uncaused behavior or predetermined, automatic behavior. This development is closely related to the prominence of a *creatio ex nihilo* notion of creativity that reduces spontaneity to either an agent's impulsive and inexplicable action, or to a preprogrammed design over which the agent has no control. Rather than suggesting a cultivated responsiveness on the part of the agent, spontaneity refers instead to actions that are unconstrained and unstudied in manner. The spontaneous emergence of novelty on such a reading, far from being virtuosic, would not seem to entail any personal cultivation at all.

If, however, we consult a Chinese-English dictionary, we find that the idea of spontaneity, like creativity, has a significantly different value. One Chinese equivalent given for "spontaneity" is *ziran* 自然. When this term is applied to human agency, the reflexive "self- (*zi* 自)" aspect of *ziran* has to be understood as persons-in-their-contextualizing-roles-and-relationships rather than as some separate and discrete self. Hence, *ziran* is always collaborative. In fact, *ziran* is the uninhibited virtuosity that defines the character and conduct of the *Zhuangzi*'s many craftsmen and enlightened exemplars as they interact efficaciously with their mediums and their environments:

> Butcher Ding was in the process of cutting up an ox for Lord Hui of Liang. Wherever hand came in contact, wherever shoulder leaned in, wherever foot trod down, wherever knee exerted pressure—the twack of meat separating from bone would echo and the twing of the knife's blade would ring out, with every stroke singing a perfect note consonant with "The Dance of the Mulberry Grove" and the "Jingshou Chorale."

"Magnificent!" exclaimed Lord Hui. "That technique could be raised to such heights!"

Butcher Ding laid his knife aside and replied, "What I really aspire to is an insight into the way of things (*dao*) that takes one far beyond any mere skill."[84]

Spontaneity is the hard-won freedom of action captured in the description of an evolving virtuosity in the life of Confucius himself:

The Master said, "From fifteen, my heartmind was set upon learning; from thirty I took my stance; from forty I was no longer doubtful; from fifty I realized the propensities of *tian*; from sixty my ear was attuned; from seventy I could give my heartmind free rein without overstepping the boundaries."[85]

In his recently published study, *The Value of Creativity: The Origins and Emergence of a Modern Belief*, the British philosopher John Hope Mason argues that "creativity" emerges as a value (such as heroism, honor, piety, and various other kinds of virtue) only in the mid-nineteenth century when developments in science and technology foster human independence, when a free-market economy encourages innovation, and when meliorative "progress" becomes an expectation.[86] But according to Hope Mason, within the Western cultural narrative the notion of creativity has had a complex history that has construed it in at least two radically different ways—indeed, a history that continues to condition the way in which we understand and use it today. In the most general and certainly not exclusive terms, one persistent assumption implicit in the Legge and Plaks readings of the *Zhongyong* is that creativity belongs to the Creator God, and connotes moral goodness, harmony, and spirituality. In this doctrine of a transcendent and perfect God, we have an equation between a *creatio ex nihilo* creativity and morality.[87] God haven spoken a world into being, "... it was good." And as *Psalms* 24 insists:

The earth is the Lord's and the fulness thereof
It is He that has made us and not we ourselves.

And *John* 1:3:

All things were made by Him; and without Him was not any thing made that was made.

Of course the history of the doctrine of *creatio ex nihilo* within the Greek, Hellenistic, and Abrahamic traditions is a complex and contested story, but to the extent that it guarantees the independent power, the absolute sovereignty, and the aseity of God, it has been a prominent theological theme and, as is illustrated by the guiding assumptions of Legge and Plaks, has had a role in shaping our common sense.

The second major tradition that colors our understanding of creativity is Promethean, where creativity is the work of a daringly original genius. Promethean creativity is the product of a struggle between the justice of Zeus and the audacious Titan pioneer of human civilization who steals the fire that makes such civilization possible. But because of the remove from God, such creativity is dark, dangerous, disruptive, and of questionable moral worth.

Hope Mason would see Kant, Coleridge, Carlyle, and Arnold as exemplars of the dominant valorization of creativity as the work of God (in its different senses), and would read Machiavelli's Prince, Goethe's Faust, Milton's Satan, the monster of Mary Shelley's "Victor" Frankenstein, and Nietzsche's *Ubermensch* as variations on a Promethean theme, and as such, attacks on the God-centered value of the term. Interestingly, creativity on both the God-centered and the Promethean models emphasizes originality and novelty more than enhanced meaning. Creativity as such issues from the imagination of a discrete agency, a single source. Either creativity is the prerogative of God and God alone, or it is the product of a wandering Promethean hero who is audacious, self-willed, fiercely independent, incapable of compromise, and prone to isolation and madness: the epitome of a solitary pride that is a challenge to divine order. This being the case, human creativity and the existing human morality are incompatible in both the God-centered and the Promethean traditions. In the former, where God has a monopoly on both creativity and morality, the emphasis falls on obedience to the will of God. Human creativity is hubris, and as such, is immoral. In the latter Promethean tradition in which Jove has a monopoly on justice but not on creativity, the herd morality of obedience is an obstacle to freedom that only human creativity can overcome, but it is a creativity

V · Confucian Human-Centered Religiousness

that requires both a *requiem aeternam deo* for a deceased God, and the creation of an audacious new morality.[88]

Bringing Hope Mason's discussion of creativity to Legge's critical reading of the *Zhongyong*, Legge clearly sees this text's strident claims about human creativity as a kind of arrogance that pits a Promethean creative sage against the aseity of God. In so interpreting the text, Legge seems to be construing the Confucian sage as heroic—proud, intrepid, solitary—an exemplar apart who accomplishes superhuman feats. For Legge, such human innovation can only be the product of a kind of cunning (*sagacitas*) as opposed to the wisdom (*sophia* or *sapientia*) that belongs properly to God.

And yet the image of the sage in the *Zhongyong* and other Confucian texts, far from being heroic, is rather one of a virtuosic collaborator and communicator who inspires the cosmos by orchestrating a thriving, inclusive human community in the ordinary business of the day. Sages like Confucius are not solitary and original. Rather, they have evolving corporate identities that have implicated within them the patterns of communal deference and meaning that are ultimately constitutive of the ethnic and national character. The sage (*sheng* 聖) appears on the oracle bones as ***[xliv]*** and later on the bronzes as ***[xlv]***, constructed in its earliest form simply from "ear" (*er* 耳) and "mouth" (*kou* 口), with the *ren* 壬 element being added in the Western Zhou script.[89] The character *sheng* 聖 shares an etymology with "listening" (*ting* 聽) and "sounding, voicing" (*sheng* 聲), and is defined in the *Shuowen* lexicon as "communicating with, pervading" (*tong* 通). The second-century text, *Understanding Popular Customs* (*Fengsutongyi* 風俗通義), defines the sage as "giving voice to and communicating": That is, sages "in listening to the voices and in understanding the feelings that are being expressed, they course through the world and orchestrate the flourishing of the myriad of things."[90] The sage is the efficacious communicator, the embodiment of culture, the religious center of a tightly bound community. The collaborative creativity that we find in the *Zhongyong* and the relational natural cosmology of ancient China broadly is a continuing *creatio in situ* rather than *ex nihilo* that references a continuing process of meaning-making rather than some initial originating cause.

Indeed, we can use the conditions of this *creatio ex nihilo* notion of

[xliv]

[xlv]

creativity, an act of unilateral originality, to distinguish this understanding of creativity from classical Chinese cosmology. First, *ex nihilo* is dependent upon discrete agency, separating an exclusive creator from its creature. In the processual cosmology of ancient China, situation and context are always prior to agency. That is, the individual as agent is a conceptual abstraction from concrete, constitutive relationships. Creativity is radically situated and reflexive, where the act of creating and self-creativity are inseparable. Since such creativity is always transactional, to communicate effectively is to participate in the continuing process of reconstituting the world.

Secondly, *ex nihilo* focuses on originality as its source of value. *In situ* creativity on the other hand emphasizes enhanced significance over originality and novelty. Shared relationships that appreciate in meaning are the source of increased significance. *In situ* creativity is prospective in that it focuses on the productivity of its applications rather than looking back retrospectively to its putative "origins" as its source of value. For natural Chinese cosmology, to the extent that creativity could be isolated and limited to a discrete and independent agent, it would wither in its meaningfulness.

Thirdly, *ex nihilo* entails the logical problem of supposedly bringing "some-thing" novel into existence that is absolutely dependent upon its creative source. In itself, the putative "some-thing" is in fact "no-thing." For *in situ* creativity, it is the growth of constitutive relationships that is the ultimate source of meaning and that in this process of growth, transforms what is initially inchoate into "something" that is increasingly distinctive.

Fourthly, the *ex nihilo* model appeals to a source of novelty that denies particularity, hybridity, history, development, and process. For *in situ* creativity, on the other hand, it is precisely growth in significance that is the substance of history, and that tells the story of human evolution through the aggregation of episodic, consummatory events. Within the process of *in situ* creativity, using the language of William James, relations, transitions, and conjunctions are all real.[91] The dynamic nature of creative experience requires appeal to consequences as well as to antecedents, to possibilities as well as to precedents. It is this forward propensity of the human experience that gives it a consummatory possibility. This *in situ* conception of creativity accounts for both cumulative products of particular experience (a kind of causality), and spontaneous variations that survive because of their consequent efficacy (accumulating significance).

Finally, *ex nihilo* creativity appeals to a void beyond the wholeness of experience, whereas *in situ* creativity entails the indeterminate "nothing" (*wu* 無) as the constant correlate of the determinate "something" (*you* 有). Together the determinate and its indeterminate penumbra constitute the ongoing process of experience. As we have seen, in a tradition in which all beginnings are fetal beginnings (*shi* 始), there is no notion of "void" but only a fecund receptivity.

We might take the classical Chinese canons, including the *Zhongyong* that we have focused upon in this chapter, as object lessons to illustrate this *in situ* notion of creativity. Most of the classical texts are not single-authored texts but are rather the work of many hands. Most of these texts borrow liberally and without attribution from the corpus of contemporaneously existing works that give them a literary context. They are usually composite documents, with their significance aggregating in lineages that stretch across generations. But the process does not end there. Redactions of these canonical texts are passed on through succeeding generations who then collaborate with these works by appending their own interlinear commentaries that make them relevant to their own time and place, thereby adding new meaning as such annotations accrue across the centuries.

This commentarial tradition is growth in meaning by generation upon generation of scholars correlating the canonical texts with the ordinary affairs of the day. It seems that the early Chinese thinkers were preoccupied with making the most of the phenomenal world of process and change construed simply as *dao* 道, "the unfolding field of experience," or *wanwu* 萬物," the ten thousand processes and events," or perhaps more simply put, "everything that is happening." These philosophers were less inclined to ask *what* makes something real or *why* things exist, and were more interested in *how* the complex relationships among the changing phenomena of their surroundings could be coordinated to achieve optimum productivity. It is this achieved personal, social, and ultimately cosmic harmony rather than any theological or teleological assumptions about origins or design that is their fundamental guiding value.

Epilogue: The Limits of Confucian Role Ethics

In this monograph I have tried to offer an interpretation of Confucian role ethics that allows the vocabulary of this enduring vision of the consummate life to speak for itself. This effort has been based on the premise that before either endorsing or rejecting a philosophical position, we must first apply the principle of charity and try as best we can to understand it on its own terms. But having attempted in these pages to give Confucian role ethics its most compelling argument, I am ultimately obliged to ask perhaps the most important philosophical question: Do we owe Confucian role ethics our allegiance? Is it a philosophical position that is persuasive and practicable?

The signature of the Confucian tradition is a commitment to an aesthetic holism that requires that we strive to take all of the conditions in the human experience into account in making determinations about the totality of any particular effect. This sense of wholeness is captured and expressed in the language of *dao* 道 where this term takes us beyond any partial grasp of a situation to reference a comprehensive understanding of how, from a particular perspective, "everything comes together" to produce the event, including the penumbra of latent possibilities implicated within the process. This comprehensiveness in understanding is alluded to in Tang Junyi's cosmological proposition that "knowing" requires both comprehending the oneness of a situation (its continuity, its uniqueness, its vectoral direction) and its multiplicity (its relationally constituted field of particulars, its multivalence, its polysemic meanings). In contrast to Aristotle's logic of knowing as an analytic grasping of the essence of something, Confucian knowing begins from a full inventory of the particular conditions relevant to any particular situation, and ends with an attempt to achieve optimal effect through the application of a cultivated imagination.

And ethical action in service to a thriving community requires the pursuit of such holistic understanding. In ethics we are inclined to assume that being moral has something to do with "according with what is right" or "being good," as though the notions of "right and wrong" and "good and bad" are available to us by appeal to some pre-existing standard: a pre-existing principle (causal) or some pre-existing ideal defined in the language of virtues (teleological). From the Confucian perspective, however, in the stead of pre-existing norms we discover a phenomenology of experience that serves as a resource for determining what it would mean to act in such a way as to enhance our relations. That is, we have to ask: What will make this situation comprised of these particular relations better, and what will make it worse? Confucian role ethics takes the substance of morality to be nothing more or less than positive growth in the constitutive relations of any particular situation.

As we have seen, in contrast with familiar Western ethical theories, Confucian role ethics does not make an appeal to putatively objective principles or to rational choice alone. Indeed, as a strategy for promoting moral conduct, it would seem to begin at the opposite end. In taking family feeling as the entry point for developing moral competence, role ethics is a program of personal growth that begins and extends outward from specific partial relations in the direction of the more impartial bonds that secure community more broadly. In this Confucian vision, ostensive principles and values ultimately emerge as abstractions from particular instances of appropriate conduct.

In general terms, I would contend that Confucian role ethics has several substantial contributions to make to the current discussion in ethics that derive from this holistic understanding of the human experience. Confucian role ethics begins by challenging a default foundational individualism with a sophisticated and, I would argue, empirically persuasive understanding of gerundive persons as they are uniquely constituted by their dynamic manifolds of relations. In this way, it offers a holistic understanding of what it means to become consummately human. Rather than beginning the determination

Epilogue: The Limits of Confucian Role Ethics 259

of appropriate moral responsiveness by isolating and applying some speculative principled ground for normativity, Confucian ethics returns the search for proper conduct to an assessment of meliorative growth in the concrete affairs of the day. The assumption here is that more abstract theoretical considerations about principles, virtues, and values must be authenticated in, and ought to owe their allegiance to, everyday human experience as it is transformed through exemplary conduct. It is historical models first, and principles as an efficient but also reductionistic way of communicating about such conduct. In thus focusing on the ordinary business of the day, Confucian ethics offers a holistic approach in considering the entire field of experience as being relevant to determining what is optimally appropriate. And Confucian ethics further reinstates the unfungible function of family relations as the generative source of moral competence. Here again, it offers a holistic basis for moral education that includes all those who begin their human sojourn in family relations and who see person and family as focus and context rather than as exclusive entities. Finally, the viability of Confucian role ethics relies upon the refinement and exercise of the moral imagination that certainly includes, but is not limited to or dominated by, rational calculation. Here too, Confucian ethics offers a holistic approach to determining proper conduct that includes all of the cognitive, affective, and somatic resources human beings have available to them in shaping their best response.

Perhaps an important lesson we might take away from Confucian role ethics is that while the search for objectivity and impartiality has a crucial role in assaying circumstances and adjudicating appropriate ethical conduct, applying such objective standards alone without adequate consideration for the specific details of any particular context is not in itself a sufficient warrant for proper conduct. Indeed, it can be fairly argued that the recent compensatory turn in Western philosophy toward applied ethics, virtue ethics, particularism, care ethics, pragmatic ethics, and so on, not to mention the fresh attention being paid to somaticity and affect as important moral considerations, is in sum directed at rehabilitating the wholeness of the lived experience and at reestablishing an appropriate balance between the abstract and the concrete by reinstating the singular value of a practical, applied wisdom.[1]

Joel Kupperman expresses his concern to bring alternative cultural resources into this turn in contemporary ethical reflection in his advocacy of what he calls "cosmopolitan ethics." He is keenly aware of the extent to which our Western narrative has leaned heavily upon an appeal to principle and rational choice rather than personal cultivation:

> [I]f the reference points are mainly Western systematic ethics of the last two and a half centuries, it is easy to conclude that the primary task of normative ethical philosophy is to arrive at principles that yield decision procedures. It might seem to follow that any project of transforming oneself into a certain sort of person is secondary to that of arriving at reliable moral decisions.... Part of what will emerge will be the limitations of any ethics that is principally concerned with fundamental principles that underlie major decisions in life.[2]

Kupperman allows that he has become aware of the limitations of a system of ethics that relies heavily upon principles to the exclusion of the contingencies of context by his familiarity with alternative cultural traditions in which other criteria are prominent:

> In other parts of the world, however, principles and putative laws have not always been assigned such a major role. Some examination of non-Western ethical traditions can undermine the ready assumption that Kant, totally immersed in Western traditions, makes about the centrality in ethics of laws and principles.[3]

In his "cosmopolitan ethics" Kupperman suggests that we can enrich the ethical discourse while developing a clearer sense of our own resources if we try to appreciate what is on offer from other traditions that have constructed robust responses to what it means to achieve moral competence:

> Aristotle and Confucius are both clear that a great many decisions about what it would be best to do cannot be viewed as decisions on principle. Many of these cases involve assessment of matters of degree, and appropriate awareness of nuances that may make a difference.[4]

But while appreciating the contribution that Confucian role ethics might make in suggesting a significantly different way of thinking about appropriate conduct, we also need to consider its limitations, at least as far as it has been articulated in our Confucian sources. Over its long history, advocates of Confucian ethics in their best attempts to achieve human flourishing have themselves often fallen short when it comes to a holistically informed understanding of how to proceed most effectively. The goal of Confucian living is captured in the expression "focusing the familiar" and "hitting the mark in the everyday" (*zhongyong* 中庸)—that is, achieving a quality of action that is "neither excessive nor insufficient" (*wuguobuji* 無過不及), a language immediately reminiscent of Traditional Chinese Medicine.[5] A familiar critique of Confucian role ethics as it has evolved historically is that it has tended to suffer from an excess of attention to intimate relations, thereby fostering a culture of corruption, and at the same time, has suffered from an insufficiency in exercising those guarantees that derive from more impartial considerations, thereby lacking the means necessary to control this corruption.

There are historical reasons for this persistent imbalance between partiality and impartiality. In the presentation of Confucian role ethics, I have relied upon our classical sources. These enduring texts first emerged in a different world far away and long ago when people lived and died within a relatively small compass. And that small radius put family and community in an uncontested position as the central forum in which human beings lived out their lives.

Positively speaking, the underlying wisdom in this Confucian tradition is simple: Family is that single human institution to which persons are most likely to give themselves utterly, and without remainder. To transform the world into a family, according to this Confucian sensibility, is to promote a model of interdependent relationships that will best accomplish the goal of getting the most out of your constitutive relations. Role ethics applies the logic that when another member of your family does better, you do better too. The only way to become a virtuosic teacher is by having exceptional students, and the more exceptional the students, the more virtuosic you become as teacher.

But of course the Confucian appeal to family as the organizing metaphor for the human experience is not altogether benign. Indeed, the preponderant emphasis upon family feeling as the source of the Confucian vision of the consummate life has led many to worry that so much personal investment in what is immediately at hand leaves few human resources for the formation of a vibrant civil society. The distinguished sociologist Ambrose King (Jin Yaoji 金耀基) explains that while Confucian persons are defined in terms of their particular relations with each other (*lun* 倫), they lack the conceptual and practical resources for relating effectively to the "group" (*qun* 群) more broadly construed:

> It seems to me that Confucian social ethics has failed to provide "viable linkage" between the individual and the *ch'ün* [*qun*], the nonfamilistic group. The root of the Confucian *Problematik* lies in the fact that the boundary between the self and the group has not been conceptually articulated.... The significant point is that in Confucianism, though the concept of group is recognized, the individual tends only to identify his moral relation with particular individuals of the group, not with the group per se. *Lun* exists only in relation to individuals, not in relation to the group.[6]

For King, the greatest limitation of Confucian ethics lies in its failure to provide the structural resources for particular persons to become fully social beings:

> Indeed, it could be argued that Confucianism does not provide the individual with ethical guidance in dealing with "strangers" with whom one has no particular relations.... It is a recognizable social phenomenon that the Chinese individual often ceases to be a "social being" in the true Confucian sense in relation to either the stranger or the *ch'ün* [*qun*] (group); that is to say, he often fails to take the stranger or the group as a serious relational object and is thus incapable of relating himself to the stranger or the group in interdependent terms.[7]

The fact that King's observations regarding the limitations of Confucian ethics are not only compelling but also immediately apparent is reinforced by the impressions of a relatively young Bertrand Russell during his 1920 sojourn to China. Russell's visit overlapped with John Dewey where both scholars gave many lectures across the country, and both had an immediate experience of Chinese life. Even as a near stranger to things Chinese, Russell observed with uncanny acuity:

> Filial piety, and the strength of the family generally, are perhaps the weakest point in Confucian ethics, the only point where the system departs seriously from common sense. Family feeling has militated against public spirit, and the authority of the old has increased the tyranny of ancient custom.[8]

Of course Russell goes much farther than King in his wholesale rejection of traditional Chinese family as an obstacle to be surmounted in the struggle for social progress. Russell is not only evaluating the family-based Confucian tradition from the external perspective of his own Western liberal assumptions, but is undoubtedly motivated in his critique by contemporaneous Chinese reformers of the New Culture Movement such as Kang Youwei and Tan Sitong who were themselves calling for the abolition of the traditional family as a necessary condition for Chinese modernization.[9] Russell's assumption here is that the intimacy of family feeling is a phase found everywhere in the process of civilization, but one that, in the fullness of time, is properly superseded.

> Filial piety is, of course, in no way peculiar to China, but has been universal at a certain stage of culture. In this respect, as in certain others, what is peculiar to China is the preservation of the old custom after a very high level of civilization had been attained. The early Greeks and Romans did not differ from the Chinese in this respect, but as their civilization advanced the family became less and less important. In China, this did not begin to happen until our own day.[10]

We might well reject Russell's universalistic claims about the irrelevance of cultural difference to the evolution of what he takes to be inevitable social patterns—again, a universal history. And if we were Confucians, we would also give careful scrutiny to Russell's own understanding of family relations as evidenced in his own personal life. But we would also have to allow that, while a community modeled on family relations might sound liberating, at the same time without the balance accorded by an appropriate regimen of institutionalized regulative ideals, such dependence on intimate relations can also be a disintegrative source of nepotism, cronyism, parochialism, and corruption.

Within this Confucian world there is another rather striking example of how the imbalance between partiality and impartiality has affected its development. One of the weaknesses that Chinese scholars themselves have directed at Confucianism as a tradition has been the tendency towards a kind of "voluntarism" that exaggerates the capacity of human purposes to transform the world while at the same time under-appreciating the resistance that the world might have to such change. Over the past generation, the Kantian scholar, Li Zehou 李

澤厚, has been one of China's more prominent and stringent social critics. Work being done by several contemporary interpretive scholars—particularly Woei Lien Chong, Gu Xin, and Liu Kang—makes a great deal of Li's rejection of "voluntarism": the naïve and even dangerous idea that the power of the human will can accomplish all things.[11] The ubiquitous image of this voluntarism as it came to shape the Maoist era is not new, but emerges out of and is consistent with the enduring Confucian premise that the possibilities for human flourishing lie with the transformative powers of the unmediated moral will. It is Li Zehou's claim that an unbridled confidence in the human moral will—a belief that has translated readily into ideologically driven mass-mobilization campaigns—has been importantly responsible for China's contemporary crises, from its impotence in dealing with Western imperialism down to the Great Leap Forward and the Great Cultural Revolution.[12]

The argument, simply put, is that Confucian philosophers from classical times have recognized a continuity between the human experience and their natural and cultural context that is captured in the mantra *tianren heyi* 天人合一. The nature of this continuity, however, has often been misunderstood. Instead of being a continuity between what is more or less subjective and more or less objective, respecting both the ability of the collective human community to transform its environment productively *and* the resistance of the natural world to this human transformation, it has been dominated by the belief that the moral subject holds almost absolute transformative powers over an infinitely malleable natural world. Such a belief has retarded an appreciation of the potential that the natural sciences hold to improve the human condition. As such, this voluntarism has become a kind of raw subjectivism that discounts the real need for collective efforts in science and technology to "humanize" nature in order to establish a productive relationship between subject and object, a relationship that Li Zehou takes to be a precondition for human freedom.

The problem of an imbalance in favor of partiality can also emerge in the evaluation of the political and cultural leadership of China. I have described Confucian ethics as being dependent upon a dynamic calculus of interrelating patterns of deference. While this aesthetic model has its appeal, it also has its dangers. The foremost concern of Confucius is with dissemblers: persons who are not what they purport to be. In an ethic in which models, rather than principles, are the final arbiters of proper conduct and cultural values—that is, appeal to the excellent person rather than an abstract standard—the most fundamental problem shifts from judging correspondence with an existing norm or compliance with a set of stipulated criteria, to an appreciation of personal excellence. This excellence can only be evaluated on the basis of analogies drawn from the cultural tradition in concert with an openness to creative discontinuities. Ultimately, excellence must be self-evident. It must inspire the appreciation of others by its own intrinsic worth.

In Confucian role ethics, excellence so defined is the only appropriate basis for privilege and responsibility. This being the case, with the ever-present danger of dissemblers, there is always a thin line between righteous moral indignation and self-righteousness, between advocacy and self-promotion. And where social and political status is a necessary condition for the cultivation of excellence, it is only a short step to construe position itself as a guarantee of moral superiority.

On the international stage within the context of cross-cultural accommodation, Confucian role ethics has much to recommend it. The notion of interdependence and the assumption that if your neighbor does better, you do better, is a productive framework within which a community of nations can work towards negotiating a common good. Confucian ethics avoids intractable moral conflict by abjuring any appeal to universals and assuming that appropriate conduct is always a matter of continuing, collateral or multilateral negotiation within the complexity of always particular circumstances. Indeed, the collaborative nature of moral conduct requires that it be mutual and accommodating.

But the imbalance on the side of partiality takes a toll on the value that Confucian role ethics might have to offer the growth of robust international relations too. The fact that human morality and value ultimately emerge out of personal participation in particular circumstances gives rise to a palpable Chinese provincialism and parochialism. This parochialism is manifest in the persistence of what we have called "the Chinatown phenomenon." The Great Wall stands as a symbol of how China continues to look inward and to be perceived by many as the Chinatown of the world. As enduring a monument to the unity of China as the Great Wall is—a China that within the wall includes fully 22.5% of the world's population—it has been built and rebuilt over the centuries in response to expanding and contracting lines of national identity, bounding within it a society of such enormous size and diversity that in its cultures and languages it bears a closer comparison to a continent like Europe or Africa than it does to any one of their countries. Indeed, there is a sense in which calling oneself "Chinese" is more akin to calling oneself "European" than it is to calling oneself French or German.

In 1987 when David Hall and I published *Thinking Through Confucius*, we observed that "the doors of 'Chinatown' China have opened just a crack after centuries of isolationism that have been interrupted only by the unwelcome incursions of the military, of profiteers, and of ineffectual missionaries."[13] A quarter of a century later in the wake of the Chinese economic miracle, much has changed, and the gates of China have certainly swung open considerably. But China still has its own understanding of its limited responsibilities for international leadership. Brad Glosserman and Scott Snyder summarize a recent survey taken among professional elites in Chinese society who come from a wide range of institutions on how they see the rise of Chinese influence in the world:

> They take great pride in China's rising international stature and accomplishments—especially in China's successful economic development. But in their responses, these Chinese elites seemed to show little sense of international responsibility or desire for global leadership. Almost all of them believe that China should be active internationally, but when asked what role their country could play, over 70 percent thought China's greatest contribution would simply flow from securing China's own stability and development. Chinese respondents overwhelmingly rejected suggestions for how Beijing might take on larger international leadership roles. Over 90 percent rejected an international leadership role for China, and two-thirds rejected the idea that China should take a special role in resolving international disputes. Our respondents even hesitated to endorse a leadership role for China in Asia. While agreeing that China has a positive regional economic influence, 95 percent claimed that China is not ready to take a regional leadership role. And over 80 percent rejected the idea that China might take leadership in promoting regional security. In discussions designed to flesh out those findings, we heard great pride in the status derived from China's growing power—and an insistence on China's right

to assert itself on specific issues—but no explanation of how their country might use its power and influence beyond pursuit of narrowly-defined national interests.[14]

This attitude of limited responsibility beyond its own borders is sometimes expressed internationally in what many perceive as self-serving and expedient policies that allow collusion with rogue nations where obvious economic motives seem to muffle what ought to be real humanitarian concerns.

In defining the Confucian project above I cited at some length the exhortation in the *Daxue*—the *Great Learning*—that begins with "personal cultivation" (*xiushen* 修身) and ultimately results in "bringing peace to the world" (*pingtianxia* 平天下). In the Chinese language, *tianxia* can mean either "the world of China" or "the world" more broadly construed. Perhaps it will only be when the Chinese leadership is seen in its actions as having resolved this semantic equivocation in favor of the latter meaning will the imbalance that has favored partiality over international responsibility undergo a necessary correction.

But Confucian philosophy does have the internal resources for such revision and growth that might give it a more global appeal. There are many important dimensions of the human experience that require impartiality, transparency, and more objective regulative ideals, and the Confucian tradition has long been aware of this need. Beginning with the distinction between "optimal appropriateness" (*yi* 義) and "personal advantage" (*li* 利) that we find as early as the *Analects* and the *Mencius*, Confucianism has struggled across its history with the seemingly necessary relationship between ethical conduct and a sense of impartiality.[15] Rather than invoking some transcendental moral standard or some faculty of impersonal reason as a strategy for claiming such impartiality—a strategy that is inevitably hobbled by the contingencies of circumstances—the Confucian tradition in developing a notion of impartiality has remained true to the family metaphor. That is, even in the distinction made between subjective and objective perspectives, impartiality is served practically by extending one's range of concern from "the master's-eye view" (*zhuguan* 主觀) that might be limited by some self-serving personal advantage (*li* 利) to "the guest's-eye view" (*keguan* 客觀) that seeks what is most appropriate for all concerned (*yi*

義). The Confucian formula of "putting oneself in the other's place" (*shu* 恕) and then "doing one's best" (*zhong* 忠) is another variation on this deferential attempt to keep one's range of concern open in determining what is moral. The point is that there are resources indigenous to the tradition on which to build more robust safeguards that can rein in the possible excesses of partiality.

In summary, in our contemporary era, perhaps the most profound insight Confucianism has to offer the world today lies in prompting us to rethink the role of family as the ground and primary site of the consummate life and by extension, of a truly robust democracy. Ironically, we might argue that at the same time, inopportune intimacy in relations is also China's primary obstacle on its own road to democratization. With so much investment in intimate and informal familial relationships, the Confucian tradition has been slow to produce the formal, more "objective" and "transparent" institutions necessary to sustain a Confucian version of democracy, and when it has produced them, these same institutions are often compromised and eroded by the excessive intervention of personal relationships.

While the familiar appeal to universals might suffer from the ambiguity of practical applications, the Confucian attempt to extend consideration to all involved is handicapped by the need for more abstract regulative ideals such as courage and justice that provide direction for what is a legitimate claim for consideration and inclusion. Indeed, as democracy emerges in China, the cure for the ills of a decidedly Confucian democracy might well be a continuing appeal to rule of law and the formal institutions of democracy to contain the excesses of those intimate relations that have their beginnings in family feeling. And who is to say that in the fullness of time, a Confucianism-inspired democracy—that is, a democracy grounded in a regimen of role ethics that does not suffer from the obvious tension between foundational individualism and social values—between the justified self-interest of discrete individuals and their commitment to the possibilities of a flourishing community—will not provide a worthy alternative to liberal democracy?

Notes

Preface
1. Rosemont (1991b), p. 72.
2. Rosemont (1991b), p. 193 wherein Fingarette responds to Rosemont.
3. Rosemont (1991b), p. 90.
4. Rosemont (1991b), p. 91.
5. Rosemont (1991b), pp. 92, 94.

I
1. *Analects* 7.1: 子曰：「述而不作，信而好古，竊比於我老彭。」The Master said, "Following the proper way, I do not forge new paths; with confidence I cherish the ancients—in these respects I am comparable to Old Peng."*
2. In anticipating cultural influence in the world, we ought not to underestimate the power of wealth. See Peerenboom (2007) for this argument.
3. For a translation of Leibniz's writings on China and for a substantial foray into interpreting this relationship between Leibniz and China, see Leibniz (1994) and Perkins (2004) respectively.
4. Perkins (2004), pp. 141–43.
5. Leibniz wrote this treatise in bad French, a failing that might have unintentionally distanced him from a God that, at least in some French salons, is associated directly with the proper use of this particular language.
6. Leibniz (1994), p. 75.
7. Leibniz (1994), p. 105.
8. Leibniz (1994), p. 46.
9. Leibniz (1994), p. 46.
10. Leibniz (1994), p. 46.
11. Leibniz (1994), pp. 46–47.

---

* Unless otherwise indicated, English translations from Chinese are the author's, and excerpts from classical Chinese texts are based on sources obtained from Donald Sturgeon's Chinese Text Project (see bibliography).

12. Leibniz (1994), pp. 46–47.
13. Leibniz (1994), p. 47.
14. Leibniz (1994), p. 46.
15. Hadot (2002), p. 46.
16. Hadot's work is certainly a timely corrective on the sins of the discipline of professional philosophy as it exists within the contemporary academy. Philosophy has become a predominantly discursive activity that seems to show little interest in the pursuit of practical wisdom, and is anachronistic in that it tends to construe its own historical narrative in these same terms. Hadot himself, in answering the question as to where and how philosophy became primarily an abstract and theoretical exercise divorced from everyday life, sees academic pedantry emerging as early as the age of Roman philosophy and reports on a clear theoretical ascent occurring in the Middle Ages with the growing dominance of philosophical commentary on Aristotle as integral to university culture. But good arguments have been made that Hadot's case is overdrawn at both ends. Even though we can find important counterexamples to some of Hadot's claims within the corridors of Western philosophy in the philosophical revolution of the twentieth century, there is no disputing Hadot's characterization of contemporary academic philosophy as largely having lost its earlier concern with spirituality and the philosophical life. And while I would endorse Hadot's exhortation that philosophers should return to the original task of self-transformation, what I find troubling is the actual content of the "spiritual exercises" and "self-transformation" that Hadot takes to be proper to the philosopher's "way of life." Hadot recommends an engagement with the practical not as an end in itself, but only as an expedient means of ultimately complying with the standards and norms of reason and ascending to, apprehending, and conforming to the demands of the abstract and theoretical. Hadot's philosophers so described in different ways and at different times still privilege the reductive rationalization of the human experience through "the lived practice of the virtues of logic, physics, and ethics" that make them better persons than the unprincipled sophists and the rest of humankind (Hadot 2002, p. 172). Allowing Hadot to speak for himself, in describing life in Plato's academy, he says:

> In Plato's time, dialectics was a debating technique subject to precise rules.... By dint of sincere effort, the interlocutors discover by themselves, and within themselves, a truth which is independent of them, insofar as they submit to the superior authority of the *logos*. Here, as in all ancient philosophy, philosophy consists in the movement by which the individual transcends himself toward something which lies beyond him. For Plato, this something was

> the *logos*; discourse which implies the demands of rationality and universality.... Plato affirms that we must exercise the superior part of the soul—which is none other than the intellect—in such a way that it achieves harmony with the universe and is assimilated to the deity.... It is an exercise of death because death is the separation of the soul and the body, and the philosopher spends his time trying to detach his soul from his body.... This exercise was, indissolubly, an *askēsis* of the body and of thought—a divestment of the passions in order to accede to the purity of intelligence. (Hadot 2002, pp. 62, 63, 66, 67)

Hadot appeals here to the *Phaedo* as an example of the spiritual exercises that constitute a distinctively philosophical way of life. But this Platonic dialogue not only explicitly denigrates the role of somaticity and the emotions in personal cultivation, but offers us a moral vision for externally related, self-sufficient individuals—individuals without the intrinsic and constitutive relations that would make them responsive to the needs of others. This putatively "philosophical" way of life seems markedly different from an aesthetic, holistic, and inclusive vision of the art of living we associate with Confucian philosophy that, without appeal to the ostensive authority of predetermined norms and principles, seeks to make ordinary life extraordinary by pragmatically optimizing its creative possibilities.

I found welcome corroboration for this criticism of Hadot in Steve Angle's comparative work on the Confucian sage. As Angle observes:

> Ideas of sagehood in Greece are often bound up with a conception of divinity, which is a realm of perfection separate from humanity. Only gods are truly wise, though humans can and should aspire after wisdom (*sophia*); those who do so are lovers of *sophia*, or "philosophers." Since these individuals love and aspire to something that is fundamentally different from our limited human knowledge, though, Greek theorists generally recognize that its pursuit requires a rupture with everyday life. They argue that people should seek to shape their lives by spiritual exercises that bring divine wisdom tantalizingly closer. For many thinkers, the best life (that is, the life of happiness or *"eudaimonia"*) is the life of contemplation (*"theōria"*). (Angle 2009, pp. 18–19)

Angle then brings Aristotle's *phronimos*—the practically wise person—into the discussion. As a distinctly different ideal that cannot easily be reconciled with *philosophia*, the *phronimos* does not allow for the continuity assumed between the Confucian categories of the consummate human being (*renzhe* 仁者), the exemplary person (*junzi* 君子) and the sage (*shengren* 聖人). Angle cites Yu (2007), p. 204 who insists that

> ... in Aristotle, the fulfillment of the practical self does not lead to the fulfillment of the theoretical self, and vice-versa. These are two

models of human flourishing that cannot be fulfilled within a single career, and Aristotle ranks the actualization of the theoretical self higher than the actualization of the practical self. In contrast, in Confucius, there is only one continuous process of the development of the relational self, in which one's virtuous character keeps deepening and perfecting.

17. An argument can be made that much of the revolution in twentieth-century philosophy, defined as it is by movements such as pragmatism, hermeneutics, applied ethics, and existentialism as only a few examples, has been a concerted attempt to reinstate "wisdom" as a philosophical value in a tradition that has invested heavily in the abstract and theoretical at the expense of ordinary life experience.
18. See Whitehead (1979), p. 10.
19. Whitehead (1938), p. 58.
20. Whitehead (1938), pp. 60–63.
21. Whitehead (1938), p. 62.
22. Whitehead (1938), p. 62.
23. After all, Pythagoras had an important contribution to make to abstract mathematics that has served humankind well. And indeed, for Socrates the philosophical problem was the opposite of Whitehead's "misplaced concreteness"—that is, he argued that the imbalance in harmony favored the concrete over the abstract. For Socrates the attainment of a Pythagorean balance lay in his passionate attempt to temper the concrete yet specious sophistic "wisdom" represented by the "will of the many" by an appeal to abstract principles as regulative ideals.
24. Hegel (1956), pp. 111–12.
25. See *Analects* 2.3 in which the ideal of communal self-ordering is to be achieved through the development of a personal sense of shame.
26. The Western-centric impact-response and tradition-modernization understanding of the dynamic of modern Chinese history that Paul Cohen (1984) attributes to post–World War II American scholarship is a good example of how powerful and influential this Hegelian interpretation of Chinese culture has been in the account given of recent Chinese history. See also Hall and Ames (1999) in which we try to take Cohen's criticism of this reading of Chinese history and his advocacy of a China-centered approach one step further. We too reject the familiar equation between modernization and Westernization, but contend that the recognition of an internal dynamic within Chinese culture is not a sufficient explanation of what must be understood in relational terms. That is, we insist upon reinstating the importance of Easternization as a factor in the evolving interdependent relationship between China and Western culture.

27. James (2000), p. 15.
28. James (1984), p. 222.
29. James (1892), p. 165.
30. Rosemont (1991a), pp. 62–63.
31. Dewey (1969–72), Vol. 1, p. 162. For the history, development, and the context of "*the* philosophical fallacy," see Tiles (1988), pp. 19–24.
32. James (2000), p. 98.
33. See Madsen (2003) and Thornton (2005).
34. Translated in Carrithers et al (1985), p. 22.
35. I will return to the topic of *the* philosophical fallacy below in chapter five when I argue against the persisting insinuation of a transcendentalism into our understanding of classical Confucian religiousness.
36. Leibniz (1994), pp. 46–47.
37. *Analects* 4.6: 我未見好仁者, and 5.11: 吾未見剛者.
38. See Hall and Ames (1987), chapter six, and Rosemont and Ames (2008), "Introduction" in which we make a similar point.
39. See Makeham (2008).
40. Dennerline (1988), p. 9.
41. Goldin (2008), p. 3.
42. Goldin (2008), p. 21.
43. Putnam (1990), p. 28.
44. Putnam (1990), p. 178.
45. Goldin (2008), p. 2n6 celebrates the work of Michael Puett and Andrew Plaks as two scholars who like him avoid making generalizations. Below in chapter five I will use Andrew Plaks's translation of the *Zhongyong* as an apposite example to argue that engaging a text without sufficient attention to its interpretive context leads to overwriting the text with our own cultural assumptions.
46. Graham (1990), p. 408.
47. Jaspers (1953), p. 2.
48. Benjamin Schwartz was famously and fondly remembered by his students with a T-shirt that had stenciled on the front the words "on the one hand" and then stenciled on the back, "… but on the other." Indeed, Puett (2002), pp. 11–13 describes Schwartz as having "maintained a delicate balance between the two paradigms," evolutionary and cultural essentialism. But since the reductionistic rationalist perspective rules out the possibility of a holistic cosmology, I would include Schwartz in the second group. Schwartz (1975) allows for Jaspers's "transcendence," but then revises the understanding of this term dramatically to fit it into a holistic Chinese cosmology. Schwartz defines transcendence as "a this-worldly" sort that can best be associated with "an immanent and cosmic and social order." While Schwartz accepts the characterization of Chinese cosmology as "rationalism,"

he insists that it is "a rationalism that is radically different from many varieties of rationalism in ancient Greece. What we have is the image of an all-embracing and inclusive order which neither negates nor reduces to some one ultimate principle that which is presumed to exist.... It is a synthetic rather than an analytic conception of order" (Schwartz 1975, p. 59). Far from externalizing gods and spirits, Schwartz insists that "the line dividing the 'divine' from the human is not sharply drawn, and it seems that humans may possess or take on qualities which are truly numinous." (Schwartz 1985, p. 25)

49. Puett (2002), p. 8.
50. Granet (1934), p. 279.
51. Puett (2002), p. 9.
52. Keightley (1978), pp. 211–12, "It is the argument of this exploratory essay that the secular values and institutions representing the great tradition of the Zhou and Han dynasties were characterized to a significant extent by habits of thinking and acting that had been sanctified at least a millennium earlier by the religious logic of the Shang theology and cult."
53. Whitehead (1938), pp. 60–63.
54. Puett (2002), p. 17.
55. Puett (2002), p. 18.
56. Puett (2002), p. 23.
57. Puett (2002), p. 25.
58. Puett (2002), pp. 24–25.
59. Thoreau (1962), Vol. 13, p. 77.
60. Puett (2002), p. 164.
61. Puett (2002), p. 162.
62. Puett (2002), p. 163.
63. Puett (2002), p. 164.
64. Puett (2002), p. 164.
65. Puett (2002), p. 166.
66. Puett (2002), p. 167.
67. See the "Jielao" 解老 and "Yulao" 喻老 chapters of the *Hanfeizi* 韓非子, and Creel (1970).
68. We have made a sustained argument for our "philosophical" interpretation of the *Daodejing* in Ames and Hall (2003).
69. Zhang Longxi (1999), p. 41.
70. Zhang Longxi (1999), p. 43.
71. Zhang Longxi (1999), p. 46.
72. Zhang Longxi (1999), p. 44.
73. Gernet (1985), p. 9.
74. Zhang Longxi (1999), p. 42.
75. Zhang Longxi (1999), p. 40.

76. See Rosemont and Ames (2009) pp. 34–35 for the clusters of terms that distinguish different ethical traditions as their peculiar *langue*—even among those traditions that share a continuous narrative.
77. In making its case for the importance of difference to an achieved harmony, the *Zuo Commentary to the Spring and Autumn Annals,* Duke Zhao 20 uses the examples of cooking, music, and an evolving cultural genealogy:

> 齊侯至自田，晏子侍于遄臺，子猶馳而造焉，公曰，唯據與我和夫，晏子對曰，據亦同也，焉得為和，公曰，和與同異乎，對曰異，和如羹焉，水火醯醢鹽梅，以烹魚肉，燀之以薪，宰夫和之，齊之以味，濟其不及，以洩其過，君子食之，以平其心，君臣亦然，君所謂可，而有否焉，臣獻其否，以成其可，君所謂否，而有可焉，臣獻其可，以去其否，是以政平而不干民無爭心，故詩曰，亦有和羹，既戒既平，鬷假無言，時靡有爭，先王之濟五味，和五聲也，以平其心，成其政也，聲亦如味，一氣，二體，三類，四物，五聲，六律，七音，八風，九歌，以相成也，清濁大小，長短疾徐，哀樂剛柔，遲速高下，出入周疏，以相濟也，君子聽之，以平其心，心平德和，故詩曰，德音不瑕，今據不然，君所謂可，據亦曰可，君所謂否，據亦曰否，若以水濟水，誰能食之，若琴瑟之專壹，誰能聽之，同之不可也如是，飲酒樂，公曰，古而無死，其樂若何，晏子對曰，古而無死，則古之樂也，君何得焉，昔爽鳩氏始居此地，季荝因之，有逢伯陵因之，蒲姑氏因之，而後大公因之，古者無死，爽鳩氏之樂，非君所願也。

The Marquis of Qi had returned from the hunt, and was being attended by Master Yan at the Chuan pavilion when Ju of Liangqiu galloped up to them. The Marquis said, "Only Ju is in harmony with me!"

"All that Ju does is agree with you," said Master Yan. "Wherein is the harmony?"

"Is there a difference between harmony and commonality?" asked the Marquis.

"There is indeed," replied Master Yan. "Harmony is like making congee. One uses water, fire, vinegar, sauce, salt, and plum to cook fish and meat, and burns firewood and stalks as fuel for the cooking process. The cook blends these ingredients harmoniously to achieve the appropriate flavor. Where it is too bland, he adds flavoring, and where it is too concentrated, he dilutes it with water. When you partake of this congee, Sir, it lifts your spirits.

"The relationship between ruler and minister is another case in point. Where the ruler considers something right and yet there is something wrong about it, the minister should point out what is wrong as a way of achieving what is right. Where the ruler considers something wrong and yet there is something right about it, the minister should point out what is right as a way of setting aside what is wrong. In such a way governing will be equitable without violating ritual propriety and the common people will not be contentious. Thus the *Book of Odes* says:

> There is indeed harmoniously blended congee;
> The kitchen has already been cautioned to bring out a balanced and even taste.
> The spirits will come to partake of it without finding cause for blame,
> And those above and below will be free of contention.

"The Former Kings blended the five flavors and harmonized the five notes to lift their spirits and to achieve success in their governing. Music functions similarly to flavoring. There is one field of sound; the two kinds of music: martial and civil; the three kinds of songs: airs of the states, odes, and hymns; the four quarters from which materials are gathered for making instruments; the five note pentatonic scale; the six pitch pipes; the seven sounds, the winds of the eight directions, and the nine ballads—all of which complement each other. There are the distinctions between clear and turbid, small and great, short and long, quick and slow, plaintive and joyous, hard and soft, delayed and rapid, high and low, beginning and ending, and intimate and distant—all of which augment each other. You listen to these, Sir, and they lift your spirits, which in turn enables you to excel harmoniously. Hence the *Book of Odes* says, 'There are no imperfections in the sound of excellence.'

"Now Ju is not acting in this way. Whatever you say is right, Ju also says is right; whatever you say is wrong, Ju also says is wrong. If you season water with water, who would want to partake of it? If you keep playing the same note on your lutes, who would want to listen to it? The inadequacy of 'commonality' lies in this."

They were drinking wine and enjoying themselves when the Marquis observed, "If from ancient times there had been no death, what then would be the extent of our joy!"

"If from ancient times there had been no death," ventured Master Yan, "there would be the joy of the ancients, and what would you, Sir, get out of that! In ancient times, the Shuangjiu clan first settled this territory, then came the Jice clan, followed by Youfeng Boling, the Pugu clan and finally by your first ancestor. If from ancient times there

had been no death, there would be the joy of the Shuangjiu clan, and I doubt that you would want that!"
78. Zhang Longxi (1999), p. 44. Actually, in Rosemont (1974) and again in Ames and Rosemont (1998), pp. 39–43 and appendix two, an argument is made that the Chinese written literary language is uniquely abstract in the sense that semantic overload contributes to a kind of productive vagueness requiring constant disambiguation on the part of the reader.
79. Zhang Longxi (1999), p. 45.
80. I am "borrowing" this distinction from Saussure because I do not want to endorse the kind of structuralism that would allow for any severe separation between *langue* and *parole*, instead siding with the sentiments of Mikhail Bakhtin who sees these two dimensions of language as mutually shaping and evolving in their always-dialectical relationship. Utterances gradually change the structure of language, and the changing structure orients and influences the utterances that it makes possible.
81. Chad Hansen and I had a most enjoyable time responding to just such a challenge by Eske Mollgaard. See Ames (2005).
82. In this story, Borges introduces a character who, with perfect memory of every detail of his day, requires fully 24 hours to remember 24 hours. Such concreteness turns Greek abstraction on its head, precluding the possibility of rising above the detail to reflect and deliberate on one's experience. For Plato, particularity cannot be thought.
83. Gadamer (1989), pp. 306–7, 374–75.
84. Whitehead argues that to take God as being more primordial than creativity has made conventional theology incoherent because the existence of a perfect, transcendent God threatens the very possibility of creativity itself. There is God's perfection, and that is all. With Whitehead's challenge to conventional ways of thinking about creativity, the word "creativity" becomes an individual entry in a 1971 supplement to the *Oxford English Dictionary* with two of the three references being made to Whitehead's *Religion in the Making*.

II

1. Sivin (1974), p. xi.
2. Granet (1934) and Graham (1989).
3. Sivin (1965), p. 110.
4. Ames and Rosemont (1998), pp. 25–26. The third chapter of this present work that searches for a vocabulary to give adequate expression to this relationally constituted person is an elaboration of this earlier collaboration.
5. James (2000), p. 76.

6. Dewey (1998), p. 40.
7. Dewey (1998), p. 41, emphasis added. To be fair to Dewey, while he might have been careless with his language here, he is not entirely insensitive to the problem of such cultural reductionism:

    They [psycho-analysts] treat phenomena which are peculiarly symptoms of the civilization of the West at the present time as if they were the necessary effects of fixed native impulses of human nature. (Dewey 1922, p. 153)

8. Nietzsche (1966), p. 20.
9. Richards (1932), pp. 89, 91–92.
10. See Ames (2001) for a development of this distinction.
11. *Analects* 7.1: 子曰：「述而不作, 信而好古, 竊比於我老彭。」 Translating *shu* 述 as "to follow the proper way" enables us to maintain the "path" (*dao* 道) metaphor that it suggests. Throughout the early corpus, the term meaning "to initiate" (*zuo* 作)—translated here as "to forge new paths"—is frequently associated with the term "sageliness" (*sheng* 聖). Hence Confucius's description of himself in this passage might be read as an expression of modesty. "Old Peng" is Peng Zu 彭祖, a minister during the Shang dynasty whom legend has it lived to be some eight hundred years old. With the name "Peng Zu"—literally, "Peng the Ancestor"—and with his remarkable longevity, Old Peng is certainly emblematic of historical continuity. See *Mozi* 63/39/19 and 81/46/50 where Confucius is taken at his word as being wholly a transmitter, and is criticized for offering the world a lifeless conservatism. This Mohist criticism of Confucianism—a position that I disagree with fundamentally—is alive and well in contemporary scholarship. Hsiao (1979), pp. 79–142 also describes this ostensive Confucian conservatism at length as "emulating the past" (*fagu* 法古). More specifically, Slingerland (2003), p. 64, in interpreting this same passage from the *Analects*, aligns himself with this same retrospective understanding of a Confucianism that harkens back to the Golden Age of the Zhou dynasty. He observes: "It is more likely that transmission is all that Confucius countenanced for people in his age, since the sagely Zhou kings established the ideal set of institutions that perfectly accord with human needs."
12. *Analects* 3.14: 子曰：「周監於二代, 郁郁乎文哉！吾從周。」See also *Analects* 8.20: 舜有臣五人而天下治。武王曰：「予有亂臣十人。」孔子曰：「才難, 不其然乎？唐虞之際, 於斯為盛。有婦人焉, 九人而已。三分天下有其二, 以服事殷。周之德, 其可謂至德也已矣。」

    Shun had only five ministers and the world was properly governed. King Wu also said, "I have ten ministers who bring proper order to the world." Confucius said, "As the saying has it: 'Human talent is hard to come by.'

Isn't it indeed the case. And it was at the transition from Yao dynasty to Shun that talented ministers were in greatest abundance. In King Wu's case with a woman, perhaps his wife, among them, there were really only nine ministers. The Zhou, with two thirds of the world in its possession, continued to submit to and serve the House of Yin. The excellence of Zhou can be said to be the highest excellence of all."

13. Keightley (1988), p. 389. Keightley is not alone here, positing a position shared by several of our most distinguished interpreters of the Shang dynasty, including Chang (1964) and Granet (1977).
14. Keightley (1988), p. 367.
15. Keightley (1988), p. 388.
16. Keightley (1988), p. 389n1.
17. Keightley (1988), p. 376.
18. Keightley (1988), p. 377.
19. Keightley (1988), pp. 374–75. It should be noted that Keightley is in fundamental disagreement on this point with Schwartz (1985), p. 19, Graham (1989), p. 320, and Henderson (1984), pp. 30–41, and more recently, Puett (2002), pp. 149–52, who find different historical reasons for insisting that correlative thinking is a much later Han-dynasty evolution in Chinese thought.
20. See Sivin (1987) and Nylan (2010).
21. Peterson (1982), p. 67.
22. Shaughnessy (1997), p. 1.
23. Shaughnessy (1997), p. 1.
24. Peterson (1982), p. 85. In response to the question "how can a divination text 'connect' with the cosmos?", Peterson allows that the word "duplicated" is "my feeble attempt to provide a necessarily inadequate name for the relationship." He goes on to describe rather clearly what I have called the holographic focus/field relationship between the cosmos and the *Yijing*:

    They are each "one of two things" exactly alike, each a double of the other, each "has in it" the other. (Peterson 1982, p. 91)

25. Peterson (1982), p. 91.
26. *Great Tradition* B8: 易之為書也，廣大悉備，有天道焉，有人道焉，有地道焉。In translating passages from the *Yijing*, I have had the benefit of consulting existing translations, particularly those of Peterson (1982), Shaughnessy (1997), and Lynn (1994).
27. The *Yijing* has served over the centuries as a heuristic for ordering the Chinese world, providing imagistic analogies and a vocabulary for reflection. Other canonical texts have functioned similarly as a source of analogy. See, for example, the "Attuning the Single Thread" (*zhengguan* 正貫) chapter of the *Chunqiufanlu* 春秋繁露 in which the *Spring and*

Autumn Annals is described in similar terms as functioning as a source for ordering the human experience:

是以必明其統於施之宜,故知其氣矣,然後能食其誌也;知其聲矣,而後能扶其精也。知其行矣,而後能遂其形也……

Thus we must be cognizant of how suitable its system is in practice. It is only when we understand its basic sentiments that we are able to digest its purposes; it is only when we understand its voice that we are able to promote its spirit; it is only when we understand its practices that we are able to follow its institutional forms.

28. *Great Tradition* A11: 是故,闔戶謂之坤;闢戶謂之乾;一闔一闢謂之變;往來不窮謂之通;見乃謂之象;形乃謂之器;制而用之,謂之法;利用出入,民咸用之,謂之神。
29. *Great Tradition* A12: 是故,形而上者謂之道,形而下者謂之器。化而裁之謂之變,推而行之謂之通,舉而錯之天下之民,謂之事業。
30. *Great Tradition* B1: 天地之大德曰生,聖人之大寶曰位。何以守位曰仁,何以聚人曰財。理財正辭,禁民為非曰義。
31. *Great Tradition* B5: 知幾其神乎?君子上交不諂,下交不瀆,其知幾乎,幾者動之微,吉之先見者也,君子見幾而作,不俟終日……君子知微知彰,知柔知剛,萬夫之望。
32. *Great Tradition* B5: 過此以往,未之或知也。窮神知化,德之盛也。
33. *Great Tradition* B2: 易窮則變,變則通,通則久。
34. *Great Tradition* A8: 聖人有以見天下之動,而觀其會通,以行其典禮。
35. *Great Tradition* B2: 黃帝、堯、舜氏作,通其變,使民不倦,神而化之,使民宜之。
36. *Great Tradition* A10: 夫易,聖人之所以極深而研幾也。唯深也,故能通天下之志。唯幾也,故能成天下之務。唯神也,故不疾而速,不行而至。
37. Ames and Hall (2001), p. 113. *Zhongyong* 32: 唯天下至誠,為能經綸天下之大經,立天下之大本,知天地之化育。夫焉有所倚?肫肫其仁!淵淵其淵!浩浩其天!苟不固聰明聖知達天德者,其孰能知之?
38. Sivin (1987) pp. 441–42 in Appendix D provides an outline of the curriculum for a Traditional Medical School.
39. Using a careful reading of Zhang Zai's *Correcting Youthful Ignorance* (*Zhengmeng* 正蒙), Kim (2008) and (2010) has constructed a sustained argument against those interpreters of *qi* who would understand it as a kind of monistic ontology.
40. Farquhar (1994), p. 34.
41. Farquhar (1999), p. 162.

42. I am using the database "Cognitive Analysis of Archaic Chinese Script Components" being constructed by Tze-wan Kwan and his team at The Chinese University of Hong Kong. These two figures are 一期殷契佚存 586 and [西周中期] CHANT: 246. The argument behind this database is compelling. With the modern Chinese character it is a commonplace that the "radicals" provide a certain degree of semantic reference—a "tree" 木 signifier indicates that a character has something to do with plants or wood, and the "heartmind" 心 signifier indicates that a character has something to do with thinking and feeling. The argument of this CUHK database is that the ancient graphic form of the characters found on the oracle bones, on the bronzes, and in the recent archaeological texts provide a degree of semantic meaning that was much reduced with the stylization and standardization of the characters as *lishu* 隸書, a degree of meaning that can in degree be recovered through careful analysis of their early graphic forms. Here Kwan underscores this "pregnant" dimension of the archaic graph for *shen* 身, "lived body." Much has been made of the archaic form of *ren* 仁 in some of the bamboo strip manuscripts that is constituted of *shen* 身 over *xin* 心, putatively challenging the commonplace that *ren* is fundamentally relational. But the early form of *shen* as a pregnant body in fact retains a profoundly relational aspect.
43. Zhang Yanhua (2007), p. 36.
44. Farquhar (1991), p. 386.
45. Farquhar (1991), p. 386.
46. Zhang Yanhua (2007), pp. 37–38.
47. Zhang Yanhua (2007), p. 41.
48. Zhang Yanhua (2007), pp. 51.
49. Granet (1934), p. 329.
50. Needham (1956), p. 291.
51. Needham (1956), p. 290.
52. Major (1993).
53. Chan (1963), p. 141.
54. 萬物負陰而抱陽，沖氣以為和。See also *Daodejing* 10 and 55.
55. See Roth (1999).
56. Wang Bi's commentary on chapter thirty-eight of the *Daodejing* is the earliest occurrence we have of this *tiyong* notion of transformation, although one can argue that the same cosmological idea was given expression in different language much earlier. For example, the *Yijing* develops the idea of "flux and persistence" (*biantong* 變通).
57. *Analects* 9.17: 子在川上，曰：「逝者如斯夫！不舍晝夜。」
58. Shun (1997), pp. 67–68.
59. Chad Hansen (1992), p. 175 is not alone among commentators who would describe Mencius on *qi* as a "moral mysticism."

60. This expression alludes to *Analects* 20.3, underscoring the relationship between understanding discourse and achieving virtuosity in one's relations:

    不知言無以知人也 。

    Someone who does not understand discourse has no way of understanding others.

61. *Mencius* 2A2: 孟子曰：「……我四十不動心。」〔公孫丑問〕曰：「不動心有道乎？……敢問夫子惡乎長？」曰：「我知言，我善養吾浩然之氣。」「敢問何謂浩然之氣？」曰：「難言也。其為氣也，至大至剛，以直養而無害，則塞于天地之閒。其為氣也，配義與道；無是，餒也。是集義所生者，非義襲而取之也。」

62. *Mencius* 7A4: 萬物皆備於我矣。反身而誠，樂莫大焉。強恕而行，求仁莫近焉。

63. See the Introduction to Ames and Hall (2001) for an extended discussion of this particular use of *cheng* 誠 as it is first found in the *Mencius* and then elaborated upon in the *Zhongyong*.

64. *Analects* 6.30: 夫仁者，己欲立而立人，己欲達而達人。能近取譬，可謂仁之方也已。

65. Zhu Xi (1969), *Mengzi* 13:2b: 此言理之本然也。大則君臣父子，小則事物細微。其當然之理無一不具於性分之內也。

66. Granet (1934), p. 478.

67. Dewey (1998), p. 41.

68. Whitehead (1933), p. 356.

69. *Zhongyong* 26: 天地之道，可壹言而盡也。其為物不貳，則其生物不測。

70. See Hall and Ames (1987), pp. 246–49, (1995) pp. 273–75, (1998) pp. 39–43, 111–12.

71. Guo (2004).

72. It should be noted that Tang Junyi himself in his preface to *The Spiritual Value of Chinese Culture* 中國文化之精神價值 (1953) repudiated some of the ideas developed in his earlier work *Collected Studies on a Comparison of Chinese and Western Philosophical Thinking* 中西哲學思想之比較研究集 (1943) from which these cosmological propositions are drawn. My own understanding of Tang's contribution is that there is indeed a greater profundity in the later work that supersedes his earlier writings, and in the following chapter I depend heavily upon this second text in appealing to Tang's understanding of what it means to become consummately human within Chinese natural cosmology. An important element in his criticism of his own work is his earlier failing to appreciate the possibilities of bringing these traditions together productively, and is not directed at his appeal to the *Book of Changes* as ground for reflecting upon Chinese natural cosmology.

73. Tang (1991), Vol. 11, p. 8: 中國文化之根本精神即將[部分與全體交融互攝]之精神；自認識上言之，即不自全體中劃出部分之精神（此自中國人之宇宙觀中最可見之）；自情意上言之，即努力以部分實現全體之精神（此自中國人之人生態度中可見之）。
74. Tang (1991), Vol. 11, pp. 9–11.
75. Tang (1991), Vol. 11, pp. 20–22.
76. *Great Tradition* A4: 故神無方而易無體。
77. Peterson (1982), p. 103.
78. In fact, at least as early as the Ming dynasty, the Chinese expression for "thing," *dongxi* 東西, is literally "east-west," underscoring the relational and contextual understanding that attends Chinese phenomonological perceptions. This traditional expression is often explained by reference to the location of open markets within population centers.
79. Tang (1991), Vol. 11, pp. 17–19.
80. Tang (1991), Vol. 11, pp. 11–16.
81. Tang (1991), Vol. 11, pp. 101–3: 中國哲人言世界，只想著我們所處的世界。我們所處的世界以外有無其他的世界……不說我們的世界是一世界 A World 亦不說這世界 The World 而只是說世界，天地，World as such 前面不加冠詞。
82. *Daodejing* 40: 反者道之動。
83. Tang Junyi (1991) Vol. 11, pp. 16–17.
84. Tang Junyi (1991) Vol. 11, pp. 22–25.
85. *Analects* 7.23: 天生德於予。

III

1. See *Analects* 12.1: "Through self-discipline and observing ritual propriety in one's roles and relations one becomes consummate in one's conduct" 克己復禮為仁.
2. "For Confucius, unless there are at least two human beings, there can be no human beings." (Fingarette 1983, p. 217)
3. *Analects* 1.2: 君子務本，本立而道生。孝弟也者，其為仁之本與！
4. Henry Rosemont and I (2009) have chosen to translate the term *xiao* 孝 as "familial reverence" rather than "filial piety." The virtue of "family reverence" as a translation is that it in degree disassociates *xiao* from the duty to God implied by "piety" and from the top-down obedience that is assumed in *paterfamilias*. "Family reverence" also has the virtue of retaining the sacred connotations and including the bottom-up direction of *xiao* that are certainly at play in the ritualized culture of ancestral sacrifice.
5. Zhu Xi (1969), *Lunyu* 1:2a: ……孝弟行於家而後仁愛及於物，所謂親親而仁民也。故為仁以孝弟為本。論性則以仁為孝弟之本。或問孝弟為仁之本，此是由孝弟可以至仁否？曰非。謂行仁自孝弟始，孝弟是仁之一事；謂之行仁之本則可，謂之仁之本則不可。蓋仁是性也，孝弟是用也。性中只有簡仁義禮智四者而已，曷嘗有孝弟來？然仁主於愛，愛莫大於愛親。故曰：孝弟也者其為仁之本與。

6. *Mencius* 7A21: 君子所性；7A30：堯舜，性之也；湯武，身之也；五霸，假之也。
7. Storch (2009), p. 54.
8. *Analects* 6.30: 能近取譬，可謂仁之方也已。
9. *Analects* 12.1: 為仁由己，而由人乎哉？
10. *Analects* 14.35:下學而上達。
11. Zhu Xi (1969): *Daxue* 1a–1b: 大學之道，在明明德，在親民，在止於至善。知止而後有定，定而後能靜，靜而後能安，安而後能慮，慮而後能得。物有本末，事有終始，知所先後，則近道矣。
12. Zhu Xi (1969): *Daxue*1b–2a: 古之欲明明德於天下者，先治其國；欲治其國者，先齊其家；欲齊其家者，先修其身；欲修其身者，先正其心；欲正其心者，先誠其意；欲誠其意者，先致其知，致 知在格物。物格而後知至，知至而後意誠，意誠而後心正，心正而後身修，身修而後家齊，家齊而後國治，國治而後天下平。
13. Dewey (1998), p. 299 describes such cultivated habits as "habitudes":

    The influence of habit is decisive because all distinctively human action has to be learned, and the very heart, blood, and sinews of learning is the creation of habitudes.... Habit does not preclude the use of thought, but it determines the channels within which it operates.

14. Zhu Xi (1969): *Daxue* 2b: 自天子以至於庶人，壹是皆以修身為本。其本亂而末治者否矣，其所厚者薄，而其所薄者厚，未之有也！
15. Lau and Chen (1992b), 43.1/164/30: 此謂知本，此謂知之至也。
16. *Analects* 7.1.
17. Tang (1991), Vol. 4, pp. 210–15.
18. *Analects* 17.21. The awareness of the dependence of the infant is reinforced by Dewey: "The dependence of habit-forming upon those habits of a group which constitute customs and institutions is a natural consequence of the helplessness of infancy." (Dewey 1998, p. 298)
19. See Kwan Tze-wan's "Multi-function Character Database" 甲骨續存 1.477.
20. As Dewey describes this emergent process with his language of "doings and undergoings": "We *use* our past experiences to construct new and better ones in the future." (Dewey 1976–83, Vol. 12, p. 134)
21. Steele (2002), p. 196.
22. *Analects* 13.3: 子路曰：「衛君待子而為政，子將奚先？」子曰：「必也正名乎！」子路曰：「有是哉，子之迂也！奚其正？」子曰：「野哉由也！君子於其所不知，蓋闕如也。名不正，則言不順；言不順，則事不成；事不成，則禮樂不興；禮樂不興，則刑罰不中；刑罰不中，則民無所措手足。故君子名之必可言也，言之必可行也。君子於其言，無所苟而已矣。」

23. The *Zuo Commentary to the Spring and Autumn Annals,* Duke Cheng 2. Cf. Legge (1960), Vol. 5, p. 344: 仲尼聞之曰，惜也，不如多與之邑，唯器與名，不可以假人，君之所司也，名以出信，信以守器，器以藏禮，禮以行義，義以生利，利以平民，政之大節也，若以假人，與人政也，政亡，則國家從之，弗可止也已。The *Hanshi waizhuan* 5.34/41/19 records of a story in which again Confucius in attendance on Ji Sun (see *Analects* 14.36) worries over the appropriate use of names. See Lau and Chen (1992a).
24. See, for example, *Analects* 3.10, 3.22, 11.6, 11.17.
25. See, for example, *Analects* 3.1, 3.2, 3.6.
26. See Mattice (2010) for a substantial argument for including both the prospective as well as the retrospective implications of *zhengming* in our understanding of this term.
27. *Great Tradition* A6: 君子居其室，出其言，善則千里之外應之，況其邇者乎，居其室，出其言不善，則千里之外違之，況其邇者乎，言出乎身，加乎民，行發乎邇，見乎遠。言行君子之樞機，樞機之發，榮辱之主也。言行，君子之所以動天地也，可不慎乎。
28. James (2000), p. 42.
29. Note the paronomastic definitions, that is, definition by semantic and phonetic association, for *ren* 仁 and *yi* 義 as *ren* 人 and *yi* 宜, respectively.
30. *Zhongyong* 20: 仁者人也，親親為大；義者宜也，尊賢為大。親親之殺，尊賢之等，禮所生也。See Ames and Hall (2001), p. 101. In deference to the Confucian commitment to family as the putative ground of moral sensibilities, we have challenged the conventional translation of the title of this text as "Doctrine of the Mean" with "Focusing the Familiar," and in so doing, have sought to underscore the cognate relationship between "family" and "familiar." It should be noted that "Doctrine of the Mean" as a translation of the title, *Zhongyong*, was introduced by James Legge in his early 1861 translation of this text, but he abandoned it himself in favor of "The State of Equilibrium and Harmony" when he translated it a second time in the 1880s as part of the *Book of Rites* (*Liji* 禮記).
31. Dennerline (1988), p. 9.
32. Tang (1991), Vol. 4, pp. 210–302. While family is largely absent as a model for social order in the Western narrative, Tang allows that Aristotle and Hegel are exceptions who do recognize the importance of family as a source of social solidarity, but is critical of their failure to understand the cosmological and religious import of family relations extended more broadly.
33. Many if not most of Chinese characters are constructed with a classifactory signifier that provides semantic information—for example, a kind of

tree 木 or something to do with thinking or feeling 心—and a second phonetic element that suggests pronunciation.

34. See Kwan Tze-wan's "Multi-function Character Database" 中山王方壺 CHANT: 9735.3 and 馬王堆, 十問, 6.
35. Putnam (1990), p. 28.
36. Zhang Yanhua (2007), p. 6.
37. *Daodejing* 13: 故貴以身為天下，若可寄天下；愛以身為天下，若可託天下。This same idea is stated negatively in *Daodejing* 26: "How could someone be the king of a huge state and treat his own person as less important than the world?" 奈何萬乘之主，而以身輕天下？
38. 身體髮膚，受之父母，不敢毀傷，孝之始也。See Rosemont and Ames (2009).
39. Lau (1992b), *Liji* 25.36/128/6: 天之所生，地之所養，無人為大。父母全而生之，子全而歸之，可謂孝矣。不虧其體，不辱其身，可謂全矣。
40. *Book of Odes* 195.
41. *Analects* 8.3: 曾子有疾，召門弟子曰：「啟予足！啟予手！《詩》云『戰戰兢兢，如臨深淵，如履薄冰。』而今而後，吾知免夫！小子！」
42. See Sivin (1995b), p. 5.
43. See, for example, *Chunqiufanlu* 23 and 46.
44. *Chunqiufanlu* 56.
45. See Zhang Zailin (2008), pp. 20–22.
46. Zhang Yanhua (2007), p. 38.
47. Lau (1992b), *Liji* 50.1/174/18: 凡禮之大體，體天地，法四時，則陰陽，順人情，故謂之禮。訾之者是不知禮之所由生也。
48. Boodberg (1953), p. 326. This might explain the abbreviated graph for *ti* 體 that is constituted by "person" (*ren* 人) and "root or trunk" (*ben* 本) as *ti* 体. See Ames (1993), p. 169.
49. Sommer (2008), p. 295.
50. Sommer (2008), p. 296.
51. Sommer (2008), p. 294.
52. Sommer (2008), p. 294.
53. Sommer (2008), p. 294.
54. See Shusterman (2008) on somaticity, especially chapters five and six on James and Dewey.
55. Tang (1991) Vol. 15, p. 99: 又禮運篇在說大同之世之理想時，人所念者，唯是人人之得其所。此中禮義之觀念，攝于此《人》之觀念之中。然在實現此志之歷程中，則必須通過人對人之禮義，然後有此人與人之各得其所。
56. See *Analects* 2.21.
57. *Analects* 3.12: 祭如在，祭神如神在。子曰：「吾不與祭，如不祭。」
58. Zhang Yanhua (2007), p. 50.

59. Zhang Yanhua (2007), p. 50.
60. *Analects* 13.28: 子路問曰：「何如斯可謂之士矣？」子曰：「切切、偲偲、怡怡如也，可謂士矣。朋友切切、偲偲，兄弟怡怡。」See Hall and Ames (1994), pp. 77–94 and (1998), pp. 257–69 for a fuller discussion of the Confucian notion of friendship.
61. *Analects* 1.8: 君子……無友不如己者 (repeated in 9.25).
62. Barnes (1984), MM. 1213a20–26. See Yu Jiyuan (2007), p. 4.
63. Barnes (1984), NE, 1157b5–1158b11. See Yu Jiyuan (2007), p. 214.
64. Barnes (1984), *NE*, 1096a11–16.
65. *Analects* 12.24: 曾子曰：「君子以文會友，以友輔仁。」
66. See Sim (2007), chapter seven *passim*.
67. *Analects* 13.23: 君子和而不同，小人同而不和。
68. *Analects* 19.22: 文武之道，未墜於地，在人。賢者識其大者，不賢者識其小者，莫不有文武之道焉。夫子焉不學？而亦何常師之有？
69. *Analects* 7.22: 子曰：「三人行，必有我師焉。擇其善者而從之，其不善者而改之。」
70. *Analects* 16.4: 益者三友，損者三友。友直，友諒，友多聞，益矣。友便辟，友善柔，友便佞，損矣。
71. See Kwan Tze-wan's "Multi-function Character Database" [西周中期] CHANT: 2735, 甲骨文合集 CHANT: 1025 and 甲骨文合集 CHANT: 1025A.
72. See Kwan Tze-wan's "Multi-function Character Database" [西周早期] CHANT: 9091.
73. *Analects* 19.3: 子夏之門人問交於子張。子張曰：「子夏云何？」對曰：「子夏曰：『可者與之，其不可者拒之。』」子張曰：「異乎吾所聞：君子尊賢而容眾，嘉善而矜不能。我之大賢與，於人何所不容？我之不賢與，人將拒我，如之何其拒人也？」
74. See especially *Analects* 12.20.
75. *Analects* 11.20: 子張問善人之道。子曰：「不踐跡，亦不入於室。」
76. *Analects* 6.7.
77. *Analects* 6.3 and 11.7.
78. *Analects* 5.9: 子謂子貢曰：「女與回也孰愈？」對曰：「賜也何敢望回。回也聞一以知十，賜也聞一以知二。」子曰：「弗如也！吾與女弗如也。」
79. *Analects* 7.24: 子曰：「二三子以我為隱乎？吾無隱乎爾。吾無行而不與二三子者，是丘也。」
80. *Analects* 9.23: 子曰：「後生可畏，焉知來者之不如今也？四十、五十而無聞焉，斯亦不足畏也已。」
81. *Analects* 11.10: 顏淵死，子哭之慟。從者曰：「子慟矣。」曰：「有慟乎？非夫人之為慟而誰為！」
82. Sim (2007), pp. 8, 13.

83. This seems to be a major concern for Sim (2007), p. 13 and *passim* in her reading of Confucius:

    The Confucian self... is so relationalistic that it is difficult to see how it could function as a source of agency or locus of responsibility as Confucian ethics demands.

84. Dewey (1998), p. 301.
85. *Xunzi* 105.29.29–31.
86. See *Analects* 4.17.
87. Fingarette (1991), pp. 198–99.
88. Wilhelm (1977), p. 37.
89. *Analects* 6.30: 夫仁者，己欲立而立人，己欲達而達人。
90. Tang (1991) Vol. 13, pp. 28–29.
91. Tang (1991) Vol. 11, pp. 22–24.
92. Tang (1991) Vol. 4, pp. 98–100: 中國自然宇宙論中，共相非第一義之理。物之存在的根本之理為生理，此生理即物之性。物之性表現於與他物感通之德量。性或生理，乃自由原則，生化原則，而非必然原則。蓋任一事象之生起，必由以前之物與其他之交感，以為其外緣。而一物與他物之如何交感或交感之形式，則非由任一物之本身所決定。因而一物之性之本身，即包含一隨所感而變化之性。
93. Tang (1991), Vol. 4, p. 100: 所謂天命之為性，非天以一指定命運規定人物之行動運化，而正是賦人物以多多少少不受自己過去之習慣所機械支配，亦不受外界之來感之力之機械支配，而隨境有一創造的生起而表現自由之性。
94. Tang (1991), Vol. 4, p. 100: 且物必愈與他物感通，而後愈有更大之創造的生起……個體的德量，由其與他物感通，新有所創造的生起而顯；亦由時時能自覺的求多所感通，求善於感通，並脫離其過去之習慣之機械支配，及外界之物之力之機械支配，而日趨宏大。但此非一般物之所能，唯人乃能之耳。
95. Tang (1991), Vol. 4, p. 22: 人者天地之心也。
96. Tang (1991), Vol. 13, p. 28: 然就一具體存在之有生，而即言其有性，則重要者不在說此存在之性質性相之為何，而是其生命存在之所向之為何。
97. Tang (1991), Vol. 13 pp. 21–22: 人之現實性不必能窮盡人之可能性，而欲知人之可能性，亦不能如人之求知其他事物之可能性，而本推論與假設以客觀知之；而當由人之內在的理想之如何實踐，與如何實現以知之。即對人性有知，自亦必有名言概念，加以表達。然此名言概念，乃順此所知，而隨機以相繼的形成。
98. Tang (1991), Vol. 13, p. 24: 如西方人之Property, Characteristics, Propensity 及 Essence 諸名之所指，皆是一定之性相性質或性向。然吾人若由人之面對天地萬物與其所體驗之內在理想，而自反省其性之何所是時，是否可言人有定性，則大成問題。因人之所面對之天地萬物與理想，皆為 變化無方者⋯⋯ 中國思想之論人性，幾於大體上共許之一義，即為直就此人性之能變化無方處，而指為人之特性之所在，此即人之靈性，而異於萬物之為一定而不靈者。

99. Tang (1991), Vol. 13, p. 21: 依吾人之意，以觀中國先哲之人性論之原始，其基本觀點，首非將人或人性，視為一所對之客觀事物，來論述其普遍性，特殊性，或可能性，而主要是就人之面對天地萬物，並面對其內部所體驗之人生理想，而自反省此人性之所是，以及天地萬物之性之何所是。緣是而依中國思想之諸人流，以觀人之性，則人雖為萬物中之一類，而不只為萬物之一類。
100. *Zhongyong* 13: 道不遠人。人之為道而遠人，不可以為道。See Ames and Hall (2001), pp. 93–94.
101. *Analects* 7.30: 子曰：「仁遠乎哉？我欲仁，斯仁至矣。」
102. Sandel (1998), p. 50.
103. Mill (1930) Book, chapter seven, section one, p. 608.
104. Such is the persistence of old ideas, even in a world in which developments in science have encouraged us think differently about things; that is, contemporary science has given us a new, ecologically informed world in which "objects are purely relational and have nothing to do with the intrinsic qualities of individual things and nothing to say about them." (Dewey 1998, p. 220)
105. Perhaps philosophers who regularly teach Leslie Stevenson's *Seven Theories of Human Nature* (revised now to "Ten Theories") are less inclined to be overwhelmed by this cultural dominant, but our best interpreters of the Chinese tradition would seem to begin here. See for example, Munro (1977), pp. 19–20, 57 in commenting on the same opening passage of the *Zhongyong* that Tang Junyi discusses above:

> This means that a person's nature being so decreed, cannot be altered through human action; it is a "given" that exists from birth. The Neo-Confucians also affirmed the fixed character of man's essential nature.... The Chinese immediately associate the panhuman with the innate and the innate with the unchangeable.

See also Schwartz (1985), pp. 175, 179 who appeals to this conventional interpretation in describing *xing* as "a 'heavenly endowed' or 'heavenly ordained' tendency, directionality, or potentiality of growth in the individual," and "an innate tendency toward growth or development in a given, predetermined direction."

In *A Taoist Theory of Chinese Thought*, Hansen (1992), concerned that "most of Graham's appreciative herd of Mencius worshipers still think that the problems of moral reform dictate Mencius' status-quo solution" (p. 194), argues that Mencius' "innatist" interpretation of *xing* precludes the possibility of moral reform all together. Hansen insists that "the content—

the detailed structure of the nature of the moral plant—is not the result of external factors.... Morality is internal in this sense" (p. 174), and hence "there is an absolutely correct thing to do in each situation" (p. 178) because "nature programs *xin* [heart-and-mind] to generate that action" (p. 177). Hansen summarizes Mencius' innatist position in the following terms:

> We could understand Mencius as arguing that humans have an entire innate moral grammar. That moral grammar enables them to process any morally neutral external structure and produce the morally right line of behavior. But moral rightness has no metaphysical basis other than its situational production by the heart. That would preserve Mencius' claim that morality is metaphysically internal rather than external. (Hansen 1992, p. 187)

Ivanhoe (1990) acknowledges the merit of Angus Graham's novel insistence that "*the proper course of development* defines human nature" (p. 34), but insists that morality is not "existential" in any sense of being dependent upon human choices, but rather is simply "the manifestation of human nature" (p. 33). "Human nature has a specific *content*.... These different parts are arranged in a very special structure and the shape of this structure emerges as an individual matures" (p. 47).

Kanaya Osamu (1966) also internalizes and essentializes *renxing*. He observes that "from this doctrine that human nature is good, in the teaching of morality there is a shift from an emphasis on being taught from above to making the main locus of teaching the internal intuitions of all people. The anticipation is that the content of education comes from within everyone and then spreads from there to perfect them" (p. 127). Kanaya also see this doctrine as a kind of human egalitarianism that challenges Confucius's more elitist discriminations.

106. *Mencius* 4B19: 人之所以異於禽於獸者幾希。
107. *Mencius* 2A6, 6A6, and 7A21.
108. Ames (1991), pp. 145–46.
109. *Mencius* 2A6: 惻隱之心，仁之端也；羞惡之心，義之端也；辭讓之心，禮之端也；是非之心，智之端也。人之有是四端也，猶其有四體也。有是四端而自謂不能者，自賊者也；謂其君不能者，賊其君者也。凡有四端於我者，知皆擴而充之矣，若火之始然，泉之始達。苟能充之，足以保四海；苟不充之，不足以事父母。
110. *Mencius* 7A21: 君子所性，雖大行不加焉，雖窮居不損焉，分定故也。君子所性，仁義禮智根於心。其生色也，睟然見於面，盎於背，施於四體，四體不言而喻。
111. *Mencius* 2A6: 人之有是四端也猶其有四體也。
112. *Mencius* 7A1: 盡其心者知其性也。知其性則知天矣。存其心養其性所以事天也。It is important to appreciate the performative implications of *zhi* 知 that I have rendered here as "to realize" rather than as simply "to know."
113. Zhang Dainian (1982), pp. 250–53.
114. *Mencius* 6A15.
115. *Mencius* 6B2: 曹交問曰：「人皆可以為堯舜，有諸？」曰：「……堯舜之道，孝弟而已矣。子服堯之服，誦堯之言，行堯之行，是堯而已矣。」
116. *Mencius* 6A6: 孟子曰：「乃若其情，則可以為善矣，乃所謂善也。若夫為不善，非才之罪也。惻隱之心，人皆有之；羞惡之心，人皆有之；恭敬之心，人皆有之；是非之心，人皆有之。惻隱之心，仁也；羞惡之心，義也；恭敬之心，禮也；是非之心，智也。仁義禮智，非由外鑠我也，我固有之也，弗思耳矣。故曰：『求則得之，舍則失之。』或相倍蓰而無算者，不能盡其才者也。」See also 2A6 for similar language.
117. Yang (1998) insists that although the notion of "forming and functioning" (*tiyong* 體用) is only applied to Confucianism in the Song dynasty, it is already there in essence in *Mencius*. As we have seen in chapter two, *tiyong* expresses the interdependence and mutuality of forming and functioning: that is, how we think and what we think about are mutually shaping. However, in Yang's analysis of Mencius's thought, he makes *xing* into something that is exclusively internal and that then emerges to be manifest in one's conduct, violating the notion of interdependence by making *xing* itself foundational and unchanging in the conduct it inspires.
118. *Mencius* 6A2: 水信無分於東西，無分於上下乎。人性之善猶水之就下也。人無有不善，水無有不下。This more careful reading was suggested to me in correspondence with Vytis Silius at Vilnius University.
119. *Mencius* 6A15: 公都子問曰：「鈞是人也，或為大人，或為小人，何也？」孟子曰：「從其大體為大人，從其小體為小人」。曰：「鈞是人也，或從其大體，或從其小體，何也？」曰：「耳目之官不思，而蔽於物，物交物，則引之而已矣。心之官則思，思則得之，不思則不得也。此天之所與我者，先立乎其大者，則其小者弗能奪也。此為大人而已矣。」
120. *Mencius* 7B24: 口之於味也，目之於色也，耳之於聲也，鼻之於臭也，四肢之於安佚也，性也，有命焉，君子不謂性也。仁之於父子也，義之於君臣也，禮之於賓主也，智之於賢者也，聖人之於天道也，命也，有性焉，君子不謂命也。
121. *Mencius* 7A36: 居移氣，養移體，大哉居乎！夫非盡人之子與？
122. *Mencius* 4B26: 天下之言性也，則故而已矣。
123. The considered understanding of *xing* 行 offered in the work of Joseph Needham and Nathan Sivin supports the translation of the title of this

text as "Five Modes of Proper Conduct" where "proper" locates the action as appropriate to a specific relationship. It also recommends an understanding of *xing* as relational activity or virtuosity in action rather than as "virtue" in the sense of a character trait. Needham (1956), pp. 243–44 writes:

> The conception of the elements was not so much one of a series of five sorts of fundamental matter (particles do not come into the question), as of five sorts of fundamental processes. Chinese thought here characteristically avoided substance and clung to relation."

Sivin (1987), p. 74, building on the insights of Needham, concludes:

> *Wu* means "five"; the pertinent meanings of *hsing* [*xing*] are "to do, to act, to move, to set in motion; action, activity, motion," etc. If the idea that *wu hsing* [*wuxing*] was first applied to moral discourse turns out to be true once the tangle of dates is unraveled, the word *hsing* must almost certainly refer to types of action based on such qualities.

124. *Mencius* 7A4: 萬物皆備於我矣。
125. Dewey is making a similar point when he remarks, "To say that some pre-existent association of human beings is prior to every particular human being who is born into the world is a commonplace." (Dewey 1922, p. 59)
126. For example, *Wuxingpian* 9 reads:

> 金聲而玉振之有德者也。金聲善也，玉音聖也。善人道也，德天道也。唯有德者然後能金聲而玉振之。

> Opening with bells, to then rally others with jade tubes is to have a moral excellence. The opening with bells is efficacy and the sound of jade tubes is sagacity. Efficacy is the human way; excellence in one's habits is the way of *tian*. Only once one has developed moral excellence can one "open with bells and rally others with jade tubes."

This passage is echoed in *Mencius* 5B1:

> 孔子聖之時者也。孔子之謂集大成。集大成也者金聲而玉振之也。金聲也者始條理也。玉振之也者終條理也。始條理者智之事也。終條理者聖之事也。

> Confucius was the sage whose actions were timely. It was Confucius who was said to bring together all accomplishments. Bringing together all accomplishments is to open with bells and rally others with jade tubes. To open with bells is to begin by effecting a coherent pattern; to rally others with jade tubes is to conclude by effecting a coherent pattern. To begin by effecting a coherent pattern is the stuff of wisdom; to conclude by effecting a coherent pattern is the stuff of sageliness.

In addition to the obvious overlap in vocabulary and metaphor, the fact that the last two lines end with the "wisdom and sagacity" theme might suggest that the *Wuxingpian* is being alluded to in this *Mencius* passage. Again there is the much debated passage in the *Xunzi* "*Contra* Twelve Philosophers" chapter, HY 16/6/10, in which Xunzi associates both Mencius and Zisizi with the doctrine of "five modes of proper conduct," and then condemns them severely for advocating such a doctrine. See Ames and Hall (2001), pp. 137–43, and for an interpretation of the relationship between these earlier moral categories and the *wuxing* 五行 five-phases cosmology, see Lloyd and Sivin (2002), p. 259.

127. *Mencius* 2A6.
128. The Mawangdui version of the *Wuxingpian* text has "wisdom" before "ritual propriety," while the Guodian text has the reverse order. The "five modes of proper conduct" (*wuxing* 五行) are the same as the "four inklings" (*siduan* 四端) of *Mencius* with "sagacity" (*sheng* 聖) added on as the fifth mode of proper conduct. The "four inklings" in the *Mencius* 2A6, 6A6, and 7A21 occur in the same order as the Guodian text as 仁義禮智 (*ren, yi, li, zhi*).
129. *Zhouli* HY 4/6b–7a states that "the court tutor instructs the crown prince in the three kinds of moral excellences (*sande* 三德) and the three modes of proper conduct (*sanxing* 三行)" 師氏……以三德教國子……教三行. The Zheng Xuan 鄭玄 commentary observes: "The expression 'morally excellent conduct' (*dexing* 德行) refers to both the inner and the outer, where that which is in the heart-and-mind is moral dispositions, and acting upon them is proper conduct" 德行，內外之稱。在心為德。施之為行.
130. *Wuxingpian* 1: 仁形於內謂之德之行，不形於內謂之行。義形於內謂之德之行，不形於內謂之行。禮形於內謂之德之行，不形於內謂之行。智形於內謂之德之行，不形於內謂之行。聖形於內謂之德之行，不形於內謂之行。德之行五，和謂之德，四行和謂之善。善人道也，德天道也。 This distinction between habituated moral conduct and mere conduct is a major theme in the *Mencius*. In *Mencius* 6B6 for example, it states that "what one has within will necessarily be expressed in external conduct" 有諸內必行諸外. The *Mencius* 2B2 has the expression "morally excellent conduct" (*dexing* 德行) and 2A3 has the passage "those who act consummately by virtue of their moral excellence are true kings" 以德行仁者王.
131. 孟子曰：「人之所以異於禽獸者希。庶民去之，君子存之。舜明於庶物，察於人倫，由仁義行，非行仁義也。」
132. *Analects* 7.23: 天生德於予.
133. 心之官則思，思則得之，不思則不得也。此天之所與我者。
134. Mead (1982), p. 156.
135. Dewey (1922), p. 176.

136. Dewey (1922), pp. 176–77.
137. Dewey (1998), p. 297.
138. Dewey (1969–72), Vol. 3, p. 304.
139. Dewey (1969–72), Vol. 4, p. 38.
140. Dewey (1922), pp. 93–94.
141. Dewey (1922), p. 94.
142. Dewey (1960), p. 173.
143. Dewey (1981–90), Vol. 7, p. 323.
144. Campbell (1995), pp. 53–55.
145. Campbell (1995), p. 40.
146. Dewey (1981–90), Vol. 1, p. 135.
147. Dewey (1958), p. 133.
148. Dewey (1981), pp. 626–27.
149. *Mencius* 7A15: 人之所不學而能者，其良能也；所不慮而知者，其良知也。孩提之童，無不知愛其親者；及其長也，無不知敬其兄也。親親，仁也；敬長，義也。無他，達之天下也。I follow Zhu Xi here in understanding *liangneng* 良能 and *liangzhi* 良知 as *benneng* 本能 and *benzhi* 本知.
150. *Mencius* 6A4, 6A5, 6A6.
151. Sullivan (2000), p. 23 observes a similar limitation in Dewey's writings with respect to gender. In spite of "Dewey's political activism on behalf of issues important to women and the affinity between his pragmatism and feminist theory due to their shared emphasis upon pluralism, perspectivism, and the connection of theory and practice, it is disappointing that Dewey never wrote much on the topic of gender." Sullivan is pointing out an inconsistency between Dewey's underlying premises and "the lack of extended, explicit attention in Dewey's voluminous corpus to, for example, the lives and experiences of women in particular, including their differences from those of men...". What makes this perhaps even more surprising is that Dewey is not unaware of the entrenched gender prejudice. He rues the palpable lack of concern for female individuality: "Writers, usually male, hold forth on the psychology of woman, as if they were dealing with a Platonic universal entity, although they habitually treat men as individuals, varying with structure and environment." (Dewey 1922, p. 153)
152. Sim (2007) pp. 40–41n34 does point out that the role of family does have a degree of importance for Aristotle 1180a29–33 and 1180b4–14, but also allows that family as a source of order is subordinate to the universal knowledge provided by law in 1180b15–20. Indeed, Sim sees the appeal to this objective standard as a way of resolving the perennial Confucian problem of corruption that emerges as a consequence of the inappropriate disposition of intimate relations. Perhaps one exception here would be

Hegel. In his *Philosophy of Right*, he develops a complex argument for the moral worth of family, and for the unity and interdependence of family members. Another exception to this claim that family is not an important consideration in the evolution of Western ethical thinking is Jane Addams who was an otherwise strong influence on Dewey. See her *Democracy and Social Ethics* (2002).

153. Dewey (1976–83), Vol. 13, pp. 230, 103.
154. The sociologist Ambrose King makes this argument. See King (1985), p. 58.
155. Rosemont and Ames (2009).
156. *Daodejing* 25: 道法自然。
157. Similarly, for Dewey (1998), p. 223:

> Potentialities cannot be known till after the interactions have occurred. There are at a given time unactualized potentialities in an individual because and in as far as there are in existence other things with which it has not as yet interacted.

Lincoln is not Lincoln independent of the circumstances of history, nor are the circumstances of history the making of Lincoln. Indeed, Lincoln is a collaboration between person and circumstances expressed as those thick habits of conduct with whom Lincoln is identified. "The idea that potentialities are inherent and fixed by relation to a predetermined end was a product of a highly restricted state of technology." (Dewey 1998, p. 224)

IV

1. For example, in her seminal essay that has underwritten much more recent work in Aristotelian naturalism, "Modern Moral Philosophy," Elizabeth Anscombe suggests that "just as *man* has so many teeth... so perhaps the species *man*, regarded not just biologically, but from the point of view of the activity of thought and choice in regard to the various departments of life... 'has' such-and-such virtues." (Anscombe (1981), p. 38.)
2. *Analects* 17.8: 子曰：「由也，女聞六言六蔽矣乎？」對曰：「未也。」「居！吾語女。好仁不好學，其蔽也愚；好知不好學，其蔽也蕩；好信不好學，其蔽也賊；好直不好學，其蔽也絞；好勇不好學，其蔽也亂；好剛不好學，其蔽也狂。」
3. *Analects* 1.6: 弟子入則孝，出則弟，謹而信，汎愛眾，而親仁。行有餘力，則以學文。
4. See Kwan Tze-wan's "Multi-function Character Database" 京津 4836 and [西周晚期] CHANT: 4324.
5. The name of this young man speaks volumes. *Zhi* 直 means "true" in the sense of being "true, upright, honest." *Gong* 躬 is a term for one's body that means specifically the deliberate public display of one's personal

merits. Sommer (2008), p. 307 in her analysis of the various designations for "body" in classical Chinese, reports that *gong* "most often signifies a body in the process of personally and consciously performing an action, usually in a ritual context before an audience, that demonstrates visually the virtuous character of the actor.... The conduct of the *gong* body is ritualized, stylized, nonspontaneous, and guided by traditional mores and social obligations." In this context, *gong* conveys a sense of priggishness—a young man who is making a conscious display of his virtues for all to see.

6. This governor of She also appears in *Analects* 13.16 that records an occasion in the 26th year of King Zhao of Chu (490 BCE) when the governor asks the itinerant Confucius about governing properly. Confucius replies: "If those near at hand are pleased, those at a distance will repair to you" 近者悦，遠者來.

7. On Zhu Xi's reading, the father is in dire straits, taking *rang* 攘 to mean "to steal when in difficult circumstances." Zhu Xi would have the father stealing out of the abject need to feed his starving children. But on such a reading, the putative "crime" of the father evaporates, and the son is just rotten. Perhaps Confucius has a more complex situation in mind.

8. *Analects* 13.18: 葉公語孔子曰：「吾黨有直躬者，其父攘羊，而子證之。」孔子曰：「吾黨之直者異於是。父為子隱，子為父隱，直在其中矣。」This passage goes to the centrality of both family reverence and moral imagination in Confucian role ethics. See interesting and amusing parodies of this anecdote in *Hanfeizi* 韓非子 (1982), 49.9.2, *Lüshichunqiu* 呂氏春秋 (1955), p. 449, and *Huainanzi* 淮南子 (1992), 13/125/14 in which the clever young man, asking to replace his aged and ailing father in detention, is much praised by the magistrate as a model son. When the magistrate allows the son to take his father's place and serve his time in jail, the young man then petitions the magistrate wondering what affect it might have on the moral fiber of the community if the magistrate continues to incarcerate what he himself has praised as a model son. The magistrate on reflection releases the son as clear evidence of the magistrate's own moral caliber.

9. See Rosemont and Ames (2008) for an extended discussion of this and similar cases in which a tension between loyalty to the family and to the state is at issue. In this article, we argue that "family reverence" (*xiao* 孝), far from being a source of corruption that compromises social morality, is itself the ultimate source of "consummate conduct" (*ren* 仁).

10. Rosemont and Ames (2008), pp. 12, 14. It is of course possible to derive generalizations from the Confucian canon, but these are a long way from claims about universal "principles" because the latter can be refuted by a single counterexample. Generalizations, however, are defeated not by a counterexample—or even several of them—but rather by a better

generalization; we should not be thinking of "all" so much as "many," or "most." Some might wish to claim that the "negative golden rule" found in *Analects* 5.12, 12.2 and 15.24 is paradigmatically a universal principle. We believe it is more correctly and incisively seen as a rough generalization about an attitude one should have for determining what is most appropriate in one's relations with others that does not presume to know from the beginning what is right for everyone. We cultivate a sense of deference (*shu* 恕) initially in our family relations, and then extend this sensibility with imagination to those who are very different from us as our lives unfold. Indeed, far from being an argument *for* universalism in ethics, it is an argument *against* it.

11. See Kwan Tze-wan's "Multi-function Character Database" 甲骨文合集 CHANT: *0601 and [西周中期] CHANT: 4199.
12. *Analects* 2.21: 或謂孔子曰:「子奚不為政?」子曰:「《書》云:『孝乎惟孝、友于兄弟,施於有政。』是亦為政,奚其為為政?」The historical records that emerge over the centuries after Confucius' death take his side by refuting the questioner's charge. A hundred years after the death of Confucius it is recorded that he was in fact Minister of Justice in the state of Lu, later still he is promoted to Prime Minister, and then during the Han dynasty, to the status of "the uncrowned king" (*suwang* 素王) of Lu.
13. *Analects* 12.11: 齊景公問政於孔子。孔子對曰:「君君,臣臣,父父,子子。」公曰:「善哉!信如君不君,臣不臣,父不父,子不子,雖有粟,吾得而食諸?」Compare 1.2 and 2.21 in which the argument is that effective familial relations are the root of both community and state.
14. See Kwan Tze-wan's "Multi-function Character Database" 甲骨文合集 CHANT: 1490, [戰國早期] CHANT: 17, 甲骨文合集 CHANT: 2929C, 甲骨文合集 CHANT: 2924A, and [商代] CHANT: 6213.
15. Ames and Hall (2001), pp. 89–90: 喜怒哀樂之未發,謂之中;發而皆中節,謂之和;中也者,天下之大本也;和也者,天下之達道也。致中和,天地位焉,萬物育焉。
16. *Analects* 1.12: 禮之用,和為貴。先王之道斯為美,小大由之。有所不行,知和而和,不以禮節之,亦不可行也。See also 12.1 and 12.15.
17. *Analects* 8.2: 子曰:「恭而無禮則勞,慎而無禮則葸,勇而無禮則亂,直而無禮則絞。君子篤於親,則民興於仁;故舊不遺,則民不偷。」
18. *Analects* 2.8: 子曰:「色難。有事弟子服其勞,有酒食先生饌,曾是以為孝乎?」
19. *Analects* 8.4: 曾子言曰:「……君子所貴乎道者三:動容貌,斯遠暴慢矣;正顏色,斯近信矣;出辭氣,斯遠鄙倍矣。籩豆之事,則有司存。」

20. *Analects* 10.4: 入公門，鞠躬如也，如不容。立不中門，行不履閾。過位，色勃如也，足躩如也，其言似不足者。攝齊升堂，鞠躬如也，屏氣似不息者。出，降一等，逞顏色，怡怡如也。沒階趨，翼如也。復其位，踧踖如也。

21. Kwan Tze-wan's "Multi-function Character Database" 甲骨文合集 CHANT: 2809 and [西周早期] CHANT: 6015.

22. *Analects* 10.19: 疾，君視之，東首，加朝服，拖紳。There is a protocol expressed here. The bed for the master of the house was usually on the western side of the southern window. When one's lord would visit, the lord would approach by ascending the stairs from the east. The eastern stairs is the place of the host, but since the lord himself is the host of the entire country, he would ascend and descend from the eastern steps.

23. See the Kwan "Multi-function Character Database" 殷虛書契前編 2.19.1 and 2840 中山王鼎 in the bibliography. The representation of this central philosophical term *ren* with a character that includes the pregnant body helps to make the argument that if in classical Confucianism ethical conduct is to be understood as that which conduces to growth in relations, then misogyny is anathema to its underlying premises.

24. *Analects* 12.1. Confucius is cognizant of the individual strengths of some of his most prominent students, but denies that they have achieved *ren* (5.8). And he is certainly unwilling to define *ren* negatively as the absence of disintegrative conduct (14.1). Aware of the tenacity and incorruptibility of certain historical models, he again is reluctant to allow that they are *ren* (5.19) by virtue of this history. In fact, it is only Yan Hui among those around him that he is willing to describe as *ren*, and one wonders if this was in fact an ascription subsequent to the early death of his favorite protégé.

25. *Analects* 17.2: 性相近也，習相遠也。

26. *Analects* 5.13: 子貢曰：「夫子之文章，可得而聞也；夫子之言性與天道，不可得而聞也。」Zigong said, "We can learn from the Master's cultural refinements, but are unlikely to hear him discourse on subjects such as our 'natural tendencies' (*xing*) or 'the way of *tian*' (*tiandao*)."

27. *Analects* 6.23.

28. James (2000), pp. 97–98.

29. *Analects* 20.2.

30. *Analects* 13.27: 子曰：「剛毅、木訥，近仁。」

31. *Analects* 17.6: 能行五者於天下，為仁矣。……恭、寬、信、敏、惠。恭則不侮，寬則得眾，信則人任焉，敏則有功，惠則足以使人。

32. *Analects* 4.4: 苟志於仁矣，無惡也。and 4.3: 唯仁者能好人，能惡人。

33. *Analects* 4.16.

34. *Analects* 17.23: 子路曰：「君子尚勇乎？」子曰：「君子義以為上。君子有勇而無義為亂，小人有勇而無義為盜。」

35. *Analects* 4.19–21.
36. All translations from the *Xiaojing* are adapted from Rosemont and Ames (2009). *Xiaojing* 1: 子曰：「夫孝，德之本也，教之所由生也。」
37. See in the bibliography the Kwan "Multi-function Character Database" 甲骨文合集 CHANT: 0039A, Small Seal Script 小篆 (康熙圖), [西周晚期] CHANT: 3937, and 甲骨文合集 CHANT: 3233.
38. *Shuowen*: 教，上所施，下所效也。
39. *Xiaojing* 1: 不敢毀傷，孝之始也。立身行道，揚名於後世，以顯父母，孝之終也。夫孝，始於事親，中於事君，終於立身。
40. Witness Sim (2007), p. 14n3 who reflects this familiar reading of Confucius when she invokes Aristotle to save Confucius from himself:

    That is, we believe today that what appears to us to be Confucius' recommendation of blind obedience and loyalty to abusive parents or tyrannical rulers impairs the recipients of such blind loyalty no less than its performers.

41. *Xiaojing* 12: 禮者，敬而已矣。故敬其父，則子悦；敬其兄，則弟悦；敬其君，則臣悦；敬一人，而千萬人悦。所敬者寡，而悦者眾，此之謂要道也。
42. *Xiaojing* 15: 曾子曰：「……敢問子從父之令，可謂孝乎？」子曰：「是何言與，是何言與！……故當不義，則子不可以不爭於父，臣不可以不爭於君。故當不義則爭之。從父之令，又焉得為孝乎！」
43. *Xunzi* 20.
44. *Analects* 4.18: 事父母幾諫。見志不從，又敬不違，勞而不怨。
45. *Analects* 12.5: 君子敬而無失，與人恭而有禮。四海之內，皆兄弟也。君子何患乎無兄弟也？
46. See Rosemont and Ames (2009), p. 3.
47. *Analects* 4.5.
48. *Analects* 5.3: 子謂子賤，「君子哉若人！魯無君子者，斯焉取斯？」See also 9.14, where Confucius claims that the model of an exemplary person living among barbarians would be transformative for them.
49. *Analects* 2.3: 子曰：「道之以政，齊之以刑，民免而無恥；道之以德，齊之以禮，有恥且格。」
50. *Analects* 12.13: 子曰：「聽訟，吾猶人也，必也使無訟乎！」
51. *Analects* 6.23: 子曰：「知者樂水，仁者樂山；知者動，仁者靜；知者樂，仁者壽。」
52. *Analects* 4.2: 仁者安仁，知者利仁。
53. Some modern dictionaries take the signifier to be "sun, day" (*ri* 日).
54. See Kwan Tze-wan's "Multi-function Character Database" 英國所藏甲骨集 2518, 甲骨文合集 30429, and [春秋早期] CHANT: 2766.
55. Karlgren (1996), p. 228.

56. *Analects* 6.20: 知之者不如好之者，好之者不如樂之者。
57. This pragmatic association between "knowing" and making one's best way forward is not lost on Dewey (2004), pp. 89–90 who makes a similar point:

    > If ideas, meanings, conceptions, notions, theories, systems are instrumental to an active reorganization of the given environment, to a removal of some specific trouble and perplexity, then the test of their validity and value lies in accomplishing this work.... That which guides us truly is true—demonstrated capacity for such guidance is precisely what is meant by truth. The adverb "truly" is more fundamental than either the adjective true, or the noun, truth. An adverb expresses a way, a mode of acting.

58. *Analects* 15.16: 不曰「如之何如之何」者，吾末如之何也已矣。
59. *Analects* 6.7: 回也，其心三月不違仁，其餘則日月至焉而已矣。
60. *Analects* 19.6: 博學而篤志，切問而近思，仁在其中矣。
61. *Analects* 4.15: 夫子之道，忠恕而已矣。
62. *Analects* 15.24: 子貢問曰：「有一言而可以終身行之者乎？」子曰：「其恕乎！己所不欲，勿施於人。」Compare *Analects* 5.12 and 12.2.
63. Chan (1963), p. 44; Tu (1989), pp. 34–36 and Dawson (1981), p. 41; Waley (1938), p. 105; Fingarette (1972), p. 55; Slingerland (2003), p. 242; Lau (1992), pp. xv–xvi.
64. See Kwan Tze-wan's "Multi-function Character Database" 甲骨文合集 CHANT: 0470.
65. *Analects* 6.30: 能近取譬，可謂仁之方也已。
66. *Book of Odes* 158; compare Karlgren (1950), p. 103.
67. *Zhongyong* 13: 道不遠人。人之為道而遠人，不可以為道。《詩》云：「伐柯伐柯，其則不遠。」執柯以伐柯，睨而視之，猶以為遠。故君子以人治人，改而止。忠恕違道不遠，施諸己而不愿，亦勿施於人。See Ames and Hall (2001), p. 94.
68. *Zhongyong* 13: 君子之道四，丘未能一焉：所求乎子以事父，未能也；所求乎臣以事君，未能也；所求乎弟以事兄，未能也；所求乎朋友先施之，未能也。庸德之行，庸言之謹，有所不足，不敢不勉，有餘不敢盡；言顧行，行顧言，君子胡不慥慥爾！
69. *Analects* 6.22, 12.1, 12.2, 12.3, 12.22, 13.19, 15.10.
70. *Analects* 11.22: 求也退，故進之；由也兼人，故退之。
71. Lau (1992), p. xvi.
72. See Kwan Tze-wan's "Multi-function Character Database" [戰國晚期] CHANT: 2840.
73. See Kwan Tze-wan's "Multi-function Character Database" 甲骨文合集 CHANT: 2456 and [西周中期] CHANT: 250.
74. See Kwan Tze-wan's "Multi-function Character Database" [春秋] CHANT: 102.
75. See the discussion under 義 in Kwan Tze-wan's "Multi-function Character

Notes

Database."

76. *Wuxingpian* 20: 故義取閒而仁取匿。剛義之方也，柔仁之方也。
77. *Analects* 4.10: 君子之於天下也，無適也，無莫也，義之與比。See also *Analects* 14.32 and 9.4. In 18.8, having surveyed the defining events of a series of cultural heroes, Confucius allows that "I am different from all of these people in that I do not have presuppositions as to what may and may not be done" 我則異於是，無可無不可.
78. *Analects* 9.4: 子絕四：毋意，毋必，毋固，毋我。
79. *Analects* 2.24: 見義不為，無勇也。
80. *Analects* 7.3: 德之不脩，學之不講，聞義不能徙，不善不能改，是吾憂也。
81. *Analects* 15.18: 義以為質，禮以行之，孫以出之，信以成之。君子哉！ The received text begins this passage with "the exemplary person," and then ends the passage by repeating it. I have followed the Dingzhou version of the *Analects* in omitting the first instance of this expression.
82. *Analects* 1.13: 信近於義，言可復也。
83. In the *Analects*, for example, see 1.4, 1.5, 1.6, 2.22, 4.22, 5.10, 14.20, 14.27, 15.6, 16.4.
84. See Kwan Tze-wan's "Multi-function Character Database" 殷墟文字甲編 2304.
85. See Kwan Tze-wan's "Multi-function Character Database" [西周早期] CHANT: 2837.
86. *Analects* 12.10: 子張問崇德⋯⋯ 子曰：「主忠信，徙義，崇德也。」
87. *Analects* 12.21: 先事後得，非崇德與？
88. Sim (2007), p. 17 for example, makes the ruler and people exclusive when she states:

> Confucius so completely embeds moral principle in customary norms and the model persons embodying and exhibiting them that he hangs all his political hopes on rule by an exemplary individual who inspires other to virtue.

But if we recall *Analects* 2.3, Confucius, on the contrary, is relying upon the achieved capacity of the people to order themselves through a sense of shame and belonging. See also (*Analects* 3.5):

> 夷狄之有君，不如諸夏之亡也。
>
> The Yi and Di barbarian tribes with rulers are not as viable as the various Chinese states without them.

V

1. Granet (1934), p. 478.
2. Tang (1991), Vol. 11, p. 241: 中國民族無含超絕意義的天的觀念。中

國人對天有個普遍的觀念，就是天與地是分不開的。

3. Needham (1956), p. 290.
4. For similar characterizations of early Chinese cosmology, see Granet (1934), p. 279, Tang (1991), Vol. 11, p. 100–103, Xiong (1985b), pp. 297, 554, Zhang Dongsun (1995a), p. 271, (1995b), pp. 285–90, Graham (1989), p. 222, Sivin (1995a), p. 3, Hansen (1992), p. 215, Kupperman (1971), p. 189. To cite an example, Girardot (1983), p. 64: "The imagery of 'mother,' 'dark female,' 'divine bird,' 'primal ancestor,' and also the primordial couple, primal giant, and 'mass of flesh' imagery, is all relevant to the development of early Taoist thought; but the essential mystical intentionality seems to favor the idea of creation always lacking any creator separate from the creation."
5. Graham (1990), p. 287.
6. For example, Csikszentmihalyi (2004), p. 161n1 attributes a kind of deism to David Hall and myself. In this interpretation, God creates the world and then lets it take its own course. Csikszentmihalyi states that our "use of the term [transcendence] is closer to the theological sense that rejects the immanence of a deity, that is, transcendence as a denial of divine interference in mundane affairs." But in fact, as we have explained the asymmetry in strict transcendence between God and world, God has a free hand in determining and sustaining the world while conversely the world does not have any effect on the perfection that is God. Hence God and world stand in a dualistic relationship. God stands independent of the world, and negates it in the sense that the world has no independent existence outside of God's perfection. An alternative to such strict transcendence is the correlative relationship between *tian* and the human experience captured in the familiar expression used to characterize classical Chinese cosmology, *tianren heyi* 天人合一, "the continuity between the natural and cultural context and the human experience." Csikszentmihalyi goes on to argue that the *Wuxingpian* describes sages as having access to *tian* in a way that makes their experience different from ordinary human experience not in degree, but in kind. In ascribing a difference in kind to the sages, he introduces a gap between human experience and *tian* that would vitiate the notion of the interdependence and inseparability of *tian* and the human experience broadly. We would argue that all human experience is transactional with *tian* but that sages are sages because they get more from and contribute more to *tian* than ordinary human beings.
7. Hall and Ames (1987), p. 13. For an example of this continuity, see Hall and Ames (1998), p. 190.
8. Whitehead's understanding of the metaphysician Plato as an abstract formist is a fair representative of the "received" Plato. It is important to stipulate *whose* Plato. Much good research is being done to rescue the

more interesting artist and ironist Plato from the received abstract formist, idealist, rationalist Plato, dominated as this latter interpretation has been by systematic metaphysics. David Hall's *Eros and Irony: A Prelude to Philosophical Anarchism* is a good example of this new literature. But it is the received Plato, filtered through Augustine and the Church fathers, and through twentieth-century scientism—interpretations that have collaborated to promote Plato as a metaphysical realist—that has exercised a defining influence on the evolution of the Western cultural narrative.

9. James (2000), pp. 41–42.
10. Sivin (1995a), p. viii.
11. See Ames (2008). This essay appears in a special issue of *Asia Major* that celebrates Sivin's work, containing therein a fuller discussion of his important contribution.
12. Sivin (1995a), p. 3.
13. Han Feizi appeals to the notion of "accountability" (*xingming* 形名)—that is, the relationship between what is claimed and what subsequently occurs—as a precept in his political philosophy. Makeham (1994) interprets the exposition of what he translates as "name and actuality" (*mingshi* 名實) as being the main theme of Xu Gan 徐幹 (170–217) in his *Zhonglun* 中論. Versions of this expression *mingshi* are to be found earlier than Xu Gan in the School of Names thinkers such as Gongsun Longzi and in the Later Mohist canons, as well as in the *Xunzi*, in the *Chunqiufanlu* 春秋繁露 attributed to Dong Zhongshu 董仲舒 (c. 179–c. 104), in the *Lunheng* 論衡 of Wang Chong 王充 (27–c. 97), and in the writings of Wang Fu 王符 (85–162) as well.
14. Sivin (1995a), p. 8.
15. Xunzi 荀子 is frequently regarded as the most dialectical of the pre-Qin philosophers, yet he too placed considerable value in the kind of consensus referenced by the expression "the art of accommodation" (*jianshu* 兼術) HY 14/5/49. See also Hall and Ames (1998), part two.
16. See Graham (1989), p. 3.
17. For a discussion of this issue in some detail see Hall and Ames (1998), "Cultural Requisites for a Theory of Truth" in our *Thinking from the Han*.
18. Herfel, Rodrigues, and Gao (2007), p. 59.
19. Herfel, Rodrigues, and Gao (2007), p. 59.
20. Redding (1998), *passim*. See also Sivin (1995a), pp. 2–3 and Hall (2000).
21. Metonymy is a figure of speech in which a word or phrase is substituted for another word or phrase with which the former is closely associated, such as in the use of "Peking" for "the Chinese government" or of "the throne" for "the sovereign ruler."
22. Graham (1989), pp. 222–23.
23. Tang (1962), p. 195.

24. See Kwan Tze-wan's "Multi-function Character Database" 甲骨文合集 CHANT: 0198A, 甲骨文合集 CHANT: 0198, and [西周晚期] CHANT: 2829.
25. *Analects* 19.21: 子貢曰：「君子之過也，如日月之食焉：過也，人皆見之；更也，人皆仰之。」
26. *Zhongyong* 32: 唯天下至誠，為能經綸天下之大經，立天下之大本，知天地之化育。夫焉有所倚？肫肫其仁！淵淵其淵！浩浩其天！苟不固聰明聖知達天德者，其孰能知之？
27. *Analects* 19.24: 叔孫武叔毀仲尼。子貢曰：「無以為也，仲尼不可毀也。他人之賢者，丘陵也，猶可踰也；仲尼，日月也，無得而踰焉。人雖欲自絕，其何傷於日月乎？多見其不知量也！」
28. *Zhongyong* 30: 仲尼祖述堯、舜，憲章文、武；上律天時，下襲水土。辟如天地之無不持載，無不覆幬，辟如四時之錯行，如日月之代明。
29. See Kwan Tze-wan's "Multi-function Character Database" 甲骨文合集 CHANT: 1132, [商代] CHANT; 5413, and 馬王堆：老子甲本卷後古佚書 344.
30. *Analects* 3.11: 或問禘之說。子曰：「不知也。知其說者之於天下也，其如示諸斯乎！」指其掌。
31. Major (1993), p. 18.
32. Zhang Dongsun (1995b), pp. 373–74.
33. I would have to allow that "principle" does perhaps work better than "pattern" or "coherence" for *li* 理 at least in carrying over the normative dimension of this term.
34. *Huainanzi* 3/18/18: 天墜未形，馮馮翼翼，洞洞灟灟，故曰太始。道生于[太始生]虛霩，虛霩生宇宙，宇宙生元氣。Compare Major (1993), p. 62.
35. Mote (1989), p. 15.
36. Schwartz (1985), p. 26.
37. See, for example, Loewe (1982), p. 63.
38. Graham (1989), p. 12. See also Mote (1972), p. 7 in his "The Cosmological Gulf Between China and the West."
39. A rather complete statement of this challenge to the claim that early Chinese cosmology offers no creation myth is to be found in Goldin (2008). On his own admission he is pitting himself against most of the prominent sinologists of the twentieth century (see not only the text itself but his footnote 6), and we are happily included in this company. In characterizing the position we outline in Hall and Ames (1995), Goldin describes us as purveyors of "an updated Orientalism" because we claim that classical Chinese "cosmology" is "acosmotic." This is a neologism that means classical Chinese cosmology posits a world that has neither a radical beginning nor constitutes a "single-ordered world," conditions of

a cosmogony that we have described as characteristic of a metaphysical transcendentalism. Goldin then rehearses a series of Chinese canonical texts that he claims exhibit a cosmogony that has an initial beginning and that is ordered by an independent principle. For example, he analyzes a cosmogonic passage from the *Huainanzi* 7/54/26 that describes "two gods who were spontaneously born" 有二神混生, a familiar metaphor for *yinyang* that we find in several *Huainanzi* passages (cf. 1/1/10 for example) that describe such "gods" as "traveling together with transformation" 神與化游. The Gao You 高誘 commentary observes: "The two gods are the *yinyang* gods, and spontaneously born means that they were born together" 二神，陰陽之神，混生，俱生也. The two spirits, far from being external to the transformative process, are numinous forces that constitute its inner yin/yang dynamic. But rather than interpreting these "gods" as the tension within the continuing procreative process that produces transformation, Goldin describes them as "*custodians* external to the created world" who, because "the Myriad Things could not have come to exist by *ziran*," therefore belong to "a time before the Myriad Things." We would aver that Goldin, in his attempt to find the basis for a single-ordered world in classical Chinese cosmology, misses our point, eliding as he does what we have called a metaphysical cosmogony that entails external agency, and a holistic, continuing genealogical cosmogony that has the energy of transformation within the process itself. He is right in observing that not all cosmogonies in the classical Greek tradition entail a single-ordered world, but Hall and I too argue that the notion of *kosmos* as a single-ordered world is relatively late, and that early Greek philosophers such as Anaximander and Empedocles, for example, have multiple world cosmogonies.

40. Girardot (1983), pp. 12–15.
41. See Major (1993), pp. 326–27.
42. Note that the phrase that precedes a second phrase is embedded in this phrase that follows from it. The text is attempting to delineate succeeding stages in this process of early beginnings. On this basis, the character *you* 有 is added to the first phrase.
43. *Huainanzi* 2/10/14: [有]有始者，有未始有有始者，有未始有夫未始有有始者，有有者，有無者，有未始有無者。
44. *Zhuangzi* 5/2/49: 有始也者，有未始有始也者，有未始有夫未始有始也者，有有也者，有無也者，有未始有無也者，有未始有夫未始有無也者。
45. Huang (2007) gives a nuanced account of early missionaries such as Ricci (1985) and more contemporary scholars such as Benjamin Schwartz (1985), Ching (1977) and Clark (2005) and (2009) who claim that *tian* and *di* as discussed in the Chinese sources reference a transcendent deity comparable

to the Christian God in many crucial aspects.
46. Fingarette (1972). See his various published papers on the *Analects* in the bibliography.
47. See Dewey (1998), pp. 401–10, "Religion versus the Religious," and Emerson (2003), "The Divinity School Address" for a perceived antagonism between real religious feelings and the institutions of structured religions. More recently, Gianni Vattimo in his *After Christianity* (2002), and Rorty (1999) in essays such as "Religion as a Conversation-stopper," both individually and again together in a Rorty and Vattimo conversation, *The Future of Religion* (2005), have taken the regimentation of institutionalized, clerical religion as the target of their sustained critique.
48. See Kwan Tze-wan's "Multi-function Character Database" 甲骨文合集 CHANT: 2041.
49. See Liu (1995), pp. 299–301.
50. *Analects* 6.22: 務民之義，敬鬼神而遠之，可謂知矣。
51. *Analects* 11.12: 季路問事鬼神。子曰：「未能事人，焉能事鬼？」敢問死。曰：「未知生，焉知死？」Keightley (1990) in his reflections on the meaning and value of death in classical China broadly, allows that death was perceived as "unproblematic." Of course, he is not claiming that the end of life was not approached with some trepidation. He means rather that death was not considered unnatural, perverse, or horrible. Chinese "natural" death as integral to the cycle of life is contrasted with the enormity of death in the Judeo-Christian tradition, where mortality is conceived as divine punishment meted out for human hubris and disobedience. While there is an uneasiness manifested in visions of the "Yellow Springs," a name for the netherworld, there is a marked absence of the morbidity and gloom that we associate with the Greek, Roman, and medieval European conceptions of death. See also Ames (1998) and (forthcoming).
52. Rorty (1989), pp. 169ff.
53. Cited in Steele (2002), p. 217.
54. Dalmiya (1998), p. 523.
55. See Ames (2003). A more sustained argument for the profundity and legitimacy of this use of religiousness is found in Henry Rosemont Jr.'s *Rationality and Religious Experience* (2001).
56. Tu (1985) develops this contrast between *creatio ex nihilo* and the continuous creativity of the Confucian world as it is directed by an "anthropocosmic vision."
57. *Zhongyong* 5: 道其不行矣夫。
58. *Zhongyong* 22: 可以與天地參矣。
59. *Zhongyong* 31: 故曰配天。
60. Dewey (1976–83), Vol. 4, p. 12.

61. Leuba (1901), p. 572.
62. Emerson (1979), p. 712.
63. Emerson (1979), p. 713.
64. Dewey (1976–83), Vol. 12, p. 186.
65. Although there is often an asymmetry in relationships, we only need to remember *Analects* 19.23 to appreciate the mutuality of the co-creative process:

    衛公孫朝問於子貢曰：「仲尼焉學？」子貢曰：「文武之道，未墜於地，在人。賢者識其大者，不賢者識其小者，莫不有文武之道焉。夫子焉不學？而亦何常師之有？」

    Gongsun Chao of Wei asked Zigong, "With whom did Confucius study?"

    Zigong replied, "The way (*dao*) of Kings Wen and Wu has not collapsed utterly—it lives in the people. Those of superior character have grasped the greater part, while those of lesser parts have grasped a bit of it. Everyone has something of Wen and Wu's way in them. Who then does the Master not learn from? Again, how could there be a single constant teacher for him?"

66. Legge (1960), pp. 383, 55. Another place in which Legge offers his personal commentary is in the *Zhuangzi* anecdote about the demise of Lord "Chaos" when order is imposed upon him by "Heedless" and "Sudden," the rulers of the north and south seas. Legge's comment is: "But surely it was better that Chaos should give place to another state. 'Heedless' and 'Sudden' did not do a bad work." (Legge 1962, p. 267)
67. Berthrong (1998), p. 1.
68. See Ames and Hall (2001), pp. 30–35 for our justification for translating *cheng* as "creativity" along with the commentarial evidence that supports such a rendering. Commentators late and soon have repeatedly defined *cheng* as "ceaselessness" and "continuity itself," and Zhu Xi in *Zhongyong* 20 glosses it as "what is genuinely real without lapse" 真實無妄 and "what the patterns of nature really are" 天理之本然, attributing to the human being "the desire to make genuinely real what cannot yet be so" 未能真實無妄而欲其真是無妄. Chan (1963), p. 96 puts these two aspects of *cheng* together as a changing, transforming reality and insists that *cheng* is "an active force that is always transforming things and completing things, drawing man and Heaven together in the same current." Tu (1989), pp. 82–83 concludes explicitly that *cheng* "can be conceived as a form of creativity" and that it "is simultaneously a self-subsistent and self-fulfilling process of creation that produces life unceasingly." While *cheng* without question entails a creative process, we will see that what in fact makes the translation of *cheng* as "creativity" problematic is the skewed way in which

"creativity" has come to be understood in the English language.
69. *Zhongyong* 25: 誠者自成也，而道自道也。誠者物之終始，不誠無物。是故君子誠之為貴。誠者非自成己而已也，所以成物也。成己，仁也；成物，知也。性之德也，合外內之道也，故時措之宜也。
70. *Zhongyong* 22: 唯天下至誠，為能盡其性；能盡其性，則能盡人之性；能盡人之性，則能盡物之性；能盡物之性，則可以贊天地之化育；可以贊天地之化育，則可以與天地參矣。
71. *Zhongyong* 31: 唯天下至聖，為能聰明睿知，足以有臨也；寬裕溫柔，足以有容也；發強剛毅，足以有執也；齊莊中正，足以有敬也；文理密察，足以有別也。溥博淵泉，而時出之。溥博如天，淵泉如淵。見而民莫不敬，言而民莫不信，行而民莫不說。是以聲名洋溢乎中國，施及蠻貊；舟車所至，人力所通，天之所覆，地之所載，日月所照，霜露所隊；凡有血氣者，莫不尊親，故曰配天。
72. Chan (1963), p. 95, for example, says of "the Way of Heaven" that it "transcends time, space, substance, and motion, and is at the same time unceasing, eternal, and evident."
73. For Goldin (2008), pp. 2–3, Andrew Plaks and Michael Puett are two contemporary scholars who challenge the scholarly consensus that China has no creation myth, and by resisting generalizations about China, avoid the reifying and essentializing of both their own cultural narrative and that of China.
74. Plaks (2003), p. 74.
75. Plaks (2003), p. 78.
76. Plaks (2003), p. 77.
77. Plaks (2003), p. 97.
78. Plaks (2003), pp. 98–99.
79. Plaks (2003), p. 78.
80. Plaks (2003), p. 80n3.
81. James (1977), p. 147.
82. Dewey (1994), p. 35.
83. Bruya (2010), p. 225.
84. See *Zhuangzi* HY 7.3.2–5: 庖丁為文惠君解牛，手之所觸，肩之所倚，足之所履，膝之所踦，砉然嚮然，奏刀騞然，莫不中音。合於《桑林》之舞，乃中《經首》之會。文惠君曰：「譆！善哉！技蓋至此乎？」庖丁釋刀對曰：「臣之所好者道也，進乎技矣。」
85. *Analects* 2.4: 子曰：「吾十有五而志于學，三十而立，四十而不惑，五十而知天命，六十而耳順，七十而從心所欲，不踰矩。」
86. There are counterexamples that come to mind from Renaissance philosophy such as Nicholas de Cusa and Vico.
87. Interestingly, the virgin birth is a repetition of the *creatio ex nihilo* model, "preserving the unity, purity, and spirituality of God." (Hope Mason 2003,

p. 26)
88. Hope Mason (2003), p. 30.
89. See Kwan Tze-wan's "Multi-function Character Database" 甲骨文合集 CHANT: 0693 and [西周中期] CHANT: 246.
90. *Fengsutongyi yiwen* 風俗通義佚文 15: 聖者聲也，通也。言其聞聲知情，通於天地，調暢萬物。See Wu (1980), p. 415.
91. This priority of the quantitatively discrete is the target of William James when in the *Principles of Psychology* he argues for the reality of "conjunctions and transitions" in the stream of consciousness. See James (1984), pp. 47–81.

Epilogue
1. For examples of care ethics, see the work of Gilligan (1982), Noddings (2003), Walker (2000), Held (2006), and the works mentioned in Tronto (1999), among others. Similarly, there is also an attempt to reinstate the fundamental importance of context in recent work in Pragmatist ethics: for example, Lekan (2003) and particularly Fesmire (2003). For moral particularism, see Hooker and Little (2000). Most recently Shusterman (2008) and (1997) and in many of his other books has argued for an educated and elegant somaticity as integral to the cultivation of the consummate life. Robert C. Solomon over a distinguished career led the discipline in arguing for and promoting literacy in the philosophy of the emotions.
2. Kupperman (2010), p. 185.
3. Kupperman (2010), p. 186.
4. Kupperman (2010), p. 200.
5. See Zhang Yanhua (2007), pp. 46–48.
6. King (1985), pp. 62–63.
7. King (1985), pp. 64–65.
8. Russell (1922), p. 40.
9. Kang (1956) and Tan (1958).
10. Russell (1922), p. 41.
11. I am indebted here to the article by Chong (1996), "Mankind and Nature in Chinese Thought: Li Zehou on the Traditional Roots of Maoist Voluntarism," and also to the responses to Chong (1999) by Li (1999) and Cauvel (1999) that appeared in a special issue of *Philosophy East and West*, guest edited by Tim Cheek.
12. Hao (1994) makes a similar point in his response to W. T. de Bary's *The Trouble with Confucianism*.
13. Hall and Ames (1987), p. 309.
14. Glosserman and Snyder (2009).
15. See, for example, *Analects* 4.16, 14.12, 14.13, 16.10, and 19.1, and

Mencius 1A1, 2A2, 7A33, 7A34, 7B31.

Bibliography of Works Cited

Addams, Jane (2002). *Democracy and Social Ethics*. Introduction by Charlene Haddock Seigfried. Urbana, IL: University of Illinois.

Ames, Roger T. (forthcoming). "War, Death and Ancient Chinese Cosmology: Thinking Through the Thickness of Culture." In *Mortality in Ancient Chinese Thought*. Edited by Amy L. Olberding and Philip J. Ivanhoe. Albany, NY: State University of New York Press.

——— (2008). "What Ever Happened to Wisdom? Confucian Philosophy of Process and 'Human Becomings.'" Special Festschrift issue of *Asia Major* in honor of Nathan Sivin. Edited by Michael Nylan, Henry Rosemont Jr., and Li Waiyee. Third Series, *21* Part 1.

——— (2005). "Getting Past the Eclipse of Philosophy in World Sinology: A Response to Eske Mollgaard." *Dao: A Journal of Comparative Philosophy*, 4(2).

——— (2003). "*Li* 禮 and the A-theistic Religiousness of Classical Confucianism." In *Confucian Spirituality*. Vol. 1. Edited by Tu Wei-ming and Mary Evelyn Tucker. New York: Crossroad Publishing Company.

——— (2001). "New Confucianism: A Native Response to Western Philosophy." In *Chinese Political Culture, 1989–2000*. Edited by Hua Shiping. Armonk, NY: M. E. Sharpe.

——— (1998). "Death as Transformation in Classical Daoism." In *Death and Philosophy*. Edited by Jeff Malpas and Robert Solomon. London and New York: Routledge.

——— (1993). "The Meaning of Body in Classical Chinese Philosophy." In *Self as Body in Asian Theory and Practice*. Edited by Roger T. Ames, Wimal Dissanayake, and Thomas P. Kasulis. Albany, NY: State University of New York Press.

——— (1991). "The Mencian Conception of *Ren xing* 人性: Does It Mean 'Human Nature'?" In *Chinese Texts and Philosophical Contexts: Essays Dedicated to Angus C. Graham*. Edited by Henry Rosemont Jr. La Salle, IL: Open Court.

Ames, Roger T. and David L. Hall (2003). *Dao De Jing: A Philosophical Translation; "Making This Life Significant."* New York: Ballantine.
——— (2001). *Focusing the Familiar: A Translation and Philosophical Interpretation of the Zhongyong.* Honolulu: University of Hawai'i Press.
Ames, Roger T. and Henry Rosemont Jr. (1998). *The Analects of Confucius: A Philosophical Translation.* New York: Ballantine.
Angle, Stephen C. (2009). *Sagehood: The Contemporary Significance of Neo-Confucian Philosophy.* New York: Oxford University Press.
Anscombe, G. E. M. (1981). "Modern Moral Philosophy." In *The Collected Philosophical Papers of G. E. M. Anscombe.* Vol. 3, *Ethics, Religion and Politics.* Minneapolis, MN: University of Minnesota Press.
Arendt, Hannah (1994). *Eichmann in Jerusalem: A Report on the Banality of Evil.* New York: Penguin.
Barnes, Johnathan (ed.) (1984). *The Complete Works of Aristotle: The Revised Oxford Translation.* Princeton: Princeton University Press.
Berthrong, John (1998). *Concerning Creativity: A Comparison of Chu Hsi, Whitehead, and Neville.* Albany, NY: State University of New York Press.
Boodberg, Peter A. (1953). "The Semasiology of Some Primary Confucian Concepts." *Philosophy East and West*, 2(4).
Bruya, Brian J. (2010). "The Rehabilitation of Spontaneity: A New Approach in Philosophy of Action." *Philosophy East and West*, 60(2).
Campbell, James (1995). *Understanding John Dewey: Nature and Cooperative Intelligence.* La Salle, IL: Open Court.
Carrithers, Michael, Steven Collins, and Steven Lukes (1985). *The Category of the Person: Anthropology, Philosophy, History.* Cambridge: Cambridge University Press.
Cauvel, Jane (1999). "The Transformative Power of Art: Li Zehou's Aesthetic Theory." *Philosophy East and West*, 49(2).
Chan, Wing-tsit (1963). *A Source Book in Chinese Philosophy.* Princeton: Princeton University Press.
Chang, Kwang-chih (1964). "Some Dualistic Phenomena in Shang Society." *Journal of Asian Studies*, 24(1).
Ching, Julia (1977). *Confucianism and Christianity: A Comparative Study.* Tokyo: Kodansha International.
Chong, Woei Lien (1999). "Combining Marx with Kant: The Philosophical Anthropology of Li Zehou." *Philosophy East and West*, 49(2).
——— (1996). "Mankind and Nature in Chinese Thought: Li Zehou on the Traditional Roots of Maoist Voluntarism." *China Information*, 11(2–3).
Clark, Kelly James (2009). "Tradition and Transcendence in Masters Kong and Rorty." In *Rorty, Pragmatism, and Confucianism: With Responses by Richard Rorty.* Edited by Huang Yong. Albany, NY: State University of New York Press.

——— (2005). "The Gods of Abraham, Isaiah, and Confucius." *Dao: A Journal of Comparative Philosophy*, 5(1).
Cohen, Paul A. (1984). *Discovering History in China: American Historial Writing on the Recent Chinese Past*. New York: Columbia University Press.
Creel, Herrlee G. (1970). *What Is Taoism? And Other Studies in Chinese Cultural History*. Chicago: Chicago University Press.
Csikszentmihalyi, Mark (2004). *Material Virtue: Ethics and the Body in Early China*. Leiden, Netherlands: Brill.
Dalmiya, Vrinda (1998). "Linguistic Erasures." *Peace Review*, 10(4).
Dawson, Raymond (1981). *Confucius*. New York: Hill and Wang.
Dennerline, Jerry (1988). *Qian Mu and the World of Seven Mansions*. New Haven: Yale University Press.
Dewey, John (2004). *Reconstruction in Philosophy*. Mineola, NY: Dover.
——— (1998). *The Essential Dewey*. Vol. 1, *Pragmatism, Education, and Democracy*. Edited by Larry Hickman and Thomas M. Alexander. Bloomington, IN: Indiana University Press.
——— (1994). *The Moral Writings of John Dewey*. Edited by James Gouinlock. New York: Prometheus Books.
——— (1981–90). *The Later Works of John Dewey, 1925–1953*. 17 vols. Edited by Jo Ann Boydston. Carbondale, IL: Southern Illinois University Press.
——— (1981). *The Philosophy of John Dewey*. Edited by John McDermott. Chicago: University of Chicago Press.
——— (1976–83). *The Middle Works of John Dewey, 1899–1924*. 15 vols. Edited by Jo Ann Boydston. Carbondale, IL: Southern Illinois University Press.
——— (1969–72). *The Early Works of John Dewey, 1892–1898*. 5 vols. Edited by Jo Ann Boydston. Carbondale, IL: Southern Illinois University Press.
——— (1960). *Reconstruction in Philosophy*. New York: Beacon Press.
——— (1958). *Experience and Nature*. New York: Dover.
——— (1922). *Human Nature and Conduct*. New York: Henry Holt and Company.
Emerson, Ralph Waldo (2003). *The Spiritual Emerson: Essential Writings*. Edited by David M. Robinson. Boston: Beacon Press.
——— (1979). "The Divinity School Address." In *The Norton Anthology of American Literature*. Vol. 1. Edited by Ronald Gottesman. New York: W. W. Norton and Company.
Farquhar, Judith (1999). "Technologies of Everyday Life: The Economy of Impotence in Reform China." *Cultural Anthropology*, 14(2).
——— (1994). *Knowing Practice: The Clinical Encounter of Chinese Medicine*. Boulder: Westview.
——— (1991). "Objects, Processes, and Female Infertility in Chinese Medicine." *Medical Anthropology Quarterly*, 5(4).

Fesmire, Steven (2003). *John Dewey and Moral Imagination: Pragmatism in Ethics*. Bloomington, IN: Indiana University Press.

Fingarette, Herbert (1991). "Reason, Spontaneity, and the *Li*." In *Chinese Texts and Philosophical Contexts: Essays Dedicated to Angus C. Graham*. Edited by Henry Rosemont Jr. La Salle, IL: Open Court.

——— (1983). "The Music of Humanity in the *Conversations of Confucius*." *Journal of Chinese Philosophy*, *10*(4).

——— (1981). "The Concept of Ideal Authority in the *Analects*." *Journal of Chinese Philosophy 7*(1).

——— (1980). "The 'One Thread' of the *Analects*." *Journal of the American Academy of Religion*, Thematic Issue S, *47*(3).

——— (1977). "The Problem of the Self in the *Analects*." *Philosophy East and West*, *29*(2).

——— (1972). *Confucius: The Secular as Sacred*. New York: Harper and Row.

——— (1966). "Human Community as Holy Rite: An Interpretation of Confucius' *Analects*." *Harvard Theological Review*, *59*(1).

Gadamer, Hans-Georg (1989). *Truth and Method*. 2nd revised edition. Translated by J. Weinsheimer and D. Marshall. New York: Crossroad.

Gernet, Jacques (1985). *China and the Christian Impact: A Conflict of Cultures*. Translated by J. Lloyd. Cambridge: Cambridge University Press.

Gilligan, Carol (1982). *In a Different Voice*. Cambridge, MA: Harvard University Press.

Girardot, N. J. (1983). *Myth and Meaning in Early Taoism: The Theme of Chaos (Hun-tun)*. Berkeley: University of California Press.

Glosserman, Brad, and Scott Snyder (2009, November 13). "Not Too Fast with China." *PacNet Newsletter*, 74.

Goldin, Paul R. (2008). "The Myth That China Has No Creation Myth." *Monumenta Serica*, *56*(1).

Graham, A. C. (1990). *Studies in Chinese Philosophy and Philosophical Literature*. Albany, NY: State University of New York Press, 1990.

——— (1989). *Disputers of the Tao: Philosophical Argument in Ancient China*. La Salle, IL: Open Court.

Granet, Marcel (1977). "Right and Left in China." In *Right and Left: Essays on Dual Symbolic Classification*. Edited by Rodney Needham. Chicago: University of Chicago Press.

——— (1934). *La pensée Chinoise*. Paris: Editions Albin Michel.

Guo Qiyong 郭齊勇 (2004). "Xiandai Xinrujia de Yixue sixiang lungang" 現代新儒家的易學思想論綱 (Contemporary Confucians on *Yijing* Thought). *Zhouyiyanzhou* 周易研究, *Zhouyi Studies*, no. 4.

Hadot, Pierre (2006). *The Veil of Isis: An Essay on the History of the Idea of Nature*. Translated by Michael Chase. Cambridge, MA: Belknap Press of Harvard University.

―― (2002). *What is Ancient Philosophy?* Translated by Michael Chase. Cambridge, MA: Belknap Press of Harvard University.

―― (1995). *Philosophy as a Way of Life: Spiritual Exercises from Socrates to Foucault.* Oxford: Blackwell.

Hall, David L. (1982). *Eros and Irony: A Prelude to Philosophical Anarchism.* Albany, NY: State University of New York.

Hall, David L., and Roger T. Ames (1999). *The Democracy of the Dead: Dewey, Confucius, and the Hope for Democracy in China.* La Salle, IL: Open Court.

―― (1998). *Thinking from the Han: Self, Truth, and Transcendence in Chinese and Western Culture.* Albany, NY: State University of New York Press.

―― (1995). *Anticipating China: Thinking Through the Narratives of Chinese and Western Culture.* Albany, NY: State University of New York Press.

―― (1994). "Confucian Friendship: The Road to Religiousness." In *The Changing Face of Friendship.* Edited by Leroy S. Rouner. Notre Dame: University of Notre Dame Press.

―― (1987). *Thinking Through Confucius.* Albany, NY: State University of New York Press.

Hanfeizi 韓非子 (1982). *Hanfeizi suoyin* 韓非子索引 (A Concordance to the *Hanfeizi*). Beijing: Zhonghua shuju.

Hansen, Chad (1992). *A Taoist Theory of Chinese Thought: A Philosophical Interpretation.* Hong Kong: Oxford University Press.

Hao, Chang (1994). "A Roundtable Discussion of *The Trouble with Confucianism* by W. Theodore de Bary." *China Review International,* 1(1).

Hegel, G. W. F. (1956). *Philosophy of History.* New York: Dover.

―― (1965). *Philosophy of Right.* Translated by T. M. Knox. Oxford: Clarendon Press.

Held, Virginia (2006). *The Ethics of Care: Personal, Political, Global.* Oxford: Oxford University Press.

Henderson, John B. (1984). *The Development and Decline of Chinese Cosmology.* New York: Columbia University Press.

Herfel, William, Dianah Rodrigues, and Yin Gao (2007). "Chinese Medicine and the Dynamic Conceptions of Health and Disease." *Journal of Chinese Philosophy,* 34, Supplement s1.

Holloway, Kenneth W. (2009). *Guodian: The Newly Discovered Seeds of Chinese Religious and Political Philosophy.* New York: Oxford University Press.

Hooker, Brad, and Margaret Little (eds.) (2000). *Moral Particularism.* Oxford: Oxford University Press.

Hope Mason, John (2003). *The Value of Creativity: The Origins and Emergence of a Modern Belief.* Aldershot, UK: Ashgate.

Hsiao, Kung-chuan (1979). *A History of Chinese Political Thought.* Vol. 1. Translated by F. W. Mote. Princeton: Princeton University Press.

Hsün Tzu (1966). Harvard-Yenching Sinological Index Series, Supplement 22. Taipei: Chinese Materials Center.

Huainanzi 淮南子 (1992). *Huainanzi zhuzisuoyin* 淮南子逐字索引 (A Concordance to the *Huainanzi*). Hong Kong: Commercial Press.

Huang Yong (2007). "Confucian Theology: Three Models." *Religion Compass*, *1*(4).

Ivanhoe, Philip J. (1990). *Ethics in the Confucian Tradition: The Thought of Mencius and Wang Yangming*. Atlanta: Scholars Press.

James, William (2000). *Pragmatism and Other Writings*. New York: Penguin.

——— (1984). *William James: The Essential Writings*. Edited by Bruce W. Wilshire. Albany: State University of New York Press.

——— (1977). *A Pluralistic Universe*. Cambridge: Harvard University Press.

——— (1892). *Principles of Psychology*. Cambridge: Harvard University Press.

Jaspers, Karl (1953). *The Origin and Goal of History*. Translated by Michael Bullock. New Haven: Yale University Press.

Kanaya Osamu 金谷治 (1966). *Mōshi* 孟子 (Mencius). Tokyo: Iwanami.

Kang Youwei 康有為 (1956). *Datongshu* 大同書 (The Book of Grand Unity). Beijing: Guji chubanshe.

Karlgren, Bernhard (1996). *Grammata serica recensa*. Taibei: SMC Publishing Inc.

——— (1950). *The Book of Odes: Chinese Text, Transcription and Translation*. Stockholm: Museum of Far Eastern Antiquities.

Keightley, David N. (1990). "Early Civilization in China: Reflections on How It Became Chinese." In *Heritage of China: Contemporary Perspectives on Chinese Civilization*. Edited by Paul S. Ropp. Berkeley: University of California Press.

——— (1988). "Shang Divination and Metaphysics." *Philosophy East and West*, *38*(4).

——— (1978). "The Religious Commitment: Shang Theology and the Genesis of Chinese Political Culture." *History of Religions*, *17*(3–4).

Kim, Jung-Yeup (2010). "A Revisionist Understanding of Zhang Zai's Development of *Qi* in the Context of his Critique of the Buddhist." *Asian Philosophy*, *20*(2).

——— (2008). "Zhang Zai and his Qi 氣 Cosmology" (doctoral dissertation). University of Hawai'i, HI.

King, Ambrose (1985). "The Individual and the Group in Confucianism: A Relational Perspective." *Individualism and Holism: Studies in Confucian and Taoist Values*. Edited by Donald Munro. Ann Arbor, MI: University of Michigan Press.

Kupperman, Joel (2010). "Why Ethical Philosophy Needs to be Comparative." *Philosophy*, *85*(2).

——— (1971). "Confucius and the Nature of Religious Ethics." *Philosophy East and West*, *21*(2).

Kwan, Tze-wan. "Multi-function Character Database" [Database of bronze and oracle bone Chinese characters]. Retrieved from http://humanum.arts.cuhk.edu.hk/Lexis/lexi-mf/

Lau, D. C. (1992). *Confucius: The Analects.* Hong Kong: Chinese University Press.

Lau, D. C. and Chen Fong Ching (1992a). Hanshiwaizhuan zhuzisuoyin 韓詩外傳逐字索引 (A Concordance to the *Hanshi waizhuan*). Hong Kong: Commercial Press.

——— (1992b). Liji zhuzisuoyin 禮記逐字索引 (A Concordance to the *Liji*). Hong Kong: Commercial Press.

Legge, James (1962). *The Texts of Taoism.* New York: Dover.

——— (1960). *The Chinese Classics.* Vols. 1–5. Hong Kong: University of Hong Kong Press.

Leibniz, Gottfried Wilhelm (1994). *Writings on China.* Translated by Daniel J. Cook and Henry Rosemont Jr. Chicago: Open Court.

Lekan, Todd (2003). *Making Morality: Pragmatist Reconstruction in Ethical Theory.* Nashville, TN: Vanderbilt University Press.

Leuba, Henry (1901). "The Contents of Religious Consciousness." *The Monist, 11*(4).

Li Zehou (1999). "Subjectivity and 'Subjectality': A Response." *Philosophy East and West,* 49(2).

Liu, Lydia H. (1995). *Translingual Practice: Literature, National Culture, and Translated Modernity: China, 1900–1937.* Stanford: Stanford University Press.

Lloyd, Geoffrey, and Nathan Sivin (2002). *The Way and the Word: Science and Medicine in Early China and Greece.* New Haven: Yale University Press.

Loewe, Michael (1982). *Chinese Ideas of Life and Death: Faith, Myth, and Reason in the Han Period (202 BC–AD 220).* London: Allen and Unwin.

Lüshichunqiu 呂氏春秋 (1955). Edited by Xu Weiyu 許維遹. Beijing: Wenxue guji kanxingshe.

Lynn, Richard John (1994). *The Classic of Changes: A New Translation of the I Ching as Interpreted by Wang Bi.* New York: Columbia University Press.

Madsen, Richard (2003). "Ethics and the Family: China/West." In *Chinese Ethics in Global Context: Moral Bases of Contemporary Societies.* Edited by Karl-Heinz Pohl and Anselm W. Muller. Leiden and Boston: Brill.

Major, John (1993). *Heaven and Earth in Early Han Thought: Chapters Three, Four, and Five of the* Huainanzi. Albany, NY: State University of New York Press.

Makeham, John (2008). *Lost Soul: "Confucianism" in Contemporary Chinese Academic Discourse.* Cambridge, MA: Harvard University Asia Center for the Harvard-Yenching Institute.

——— (1994). *Name and Actuality in Early Chinese Thought.* Albany, NY: State University of New York Press.

Mattice, Sarah A. (2010). "On 'Rectifying' Rectification: Reconsidering *Zhengming* in Light of Confucian Role Ethics." *Asian Philosophy,* 20(3).

Mead, George Herbert (1982). *The Individual and the Social Self: Unpublished Work of George Herbert Mead*. Edited by David L. Miller. Chicago: University of Chicago Press.

Mill, John Stuart (1930). *A System of Logic, Ratiocinative and Inductive: Being a Connected View of the Principles of Evidence and the Methods of Scientific Investigation*. 8th edition. London, New York: Longmans, Green.

Mozi 墨子 (1948). In Harvard-Yenching Sinological Series, Supplement 21. Beijing: Harvard-Yenching Institute of Harvard University.

Mote, Frederick (1989). *Intellectual Foundations of China*. New York: Knopf.

——— (1972). "The Cosmological Gulf Between China and the West." In *Transition and Permanence: Chinese History and Culture*. Edited by David C. Buxbaum and Frederick W. Mote. Hong Kong: Cathay Press.

Munro, Donald J. (1977). *The Concept of Man in Contemporary China*. Ann Arbor, MI: University of Michigan Press.

Needham, Joseph (1956). *Science and Civilisation in China*. Vol. 2, *History of Scientific Thought*. Cambridge: Cambridge University Press.

Nietzsche, Friedrich (1966). *Beyond Good and Evil*. Translated by Walter Kaufmann. New York: Vintage.

Noddings, Nel (2003). *Caring*. Berkeley and Los Angeles: University of California Press.

Nylan, Michael (2010). *China's Early Empires: A Re-appraisal*. Edited by Michael Nylan and Michael Loewe. Cambridge: Cambridge University Press.

Peerenboom, Randall (2007). *China Modernizes: Threat to the West or Model for the Rest?* Oxford: Oxford University Press.

Perkins, Franklin (2004). *Leibniz and China: A Commerce of Light*. Cambridge: Cambridge University Press.

Peterson, Willard J. (1982). "Making Connections: 'Commentary on the Attached Verbalizations' of the *Book of Change*." *Harvard Journal of Asiatic Studies*, 42(1).

Plaks, Andrew (trans.) (2003). Ta Hsüeh *and* Chung Yung *(*The Highest Order of Cultivation *and* On the Practice of the Mean*)*. London: Penguin.

Puett, Michael (2002). *To Become a God: Cosmology, Sacrifice, and Self-Divinization in Early China*. Cambridge: Harvard University Asia Center.

Putnam, Hillary (1990). *Realism with a Human Face*. Cambridge, MA: Harvard University Press.

Redding, Jean-Paul (1998, May 28–30). Paper delivered at conference Thinking Through Comparisons: Ancient Greece and China: "Words for Atoms, Atoms for Words: Comparative Considerations on the Origins of Atomism in Ancient Greece and the Absence of Atomism in Ancient China." University of Oregon, OR.

Richards, I. A. (1932). *Mencius on the Mind: Experiments in Multiple Definition*. London: Kegan Paul, Trench, Trubner & Co., Ltd.

Ricci, Matteo (1985). *The True Meaning of the Lord of Heaven*. Taibei: Ricci Institute.

Rorty, Richard (1999). *Philosophy and Social Hope*. New York: Penguin.

——— (1989). *Contingency, Irony, and Solidarity*. Cambridge: Cambridge University Press.

Rorty, Richard and Gianni Vattimo (2005). *The Future of Religion*. New York: Columbia University Press.

Rosemont, Henry Jr. (2001). *Rationality and Religious Experience: The Continuing Relevance of the World's Spiritual Traditions*. La Salle, IL: Open Court.

——— (1991a). *The Chinese Mirror: Moral Reflections on Political Economy and Society*. La Salle, IL: Open Court.

——— (1991b). "Rights-bearing Individuals and Role-bearing Persons." In *Rules, Rituals, and Responsibility: Essays Dedicated to Herbert Fingarette*. Edited by Mary I. Bockover. La Salle, IL: Open Court.

——— (1976). "Review of *Confucius: The Secular as Sacred* by Herbert Fingarette." *Philosophy East and West*, 26(4).

——— (1974). "On Representing Abstractions in Archaic Chinese." *Philosophy East and West*, 24(1).

Rosemont, Henry Jr., and Roger T. Ames (2009). *The Chinese Classic of Family Reverence: A Philosophical Translation of the* Xiaojing. Honolulu: University of Hawai'i Press.

——— (2008). "Family Reverence (*xiao* 孝) as the Source of Consummatory Conduct (*ren* 仁)." *Dao: A Journal of Comparative Philosophy*, 7(1).

Roth, Harold D. (1999). *Original Tao: Inward Training* (Nei-yeh) *and the Foundations of Taoist Mysticism*. New York: Columbia University Press.

Russell, Bertrand (1922). *The Problem of China*. New York: The Century Co. London: George Allen and Unwin.

Sandel, Michael (1998). *Liberalism and the Limits of Justice*. Cambridge: Cambridge University Press.

Schwartz, Benjamin (1985). *The World of Thought in Ancient China*. Cambridge, MA: Harvard University Press.

——— (1975). "Transcendence in Ancient China." Daedalus, *104*(2).

Shaughnessy, Edward L. (trans.) (1997). *I Ching: The Classic of Changes*. New York: Ballantine.

Shun, Kwong-loi (1997). *Mencius and Early Chinese Thought*. Stanford: Stanford University Press.

Shusterman, Richard (2008). *Body Consciousness: A Philosophy of Mindfulness and Somaesthetics*. Cambridge: Cambridge University Press.

——— (1997). *Practicing Philosophy: Pragmatism and the Philosophical Life*. New York: Routledge.

Sim, May (2007). *Remastering Morals with Aristotle and Confucius*. Cambridge: Cambridge University Press.

Sivin, Nathan (1995a). *Medicine, Philosophy and Religion in Ancient China: Researches and Reflections*. Aldershot, UK: Variorum.

——— (1995b). "State, Cosmos, and Body in the Last Three Centuries B.C." *Harvard Journal of Asiatic Studies*, *55*(1).

——— (1987). *Traditional Medicine in Contemporary China*. Ann Arbor, MI: University of Michigan Center for Chinese Studies.

——— (1974). Forward to Manfred Porkert, *The Theoretical Foundations of Chinese Medicine*. Cambridge, MA: MIT Press.

——— (1965). "Chinese Alchemy and the Manipulation of Time." *Earlham Review*, *I*.

Slingerland, Edward (trans.) (2003). *Confucius Analects: With Selections from Traditional Commentaries*. Indianapolis: Hackett Publishing.

Sommer, Deborah (2008). "Boundaries of the *Ti* Body." *Asia Major* (Third Series), *21*(1).

Steele, David Ramsey (ed.) (2002). *Genius in Their Own Words: The Intellectual Journeys of Seven Great 20th-Century Thinkers*. Chicago: Open Court.

Stevenson, Leslie (1974). *Seven Theories of Human Nature*. Oxford: Oxford University Press.

Storch, Tatyana (2009). *Japan Under Snow: Poems in Russian and English*. Philadelphia: The Coast

Sturgeon, Donald. "Chinese Text Project" [Database of Classical Chinese Texts and Translations]. Retrieved from http://www.ctext.org..

Sullivan, Shannon (2000). "Reconfiguring Gender with John Dewey: Habit, Bodies, and Cultural Change." *Hypatia*, *15*(1).

Tan Sitong 譚嗣同 (1958). *Renxue* 仁學 (A Study of Becoming Consummately Human). Beijing: Zhonghua shuju.

Tang Junyi 唐君毅 (1991). *Tang Junyi quanji* 唐君毅全集 (The Complete Works of Tang Junyi). 30 vols. Taibei: Xuesheng shuju.

——— (1962). "The T'ien Ming [*Tianming*] (Heavenly Ordinance) in Pre-Ch'in [Qin] China." *Philosophy East and West*, *11*(4).

Thoreau, Henry D. (1962). *The Journal of Henry D. Thoreau*. 14 vols. Edited by Bradford Torrey and Francis H. Allen. New York: Dover.

Thornton, Arland (2005). *Reading History Sideways: The Fallacy and Enduring Impact of the Developmental Paradigm on Family Life*. Chicago: University of Chicago Press.

Tiles, James. E. (1988). *Dewey*. London: Routledge.

Tronto, Joan C. (1999). "Care Ethics: Moving Forward." *Hypatia*, *14*(1).

Tu, Wei-ming (1989). *Centrality and Commonality: An Essay on Confucian Religiousness*. Albany, NY: State University of New York Press.

——— (1985). *Confucian Thought: Selfhood as Creative Transformation*. Albany, NY: State University of New York Press.

——— (1979). *Humanity and Self-Cultivation: Essays in Confucian Thought*. Berkeley: Asian Humanities Press.

Vattimo, Gianni (2002). *After Christianity*. New York: Columbia University Press.

Waley, Arthur (1938). *The Analects of Confucius*. London: George Allen and Unwin.

Walker, Margaret Urban (ed.) (2000). *Mother Time: Women, Aging, and Ethics*. Lanham, MD: Rowman and Littlefield.

Whitehead, Alfred North (1979). *Process and Reality: An Essay in Cosmology*. Donald Sherbourne corrected edition. New York: Free Press.

——— (1938). *Modes of Thought*. New York: Macmillan.

——— (1933). *Adventures of Ideas*. New York: Macmillan.

Wilhelm, Hellmut (1977). *Heaven, Earth, and Man in the Book of Changes*. Seattle: University of Seattle Press.

Wu Shuping 吳樹平 (1980). *Fengsutongyi jiaoshi* 風俗通義校釋 (A Critical Edition of Understanding the Meaning of Popular Customs). Tianjin: Tianjin renmin chubanshe.

Xiong Shili 熊十力 (1985a). *Tuihuoxianzongji* 推惑顯宗記 (Getting Past Doubts and Demonstrating the Basics). Taibei: Xuesheng shuju.

——— (1985b). *Xinweishilun* 新唯識論 (A New Discourse on Consciousness Only). Beijing: Zhonghua shuju.

Xunzi 荀子 (1994). *Xunzi: A Translation and Study of the Complete Works*. Vol. 3. Translated by John Knoblock. Stanford: Stanford University Press.

Xunzi (1966). See *Hsün Tzu*.

Yang Zebo 楊澤波 (1998). *Mengzi pingzhuan* 孟子評傳 (A Critical Biography of Mencius). Nanjing: Nanjing daxue chubanshe.

Yu, Jiyuan (2007). *The Ethics of Confucius and Aristotle: Mirrors of Virtue*. New York: Routledge.

Zhang, Longxi 張隆溪 (1999). "Translating Cultures: China and the West." In *Chinese Thought in a Global Context: A Dialogue Between Chinese and Western Philosophical Approaches*. Edited by Karl-Heinz Pohl. Leiden, Netherlands: Brill.

Zhang, Yanhua (2007). *Transforming Emotions with Chinese Medicine: An Ethnographic Account from Contemporary China*. Albany, NY: State University of New York Press.

Zhang Dainian 張岱年 (1982). *Zhongguozhexue dagang* 中國哲學大綱 (An Outline of Chinese Philosophy). Beijing: Zhongguo shehui kexueyuan chubanshe.

Zhang Dongsun 張東蓀 (1995a). *Zhishi yu wenhua: Zhang Dongsun wenhua lunzhu jiyao* 知識與文化：張東蓀文化論著輯要 (Knowledge and Culture: The Essential Writings of Zhang Dongsun on Culture). Edited by Zhang Yaonan 張耀南. Beijing: Zhongguo guangbo dianshi chubanshe.

——— (1995b). *Lixing yu liangzhi: Zhang Dongsun wenxuan* 理性與良知：張東蓀文選 (Rationality and Conscience: Selections from the Writings of Zhang Dongsun). Edited by Zhang Rulun 張汝倫. Shanghai: Shanghai yuandong chubanshe.

Zhang Zailin 張再林 (2008). *Zuoweishentizhexue de Zhongguogudaizhexue* 作為身體哲學的中國古代哲學 (Traditional Chinese Philosophy as the Philosophy of Body). Beijing: China Social Science Press.

Zhu Xi 朱熹 (1969). *Sishu jizhu* 四書集註 (Collected Commentaries on the *Four Books*). Taibei: Yiwen yinshuguan.

Index

abstraction, 144, 159–63, 168–71, 277n78; and European culture, 5–13; Leibniz on, 6; Whitehead on "the perils of," 10–13, 32–33; Zhang Longxi on, 30–35
achieving propriety in one's roles and relations (*li* 禮). See *li* 禮 (achieving propriety in one's roles and relations)
Addams, Jane, 295n152
Analects (*Lunyu* 論語), 46, 67, 87, 88, 89–91, 95, 100–101, 103, 108, 112–13, 126, 146, 163, 170, 174, 176, 183, 188, 193, 196, 198, 203, 267; on friendship, 114–121; on *tian* 天 ("heaven"), 222
analogy, 35–40; associative and contrastive, 38–40; wholesale and retail, 38–40
Angle, Stephen, 271–72n16
Arendt, Hannah, 235
Arnold, Matthew, 252
Aristotle, 10, 32, 38–39, 43–44, 61, 64, 87, 193, 212–13, 249, 257, 260, 270–72n16, 285n32, 294n152; on friendship, 115–16; on the human being, 121–22, 150
ars contextualis, 53, 77, 84
Axial Age, 24–25

Bacon, Francis, 37
ben 本 (root), 88–94, 154
Bentham, Jeremy, 165
Berthrong, John, 242
biantong 變通 (flux and persistence), 24, 34, 51, 53–54, 57, 72; as common sense, 46
body. See *ti* 體 (body, embodying); *shen* 身 and *shenti* 身體 (lived-body)
Boodberg, Peter, 109
Book of Changes (*Yijing* 易經), 5, 24, 48, 63, 78, 80, 279n27; and correlative cosmology, 49–55. See also Great Tradition (*Dazhuan* 大傳) commentary on the *Book of Changes* (*Yijing* 易經)
Book of Documents (*Shujing* 書經), 167
Book of Odes (*Shijing* 詩經), 109, 197
Book of Rites (*Liji* 禮記), 94, 107–9, 130
Borges, Jorge Luis, 17, 37, 277n82
Bruya, Brian, 249–50
Buddhism, 3, 89–90

Campbell, James, 150
Carlyle, Thomas, 252
Caroll, Lewis, 17
categories, 62–63
causality (*shi* 勢). See *shi* 勢 (casuality)
Chan, Wing-tsit, 63, 195, 307n68, 308n72
Chang, K. C., 25, 279n13
cheng 誠 (sincerity, integrity, creativity), 67–68, 206, 307n68; defined, 126–27; in the *Zhongyong*

中庸 (*Focusing the Familiar*), 243–44
Cheng brothers 二程, 89–91
chi 恥 (a sense of shame), 172–74
Ch'ien Mu Lectures 2008, xiii. *See also* Qian Mu 錢穆
Chinatown phenomenon, the, 265–66
Chong, Woei Lien, 264
Classic of Family Reverence (*Xiaojing* 孝經), 107, 183–88
Cohen, Paul, 272n26
Coleridge, Samuel Taylor, 252
common sense, 41–49, 65–66, 135
Confucianism: as an aestheticism, 171–74, 189–93; a Cartesian interpretation of, 36; a Christianized interpretation of, 19–20, 36, 38, 224–25; contributions of, 258–61; creativity as *in situ* in, 76–77, 126–28; and democracy, 4, 268; a depreciated version of, 18–20; epistemology in, 75–76; on equality, 122–23; family as governing metaphor in, 96–99; on freedom, 122; a Greek interpretation of, 36; on justice, 123; on language, 100–102; Leibniz on, 5–9; the limits of role ethics in, 257–68; and a new cultural order, 2, 4–5; and Orientalism, 20; personal identity in, 102–14; a pragmatic interpretation of, 36, 38; as preemptive, 189–93; the project of, 92–96, 136–37; radical empiricism in, 94–96; religiousness in, 52–55, 68–72, 81–85, 92, 211–55, 306n47; on *renxing* 人性 ("human nature," natural tendencies), 128–34; as *ruxue* 儒學 (literati learning), 1

Confucius (Kongfuzi 孔夫子), 1–2, 46, 91–92, 100–101, 121, 161–64, 171, 186–87, 189–91, 193–94, 209–10, 236, 260, 264, 297n12, 298n24, 301n77, 301n88; on *chi* 恥 (a sense of shame), 172–74; on family, 167–68; on friendship, 114–21; on religiousness, 233–34; on *ren* 仁 (consummate person/conduct), 123–28, 175–83; the roles of, 95–97; on *shu* 恕 (putting oneself in the other's place), 199–200; on *tian* 天 ("heaven"), 222–23; on *yi* 義 (optimal appropriateness), 203–4
consummate person/conduct (*ren* 仁). *See ren* 仁 (consummate person/conduct)
cosmology, correlative, 24–30, 33–34, 41–49; as an aesthetic vision, 78–79, 160; and *ben* 本 (root), 94, 154; Benjamin Schwartz on, 273–74; and the *Book of Changes* (*Yijing* 易經), 49–55; and causality, 156–57; and cosmogony, 225–31, 304n39; and *creatio in situ*, 241–55; David Keightley on, 47–49; and ecology, 61–66; and focus (*de* 德)/field (*dao* 道), 66–76, 78–79; as genealogical, 225–31, 304n39; as gerundive, 218–21; individuation in, 75–76, 79–80; Michael Puett on, 25–29; as a moral cosmology, 66–69; and objectivity, 216–18; and particularity, 207–10, 217; and potential, 155–56; and process, 77–85; and *qi* 氣 (vital energy), 56–71, 79–80; as a religious cosmology, 69–72; and source, 154–55; Tang Junyi on, 77–85;

and Traditional Chinese Medicine (TCM), 56–61, 217; and transcendence, 211–55
creativity, 248–55; as *creatio ex nihilo*, 251–55; as *creatio in situ*, 76–77, 121–28, 225–31, 236, 241–55, 307n65; as *huasheng* 化生 (transforming into something else), 110–11; John Hope Mason on, 251–53; as *paisheng* 派生 (birthing of a distinct thing), 110–11; Promethean, 252–53
Creel, Herrlee G., 30
Csikszentmihalyi, Mark, 302n6

Dalmiya, Vrinda, 235
dao 道, 116, 184, 186, 194–95, 197, 219, 224–26, 255, 257–58; in the *Daodejing*, 82; and *de* 德 (excelling morally), 206–10; as situational, 192–93; as source, 154–55, 225–31; in the *Zhongyong* 中庸 (*Focusing the Familiar*), 245–48
Daodejing 道德經, 64, 82, 207, 210; on source, 155; on valuing one's person (*guishen* 貴身), 107
Dawson, Raymond, 195
de 德 (excelling morally), 133, 183, 224–25; and Confucian role ethics, 206–10; defined, 206–10; in *Five Modes of Proper Conduct* (*Wuxingpian* 五行篇), 143–47
de Caballero, Antonio, 31
Descartes, Rene, 15
Dewey, John, 76, 122, 160–61, 175, 232, 245, 262, 278n7, 284n13, 284n18, 284n20, 289n104, 292n125, 294n151, 295n157, 300n57; on common sense, 43–44; on *the* philosophical fallacy, 15–18, 273; on religiousness, 238–40, 306n47

di 帝 (thearch), 221–25
Discourses on the States (*Guoyu* 國語), 65
Doctrine of the Mean. See *Zhongyong* 中庸 (*Focusing the Familiar*)
Dong Zhongshu 董仲舒, 108, 279–80n27
Duan Yucai 段玉裁, 202

Eichmann, Adolf, 235
Eliot, T. S., 39
Emerson, Ralph Waldo, 232; on religiousness, 240, 306n47
empiricism, radical, 94–96
Epicurus, 10, 249
epistemology, Confucian, 75–76, 190–93, 218–21, 225–31, 257–58
essentialism, 24–28, 30–35, 70, 87–89
exemplary person (*junzi* 君子). See *junzi* 君子 (exemplary person)

family, 187–88, 294n152; Aristotle on, 153; Confucius on, 167–68; discursive nature of relations in, 97–102; as governing metaphor, 96–99, 153–54, 175; and morality, 169–71; Plato on, 153; Qian Mu on, 104; relations in, 103–4; and religiousness, 232–33; roles as norms in, 183–88; in the Western philosophical narrative, 153–54, 175
family reverence (*xiao* 孝). See *xiao* 孝 (family reverence)
Fang Dongmei 方東美, 4
Farquhar, Judith, 57–59
feelings (*qing* 情). See *qing* (feelings 情)
Fesmire, Steven, 309n1
filial piety. See *xiao* 孝 (family reverence)

Fingarette, Herbert, xiv–xv, 125, 195, 231
Five Modes of Proper Conduct (*Wuxingpian* 五行篇), 203, 291n123; and the *Mencius* (*Mengzi* 孟子), 138, 143–47, 292n126, 293n130
flux and persistence (*biantong* 變通), 24, 81, 281n56
focus (*de* 德)/field (*dao* 道) cosmology, 66–76, 78–79, 175
Focusing the Familiar. See *Zhongyong* 中庸 (*Focusing the Familiar*)
forming and functioning (*tiyong* 體用). See *tiyong* 體用 (forming and functioning)
Forster, E. M., 39
Four Books, 46, 87, 89, 103, 236
four inklings (*siduan* 四端). See *siduan* 四端 (four inklings)
fraternal deference (*ti* 悌/弟). See *ti* 悌/弟 (fraternal deference)
friendship, 114–21; Aristotle on, 115–16; Christianity on, 115; Confucius on, 114–21; as *peng* 朋, 117–18; Plato on, 115–16; Whitehead on, 11–13; as *you* 友, 118
Frost, Robert, 36, 39
Fry, Roger, 39
Fung Yu-lan, 24
Fu Xi 伏羲, 53–54

Gadamer, Hans-Georg, 22, 37, 99, 234, 249
generalizations, informed cultural, 20–40, 296n10; Hans-Georg Gadamer on, 37; Michael Puett on, 24–30; Paul Goldin on, 21; Zhang Longxi on, 30–35
Genesis, 230
Gernet, Jacques, 31, 33

Gilligan, Carol, 309n1
Girardot, Norman, 228–29, 302n4
Glosserman, Brad, 266–67
God, Abrahamic conception of, 31–35, 92, 211–19, 221–25, 230–31, 236–40, 242, 245–48, 251–53
Goethe, J. W., 252
Goldin, Paul, 21, 28, 273n45, 308n73; and cosmogonies, 228, 304n39; on generalizations, 21; and naïve realism, 21
Graham, A. C., 23–25, 27, 41, 212, 216, 219, 228, 279n19
Granet, Marcel, 25–27, 41, 63, 72, 211, 213, 218, 278n13
Great Learning (*Daxue* 大學), 97, 103, 133, 165, 183–84; and the Confucian project, 46, 66, 71, 87, 92–96, 267
Great Tradition (*Dazhuan* 大傳) commentary on the *Book of Changes* (*Yijing* 易經), xiii, 48, 78, 80, 99, 128; and correlative cosmology, 49–55
Guanzi 管子, 64
Guo Qiyong 郭齊勇, 77–78
Gu Xin, 264

Hadot, Pierre, 9, 270–72n16
Hall, David, and Roger Ames, 25–27, 212, 241, 266, 272n26, 285n30, 304n39, 307n68
Hanfeizi 韓非子, 30
Hansen, Chad, 277n81, 281n59, 289n105
harmony. See *he* 和 (harmony)
he 和 (harmony), 84–85, 112–14, 165, 168–71, 275–77n77
heartmind (*xin* 心). See *xin* 心 (heartmind)
"heaven." See *tian* 天 ("heaven")
Hegel, G. W. F., 4, 285n32, 294n152;

Index

on Chinese ethics, 13–14
Heidegger, Martin, 36–37, 70, 207–8
Held, Virginia, 309n1
historiography, 17, 249
Hope Mason, John, 251–53
Hsiao Kung-ch'uan, 278n11
Huainanzi 淮南子, 225–31
Huang Yong, 305n45
human *becoming*, 87–92, 121–28
"human nature" (*renxing* 人性). *See renxing* 人性 ("human nature," natural tendencies)
Hume, David, 245

identity, achieving personal, 102–14, 147–54
individualism, foundational, xiv, 88, 135, 164–65; Henry Rosemont on, 15; and human rights, xv; John Dewey's rejection of, 147–54; John Stuart Mill on, 135; Marcel Mauss on, 17–18
Ivanhoe, P. J., 290n105

James, William, 14–17, 147, 179–80, 214, 254, 309n91; on the "block universe," 42–43, 248; on common sense, 42–44; on substance, 102–3
Jaspers, Karl, 24–25
Jesus, 240
jian 諫 (remonstrance), 164, 186–87
junzi 君子 (exemplary person), 46, 69–70, 78, 85, 88, 102, 116, 126, 188, 197, 235

Kanaya Osamu, 290n105
Kang Youwei, 263
Kant, Immanuel, 4, 14, 136, 165, 252, 260, 263
Karlgren, Bernhard, 191
Keightley, David, 26, 274n52, 279n13, 279n19, 306n51; on correlative cosmology, 47–49
Kierkegaard, Soren, 16
Kim, Jung-Yeup, 280n39
King, Ambrose (Jin Yaoji 金耀基), 35, 261–63
Kupperman, Joel, 259–60
Kwan Tze-wan, 281n42

language, proper use of (*zhengming* 正名). *See zhengming* 正名 (the proper use of language)
langue (language), 34–35
Lau, D. C., xvii, 105, 141, 195, 241; on *zhong* 忠 (doing one's utmost), 200–201
learning (*xue* 學). *See xue* 學 (learning)
Legalists, 2
Legge, James, 241–43, 245–48, 251, 253, 285n30, 307n66
Leibniz, Gottfried Wilhelm, 5–9, 18; on abstraction, 5–9; on generalizations, 5–9, 21; rationality and, 13–15
Lekan, Todd, 309n1
Leuba, Henry, 239–40
li 禮 (achieving propriety in one's roles and relations), 7, 22, 35, 46, 78, 89, 98, 111–14, 144–45, 155, 170–71, 224–25; the aesthetics of, 171–74; and body, 173–74; as *chi* 恥 (a sense of shame), 171–74; and Confucian religiousness, 231–36; defined, 173–74, 232–33; and law, 14; and *ti* 體 (body), 109–14; and *yue* 樂 (musicality), 73–74
Liji 禮記 (*Book of Rites*). *See Book of Rites* (*Liji* 禮記)
Liu Kang, 264
Li Zehou 李澤厚, 263–64

Locke, John, 136
lun 倫 (roles), 175–80, 261–63; of Confucius, 95–96; as constitutive, 96–99; as norms, 159–60, 168, 183–88

Machiavelli, Niccolo, 252
Major, John, 223, 229
Marxism, 3
Mauss, Marcel, 17–18
Mead, George Herbert, 147
meaning, the source of, 12, 205, 231–35
Mencius (*Mengzi* 孟子), 66–69, 103, 267, 291n117; on *ben* 本 (root), 150; *Five Modes of Proper Conduct* (*Wuxingpian* 五行篇), 138, 143–47, 292n126, 293n130; on *li* 禮 (achieving propriety in one's roles and relations); *ming* 命 (basic conditions) distinguished from *xing* 性 ("nature," natural tendencies), 142–43; on *renxing* 人性 ("human nature," natural tendencies), 87–91, 134–45; on *siduan* 四端 (four inklings), 137–40, 150–52; on *xin* 心 (heartmind), 138–39
Mill, John Stuart, 135–36, 165
Milton, John, 252
Mohists, 2
moral imagination, 163–68, 189–200
Mote, Frederick, 25, 226
Mou Zongsan 牟宗三, 4
Munro, Donald, 289n105

Needham, Joseph, 25, 63, 211, 291n123
neo-Confucianism, 3
New Confucians (*xinruxuejia* 新儒學家), 3, 77–78, 133
New Culture Movement, 5, 263

Nietzsche, Friedrich, 47, 252; on "philosophy of grammar," 44–45
Noddings, Nel, 309n1
Nylan, Michael, 49

Orientalism, 2–22, 304n39

Parmenides, 212–13
parole (speech), 34–35
Peerenboom, Randall, 269n2
person: the Confucian conception of relational, xiv, 72–76, 78–79, 83–85, 88–147, 191; John Dewey on, 147–54; the pragmatic conception of relational, 147–54
Peterson, Willard, 50–51, 279n24
philosophical fallacy and John Dewey, the, 15–18, 273
philosophy: as the love of knowledge (*philoepisteme*), 8–13; as the love of wisdom (*philosophia*), 8–13
Plaks, Andrew, 245–48, 251, 273n45, 308n73
Plato, 10, 32, 38, 43–44, 76, 87, 212–13, 231, 271–72, 302n8; on friendship, 115–16
Pope, Alexander, 36
potential: Aristotle on, 150; defined, 155–56; Dewey on, 295n157
Pound, Ezra, 39
Pragmatism, and the relational conception of person, 147–54
principles, 224–25, 296–97n10; as generalizations, 180–83; the source of, 159–63
Puett, Michael, 273n45, 279n19, 308n73; on the "cultural-essentialist model" of Chinese cosmology, 27–30; on the *Daodejing* 道德經, 28–30; on the "evolutionary model" of Chinese cosmology, 24–27; on the

Taiyishengshui 太一生水, 28–30
Putnam, Hilary, 21–22, 28, 106
Pythagoras, 9, 42, 87, 272

qi 氣 (vital energy), 56–71, 79–80; as common sense, 65–66; in the *Mencius* (*Mengzi* 孟子), 66–69
Qian Mu 錢穆, 20–21, 35; on *li* 禮 (achieving propriety in one's roles and relations), 103–4
qing 情 (feelings), 88, 113–14, 169–70

rationality, Western Enlightenment, 13–18
realism, metaphysical, 8, 41, 43, 45, 135, 213
realism, naïve, 21–22
relationality: the discursive nature of, 97–102, 151–53; the nature of, 71–76; as the source of morality, 258
religions, Abrahamic, xiv, 19–20, 91–92
religiousness, Confucian, xiv, 52–55, 68–72, 81–85, 92, 211–55; Confucius on, 233–34
remonstrance (*jian* 諫). *See jian* 諫 (remonstrance)
ren 仁 (consummate person/conduct), 46, 67, 78, 85, 87–88, 101, 103, 120, 126, 129, 133, 144–45, 155–56, 165, 183, 203, 224–25, 298n23; as authoritative person/conduct, 178–79; as benevolence, 177; and Confucian role ethics, 193–94; and *de* 德 (excelling morally), 208; defined, 123–24, 175–80; as expedience in conduct, 179–80; as humaneness, 177–78; as relational virtuosity, 181–83; as self-loving (*ziai* 自愛), 124–25, 127–28, 140; and *shu* 恕 (putting oneself in the other's place), 195; and *xiao* 孝 (family reverence), 88–92, 188; and *zhi* 知/智 (wisdom), 189–94
Ricci, Matteo, 3, 8
Richards, I. A., 45
righteousness. *See yi* 義 (optimal appropriateness)
ritual propriety. *See li* 禮 (achieving propriety in one's roles and relations)
Roetz, Heiner, 24
roles (*lun* 倫). *See lun* 倫 (roles)
root (*ben* 本). *See ben* 本 (root)
Rorty, Richard, 232, 234, 249, 306n47
Rosemont, Henry, Jr., xv, 42, 164–65, 241, 283n4, 306n55; on Confucian role ethics, xv–xvii, 122, 154; on individualism, 15
Roth, Harold, 229
Russell, Bertrand, 35, 262–63
ruxue 儒學 (literati learning), Confucianism as, 1

sage (*shengren* 聖人). *See shengren* 聖人 (sage)
Sandel, Michael, 135
Sapir-Whorf hypothesis, 44, 47
Saussure, Ferdinand de, 34–35, 277n80
Schafer, Edward, 223
Schleiermacher, F. D. E., 237
Schwartz, Benjamin, 226, 273–74n48, 289n105
shame, a sense of (*chi* 恥). *See chi* 恥 (a sense of shame)
Shaughnessy, Edward, 50
Shelley, Mary, 252
shen 身 and *shenti* 身體 (lived-body), 57–61, 106–7, 111; and *jingshen*

精神 (human vitality), 109; as pregnant body, 58
shengren 聖人 (sage), 85, 93–94, 134, 139–40, 144–46, 244–45; defined, 253
Shen Nong 神農, 53–54
shi 勢 (causality), 156–57
shu 恕 (putting oneself in the other's place), 194–200, 268, 296–97n10; and Confucius, 199–200; defined, 195–96; and the Golden Rule, 198–99; and *ren* 仁 (consummate person/conduct), 195, 197–98; and *yi* 義 (optimal appropriateness), 201–2; in the *Zhongyong* 中庸 (*Focusing the Familiar*), 197–200
Shun, Kwong-loi, 65
Shuowen 說文 lexicon, 127, 195, 200, 203, 206, 221, 232–33
Shusterman, Richard, 309n1
siduan 四端 (four inklings), 137–40, 150–52; as *de* 德 (excelling morally), 143–47
Sim, May, 116, 121, 288n83, 294–95n152, 299n40, 301n88
sincerity (*cheng* 誠). See *cheng* 誠 (sincerity, integrity, creativity)
Sivin, Nathan, 41–42, 49, 108, 214–17, 291–92n123
Slingerland, Edward, 195, 278n11
Snyder, Scott, 266–67
Socrates, 272n23
Solomon, Robert C., 18, 309n1
Sommer, Deborah, 109–11, 295n5
soul, 87, 96, 103, 111, 121–22, 147–48, 213
source, definition of, 154–55
Spinoza, Baruch, 191
spontaneity, 249–52
Storch, Tanya, 90–91
Strachey, Lytton, 39

Sullivan, Shannon, 294n151
Tang Junyi 唐君毅, xiii, xvii, 4, 111–12, 135, 211, 257; on correlative cosmology, 77–85, 160, 282n72; on family, 104–5, 285n32; on *renxing* 人性 ("human nature," natural tendencies), 128–34, 147–48; on *tianming* 天命 (the mandate of *tian*), 220–21; on the *Zhongyong* 中庸 (*Focusing the Familiar*), 129–30
Tan Sitong 譚嗣同, 263
Theogony, 230
thinking, correlative/analogical, 194–200; as common sense, 41–49
Thoreau, Henry, 28
ti 體 (body, embodying), 21–22, 111, 231, 295n5; and *li* 禮 (achieving propriety in one's roles and relations), 109–14; as metaphor, 108–9; and personal identity, 102–14; and *qi* 氣 (vital energy), 57–61; variants on the character, 106–7
ti 悌/弟 (fraternal deference), 88–89, 187–88, 196
tian 天 ("heaven"), 85, 129–30, 133, 211, 219; and Confucius, 222–23; defined, 221–25
tianming 天命 (the mandate of *tiun*), 220–21
tianren heyi 天人合一 (the continuity between the religious, natural, and cultural context and the human experience), 53–54, 92, 156, 264, 302n6
Timaeus, 230
tiyong 體用 (forming and functioning), 34, 57, 63–65, 72, 81, 281n56
Traditional Chinese Medicine (TCM), xiii, 78, 127, 217, 261; and

correlative cosmology, 56–62
transcendence, 24–25, 47–48, 55, 245–48, 273n48, 304–5n39; and correlative cosmology, 211–55; defined, 212–13; John Dewey's critique of, 238–39; Mark Csikszentmihalyi on, 302n6
Tronto, Joan C., 309n1
True Goody (Zhigong 直躬), 163–68, 295n5, 296n8
Tu Wei-ming, 195, 306n56, 307n68

understanding, narrative and analytic, 45–46

value, defined, 159–63
Vattimo, Gianni, 232, 306n47
virtue. See de 德 (excelling morally)
virtues: the source of, 159–63, 295n1; as virtuosity, 180–83

Waley, Arthur, 39, 195
Walker, Margaret Urban, 309n1
Wang Bi 王弼, 65, 281n56
Wang Guowei 王國維, 223
Weber, Max, 24
Whitehead, A. N., 4, 32, 302n8; on creativity, 38–39, 277n84; and the fallacy of misplaced concreteness, 10–13, 168; on friendship, 11–13; on the ontological principle, 76–77; on rational/logical and aesthetic order, 11, 26
Wilhelm, Hellmut, 126
wisdom. See zhi 知/智 (wisdom)
Wittgenstein, Ludwig, 23
Woolf, Virginia, 39
Wright, Arthur, 31, 33
Wuxingpian 五行篇 (*Five Modes of Proper Conduct*). See *Five Modes of Proper Conduct* (*Wuxingpian* 五行篇)

xiao 孝 (family reverence), 19, 46, 78, 108, 111–12, 164, 171, 183–88, 196, 224–25, 233, 283n4; Bertrand Russell's critique of, 262–63; cognates of, 104; defined, 183–84; distinguished from *paterfamilias*, 185–86; and *jian* 諫 (remonstrance), 186–87; and *jiao* 教 (education), 183–84; as the root of *ren* 仁 (consummate person/conduct), 88–92, 296n9; and *zhong* 忠 (political loyalty), 188
Xiaojing 孝經 (*Classic of Family Reverence*). See *Classic of Family Reverence* (*Xiaojing* 孝經)
xin 心 (heartmind), 127–28, 145–46, 151, 201; as an analogy for person, 59–61, 105–6; Mencius on, 138–39
xin 信 (making good on one's word), 205–6
xing 性 ("nature," natural tendencies), 73–74, 83–85, 89, 289n105; defined, 128–34, 155–57; as initial conditions, 73, 74, 129, 178; Mencius on, 134–45; Tang Junyi on, 128–34, 147–48
Xiong Shili 熊十力, 4
xue 學 (learning), 120; defined, 162–63; in the *Great Learning* (*Daxue* 大學), 93–96; as personal growth, 161–63
Xunzi 荀子, 2, 123–24, 187, 293n126, 303n15
Xu Zhongshu 徐中舒, 223

Yan Fu 嚴復, 3
Yang Zebo 楊澤波, 291n117
Yan Hui 顏回, 119–21, 124, 194, 298n24
yi 義 (optimal appropriateness),

46, 67, 78, 89, 102–3, 111–12, 133, 144–45, 156, 164–65, 181, 224–25; and boldness (*yong* 勇), 182–83; and Confucian role ethics, 201–5; defined, 201–5; and personal advantage (*li* 利), 182, 267–68

Yu Jiyuan, 271–72n16

Zeng, Master (Zengzi 曾子), 108, 116, 172, 186–87, 194–95
Zhang Dainian 張岱年, 139–40
Zhang Dongsun 張東蓀, 224
Zhang Longxi 張隆溪, 30–35
Zhang Yanhua 張燕華, 58–60, 106–7, 109, 113–14
zhengming 正名 (the proper use of language), 100–102, 215–16, 303n13
zhi 直 (true, upright), 163–68; defined, 165–66
zhi 知/智 (wisdom), 89, 144–45, 155; defined, 190–91; as productive correlations, 62–64; and *ren* 仁 (consummate person/conduct), 190–94
Zhigong 直躬 (True Goody). *See* True Goody (Zhigong 直躬)

zhong 中 (centering, equilibrium), 169–70
zhong 忠 (doing one's utmost), 194, 197; D. C. Lau on, 200–201; defined, 200–201; and *yi* 義 (optimal appropriateness), 201–2
Zhongyong 中庸 (*Focusing the Familiar*), 55, 76, 87, 103, 134, 210, 234, 285n30; Andrew Plaks on, 245–48, 251; on *cheng* 誠 (sincerity, integrity, creativity), 243–44; creativity in, 38–39, 241–55; feelings in, 169–70; on harmony (*he* 和) and centering, equilibrium (*zhong* 中), 169–70; James Legge on, 241–43, 245–48, 251; on religiousness, 236–37; on *shu* 恕 (putting oneself in the other's place), 197–200; Tang Junyi on, 129–30; on *tian* 天 ("heaven"), 222–23
Zhuangzi 莊子, 229–30, 250–51
Zhu Xi 朱熹, 46, 55, 68, 89, 236, 296n7, 307n68
Zisizi 子思子, 88
Zuo Commentary to the Spring and Autumn Annals (*Zuozhuan* 左傳), 65, 100–101, 275–77n77

www.ingramcontent.com/pod-product-compliance
Lightning Source LLC
Chambersburg PA
CBHW030127240426
43672CB00005B/51